Essentials
|||| || |||||| || ||| || ||||||||| ||||| |||| |||
W9-BGZ-593

of PSYCHOLOGICAL ASSESSMENT Series

Everything you need to know to administer, score, and interpret the major psychological tests.

I'd like to order the following
ESSENTIALS OF PSYCHOLOGICAL ASSESSMENT:

All titles are $34.95 each*

- ❑ WAIS®-III Assessment / 0471-28295-2
- ❑ WISC-III® and WPPSI-R® Assessment / 0471-34501-6
- ❑ WJ III® Cognitive Abilities Assessment / 0471-34466-4
- ❑ Cross-Battery Assessment / 0471-38264-7
- ❑ Cognitive Assessment with KAIT & Other Kaufman Measures / 0471-38317-1
- ❑ Nonverbal Assessment / 0471-38318-X
- ❑ PAI® Assessment / 0471-08463-8
- ❑ CAS Assessment / 0471-29015-7
- ❑ MMPI-2™ Assessment / 0471-34533-4
- ❑ Myers-Briggs Type Indicator® Assessment / 0471-33239-9
- ❑ Rorschach® Assessment / 0471-33146-5
- ❑ Millon™ Inventories Assessment, Second Edition / 0471-21891-X
- ❑ TAT and Other Storytelling Techniques / 0471-39469-6
- ❑ MMPI-A™ Assessment / 0471-39815-2
- ❑ NEPSY® Assessment / 0471-32690-9
- ❑ Neuropsychological Assessment / 0471-40522-1
- ❑ WJ III® Tests of Achievement Assessment / 0471-33059-0
- ❑ Individual Achievement Assessment / 0471-32432-9
- ❑ WMS®-III Assessment / 0471-38080-6
- ❑ Behavioral Assessment / 0471-35367-1
- ❑ Forensic Assessment / 0471-33186-4
- ❑ Bayley Scales of Infant Development—II Assessment / 0471-32651-8
- ❑ Career Interest Assessment / 0471-35365-5
- ❑ WPPSI™-III Assessment / 0471-28895-0
- ❑ 16PF® Assessment / 0471-23424-9
- ❑ Assessment Report Writing / 0471-39487-4
- ❑ Stanford-Binet Intelligence Scales (SB5) Assessment / 0471-22404-9
- ❑ WISC®-IV Assessment / 0471-47691-9

Please complete the order form on the back

TO ORDER BY PHONE, CALL TOLL FREE 1-877-762-2974
To order online: www.wiley.com/essentials
To order by mail refer to order form on next page

Essentials

of **PSYCHOLOGICAL ASSESSMENT** Series

Order Form

Please send this order form with your payment (credit card or check) to:

John Wiley & Sons, Inc.
Attn: J. Knott
111 River Street
Hoboken, NJ 07030-5774

Name _____

Affiliation _____

Address _____

City/State/Zip _____

Phone _____

E-mail _____

❑ Please add me to your e-mailing list

Quantity of Book(s) ordered _____ x $34.95* each

Shipping charges:	Surface	2-Day	1-Day	
First Item	$5.00	$10.50	$17.50	
Each additional item	$3.00	$3.00	$4.00	**Total $_____**

For orders greater than 15 items, please contact Customer Care at 1-877-762-2974.

Payment Method: ❑ Check ❑ Credit Card (*All orders subject to credit approval*)
❑ MasterCard ❑ Visa ❑ American Express

Card Number _____ Exp. Date_____

Signature _____

* Prices subject to change.

WILEY

Essentials

of WISC®-IV Assessment

Dawn P. Flanagan

Alan S. Kaufman

John Wiley & Sons, Inc.

Published by John Wiley & Sons, Inc., Hoboken, New Jersey.
Published simultaneously in Canada.

Library of Congress Cataloging-in-Publication Data:

Flanagan, Dawn P.
    Essentials of WISC-IV assessment / Dawn P. Flanagan, Alan S. Kaufman.
      p. cm.
    Includes bibliographical references and indexes.
    ISBN 0-471-47691-9 (pbk.)
      1. Wechsler Intelligence Scale for Children I. Kaufman, Alan S., 1944– II. Title.

BF432.5.W42F58 2004
155.4'1393—dc22
                                                                    2004011577

Printed in the United States of America

10 9 8 7 6 5 4

For my little Megan,

The Sunshine in your smile warms my heart
You fill each day with joy
And my life with precious love
You are an angel
You are a blessing from above

Love,
Mommy

For Nadeen,

Mon coeur d'ouvre à ta voix	My heart at your dear voice
Comme s'ouvrent les fleurs,	Does unfold and rejoice
Aux baisers de l'aurore!	Like a flower when dawn is smiling!
Mais, ô mon bien ai mé	You can my weeping stay.
Pom mieux secher mes pleurs	My sadness charm away
Avec ta voix parle encore!	With your tones so beguiling!
Ainsi qu'on voit des bles	As when a field of grain
Les é pis enduler	Like the waves on the main,
Sous la brise légère,	In the breeze is swaying, bounding,
Ainsi frémit mon coeur.	So all my heart is swayed.

Samson et Dalila, Act II, Scene III
Camille Saint-Saëns (libretto by Ferdinand Lemaire)

With love always,
Alan

Essentials of Psychological Assessment Series

Series Editors, Alan S. Kaufman and Nadeen L. Kaufman

CONTENTS

SERIES PREFACE

n the *Essentials of Psychological Assessment* series, we have attempted to provide
the reader with books that will deliver key practical information in the most efficient and accessible style. The series features instruments in a variety of domains, such as cognition, personality, education, and neuropsychology. For the
experienced clinician, books in the series will offer a concise yet thorough way
to master utilization of the continuously evolving supply of new and revised instruments, as well as a convenient method for keeping up-to-date on the tried-
and-true measures. The novice will find here a prioritized assembly of all the
information and techniques that must be at one's fingertips to begin the complicated process of individual psychological diagnosis.

Wherever feasible, visual shortcuts to highlight key points are utilized alongside systematic, step-by-step guidelines. Chapters are focused and succinct. Topics are targeted for an easy understanding of the essentials of administration,
scoring, interpretation, and clinical application. Theory and research are continually woven into the fabric of each book but always to enhance clinical inference,
never to sidetrack or overwhelm. We have long been advocates of what has been
called intelligent testing—the notion that a profile of test scores is meaningless
unless it is brought to life by the clinical observations and astute detective work
of knowledgeable examiners. Test profiles must be used to make a difference in
the child's or adult's life, or why bother to test? We want this series to help our
readers become the best intelligent testers they can be.

In this *Essentials* book on the WISC-IV, the authors apply a fresh, new
theory-based approach to interpret the latest edition of an old favorite. Just as
the publishers of the fourth edition of the WISC departed from Wechsler's tra-

ditional Verbal-Performance IQ discrepancy approach, so too do Dawn Flanagan and Alan Kaufman bring innovation into the crucial task of making test
profiles come alive for clinicians in every discipline.

Alan S. Kaufman, PhD, and Nadeen L. Kaufman, EdD, Series Editors
Yale University School of Medicine

One

INTRODUCTION AND OVERVIEW

There are more individually administered tests of intelligence and IQ available today than were available at any other time in the history of psychological assessment and applied measurement. Despite all the innovations and exemplary quantitative and qualitative characteristics of new and recently revised intelligence tests, the Wechsler scales continue to reign supreme. In fact, the Wechsler Intelligence Scale for Children–Fourth Edition (WISC-IV), like its predecessor—the WISC-III—will very likely become the most widely used measure of intelligence the world over. Because the latest edition of the WISC represents the most substantial revision of any Wechsler scale to date, our task of developing an interpretive system for the WISC-IV that is both psychometrically and theoretically defensible was made more difficult as compared to past endeavors (e.g., Flanagan, McGrew, & Ortiz, 2000; Kaufman & Lichtenberger, 2002). More specifically, the elimination of the Verbal and Performance IQs required us to reconceptualize previous systems completely. Also, the proliferation of anti-profile research and writing, primarily by Glutting, Watkins, and colleagues, and the anti-profile sentiment that currently characterizes the field, impelled us to have to deal with the interpretive system not just as an empirical, logical, and theoretical endeavor, but also as a controversial topic. Finally, the nature of the contemporary scene, which is undergoing substantial changes in test usage based on the ultimate wording of the Individuals with Disabilities Education Act (IDEA) legislation and its implementation, forced us to think out of the box with an eye toward the future. Thus, our overarching goal for this book, albeit grand, was to anticipate what "best practices" in the use of the Wechsler scales would be in the coming decade.

Similar to our previous writings on the Wechsler scales, our main objective was to provide a comprehensive and user-friendly reference for those who use the WISC-IV. This book was developed specifically for those who test children between the ages of 6 and 16 and wish to learn the "essentials" of WISC-IV assessment and interpretation in a direct and systematic manner. The main topics included in this book are administration, scoring, interpretation, and clinical application of the WISC-IV. In addition, this book highlights the most salient strengths and limitations of this newest arrival to the Wechsler family of instruments. Throughout the book, important information and key points are highlighted in Rapid Reference, Caution, and Don't Forget boxes. In addition, tables and figures are used to summarize critical information, and to explain important concepts and procedures, respectively. Finally, each chapter contains a set of Test Yourself questions that are designed to help you consolidate what you have read. We believe you will find the information contained in this book quite useful for the competent practice of WISC-IV administration, scoring, and interpretation.

This chapter provides a brief overview of historical and contemporary views of the Wechsler scales as well as a brief historical account of Wechsler scale interpretation. In addition, the WISC-IV is described and its most salient new features are highlighted. Finally, a brief summary of the controversy surrounding profile interpretation with the Wechsler scales is provided, followed by a comprehensive rationale for the interpretive method described in this book.

HISTORICAL AND CONTEMPORARY VIEWS OF THE WECHSLER SCALES

Within the field of psychological assessment, the clinical and psychometric features of the Wechsler intelligence scales have propelled these instruments to positions of dominance and popularity unrivaled in the history of intellectual assessment (Alfonso et al., 2000; Flanagan et al., 2000; Kaufman, 2003). The concepts, methods, and procedures inherent in the design of the Wechsler scales have been so influential that they have guided most of the test development and research in the field over more than a half century (Flanagan et al.). Virtually every reviewer of these scales, including those who have voiced significant concerns about them, have acknowledged the monumental impact that they have had on scientific inquiry into the nature of human intelligence and the structure of cognitive abilities. For example, despite the critical content and tone of their "Just Say No" to Wechsler subtest analysis article, McDermott, Fantuzzo, and Glutting (1990) assert their "deep respect for most of the Wechsler heritage" by stating that "were we to say everything we might about the Wechsler scales and their contributions to research and practice, by far our comments would be quite positive" (p. 291).

Likewise, Kamphaus (1993) observed that praise flows from the pages of most reviews that have been written about the Wechsler scales. Kaufman's (1994b) review, entitled "King WISC the Third Assumes the Throne," is a good example of the Wechsler scales' unrivaled position of authority and dominance in the field

(Flanagan et al., 2001). Although the strengths of the Wechsler scales have always outweighed their weaknesses, critics have identified some salient limitations of these instruments, particularly as they apply to their adherence to contemporary theory and research (e.g., Braden, 1995; Little, 1992; McGrew, 1994; Shaw, Swerdlik, & Laurent, 1993; Sternberg, 1993; Witt & Gresham, 1985). Nevertheless, it remains clear that when viewed from an historical perspective, the importance, influence, and contribution of David Wechsler's scales to the science of intellectual assessment can be neither disputed nor diminished. The following paragraphs provide historical information about the nature of the Wechsler scales and summarize important developments that have occurred over several decades in attempts to derive meaning from the Wechsler IQs and scaled scores.

Brief History of Intelligence Test Development

Interest in testing intelligence developed in the latter half of the 19th century. Sir Francis Galton developed the first comprehensive test of intelligence (Kaufman, 2000b) and is regarded as the father of the testing movement. Galton theorized that because people take in information through their senses, the most intelligent people must have the best developed senses; his interest was in studying gifted people. Galton's scientific background led him to develop tasks that he could measure with accuracy. These were sensory and motor tasks, and although they were highly reliable, they proved ultimately to have limited validity as measures of the complex construct of intelligence.

Alfred Binet and his colleagues developed tasks to measure the intelligence of children within the Paris public schools shortly after the end of the 19th century (Binet & Simon, 1905). In Binet's view, simple tasks like Galton's did not discriminate between adults and children and were not sufficiently complex to measure human intellect. In contrast to Galton's sensory-motor tasks, Binet's were primarily language oriented, emphasizing judgment, memory, comprehension, and reasoning. In the 1908 revision of his scale, Binet (Binet & Simon, 1908) included age levels ranging from 3 to 13 years; in its next revision in 1911, the Binet-Simon scale was extended to age 15 and included five ungraded adult tests (Kaufman, 1990a).

The Binet-Simon scale was adapted and translated for use in the United States by Lewis Terman (1916). Binet's test was also adapted by other Americans (e.g., Goddard, Kuhlmann, Wallin, and Yerkes). Many of the adaptations of Binet's test were of virtual word-for-word translations; however, Terman had both the foresight to adapt the French test to American culture and the insight and patience to obtain a careful standardization sample of American children and adolescents (Kaufman, 2000b). Terman's Stanford-Binet and its revisions (Terman & Merrill,

1937, 1960) led the field as the most popular IQ tests in the United States for nearly 40 years. The latest edition of the Stanford-Binet—the Stanford-Binet Intelligence Scales, Fifth Edition (SB5; Roid, 2003)—is a testament to its continued popularity and longevity in the field of intellectual assessment.

The assessment of children expanded rapidly to the assessment of adults when the United States entered World War I in 1917 (Anastasi & Urbina, 1997). The military needed a method by which to select officers and place recruits, so Arthur Otis (one of Terman's graduate students) helped to develop a group-administered IQ test that had verbal content quite similar to that of Stanford-Binet tasks. This was called the Army Alpha. A group-administered test consisting of nonverbal items (Army Beta) was developed to assess immigrants who spoke little English. Ultimately, army psychologists developed the individually administered Army Performance Scale Examination to assess those who simply could not be tested validly on the group-administered Alpha or Beta tests (or who were suspected of malingering). Many of the nonverbal tasks included in the Beta and the individual examination had names (e.g., Picture Completion, Picture Arrangement, Digit Symbol, Mazes) that may look familiar to psychologists today.

David Wechsler became an important contributor to the field of assessment in the mid-1930s. Wechsler's approach combined his strong clinical skills and statistical training (he studied under Charles Spearman and Karl Pearson in England) with his extensive experience in testing, which he gained as a World War I examiner. The direction that Wechsler took gave equal weight to the Stanford-Binet/Army Alpha system (Verbal Scale) and to the Performance Scale Examination/Army Beta system (Performance Scale). The focus that Wechsler had in creating his battery was one of obtaining dynamic clinical information from a set of tasks. This focus went well beyond the earlier use of tests simply as psychometric tools. The first in the Wechsler series of tests was the Wechsler-Bellevue Intelligence Scale (Wechsler, 1939). In 1946 Form II of the Wechsler-Bellevue was developed, and the Wechsler Intelligence Scale for Children (WISC; Wechsler, 1949) was a subsequent downward extension of Form II that covered the age range of 5 to 15 years. Ultimately, the WISC became one of the most frequently used tests in the measurement of intellectual functioning (Stott & Ball, 1965). Although the practice of using tests designed for school-age children in assessing preschoolers was criticized because of the level of difficulty for very young children, the downward extension of such tests was not uncommon prior to the development of tests specifically for children under age 5 (Kelley & Surbeck, 1991).

The primary focus of the testing movement until the 1960s was the assessment of children in public school and adults entering the military (Parker, 1981). However, in the 1960s the U.S. federal government's increasing involvement in educa-

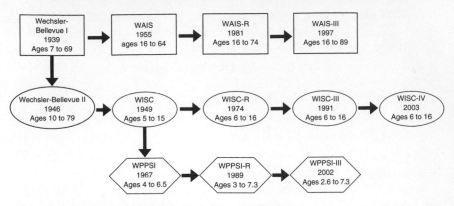

Figure 1.1 History of Wechsler Intelligence Scales

Note: WPPSI = Wechsler Preschool and Primary Scale of Intelligence; WISC = Wechsler Intelligence Scale for Children; WAIS = Wechsler Adult Intelligence Scale. From A. S. Kaufman & E. O. Lichtenberger, *Essentials of WISC-III and WPPSI-R Assessment.* Copyright © 2000. John Wiley & Sons, Inc. This material is used by permission of John Wiley & Sons, Inc.

tion spurred growth in the testing of preschool children. The development of government programs such as Head Start focused attention on the need for effective program evaluation and the adequacy of preschool assessment instruments (Kelley & Surbeck, 1991). In 1967 the Wechsler Preschool and Primary Scale of Intelligence (WPPSI) was developed as a downward extension of certain WISC subtests but provided simpler items and an appropriate age-standardization sample. However, because the WPPSI accommodated the narrow 4:0- to 6:5-year age range, it failed to meet the needs of program evaluations because most new programs were for ages 3 to 5 years.

Public Law 94-142, the Education for All Handicapped Children Act of 1975, played an important role in the continued development of cognitive assessment instruments. This law and subsequent legislation (IDEA of 1991 and IDEA Amendments in 1997) included provisions that required an individualized education program (IEP) for each disabled child (Sattler, 2001). A key feature of the development of the IEP is the evaluation and diagnosis of the child's level of functioning. Thus these laws directly affected the continued development of standardized tests such as the WPPSI and WISC. The WISC has had three revisions (1974, 1991, 2003), and the WPPSI has had two (1989, 2002). The WISC-IV is the great-great-grandchild of the 1946 Wechsler-Bellevue Form II; it is also a cousin of the Wechsler Adult Intelligence Scale–Third Edition (WAIS-III), which traces its lineage to Form I of the Wechsler-Bellevue. Figure 1.1 shows the history of the Wechsler scales.

DON'T FORGET

Origin of WISC-IV Subtests

Verbal Comprehension Index (VCI)

	Historical Source of Subtest
Vocabulary	Stanford-Binet
Similarities	Stanford-Binet
Comprehension	Stanford-Binet/Army Alpha
(Information)	Army Alpha
(Word Reasoning)	Kaplan's Word Context Test (Werner & Kaplan, 1950)

Perceptual Reasoning Index (PRI)

	Historical Source of Subtest
Block Design	Kohs (1923)
Matrix Reasoning	Raven's Progressive Matrices (1938)
Picture Concepts	Novel task developed by The Psychological Corporation
(Picture Completion)	Army Beta/Army Performance Scale Examination

Working Memory Index (WMI)

	Historical Source of Subtest
Digit Span	Stanford-Binet
Letter-Number Sequencing	Gold, Carpenter, Randolph, Goldberg, and Weinberger (1997)
(Arithmetic)	Stanford-Binet/Army Alpha

Processing Speed Index (PRI)

	Historical Source of Subtest
Coding	Army Beta/Army Performance Scale Examination
Symbol Search	Schneider and Shiffrin (1977) and S. Sternberg (1966)
(Cancellation)	Diller et al. (1974), Moran and Mefford (1959), and Talland and Schwab (1964)

Source: From A. S. Kaufman & E. O. Lichtenberger, *Essentials of WISC-III and WPPSI-R Assessment.* Copyright © 2000 John Wiley & Sons, Inc. This material is used by permission of John Wiley & Sons, Inc. *Note:* Supplementary subtests appear in parentheses.

In addition to the Wechsler scales and SB5, the Woodcock-Johnson Tests of Cognitive Ability (originally published in 1977) is in its third edition (WJ III; Woodcock, McGrew, & Mather, 2001), and the Kaufman Assessment Battery for Children (K-ABC; published in 1983) is in its second edition (KABC-II; Kaufman & Kaufman, 2004a). Other intelligence tests that have joined the contemporary scene include the Differential Abilities Scale (DAS; Elliott, 1991), the Cognitive Assessment System (CAS; Naglieri & Das, 1997), the Universal Non-verbal Intelligence Test (UNIT; Bracken & McCallum, 1997) and the Reynolds Intellectual Ability Scale (RIAS; Reynolds & Kamphaus, 2003). What is most striking about recently revised and new tests of intelligence is their generally close alliance with theory, particularly the Cattell-Horn-Carroll (CHC) theory. (See Appendix A for detailed definitions of the CHC abilities and Appendix B for a list of major intelligence tests and the CHC abilities they measure.) For a complete discussion of contemporary intelligence tests and their underlying theoretical models, see Flanagan and Harrison (in press).

Brief History of Intelligence Test Interpretation

Randy Kamphaus and his colleagues provided a detailed historical account of the many approaches that have been used to interpret an individual's performance on the Wechsler scales (Kamphaus, Petoskey, & Morgan, 1997; Kamphaus, Winsor, Rowe, & Kim, in press). These authors describe the history of intelligence test interpretation in terms of four "waves": (1) quantification of general level; (2) clinical profile analysis; (3) psychometric profile analysis; and (4) application of theory to intelligence test interpretation. Kamphaus and colleagues' organizational framework is used here to demonstrate the evolution of Wechsler test interpretation.

The First Wave: Quantification of General Level

Intelligence tests, particularly the Stanford-Binet, were used widely because they offered an objective method of differentiating groups of people on the basis of their general intelligence. According to Kamphaus and colleagues (1997; Kamphaus et al., in press), this represented the first wave of intelligence test interpretation and was driven by practical considerations regarding the need to classify individuals into separate groups.

During the first wave, the omnibus IQ was the focus of intelligence test interpretation. The prevalent influence of Spearman's g theory of intelligence and the age-based Stanford-Binet scale, coupled with the fact that factor analytic and other psychometric methods were not yet available for investigating multiple cognitive abilities, contributed to the almost exclusive use of global IQ for classification purposes. Hence, a number of classification systems were proposed for organizing individuals according to their global IQs.

Early classification systems included labels that corresponded to medical and legal terms, such as "idiot," "imbecile," and "moron." Although the Wechsler scales did not contribute to the early classification efforts during most of the first wave of test interpretation, Wechsler eventually made his contribution. Specifically, he proposed a classification system that relied less on evaluative labels (although it still contained the terms "defective" and "borderline") and more on meaningful deviations from the mean, reflecting the "prevalence of certain intelligence levels in the country at that time" (Kamphaus et al., 1997, p. 35). With some refinements over the years, interpretation of intelligence tests continue to be based on this type of classification system. That is, distinctions are still made between individuals who are mentally retarded and gifted, for example. Our classification categories are quite different from earlier classification systems, as you will see in Chapter 4.

It appears that Wechsler accepted the prevailing ideas regarding *g* and the conceptualization of intelligence as a global entity, consistent with those already put forth by Terman, Binet, Spearman, and others (Reynolds & Kaufman, 1990), when he offered his own definition of intelligence. According to Wechsler (1939), *intelligence* is "the aggregate or global capacity of the individual to act purposefully, to think rationally and to deal effectively with his environment" (p. 3). He concluded that this definition "avoids singling out any ability, however esteemed (e.g., abstract reasoning), as crucial or overwhelmingly important" (p. 3) and implies that any one intelligence subtest is readily interchangeable with another.

The Second Wave: Clinical Profile Analysis

Kamphaus and colleagues (1997; Kamphaus et al., in press) identified the second wave of interpretation as *clinical profile analysis* and stated that the publication of the Wechsler-Bellevue (W-B; Wechsler, 1939) was pivotal in spawning this approach to interpretation. Clinical profile analysis was a method designed to go beyond global IQ and interpret more specific aspects of an individual's cognitive capabilities through the analysis of patterns of subtest scaled scores.

The Wechsler-Bellevue Intelligence Scale, Form I (W-B I), published in 1939 (an alternate form—the W-B II—was published in 1946), represented an approach to intellectual assessment in adults that was clearly differentiated from other instruments available at that time (e.g., the Binet scales). The W-B was composed of 11 separate subtests, including Information, Comprehension, Arithmetic, Digit Span, Similarities, Vocabulary, Picture Completion, Picture Arrangement, Block Design, Digit Symbol, and Coding. (The Vocabulary subtest was an alternate for W-B I.)

Perhaps the most notable feature introduced with the W-B, which advanced interpretation beyond classification of global IQ, was the grouping of subtests into Verbal and Performance composites. The Verbal-Performance dichotomy represented an organizational structure that was based on the notion that intelligence could be expressed and measured through both verbal and nonverbal communication modalities. To clarify the Verbal-Performance distinction, Wechsler asserted that this dichotomy "does not imply that these are the only abilities involved in the tests. Nor does it presume that there are different kinds of intelligence, e.g., verbal, manipulative, etc. It merely implies that these are different ways in which intelligence may manifest itself" (Wechsler, 1958, p. 64).

Another important feature pioneered in the W-B revolved around the construction and organization of subtests. At the time, the Binet scale was ordered and administered sequentially according to developmental age, irrespective of the task. In contrast, Wechsler utilized only 11 subtests, each scored by points rather than age, and each with sufficient range of item difficulties to encompass the entire age range of the scale.

In his writings, Wechsler often shifted between conceptualizing intelligence as either a singular entity (the first wave) or a collection of specific mental abilities. At times he appeared to encourage the practice of subtest-level interpretation, suggesting that each subtest measured a relatively distinct cognitive ability (McDermott et al., 1990). To many, this position appeared to contradict his prior attempts not to equate general intelligence with the sum of separate cognitive or intellectual abilities. This shift in viewpoint may have been responsible, in part, for the development of interpretive methods such as profile analysis (Flanagan et al., 2001).

Without a doubt, the innovations found in the W-B were impressive, practical, and in many ways, superior, to other intelligence tests available in 1939. More importantly, the structure and organization of the W-B scale provided the impetus for Rapaport, Gill, and Schafer's (1945–1946) innovative approaches to test interpretation, which included an attempt to understand the meaning behind the shape of a person's profile of scores. According to Kamphaus and colleagues (1997; Kamphaus et al., in press), a new method of test interpretation had developed under the assumption that "patterns of high and low subtest scores could presumably reveal diagnostic and psychotherapeutic considerations" (Kamphaus et al., 1997, p. 36). Thus, during the second wave of intelligence test interpretation, the W-B (1939) was the focal point from which a variety of interpretive procedures were developed for deriving diagnostic and prescriptive meaning from the shape of subtest profiles and the difference between Verbal and Performance IQs.

In addition to the scope of Rapaport and colleagues' (1945–1946) diagnostic suggestions, their approach to understanding profile shape led to a flurry of investigations that sought to identify the psychological functions underlying an infinite number of profile patterns and their relationships to each other. Perhaps as a consequence of the clinical appeal of Rapaport and colleagues' approach,

Wechsler (1944) helped to relegate general-level assessment to the back burner while increasing the heat on clinical profile analysis.

The search for meaning in subtest profiles and IQ differences was applied to the WISC (Wechsler, 1949), a downward extension of the W-B II. The WISC was composed of the same 11 subtests used in the W-B II but was modified to assess intellectual functioning in children within the age range of 5 to 15 years. Subtests were grouped into the verbal and performance categories, as they were in the W-B II, with Information, Comprehension, Arithmetic, Digit Span, Similarities, and Vocabulary composing the Verbal Scale and Picture Completion, Picture Arrangement, Block Design, Digit Symbol, and Coding composing the Performance Scale. The WISC provided scaled scores for each subtest and yielded the same composites as the W-B II: Full Scale IQ (FSIQ), Verbal IQ (VIQ), and Performance IQ (PIQ).

Although the search for diagnostic meaning in subtest profiles and IQ differences was a more sophisticated approach to intelligence test interpretation as compared to the interpretive method of the first wave, it also created methodological problems. For example, with enough practice, just about any astute clinician could provide a seemingly rational interpretation of an obtained profile to fit the known functional patterns of the examinee. Nonetheless, analysis of profile shape and IQ differences did not result in diagnostic validity for the WISC. The next wave in intelligence test interpretation sought to address the methodological flaws in the clinical-profile analysis method (Kamphaus et al., 1997; Kamphaus et al., in press).

The Third Wave: Psychometric Profile Analysis

In 1955, the original W-B was revised and updated and its new name—Wechsler Adult Intelligence Scale (WAIS; Wechsler, 1955)—was aligned with the existing juvenile version (i.e., WISC). Major changes and revisions included (1) incorporating Forms I and II of the W-B into a single scale with a broader range of item difficulties; (2) realigning the target age range to include ages 16 years and older (which eliminated overlap with the WISC, creating a larger and more representative norm sample); and (3) refining the subtests to improve reliability.

Within this general time period, technological developments in the form of computers and readily accessible statistical software packages to assist with intelligence test interpretation provided the impetus for what Kamphaus and colleagues (1997; Kamphaus et al., in press) called the "third wave" of interpretation—*psychometric profile analysis*. The work of Cohen (1959), which was based primarily on the WISC and the then-new WAIS (Wechsler, 1955), sharply criticized the clinical-profile analysis tradition that defined the second wave. For example, Cohen's factor analytic procedures revealed a viable three-factor solution for the WAIS that challenged the dichotomous Verbal-Performance model and remained the *de facto* standard for the Wechsler scales for decades and for the WISC, in particular, until its third and fourth editions. The labels used by Cohen for the three Wechsler factors that emerged in his factor analysis of the WISC subtests (i.e., Verbal Comprehension, Perceptual Organization, and Freedom from Distractibility) were the names of the Indexes on two subsequent editions of this test (WISC-R and WISC-III), spanning more than two decades.

By examining and removing the variance shared between subtests, Cohen demonstrated that the majority of Wechsler subtests had very poor *specificity* (i.e., reliable, specific variance). Thus, the frequent clinical practice of interpreting individual subtests as reliable measures of a *presumed* construct was not supported. Kamphaus and colleagues (1997; Kamphaus et al., in press) summarize Cohen's significant contributions, which largely defined the third wave of test interpretation, as threefold: (1) empirical support for the FSIQ based on analysis of shared variance between subtests; (2) development of the three-factor solution for interpretation of the Wechsler scales; and (3) revelation of limited subtest specificity, questioning individual subtest interpretation.

The most vigorous and elegant application of psychometric profile analysis to intelligence test interpretation occurred with the revision of the venerable WISC as the Wechsler Intelligence Scale for Children–Revised (WISC-R; Wechsler, 1974). Briefly, the WISC-R utilized a larger, more representative norm sample than its predecessor; included more contemporary-looking graphics and updated items; eliminated content that was differentially familiar to specific groups; and included improved scoring and administration procedures. "Armed with the WISC-R, Kaufman (1979) articulated the essence of the psychometric profile approach to intelligence test interpretation in his seminal book, *Intelligent Testing with the WISC-R* (which was superseded by *Intelligent Testing with the WISC-III;* Kaufman, 1994)" (Flanagan et al., 2000, p. 6).

Kaufman emphasized flexibility in interpretation and provided a logical and systematic approach that utilized principles from measurement theory (Flanagan & Alfonso, 2000). His approach was more complex than previous ones and required the examiner to have a greater level of psychometric expertise than might ordinarily be possessed by the average psychologist (Flanagan et al., 2000). Anastasi (1988) lauded and recognized that "the basic approach described by Kaufman undoubtedly represents a major contribution to the clinical use of intelligence tests. Nevertheless, it should be recognized that its implementation requires a sophisticated clinician who is well informed in several fields of psychology" (p. 484).

In some respects, publication of Kaufman's work can be viewed as an indictment against the poorly reasoned and unsubstantiated interpretation of the Wechsler scales that had sprung up in the second wave (clinical profile analysis; Flanagan et al., 2000). Kaufman's ultimate message centered on the notion that interpretation of Wechsler intelligence test performance must be conducted with a higher than usual degree of psychometric precision and based on credible and dependable evidence, rather than merely the clinical lore that surrounded earlier interpretive methods.

Despite the enormous body of literature that has mounted over the years regarding profile analysis of the Wechsler scales, this form of interpretation, even when upgraded with the rigor of psychometrics, has been regarded as a perilous endeavor primarily because it lacks empirical support and is not grounded in a well-validated theory of intelligence. With over 75 different profile types discussed in a variety of areas, including neuropsychology, personality, learning disabilities, and juvenile delinquency (McDermott et al., 1990), there is considerable temptation to believe that the findings of this type of analysis alone are reliable. Nevertheless, many studies (e.g., Hale, 1979; Hale & Landino, 1981; Hale & Saxe, 1983) have demonstrated consistently that "profile and scatter analysis is not defensible" (Kavale & Forness, 1984, p. 136; also see Glutting, McDermott, Watkins, Kush, & Konold, 1997). In a meta-analysis of 119 studies of the WISC-R subtest data, Mueller, Dennis, and Short (1986) concluded that using profile analysis with the WISC-R in an attempt to differentiate various diagnostic groups is clearly not warranted. Recent evaluations regarding the merits of profile analysis have produced similar results (e.g., Glutting, McDermott, & Konold, 1997; Glutting, McDermott, Watkins, et al., 1997; Kamphaus, 1993; McDermott, Fantuzzo, Glutting, Watkins, & Baggaley, 1992; Watkins & Kush, 1994). The nature of the controversy surrounding clinical profile analysis is discussed later in this chapter.

The Fourth Wave: Application of Theory

Although the third wave of intelligence test interpretation did not meet with great success in terms of establishing validity evidence for profile analysis, the psychometric approach provided the foundation necessary to catapult to the fourth and present wave of intelligence test interpretation, described by Kamphaus and colleagues (1997; Kamphaus et al., in press) as "application of theory." The need to integrate theory and research in the intelligence test interpretation process was articulated best by Kaufman (1979). Specifically, Kaufman commented that problems with intelligence test interpretation can be attributed largely to the lack of a specific theoretical base to guide this practice. He suggested that it was possible to enhance interpretation significantly by reorganizing subtests into clusters specified by a particular theory. In essence, the end of the third wave of intelligence test interpretation and the beginning of the fourth wave was marked by Kaufman's pleas for practitioners to ground their interpretations in theory, as well as by his efforts to demonstrate the importance of linking intellectual measurement tools to empirically supported and well-established conceptualizations of human cognitive abilities (Flanagan et al., 2000).

Despite efforts to meld theory with intelligence test development and interpretation, the WISC-III (Wechsler, 1991), published nearly two decades after the WISC-R (Wechsler, 1974), failed to ride the fourth, "theoretical" wave of test interpretation. That is, the third edition of the WISC did not change substantially from its predecessor and was not overtly linked to theory. Changes to the basic structure, item content, and organization of the WISC-III were relatively minimal, with the most obvious changes being cosmetic. However, the WISC-III did introduce one new subtest (Symbol Search) and four new Indexes, namely Verbal Comprehension (VC), Perceptual Organization (PO), Freedom from Distractibility (FD), and Processing Speed (PS), to supplement the subtest scaled scores and the FSIQ, VIQ, and PIQ. As with the WISC-R, Kaufman provided a systematic approach to interpreting the WISC-III in a manner that emphasized psychometric rigor and theory-based methods (Kaufman, 1994; Kaufman & Lichtenberger, 2000).

Similar to Kaufman's efforts to narrow the theory-practice gap in intelligence test development and interpretation, Flanagan and colleagues (Flanagan & Ortiz, 2001; Flanagan et al., 2000; McGrew & Flanagan, 1998) developed a method of assessment and interpretation called the "Cross-Battery approach" and applied it to the Wechsler scales and other major intelligence tests. This method is grounded in CHC theory and provides a series of steps and guidelines that are designed to ensure that science and practice are closely linked in the measurement and interpretation of cognitive abilities. According to McGrew (in press), the Cross-Battery approach "infused CHC theory into the minds of assessment practitioners and university training programs, regardless of their choice of favorite intelligence battery (e.g., CAS, DAS, K-ABC, SB4, WISC-III)." Kaufman's (2001) description of the Cross-Battery approach as an interpretive method that (1) has "research as its foundation," (2) "add[ed] theory to psychometrics," and (3) "improve[d] the quality of the psychometric assessment of intelligence" is consistent with Kamphaus's (1997; Kamphaus et al., in press) fourth wave of intelligence test interpretation (i.e., application to theory).

Despite the availability of theory-based systems for interpreting the WISC-III (and other intelligence tests), the inertia of tradition was strong, leading many practitioners to continue using interpretive methods of the second and third waves (Alfonso et al., 2000). A few critics, however, did not succumb and instead evaluated this latest version of the WISC according to the most current and dependable evidence of science. These reviews were not positive and their conclusions were remarkably similar—the newly published WISC-III was *outdated*. According to Kamphaus (1993), "The Wechsler-III's history is also its greatest liability. Much has been learned about children's cognitive development since the conceptualization of the Wechsler scales, and yet few of these findings have been incorporated into revisions." Similarly, Shaw, Swerdlik, and Laurent (1993) concluded, "Despite more than 50 years of advancement of theories of intelligence, the Wechsler philosophy of intelligence . . . written in 1939, remains the guiding principle of the WISC-III. . . . [T]he latest incarnation of David Wechsler's test may be nothing more than a new and improved dinosaur."

Notwithstanding initial criticisms, the several years that followed the publication of the WISC-III can be described as the calm before the storm. That is, the WISC-III remained the dominant intelligence test for use with children aged 6 to 16 with little more in the way of critical analysis and review. With the advent of the 21st century, however, the CHC storm hit and has not changed its course to date. In the past five years, revisions of three major intelligence tests were published, each having CHC theory at its base (i.e., WJ III, SB5, KABC-II). Never before in the history of intelligence testing has a single theory (indeed any theory) played so prominent a role in test development and interpretation. Amidst the publication of these CHC-based instruments was the publication of the WISC-IV. Was it structurally different from the WISC-III? Did it have theory at its base? These questions will be answered in the paragraphs that follow; suffice it to say that the WISC-IV represents the most significant revision of any Wechsler scale in the history of the Wechsler lineage, primarily because of its closer alliance with theory. A brief timeline of the revisions to the Wechsler scales, from the mid-1940s to the present day, and their correspondence to interpretive approaches, is located in Figure 1.2.

Although we have associated our own methods of Wechsler scale interpretation with the fourth wave—application to theory—our methods continue to be criticized because they include an intra-individual analysis component. We believe these criticisms are largely unfounded, primarily because our methods have not been critiqued as a whole, but rather Watkins and colleagues have critiqued only one aspect of our systems—intra-individual analysis—and conclude that because their research shows that ipsative subtest scores are less reliable and less stable than normative subtest scores, any conclusions that are drawn from ipsative analysis are unsupported. Notwithstanding the problems with this

Clinical Profile Analysis (Second Wave)

- Interpretation of Verbal/Performance differences
- Interpretation of the shape of the subtest profiles
- Interpretation of both subtest scores and item responses
- Subtest profiles believed to reveal diagnostic information
- Rapaport et al.'s (1945/1946) work had significant impact

Psychometric Profile Analysis (Third Wave)

- Application of psychometric information to interpretation
- Interpretation of empirically based factors
- Incorporation of subtest specificity in interpretation
- Deemphasis on subtest interpretation
- Validity of profile analysis questioned
- Cohen's (1959) work had significant impact
- Bannatyne's (1974) recategorization of subtests
- Kaufman's (1979) "intelligent" testing approach

Applying Theory to Interpretation (Fourth Wave)

- Theoretical grouping of subtests
- Interpretation based on CHC theory
- Interpretation based on PASS theory (Naglieri & Das, 1997)
- Confirmatory hypothesis validation
- Kaufman (1979, 1994) "intelligent" testing approach
- Kamphaus (1993) confirmatory approach
- McGrew & Flanagan (1998) cross-battery approach
- Flanagan, McGrew, & Ortiz (2000) Wechsler book
- Flanagan & Ortiz (2001) CHC cross-battery approach
- Kaufman & Lichtenberger (2000) *Essentials of WPPSI-R and WISC-III Assessment*

W-B Form I 1939

- Verbal/Performance dichotomy
- Use of subtest scaled scores
- Deviation IQ (FSIQ, VIQ, PIQ)

W-B Form II 1946

- Parallel/alternate form for reliably testing after short time interval

WAIS 1955

- Name consistent with WISC
- Realigned age range to eliminate WISC overlap
- More representative norm sample
- Merged W-B I and II into single scale
- Broader age range
- Improved subtest reliability

WAIS-R 1981

- New norm sample
- Revised graphics
- More durable materials
- Updated item content

WAIS-III 1997

- New and more inclusive norm sample
- Revised graphics
- VC, PO and PS Indexes
- Introduction of WM Index
- Elimination of FD Index
- Decreased time emphasis
- Addition of Matrix Reasoning and Letter-Number Sequencing subtests

Figure I.2 Timeline of Revisions to Wechsler Scales and Corresponding Interpretive Methods

Source: Wechsler Intelligence Scales for Children: Fourth Edition. Copyright © 2004 by Harcourt Assessment, Inc. Reproduced by permission. All rights reserved.

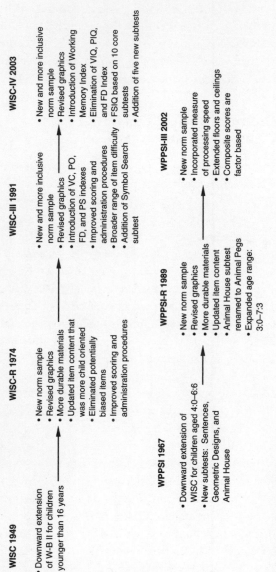

WISC 1949
- Downward extension of W-B II for children younger than 16 years

WISC-R 1974
- New norm sample
- Revised graphics
- More durable materials
- Updated item content that was more child oriented
- Eliminated potentially biased items
- Improved scoring and administration procedures

WISC-III 1991
- New and more inclusive norm sample
- Revised graphics
- Introduction of VC, PO, FD, and PS indexes
- Improved scoring and administration procedures
- Broader range of item difficulty
- Addition of Symbol Search subtest

WISC-IV 2003
- New and more inclusive norm sample
- Revised graphics
- Introduction of Working Memory Index
- Elimination of VIQ, PIQ, and FD Index
- FSIQ based on 10 core subtests
- Addition of five new subtests

WPPSI 1967
- Downward extension of WISC for children aged 4:0–6:6
- New subtests: Sentences, Geometric Designs, and Animal House

WPPSI-R 1989
- New norm sample
- Revised graphics
- More durable materials
- Updated item content
- Animal House subtest renamed to Animal Pegs
- Expanded age range: 3:0–7:3

WPPSI-III 2002
- New norm sample
- Incorporated measure of processing speed
- Extended floors and ceilings
- Composite scores are factor based

Figure 1.2 (Continued)

Note: The first wave of interpretation (quantification of general level) is omitted from this figure due to space limitations and the fact that the publication of the first Wechsler Scale did not occur until near the end of that wave. W-B = Wechsler-Bellevue; FSIQ = Full Scale IQ; VIQ = Verbal IQ; PIQ = Performance IQ; VC = Verbal Comprehension; PO = Perceptual Organization; FD = Freedom from Distractibility; PS = Processing Speed; WMI = Working Memory Index. See Figure 1.1 note for other abbreviations.

conclusion, our current interpretive approaches do not involve subtest-level analysis. The intra-individual analysis component of our interpretive approaches focuses on cluster-level, not subtest-level, analysis (Flanagan & Ortiz, 2001; Kaufman & Kaufman, 2004a). Because there is continued debate about the utility of intra-individual analysis, especially as it applies to Wechsler test interpretation, the following section provides a brief review of the most salient debate issues as well as a justification for the interpretive approach we advocate in Chapter 4.

THE CONTINUING DEBATE ABOUT THE UTILITY OF INTRA-INDIVIDUAL (IPSATIVE) ANALYSIS

Since the early 1990s, Glutting, McDermott, and colleagues "have used their research as an obstacle for clinicians, as purveyors of gloom-and-doom for anyone foolish enough to engage in profile interpretation" (Kaufman, 2000a, p. xv). These researchers have shown that ipsative scores have poor reliability, are not stable over time, and do not add anything to the prediction of achievement after g (or general intelligence) is accounted for. Thus, Glutting and colleagues believe that ipsative analysis has virtually no utility with regard to (1) understanding a child's unique pattern of cognitive strengths and weaknesses and (2) aiding in developing educational interventions. It is beyond the scope of this chapter to provide a detailed discussion of the numerous arguments that have been made for and against ipsative analysis in the past decade. Therefore, we only comment briefly on the whole of Glutting and colleagues' research and then describe how our interpretive method, which includes (but by no means is defined by) intra-individual analysis, differs substantially from previous interpretive methods.

In much of their writing, Glutting and colleagues have assumed incorrectly that all cognitive abilities represent enduring traits and, therefore, ought to remain stable over time. They further assume that interpretations of test data are made in a vacuum—that data from multiple sources, no matter how compelling, cannot influence the findings generated from an ipsative analysis of scores from a single intelligence battery. Furthermore, the method of test interpretation initially developed by Kaufman (1979) remains the focus of Glutting and colleagues' research, despite the fact that it has changed considerably in recent years (Kaufman & Lichtenberger, 2002; Kaufman, Lichtenberger, Fletcher-Janzen, & Kaufman, in press). Interestingly, these changes reflect, in part, the research of Glutting and colleagues (e.g., McDermott et al., 1992). Perhaps most disturbing is the fact that these researchers continue their cries of "Just Say No" to *any* type of interpretation of test scores beyond a global IQ, and offer *no* recommendations regarding how clinicians can make sense out of an individual's scaled score profile.

We, on the other hand, recognize the onerous task facing clinicians in their daily work of identifying the presumptive cause of a child's learning difficulties. Hence we provide clinicians with guidance in the test-interpretation process that is based on theory, research, psychometrics, and clinical experience. What Glutting and colleagues have yet to realize is that our interpretive method extends far beyond the identification of intra-individual (or ipsative) strengths and weaknesses.

Despite its inherent flaws, we believe that intra-individual analysis has not fared well because it historically has not been grounded in contemporary theory and research and it has not been linked to psychometrically defensible procedures for interpretation (Flanagan & Ortiz, 2001). When theory and research are used to guide interpretation and when psychometrically defensible interpretive procedures are employed, *some* of the limitations of the intra-individual approach are circumvented, resulting in the derivation of useful information. Indeed, when an interpretive approach is grounded in contemporary theory and research, practitioners are in a much better position to draw clear and useful conclusions from the data (Carroll, 1998; Daniel, 1997; Kamphaus, 1993; Kamphaus et al., 1997; Keith, 1988).

The findings of an intra-individual analysis are not the end of the interpretation process, but only the beginning. We do find many flaws with the purely empirical approach that Glutting and colleagues have used to evaluate the traditional approach to profile interpretation. Nonetheless, we have taken quite seriously many of the criticisms of a purely ipsative method of profile analysis that have appeared in the literature in articles by Watkins, Glutting, and their colleagues (e.g., McDermott et al., 1992). Indeed, one of us (DPF) has been frankly critical of ipsative analysis that ignores normative analysis (Flanagan & Ortiz, 2002a, 2002b). We have relied on all of these criticisms to modify and enhance our interpretive method. Following are a few of the most salient ways in which we and our colleagues have attempted to improve the practice of ipsative analysis (Flanagan & Ortiz, 2001; Kaufman & Kaufman, 2004).

First, we recommend interpreting test data within the context of a well-validated theory. Use of the CHC theory of the structure of cognitive abilities is becoming commonplace in test construction and interpretation because it is the best-supported theory within the psychometric tradition (Daniel, 1997; Flanagan & Ortiz, 2001). Without knowledge of theory and an understanding of its research base, there is virtually no information available to inform interpretation.

Second, we recommend using composites or clusters, rather than subtests, in intra-individual analysis. Additionally, the clusters that are used in the analysis must represent *unitary* abilities, meaning that the magnitude of the difference between the highest and lowest score in the cluster is not statistically significant (p < .01; see Chapter 4 for an explanation). Furthermore, the clusters that are included in the interpretive analysis should represent basic primary factors in mental organization (e.g., visual processing, short-term memory). When the variance that is common to all clusters (as opposed to subtests) is removed during ipsatization, *proportionately more reliable variance remains*. And it is precisely this shared, reliable variance that we believe ought to be interpreted because it represents the construct that was intended to be measured by the cluster. For example, when the following clusters are ipsatized—Fluid Reasoning *(Gf)*, Crystallized Intelligence *(Gc)*, Short-Term Memory *(Gsm)*, Visual Processing *(Gv)*, and Long-Term Storage and Retrieval *(Glr)*—the variance that is common to all of them (presumably *g*) is removed, leaving the variance that is shared by the two or more tests that compose each cluster. That is, if the *Gf* cluster emerged as a significant relative weakness, then our interpretation would focus on what is common to the *Gf* tests (viz., reasoning). The number of research investigations examining the relationship between broad CHC clusters and various outcome criteria (e.g., academic achievement) is beginning to provide significant validation evidence that may be used to inform the interpretive process (Flanagan, 2000; Floyd, Evans, & McGrew, 2003; McGrew, Flanagan, Keith, & Vanderwood, 1997; Vanderwood, McGrew, Flanagan, & Keith, 2002). Much less corresponding validity evidence is available to support traditional ipsative (subtest) analysis.

Third, we believe that a common pitfall in the intra-individual approach to interpretation is the failure to examine the scores associated with an identified "relative weakness" in comparison to most people. That is, if a relative weakness revealed through ipsative analysis falls well within the average range of functioning compared to most people, then its clinical meaningfulness is called into question. For example, despite presumptions of disability, average ability is achieved by most people and most people are not disabled. Therefore, a relative weakness that falls in the average range of ability compared to same-age peers will suggest a different interpretation than a relative weakness that falls in the deficient range of functioning relative to most people.

Fourth, we believe that the lack of stability in an individual's scaled score profile over an extended period of time (e.g., the three years spanning initial evaluation and reevaluation) is not unusual, let alone a significant flaw of intra-individual analysis. A great deal happens in three years: The effects of intervention. Developmental changes. Regression to the mean. Changes in what some subtests measure at different ages. The group data that have been analyzed by Glutting and colleagues do not have implications for the individual method of profile interpretation that we advocate. The strengths and weaknesses that we believe might have useful applications for developing educational interventions are based on cognitive functioning at a particular point in time. They need to be cross-validated at that time to verify that any supposed cognitive strengths or weaknesses are consistent with the wealth of observational, referral, background, and other-test data that are available for each child who is evaluated. Only then will those data-based findings inform diagnosis and be applied to help the child.

The simple finding that reevaluation data at age 13 do not support the stability of children's data-based strengths and weaknesses at age 10 says *nothing* about the validity of the intra-individual interpretive approach. If one's blood pressure is "high" when assessed in January and is "normal" when assessed three months later, does this suggest that the physician's categories (e.g., high, normal, low) are unreliable? Does it suggest that the blood-pressure monitor is unreliable? Or does it suggest that the medication prescribed to reduce the individual's blood pressure was effective?

Despite the pains taken to elevate the use of ipsative analysis to a more respectable level, by linking it to normative analysis and recommending that only unitary, theoretically derived clusters be used, one undeniable fact remains. The intra-individual analysis does not diagnose—clinicians do. Clinicians, like medical doctors, will not cease to compare scores, nor should they:

> Would one want a physician, for example, not to look at patterns of test results just because they in and of themselves do not diagnose a disorder? Would you tell a physician not to take your blood pressure and heart rate and compare them because these two scores in and of themselves do not differentially diagnose kidney disease from heart disease? (Prifitera, Weiss, & Saklofske, 1998, p. 6)

Comparing scores from tests, whether psychological or medical, is a necessary component of any test interpretation process. Why? We believe it is because comparing scores assists in making diagnoses when such comparisons are made using psychometric information (e.g., base-rate data) as well as numerous other sources of data, as mentioned previously (e.g., Ackerman & Dykman, 1995; Hale, Fiorello, Kavanagh, Hoeppner, & Gaither, 2001). The learning disability literature appears to support our contention. For example, the *double-deficit hypothesis* states that individuals with reading disability have two main deficits relative to their abilities in other cognitive areas, including phonological processing and rate or rapid automatized naming (e.g., Wolf & Bowers, 2000). Moreover, in an evaluation of subtypes of reading disability, Morris and colleagues (1998) found that "phonological processing, verbal short-term memory and rate (or rapid automatized naming)" represented the most common profile, meaning that these three abilities were significantly lower for individuals with reading disability as compared to their performance on other measures of ability. Similarly, other researchers have argued for profile analysis beyond the factor or Index level (e.g., Kramer, 1993; Nyden, Billstedt, Hjelmquist, & Gillberg, 2001), stating that important data would be lost if analysis ceased at the global ability level.

Indeed, this is not the first place that the flaws of the purely empirical approaches advocated by Glutting, McDermott, Watkins, Canivez, and others have been articulated, especially regarding the power of their group-data methodology for dismissing individual-data assessment. Anastasi and Urbina (1997) state,

> One problem with several of the negative reviews of Kaufman's approach is that they seem to assume that clinicians will use it to make decisions based solely on the magnitude of scores and score differences. While it is true that the mechanical application of profile analysis techniques can be very misleading, this assumption is quite contrary to what Kaufman recommends, as well as to the principles of sound assessment practice. (p. 513)

The next and final section of this chapter provides specific information about the new WISC-IV from a qualitative, quantitative, and theoretical perspective.

DESCRIPTION OF THE WISC-IV

Several issues prompted the revision of the WISC-III. These issues are detailed clearly in the *WISC-IV Technical and Interpretive Manual* (The Psychological Corporation, 2003, pp. 5–18). Table 1.1 provides general information about the WISC-IV. In addition, Rapid Reference 1.1 lists the key features of the WISC-IV, and Rapid Reference 1.2 lists the most salient changes from the WISC-III to WISC-IV. Finally, Rapid References 1.3 and 1.4 include the CHC broad and narrow ability classifications of the WISC-IV subtests.

Although you will recognize many traditional WISC subtests on the WISC-IV, you will also find five new ones. The WISC-IV has a total of 15 subtests—10 core-battery subtests and five supplemental subtests. Table 1.2 lists and describes each WISC-IV subtest.

Structure of the WISC-IV

The WISC-IV has been modified in terms of its overall structure. Figure 1.3 depicts the theoretical and scoring structure of the WISC-IV as reported in the *WISC-IV Technical and Interpretive Manual* (The Psychological Corporation, 2003). Several structural changes from the WISC-III are noteworthy.

Table 1.1 The WISC-IV At A Glance

GENERAL INFORMATION

Author	David Wechsler (1896–1981)
Publication Date(s)	1949, 1974, 1991, 2003
Age Range	6:0 to 16:11
Administration Time	65 to 80 minutes
Qualification of Examiners	Graduate- or professional-level training in psychological assessment
Publisher	The Psychological Corporation 555 Academic Court San Antonio, TX 78204-2498 Ordering Phone No. 1-800-211-8378 http://www.PsychCorp.com
Price	**WISC-IV™ Basic Kit** Includes Administration and Scoring Manual, Technical and Interpretive Manual, Stimulus Book 1, Record Form (pkg. of 25), Response Booklet 1 (Coding and Symbol Search; pkg. of 25), Response Booklet 2 (Cancellation; pkg. of 25), Blocks, Symbol Search Scoring Template, Coding Scoring Template, and Cancellation Scoring Templates. $799.00 (in box) or $850.00 (in hard- or soft-sided cases) **WISC-IV™ Scoring Assistant®** $185.00 **WISC-IV™ Writer™** $385.00

COMPOSITE MEASURE INFORMATION

Global Ability	Full Scale IQ (FSIQ)
Lower-Order Composites	Verbal Comprehension Index (VCI) Perceptual Reasoning Index (PRI) Working Memory Index (WMI) Processing Speed Index (PSI)

SCORE INFORMATION

Available Scores	Standard Scaled Percentile Age Equivalent
Range of Standard Scores for Total Test Composite	40–160 (ages 6:0 to 16:11)

(continued)

Table 1.1 (Continued)

NORMING INFORMATION

Standardization Sample Size	2,200
Sample Collection Dates	Aug. 2001–Oct. 2002
Average Number per Age Interval	200
Age Blocks in Norm Table	4 months (ages 6:0 to 16:11)
Demographic Variables	Age Gender (male, female) Geographic region (four regions) Race/ethnicity (White; African American; Hispanic; Asian; other) Socioeconomic status (parental education)
Types of Validity Evidence in Test Manual	Test content Response processes Internal structure Relationships with other variables Consequences of testing

≡Rapid Reference 1.1

....

Key Features Listed in the *WISC-IV Administration and Scoring Manual* (Wechsler, 2003)

- Includes several process scores that may enhance its clinical utility (see Chapters 6 and 7 for a discussion)
- Special-group studies were designed to improve its clinical utility
- Statistical linkage with measures of achievement (e.g., WIAT-II)
- Includes supplemental tests for core battery tests
- Provides computer scoring and interpretive profiling report
- Ability-Achievement discrepancy analysis available for FSIQ, VCI, and PRI with WIAT-II
- Wechsler Abbreviated Scale of Intelligence (WASI) prediction table (WASI FSIQ-4 and predicted WISC-IV FSIQ range at 68% and 90% confidence interval)
- Twelve subtests on WISC-III yielded four Indexes; 10 subtests on WISC-IV yield four Indexes
- Two manuals included in kit (Administration and Scoring; Technical and Interpretive)

≡Rapid Reference 1.2

Changes from the WISC-III to the WISC-IV

- Structural foundation updated to include measures of *Gf* and additional measures of *Gsm* (i.e., Letter-Number Sequencing) and *Gs* (i.e., Cancellation)
- Scoring criteria modified to be more straightforward
- Picture Arrangement, Object Assembly, and Mazes deleted (to reduce emphasis on time)
- Items added to improve floors and ceilings of subtests
- Instructions to examiners more understandable
- Artwork updated to be more attractive and engaging to children
- Increased developmental appropriateness (instructions modified; teaching, sample, and/or practice items for each subtest)
- Norms updated
- Outdated items replaced
- Manual expanded to include interpretation guidelines and more extensive validity information
- Weight of kit reduced by elimination of most manipulatives
- Arithmetic and Information moved to supplemental status
- Five new subtests added: Word Reasoning, Matrix Reasoning, Picture Concepts, Letter-Number Sequencing, and Cancellation
- VIQ and PIQ dropped
- Freedom from Distractibility (FD) Index replaced with a Working Memory Index
- Perceptual Organization Index (POI) renamed Perceptual Reasoning Index (PRI)

Source: Information in this table is from the *WISC-IV Technical and Interpretive Manual* (The Psychological Corporation, 2003).

- The VCI is now composed of three subtests rather than four. Information is now a supplemental subtest.
- The POI has been renamed the PRI. In addition to Block Design, the PRI is composed of two new subtests, Matrix Reasoning and Picture Concepts. Picture Completion is now a supplemental subtest. Object Assembly, Picture Arrangement, and Mazes have been dropped.
- The FD Index has been renamed the WMI. The WMI is composed of Digit Span and the new Letter-Number Sequencing subtest. Arithmetic, which was formerly part of the FD Index, is now a supplemental subtest.

≡ Rapid Reference 1.3

WISC-IV Classifications

Subtest	Broad Ability Classifications Based on CFA of WISC-IV Standardization Data[a]		Broad and Narrow Ability Classifications Based on Expert Consensus[b]	
1. Block Design	**Gv**		**Gv**	**Spatial Relations**
2. Similarities	**Gc**		**Gc**	**Language Development**
				Lexical Knowledge
3. Digit Span	**Gsm**		**Gsm**	**Memory Span**
				Working Memory
4. Picture Concepts	**Gf**		**Gf**	**Induction**
			Gc	General Information
5. Coding	**Gs**		**Gs**	**Rate-of-Test-Taking**
6. Vocabulary	**Gc**		**Gc**	**Lexical Knowledge**
7. Letter-Number Sequencing	**Gsm**		**Gsm**	**Working Memory**
8. Matrix Reasoning	**Gf**, Gv		**Gf**	**Induction and General Sequential Reasoning**

(continued)

Subtest	Primary/Secondary	Code	Classification
9. Comprehension	*Gc*	**Gc**	**General Information**
10. Symbol Search	**Gs**, *Gv*	**Gs**	**Perceptual Speed**
			Rate-of-Test-Taking
11. Picture Completion	**Gv**, *Gc*	**Gc**	**General Information**
		Gv	Flexibility of Closure
12. Cancellation	**Gs**	**Gs**	**Perceptual Speed**
			Rate-of-Test-Taking
13. Information	**Gc**	**Gc**	**General Information**
14. Arithmetic	**Gf (especially older children)**	**Gq**	**Math Achievement**
	Gsm (especially younger children)	*Gf*	Quantitative Reasoning
15. Word Reasoning	**Gc**	**Gc**	**Lexical Knowledge**
		Gf	Induction

Note: Primary classifications appear in bold type. Secondary classifications appear in regular type. CFA = Confirmatory Factor Analysis.

[a] Keith, Fine, Taub, Reynolds, and Kranzler (2004).

[b] Caltabiano and Flanagan (2004).

≡Rapid Reference 1.4

The Psychological Corporation's *a Posteriori* WISC-IV CHC Classifications

Subtest	Broad Ability Classifications of the WISC-IV Subtests (TPC®)[a]
Block Design	Gv
Similarities	Gf
Digit Span	Gsm
Picture Concepts	Gf
Coding	Gs
Vocabulary	Gc, Glr
Letter-Number Sequencing	Gsm
Matrix Reasoning	Gf
Comprehension	Gc[b]
Symbol Search	Gs
Picture Completion	Gv
Cancellation	Gs
Information	Gc, Glr
Arithmetic	Gq, Gsm
Word Reasoning	Gf

Note: TPC® = The Psychological Corporation.

[a] CHC constructs corresponding to WISC-IV Indexes were provided by The Psychological Corporation® after the publication of the WISC-IV and were obtained from a list of "WISC-IV Frequently Asked Questions (FAQs)" appearing on the Harcourt Web site.

[b] A classification for the WISC-IV Comprehension subtest was not available from the Harcourt Web site. The Gc classification denoted for the WISC-IV Comprehension subtest was based on previous classifications (e.g., Flanagan et al., 2000).

- The PSI remained unchanged. However, a new speed-of-processing test—Cancellation—was added as a supplemental subtest.
- The four Indexes are derived from 10 subtests rather than 12.

The *WISC-IV Technical and Interpretive Manual* (The Psychological Corporation, 2003) provided a series of exploratory and confirmatory factor analyses that offered support for the factor structure of the test depicted in Figure 1.3. Specifi-

Table 1.2 WISC-IV Subtest Definitions

Subtest	Description
1. Block Design (BD)	The examinee is required to replicate a set of modeled or printed two-dimensional geometric patterns using red-and-white blocks within a specified time limit.
2. Similarities (SI)	The examinee is required to describe how two words that represent common objects or concepts are similar.
3. Digit Span (DS)	On Digit Span Forward, the examinee is required to repeat numbers verbatim as stated by the examiner. On Digit Span Backward, the examinee is required to repeat numbers in the reverse order as stated by the examiner.
4. Picture Concepts (PCn)	The examinee is required to choose one picture, from among two or three rows of pictures presented, to form a group with a common characteristic.
5. Coding (CD)	The examinee is required to copy symbols that are paired with either geometric shapes or numbers using a key within a specified time limit.
6. Vocabulary (VC)	The examinee is required to name pictures or provide definitions for words.
7. Letter-Number Sequencing (LN)	The examinee is read a number and letter sequence and is required to recall numbers in ascending order and letters in alphabetical order.
8. Matrix Reasoning (MR)	The examinee is required to complete the missing portion of a picture matrix by selecting one of five response options.
9. Comprehension (CO)	The examinee is required to answer a series of questions based on his or her understanding of general principles and social situations.
10. Symbol Search (SS)	The examinee is required to scan a search group and indicate the presence or absence of a target symbol(s) within a specified time limit.
11. *Picture Completion (PCm)*	The examinee is required to view a picture and name the essential missing part of the picture within a specified time limit.
12. *Cancellation (CA)*	The examinee is required to scan both a random and a nonrandom arrangement of pictures and mark target pictures within a specified time limit.
13. *Information (IN)*	The examinee is required to answer questions that address a wide range of general-knowledge topics.
14. *Arithmetic (AR)*	The examinee is required to mentally solve a variety of orally presented arithmetic problems within a specified time limit.
15. *Word Reasoning (WR)*	The examinee is required to identify a common concept being described by a series of clues.

Note: Subtests printed in italics are supplemental.

cally, four factors underlie the WISC-IV, namely Verbal Comprehension, Perceptual Reasoning, Working Memory, and Processing Speed. The structural validity of the WISC-IV is discussed further below.

Standardization and Psychometric Properties of the WISC-IV

Standardization

The WISC-IV was standardized on a sample of 2,200 children who were chosen to match closely the 2002 U.S. Census data on the variables of age, gender, geographic region, ethnicity, and socioeconomic status (parental education). The standardization sample was divided into 11 age groups, each composed of 200 children. The sample was split equally between boys and girls (see Table 1.1).

Reliability

The reliability of the WISC-IV is presented in its *Technical and Interpretive Manual* (The Psychological Corporation, 2003, Table 4.1, p. 34) and is summarized in Rapid Reference 1.5. The average internal consistency coefficients are 0.94 for VCI, 0.92 for PRI, .92 for WMI, .88 for PSI, and 0.97 for FSIQ. Internal consistency values for individual subtests across all ages ranged from 0.72 for Coding (for ages 6 and 7) to .94 for Vocabulary (for age 15). The median internal consistency values for the individual subtests ranged from .79 (Symbol Search, Cancellation) to .90 (Letter-Number Sequencing).

The WISC-IV is a stable instrument with average test-retest coefficients (corrected for variability of the sample) of 0.93, 0.89, 0.89, 0.86, and 0.93 for the VCI, PRI, WMI, PSI, and FSIQ, respectively (The Psychological Corporation, 2003, Table 4.4, p. 40). Rapid Reference 1.6 shows one-month practice effects (gains from test to retest) for the WISC-IV Indexes and FSIQ for three separate age groups (i.e., 6–7, 8–11, and 12–16) and the overall sample. In general, practice effects are largest for ages 6–7 and become smaller with increasing age. As may be seen in Rapid Reference 1.6, average FSIQ gains dropped from about 8 points (ages 6–7) to 6 points (ages 8–11) to 4 points (ages 12–16). Rapid Reference 1.7 shows the WISC-IV subtests that demonstrated relatively large gains from test to retest. For ages 6–7, Coding and Symbol Search showed the largest gains, while Picture Completion showed the largest gains at ages 8–16. Other interesting facts about one-month practice effects on the WISC-IV are found in Rapid Reference 1.8.

G-Loadings

G-loadings are an important indicator of the degree to which a subtest measures general intelligence. Additionally, *g*-loadings aid in determining the extent to

≡Rapid Reference 1.5

Average Reliability Coefficients of WISC-IV Subtests, Process Scores, and Composite Scales, Based on Total Sample

	Overall Reliability[a]
Subtest	
Block Design	.86
Similarities	.86
Digit Span	.87
Picture Concepts	.82
Coding	.85
Vocabulary	.89
Letter-Number Sequencing	.90
Matrix Reasoning	.89
Comprehension	.81
Symbol Search	.79
Picture Completion	.84
Cancellation	.79
Information	.86
Arithmetic	.88
Word Reasoning	.80
Process Score	
Block Design No Time Bonus	.84
Digit Span Forward	.83
Digit Span Backward	.80
Cancellation Random	.70
Cancellation Structured	.75
Composite Scale	
Verbal Comprehension Index	.94
Perceptual Reasoning Index	.92
Working Memory Index	.92
Processing Speed Index	.88
Full Scale	.97

Source: Information in this table was reproduced from the *WISC-IV Technical and Interpretive Manual* (The Psychological Corporation, 2003).

[a]Average reliability coefficients were calculated with Fisher's z transformation.

≡Rapid Reference 1.6

One-Month Practice Effects for the WISC-IV Indexes and Full Scale IQ (Total N = 243)

Scale	Ages 6-7	Ages 8-11	Ages 12-16	All Ages
VCI	+3.4	+2.2	+1.7	+2.1
	(.31 SD)	(.20 SD)	(.14 SD)	(.18 SD)
PRI	+6.4	+4.2	+5.4	+5.2
	(.46 SD)	(.34 SD)	(.38 SD)	(.39 SD)
WMI	+4.7	+2.8	+1.6	+2.6
	(.33 SD)	(.22 SD)	(.12 SD)	(.20 SD)
PSI	+10.9	+8.2	+4.7	+7.1
	(.72 SD)	(.60 SD)	(.35 SD)	(.51 SD)
FSIQ	+8.3	+5.8	+4.3	+5.6
	(.62 SD)	(.53 SD)	(.34 SD)	(.46 SD)

Source: Data are from WISC-IV Technical and Interpretive Manual (The Psychological Corporation, 2003, Table 4.4).

Note: Intervals ranged from 13 to 63 days with a mean of 32 days.

which a single subtest score can be expected to vary from other scores within a profile. The WISC-IV subtest g-loadings are provided in Appendix C. Table C.1 in Appendix C provides WISC-IV subtest g-loadings by age groups and overall sample. These g-loadings represent the unrotated loadings on the first factor using the principle factor analysis method. This method assumes that g influences the subtests indirectly through its relationship with the four factors. Table C.1 shows that the VCI subtests generally have the highest g-loadings at every age, followed by the PRI, WMI, and PSI subtests. Arithmetic, however, has g-loadings that are more consistent with the VCI subtest loadings as compared to the WMI core battery subtests. Table C.2 in Appendix C includes g loadings for the overall sample from the last column in Table C.1 alongside g-loadings based on confirmatory factor analysis (CFA) using a nested factors model. This latter method assumes that each subtest has a distinct and direct relationship with both g and a broad ability (factor; Keith, personal communication, March 2004). Therefore, the g-loadings in the second column of Table C.2 were derived in a manner more consistent with the factor and scoring structure of the WISC-IV. Table C.2 shows that subtest g-loadings are generally consistent across methods, with two

Rapid Reference 1.7

One-Month Practice Effects for the Separate WISC-IV Scaled Scores: Subtests with Relatively Large Gains from Test to Retest

Ages 6–7	Ages 8–11	Ages 12–16
Coding (+0.65 SD)	Picture Completion (+0.68 SD)	Picture Completion (+0.58 SD)
Symbol Search (+0.62 SD)	Symbol Search (+0.52 SD)	Cancellation (+0.44 SD)
Picture Completion (+0.58 SD)	Picture Concepts (+0.52 SD)	Coding (+0.40 SD)
Arithmetic (+0.57 SD)	Cancellation (+0.47 SD)	Block Design (+0.40 SD)
Picture Concepts (+0.50 SD)	Block Design (+0.40 SD)	Picture Concepts (+0.35 SD)
Block Design (+0.45 SD)		
Similarities (+0.45 SD)		
Word Reasoning (+0.42 SD)		
Letter-Number Sequencing (+0.39 SD)		

Source: Data are from *WISC-IV Technical and Interpretive Manual* (The Psychological Corporation, 2003, Table 4.4).

Note: Relatively large gains are defined as at least 0.33 SD (a gain from test to retest of approximately 1.0 scaled score point, depending on the precise SDs at each age). Gains are listed by the magnitude of the gain for each age group. Intervals ranged from 13 to 63 days with a mean of 32 days.

⚡Rapid Reference 1.8

Interesting Facts about One-Month Practice Effects on the WISC-IV

- WISC-IV practice effects (gains from test to retest) are largest for ages 6–7 and become smaller with increasing age. Average FSIQ gains dropped from about 8 points (ages 6–7) to 6 points (ages 8–11) to 4 points (ages 12–16). See Rapid Reference 1.6.

- The age-related changes in practice effects held for VCI, WMI, and PSI, but not for PRI. The PRI, which measures the "performance" abilities that traditionally yield the largest practice effects, averaged test-retest gains of about 5 points across the age range (see Rapid Reference 1.6).

- Despite the very large practice effect of 11 points (.72 SD) for ages 6–7 on PSI, this age group showed no practice effect at all on Cancellation, the supplemental Processing Speed subtest. In contrast, Cancellation produced among the largest practice effects for ages 8–16 (effect sizes of about 0.45 SD; see Rapid Reference 1.7).

- Arithmetic and Letter-Number Sequencing, both measures of Working Memory, had substantial practice effects at ages 6–7 (see Rapid Reference 1.7), but yielded little or no gains for all other age groups.

- Picture Completion had by far the largest practice effect for all ages combined (0.60 SD). It joins Picture Concepts and Block Design as the only WISC-IV subtests to yield relatively large test-retest gains for each age group studied: 6–7, 8–11, and 12–16 (see Rapid Reference 1.7).

- Practice effects for Digits Forward and Digits Backward varied as a function of age. For ages 6–11, test-retest gains were larger for Digits Backward (effect size of 0.19 SD vs. 0.12 SD for Digits Forward). For ages 12–13, gains were about equal for Digits Forward and Digits Backward. For ages 14–16, test-retest gains were larger for Digits Forward (effect size of 0.29 SD vs. 0.11 SD for Digits Backward).

exceptions—both Word Reasoning and Comprehension had high g-loadings (.70 or greater) based on the principle factor analysis method, and medium g-loadings (.51 to .69) based on the CFA (nested factors) method. These g-loadings may be useful in generating hypotheses about fluctuations in a child's scaled score profile.

Structural Validity

As stated previously, the structural validity of the WISC-IV is supported by the factor analytic studies described in the *WISC-IV Technical and Interpretive Manual* (The Psychological Corporation, 2003; see Figure 1.2 in this chapter). However, the manual did not provide information about the stability or invariance of this factor structure across age. In addition, because The Psychological Corporation did not provide factor loadings and factor correlations for the confirmatory factor analyses presented in the manual, additional analyses were needed to clarify the nature of the cognitive constructs measured by the test.

Recently, Keith et al. (2004) investigated whether the WISC-IV measured the same constructs across its 11-year age span, as well as the nature of those constructs using the WISC-IV standardization data. Results of their analyses indicated that the WISC-IV measures the same constructs across the age range of the test. These constructs are represented by the large ovals in Figure 1.3. However, according to Keith and colleagues, the factor structure of the WISC-IV (depicted in Figure 1.3) is not a good explanation of the constructs measured by the test. Rather, based on a comparison of theory-derived alternative models with the one depicted in Figure 1.3, Keith and colleagues found that a factor structure more consistent with CHC theory provided a better fit to the WISC-IV standardization data. See Appendix A for detailed definitions of the CHC abilities.

According to Keith and colleagues (2004), the WISC-IV measures Crystallized Ability *(Gc)*, Visual Processing *(Gv)*, Fluid Reasoning *(Gf)*, Short-Term Memory *(Gsm)*, and Processing Speed *(Gs)*. These findings are depicted in Figure 1.4 and are consistent with the results of a recently conducted content validity study of the WISC-IV, based on CHC theory, that used an expert consensus format (Caltabiano & Flanagan, 2004). Rapid Reference 1.3 summarizes the results of the studies conducted by Keith and colleagues (2004) and Caltabiano and Flanagan (2004). Although The Psychological Corporation identified four factors to describe the constructs underlying the WISC-IV, Rapid Reference 1.3 shows that Keith and colleagues and Caltabiano and Flanagan found five. In addition, the results of these latter two studies were consistent, with the exception of the CHC abilities presumed to underlie the Arithmetic subtest. Keith and colleagues described this test as *Gf* and *Gsm,* and Caltabiano and Flanagan classified this test as Quantitative Knowledge *(Gq)* and *Gf.* Interestingly, following the publication of the WISC-IV and its *WISC-IV Technical and Interpretive Manual* (The Psychological Corporation, 2003), The Psychological Corporation classified all of the WISC-IV subtests according to CHC theory on its Web page. These classifications are located in Rapid Reference 1.4, which shows that the classifications offered by The Psychological Corporation are similar to those provided in Rapid Reference 1.3, with only a few exceptions. That is, The Psychological Corporation classified Similarities and Word Reasoning as primarily measures of *Gf* and Arithmetic as primarily a measure of *Gq* and *Gsm.*

Although the factor analyses conducted by The Psychological Corporation and Keith and colleagues (2004) differ, it is important to understand that there is no one "right" method of factor analysis. Indeed, the factor analyses, particularly

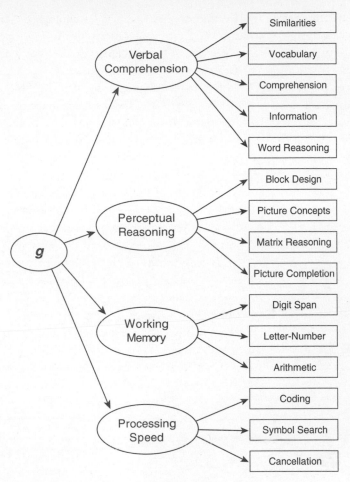

Figure 1.3 The Organization of the WISC-IV

the exploratory factor analyses, summarized in the *WISC-IV Technical and Interpretive Manual* provide strong support for the WISC-IV four-factor structure, while the confirmatory factor analyses conducted by Keith and colleagues provide strong support for a five-factor structure. Therefore, our interpretive system permits examiners to interpret the WISC-IV according to either four or five factors. The latter option is made possible by the inclusion of clinical clusters and supplementary norms tables in our interpretive system (Chapter 4, Step 7).

Briefly, based on the results of independent factor analyses, expert consensus content validity findings, the CHC classifications of the WISC-IV subtests of-

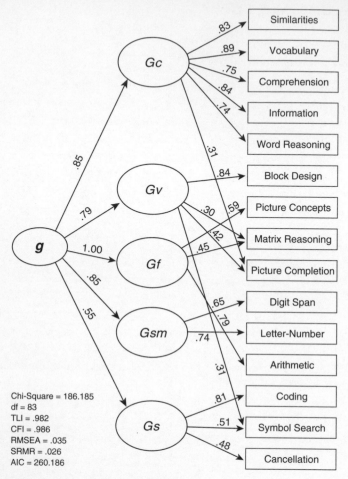

Figure 1.4 CHC Structure of the WISC-IV

Source: Keith et al. (2004). Printed with permission from authors.

Note: df = degrees of freedom; TLI = Tucker Lewis Index; CFI = Comparative Fit Index; RMSEA = Root Mean Square Error of Approximation; SRMR = Standardized Root Mean Square Residual; AIC = Akaike Information Criterion.

fered by The Psychological Corporation (see Rapid References 1.3 and 1.4), and our own clinical judgment, we developed eight new clinical clusters:

1. Fluid Reasoning *(Gf)*
2. Visual Processing *(Gv)*
3. Nonverbal Fluid Reasoning *(Gf-nonverbal)*
4. Verbal Fluid Reasoning *(Gf-verbal)*

5. Lexical Knowledge (*Gc*-VL)
6. General Information (*Gc*-KO)
7. Long-Term Memory (*Gc*-LTM)
8. Short-Term Memory (*Gsm*-MW)

These clinical clusters may be used in what we call "Planned Clinical Comparisons" to gain information about a child's cognitive capabilities beyond the four Indexes and FSIQ, as well as to generate hypotheses about cognitive performance to be verified through other data sources. Figure 1.5 provides a *selective testing table* that may be used by the examiner to identify the different combinations of WISC-IV subtests that compose the four Indexes, FSIQ, and new clinical clusters. Use of the clinical clusters in Planned Clinical Comparisons are discussed as an optional interpretive step in Chapter 4.

Relationship to Other Wechsler Scales

In addition to factor analysis and content validity research, the validity of the WISC-IV is supported by correlations with other global measures. Rapid Reference 1.9 shows the correlations between the WISC-IV FSIQ and the WISC-III FSIQ (.89) as well as the FSIQs from other Wechsler scales (i.e., WPPSI-III, WAIS-III, and WASI). Not surprisingly, the WISC-IV FSIQ is highly correlated with the FSIQs of other Wechsler scales.

The WISC-IV also shows good to excellent convergent/discriminant validity evidence. Rapid Reference 1.10 shows that the VCI has an average correlation of .83 with other measures of verbal ability compared to a mean of .61 with measures of perceptual abilities. Similarly, Rapid Reference 1.10 shows that the PRI has an average correlation of .76 with other measures of visual-perceptual ability compared to a mean of .61 with measures of verbal abilities.

Relationship to WIAT-II

The validity of the WISC-IV was investigated further through an examination of its relationship to academic achievement. Rapid Reference 1.11 includes the correlations between the WISC-IV Indexes and FSIQ with the WIAT-II Achievement Composites. This Rapid Reference shows that the correlations between the FSIQ and WIAT-II Composites ranged from .75 (Oral Language) to .78 (Reading and Math), indicating that the WISC-IV FSIQ explains 56 to 60% of the variance in these achievement domains. The correlation between the FSIQ and WIAT-II Total Achievement Score is .87 (76% of variance explained), which is about as high as the correlation between the WISC-IV FSIQ and the FSIQs of other Wechsler scales (i.e., .89; see Rapid Reference 1.9). These correlations are among the highest ever reported between global IQ and achievement. According to Kenny (1979), "Even highly developed causal

New Clinical Clusters

Subtest	Full Scale IQ (FSIQ)	Verbal Comprehension Index (VCI)	Perceptual Reasoning Index (PRI)	Working Memory Index (WMI)	Processing Speed Index (PSI)	Fluid Reasoning (Gf) Cluster	Visual Processing (Gv) Cluster	Verbal Fluid Reasoning (Gf-verbal) Cluster	Nonverbal Fluid Reasoning (Gf-nonverbal) Cluster	Lexical Knowledge (Gc-VL) Cluster	General Information (Gc-K0) Cluster	Long-Term Memory (Gc-LTM) Cluster	Short-Term Memory (Gsm-WM) Cluster [a]
1. Block Design	•		•				•						
2. Similarities	•	•						•					
3. Digit Span	•			•									•
4. Picture Concepts	•		•			•			•				
5. Coding	•				•								
6. Vocabulary	•	•								•		•	
7. Letter-Number Sequencing	•			•									•
8. Matrix Reasoning	•		•			•			•				
9. Comprehension	•	•									•		
10. Symbol Search	•				•								
11. Picture Completion							•						
12. Cancellation													
13. Information											•	•	
14. Arithmetic													
15. Word Reasoning								•		•			

[a] The Short-Term Memory (Gsm-WM) Cluster is identical to the WISC-IV Working Memory Index.

Figure 1.5 Selective Testing Table

models do not explain behavior very well. A good rule of thumb is that one is fooling oneself if more than 50% of the variance is predicted" (p. 9). It is likely that either overlapping content or standard deviations > 15 or some combination thereof led to spuriously high correlations.

Rapid Reference 1.12 summarizes the WISC-IV subtests that are the best and worst predictors of WIAT-II Achievement Composites. In general, Arithmetic, Vocabulary, and Information are the best predictors of the WIAT-II Composites; and Picture Concepts along with Coding and Cancellation (i.e., the Processing Speed subtests) are the worst predictors of these same composites.

≋Rapid Reference 1.9

Correlation of Full Scale IQs: WISC-IV and Other Wechsler Scales

	WISC-IV
WISC-III (N = 233)	.89
WPPSI-III (N = 144)	.89
WAIS-III (N = 183)	.89
WASI (N = 254)	.86

Note: All values are corrected for the variability of the standardization sample. Coefficients are from *WISC-IV Technical and Interpretive Manual* (The Psychological Corporation, 2003, Tables 5.8, 5.10, 5.12, and 5.14).

In addition to the validity evidence summarized previously, the *WISC-IV Technical and Interpretive Manual* provides a number of special-group studies to investigate the diagnostic utility of the instrument. These studies are discussed in detail in Chapter 6. Overall, the WISC-IV is a reliable and valid measure of a select number of cognitive abilities (viz., Verbal Comprehension *[Gc]*, Perceptual Reasoning *[Gf, Gv]*; Working Memory *[Gsm]*; and Processing Speed *[Gs]*).

Other Quantitative and Qualitative Characteristics of the WISC-IV

Appendix D provides a quick reference to key quantitative and qualitative features of the WISC-IV subtests that may aid in interpretation. Several quantitative characteristics are *evaluated* in Table D.1 according to commonly accepted criteria, including internal consistency and test-retest reliabilities, *g*-loadings, subtest floors and ceilings, and item gradients. Table D.1 also includes important qualitative characteristics of the WISC-IV subtests. Specifically, each subtest is classified according to degree of cultural loading and linguistic demand. Also, a list of the most probable factors that influence subtest performance is provided for each subtest. Table D.2 of this appendix provides definitions of the quantitative and qualitative characteristics included in Table D.1 along with an explanation of the criteria used to (1) evaluate the quantitative characteristics and (2) classify the WISC-IV subtests according to select qualitative characteristics. Finally, Table D.2 provides a brief description of the interpretive relevance of each characteristic included in

≡*Rapid Reference 1.10*

Convergent/Discriminant Validity of the WISC-IV Verbal Comprehension Index (VCI) and Perceptual Reasoning Index (PRI)

	WISC-IV	
	VCI	PRI
WPPSI-III (*N* = 182, ages 6–7)		
Verbal IQ	**.83**	.63
Performance IQ	.65	**.79**
General Language Composite (GLC)	**.68**	.53
WISC-III (*N* = 244, ages 6–16)		
Verbal Comprehension Index (VCI)	**.88**	.59
Perceptual Organization Index (POI)	.62	**.72**
Verbal IQ	**.87**	.64
Performance IQ	.61	**.74**
WAIS-III (*N* = 198, age 16)		
Verbal Comprehension Index (VCI)	**.86**	.64
Perceptual Organization Index (POI)	.57	**.76**
Verbal IQ	**.86**	.69
Performance IQ	.61	**.76**
WASI-4 subtests (*N* = 260, ages 6–16)		
Verbal IQ	**.85**	.61
Performance IQ	.60	**.78**

Source: Convergent values are from the *WISC-IV Technical and Interpretive Manual* (The Psychological Corporation, 2003, Tables 5.8, 5.10, 5.12, and 5.14). The divergent values (VCI with visual-perceptual ability, PRI with verbal ability) were provided by The Psychological Corporation. *Wechsler Intelligence Scale for Children: Fourth Edition.* Copyright © 2004 by Harcourt Assessment, Inc. Reproduced by permission. All rights reserved. *Wechsler Intelligence Scale for Children, WISC* and *WISC-IV* are trademarks of Harcourt Assessment, Inc., registered in the United States of America and/or other jurisdictions.

Note: Correlations of WISC-IV VCI and PRI with other measures of Wechsler's Verbal and Visual-Perceptual ability (average corrected correlations across two testing orders), respectively, are printed in bold. Coefficients in bold denote convergent validity of WISC-IV VCI and PRI. All values are corrected for the variability of the standardization sample.

Rapid Reference 1.11

WISC-IV Indexes and Full Scale IQ: Correlations with WIAT-II Achievement Composites

WIAT-II Composite	VCI	PRI	WMI	PSI	FSIQ
Reading	.74	.63	.66	.50	.78
Math	.68	.67	.64	.53	.78
Written Language	.67	.61	.64	.55	.76
Oral Language	.75	.63	.57	.49	.75
Total Achievement	.80	.71	.71	.58	.87

Note: All values are corrected for the variability of the standardization sample. Coefficients are from *WISC-IV Technical and Interpretive Manual* (The Psychological Corporation, 2003, Table 5.15). Sample sizes range from 538 to 548.

Table D.1. The information included in Appendix D may be used to assist in the generation of hypotheses about a child's unique profile of cognitive capabilities.

CONCLUSION

The contributions to the science of intellectual assessment made by David Wechsler through his intelligence scales are many and substantial, if not landmark. Although he is not recognized as an important theoretician, this neither detracts from his accomplishments nor diminishes his innovations in applied psychometrics. Wechsler was a well known clinician and, as such, he intentionally placed significant importance on developing tasks that had practical, clinical value, and not merely theoretical value. Thus, the driving force behind the development of the Wechsler scales was no doubt based more on practical considerations rather than theoretical ones. Zachary (1990) stated, "[W]hen David Wechsler published the original Wechsler-Bellevue scales in 1939, he said relatively little about the theoretical underpinnings of his new instrument; rather, he followed a pragmatic approach. He selected a set of tasks that were easy to administer and score. . . ." (p. 276). Detterman (1985) also attributed much of the popularity of the Wechsler family of tests to their "ease of administration fostered by an organization of subtests that are brief . . . and have long clinical histories" (p. 1715). For better or worse, Wechsler's primary motivation for constructing his tests was to create an efficient, easy-to-use tool for clinical purposes; opera-

≡ Rapid Reference 1.12

WISC-IV Subtests: The Best and Worst Predictors of WIAT-II Achievement Composites

Reading	Math	Written Language	Oral Language	Total Achievement
BEST				
Vocabulary (.72)	Arithmetic (.74)	Arithmetic (.67)	Vocabulary (.73)	Vocabulary (.76)
Information (.68)	Information (.67)	Vocabulary (.64)	Information (.69)	Information (.75)
Arithmetic (.68)	Vocabulary (.64)	Information (.62)	Similarities (.67)	Arithmetic (.75)
WORST				
Picture Concepts (.42)	Picture Concepts (.42)	Picture Concepts (.41)	Picture Concepts (.41)	Picture Concepts (.47)
Coding (.40)	Coding (.42)	Picture Completion (.40)	Coding (.38)	Coding (.45)
Cancellation (.14)	Cancellation (.11)	Cancellation (.14)	Cancellation (.15)	Cancellation (.15)

Note: Correlations of WISC-IV scaled scores with WIAT-II achievement composite standard scores are repeated in parentheses. All values are corrected for the variability of the standardization sample. Coefficients are from *WISC-IV Technical and Interpretive Manual* (The Psychological Corporation, 2003, Table 5.15). Sample sizes range from 531 to 548, except for the Arithmetic subtest ($N = 301$).

tionalizing them according to a specific theory of intelligence was not of paramount importance.

Despite these accomplishments and accolades, under the critical eye of subsequent advancements in the field, the failure of the Wechsler scales to keep abreast of contemporary intelligence research cannot be ignored. It is clear that meaningful use and interpretation of the Wechsler scales require the adoption of a fourth-wave approach in which contemporary theory, research, and measurement principles are integrated.

We believe that clinical judgment and experience alone are insufficient stanchions upon which defensible interpretations can be built. Application of contemporary theory and research to intelligence test use and interpretation is needed. The interpretive approach offered in this book has considerable promise as an efficient, theoretically and statistically defensible method for assessing and interpreting the array of cognitive abilities underlying the WISC-IV. The subsequent chapters of this book demonstrate how the principles and procedures of both Kaufman's and Flanagan's interpretive methods have been integrated to advance the science of measuring and interpreting cognitive abilities using the WISC-IV.

COMPREHENSIVE REFERENCES ON THE WISC-IV

The *WISC-IV Technical and Interpretive Manual* (The Psychological Corporation, 2003) provides important information about the development of the test and includes descriptions of the subtests and scales, as well as detailed information on standardization, reliability, and validity.

Also see the following resources:

- Sattler, J. M., & Dumont, R. (2004). *Assessment of Children: WISC-IV and WPPSI-III Supplement.* La Mesa, CA: Jerome M. Sattler.
- Prifitera, A., Saklofske, D. H., Weiss, L. G., & Rolfhus, E. (Eds.). (in press). *WISC-IV Clinical Use and Interpretation: Scientist-Practitioner Perspective (Practical Resources for the Mental Health Professional).* San Diego, CA: Academic Press.

☚ TEST YOURSELF ☚

1. **Picture Arrangement, Object Assembly, and Mazes were deleted from the WISC-IV battery for which one of the following reasons:**
   (a) Because they are most valid for preschool children
   (b) To deemphasize the timed nature of the battery
   (c) Because surveys regarding WISC-IV development revealed that children did not like these tests
   (d) Because these tests were deemed unfair to language impaired children

2. **The Block Design subtest is primarily a measure of which of the following CHC abilities:**
   (a) Visual Processing *(Gv)*
   (b) Fluid Reasoning *(Gf)*
   (c) Working Memory (*Gsm*-MW)
   (d) Processing Speed *(Gs)*

3. **The average reliability of the WISC-IV core battery subtests can be best described as**
   (a) high.
   (b) low.
   (c) medium.
   (d) unacceptable.

4. **Which of the following WISC-IV indexes is the best predictor of written language achievement?**
   (a) VCI
   (b) PRI
   (c) WMI
   (d) PSI

5. **The WISC-IV represents the most substantial revision of the Wechsler scales to date.** True or False?

6. **Cohen's significant contributions that largely defined the third wave of test interpretation included which of the following:**
   (a) Empirical support for the FSIQ based on analysis of shared variance between subtests
   (b) Development of the three-factor solution for interpretation of the Wechsler scales
   (c) Revelation of limited subtest specificity, questioning individual subtest interpretation
   (d) All of the above

7. **Kaufman's and Flanagan's intra-individual (ipsative) analysis method has improved upon traditional ipsative methods in several ways. One major difference between their approach and traditional approaches is that they recommend using composites or clusters, rather than subtests, in intra-individual analysis.** True or False?

Answers: 1. b; 2. a; 3. c; 4. a; 5. True; 6. d; 7. True

Two

HOW TO ADMINISTER THE WISC-IV

Both standardized and nonstandardized procedures should be used together to uncover a child's true abilities. Norm-referenced tests, such as the WISC-IV, provide information to allow the examiner to compare an individual's performance to the performance of a norm group. To obtain accurate scores from a norm-referenced test, standardized procedures need to be followed under a set of standard conditions. When an examiner adheres to these standard procedures and conditions, a fair comparison of the examinee's level of ability can be made to the "normative group"—that is, a representative sample of same-age peers from the general population. As will be discussed throughout this book, however, nonstandardized procedures such as interviews, behavioral observations, and informal assessments should be used alongside standardized tests to provide an integrated and complete picture of a child. Simply taking a snapshot of a child's abilities through a time-limited sample of performance, as is done during the administration of any standardized test, including the WISC-IV, does not provide sufficient information about the child for the purposes of diagnosing and making recommendations.

APPROPRIATE TESTING CONDITIONS

Testing Environment

There are some issues regarding the testing environment that should be considered whether you are testing a child or an adolescent. For a child of any age, it is important to have a testing environment that is relatively bland and free of distractions, both visual and auditory. For example, the surroundings should not have too many toys or windows. However, the surroundings should not be so formal or adult-like that the child or adolescent feels like he or she is in a medical examination room. The testing environment should be comfortable for both you and the examinee. In most situations, only the examiner and the examinee should be in the testing room during the evaluation.

In order to test an examinee with the WISC-IV in a manner consistent with standardized procedures, it is necessary to sit at a table. However, in some cases we have found that when testing a highly energetic young child, it may be advantageous to be prepared to move the testing materials to another location, such as the floor, where the child will best attend to you. With some children, it may be necessary to fluctuate between highly structured testing activities at a table and more informal activities that can be done on the floor. In any case, it is a good idea to use a clipboard, as it provides a smooth writing surface and it can be transported to the floor or other locations, if necessary.

Testing Materials

During testing, we recommend that you sit either opposite the child or at a 90-degree angle from the child in order to most easily view the test-taking behaviors and manipulate the test materials. The testing manual may be propped up on the table and positioned as a shield behind which the Record Form can be placed. This positioning allows the examiner to read the directions easily and prevents the child from being distracted by what the examiner is writing on the Record Form. Only the testing materials that are in immediate use should be visible to the examinee. Stimulus materials can distract young children easily if they are in view. We recommend that you keep other testing materials on the floor or on a chair beside you so that they are readily available to you, but out of the child's view.

Because the WISC-IV contains several materials, including one stimulus book, two pencils, nine blocks, two manuals, two response booklets, three scoring keys, and one Record Form, we recommend that you double-check that all necessary materials are present prior to beginning the testing. A few materials are not contained in the WISC-IV test kit

DON'T FORGET

....

Keys to Preparing to Administer the WISC-IV

- Quiet, distraction-free room with table and chairs
- Smooth writing surface
- Stopwatch

Useful materials not in the kit:

- Clipboard
- Extra paper and writing utensils (for recording observations)

Source: From A. S. Kaufman & E. O. Lichtenberger, *Essentials of WISC-III and WPPSI-R Assessment.* Copyright © 2000 John Wiley & Sons, Inc. This material is used by permission of John Wiley & Sons, Inc.

and, therefore, you will need to bring these yourself: a stopwatch, a clipboard, and extra paper for taking notes.

RAPPORT WITH EXAMINEE

Establishing Rapport

When working with children and adolescents, building rapport is crucial to obtaining valid testing results. Even the most experienced examiners may find that it is challenging to juggle the maintenance of rapport with adherence to standardized procedures. When interacting with the child initially, it is important to allow him or her enough time to become accustomed to you before beginning the evaluation. Addressing the child by his or her name, telling the child your name, and spending a reasonable amount of time interacting with the child prior to testing (e.g., discussing the child's interests and hobbies) can aid in establishing rapport (Kaufman & Kaufman, 1993). When conversing with the child, you should remember to be open, honest, and genuine. Any comments that you may make upon initially meeting the child, or throughout testing, should be mildly positive. That is, too much interest in or praise of a child's conversation, appearance, and so on may be viewed suspiciously, especially by adolescents.

In addition to being given time to accustom themselves to you, children must also be given time to become accustomed to the testing situation itself. It is important to note that the manner in which you or, in some cases, a parent or caregiver have introduced the child to the testing situation can have either positive or negative effects throughout the evaluation. Therefore, we encourage examiners and parents to explain to children ahead of time what they should expect during the evaluation. Such explanations can alleviate any anticipatory anxiety that the child may have. For example, it is good to let the child know that the examiner will be showing him or her blocks and books containing pictures and words and will be asking some questions. We advise examiners (and parents) not to use the word "test" when introducing the situation to the child because the word has a negative connotation for many children and can elicit a fear reaction. However, if a child asks directly, "Am I going to take a test?" then it is best not to lie, but rather explain to the child, "Most of the things you are going to be doing are not like the tests you take at school. In fact, lots of kids think that these special kinds of tests are pretty fun." Examiners should also be sure to explain that no one gets all of the questions and problems right, that some questions are easy and some are difficult for everyone, and that what may start off as a fairly easy task could become rather difficult.

Although an examiner should retain control of the testing situation at all times,

DON'T FORGET

Keys to Establishing Positive Rapport

- Effectively introduce the child to the testing activities.
- Avoid the word "test."
- Explain the purpose of the assessment following the standardized instructions on page 59 of the *WISC-IV Administration and Scoring Manual* (Wechsler, 2003).
- Allow the child ample time to adjust to the testing situation.
- Achieve a balance between professional (formal) and friendly (informal) demeanor.
- Correct any misperceptions that the child may have about the purpose of testing.
- Describe your role clearly and maintain control of the testing situation at all times.
- Tell examinees that you may use a stopwatch and will record their answers.

Source: From A. S. Kaufman & E. O. Lichtenberger, *Essentials of WISC-III and WPPSI-R Assessment.* Copyright © 2000 John Wiley & Sons, Inc. This material is used by permission of John Wiley & Sons, Inc.

it is important that the examiner is flexible in structuring the assessment sessions according to the child's needs. Some children may need frequent breaks due to a medical condition (e.g., cerebral palsy), and others may fatigue easily and require several short evaluation sessions (e.g., individuals with Attention-Deficit/Hyperactivity Disorder, or ADHD) and so forth. Examiners should obtain sufficient information about a child's medical and behavioral history prior to evaluating him or her to ensure the validity of the findings. Examiners should also remember not to talk down to children of any age. Rather, they should try to adjust their vocabulary appropriately to the child's age level. Adolescents may become particularly uncooperative if they are treated like younger children. With teenagers, it is important to try to initiate a conversation that is interesting to them but does not appear overly invasive, showing respect for their boundaries. A balance between formality and informality—between being professional and being friendly— should be achieved when testing both children and adolescents. The Don't Forget box above summarizes key points in establishing positive rapport.

Maintaining Rapport

Getting the attention of a child is often not as difficult as keeping his or her attention and motivation. This is when the delicate balance between rapport and adherence to standardized test procedures becomes especially important. Providing frequent praise for a child's efforts is important for maintaining his or her attention and motivation. The examiner should pay close attention to signs of waning attention, frustration, or lack of motivation. Such signs may be verbal (e.g., "How much longer?" or "These are too hard") or nonverbal (e.g., increased fidgeting, sighing, grimacing). These observations are signals to the examiner that it may be necessary to increase encouragement and praise or perhaps to take a break. See the Caution box below for a list of ways to give appropriate feedback and encouragement.

Encouragement and praise may be delivered in many different ways (e.g., an understanding smile, a pat on the hand, saying "We've got a lot more fun things to do," "You're working so hard," "Wow, you're a hard worker"). However, it is important that praise not be overly repetitive, as it will lose its reinforcing effects. Likewise, be careful when praising a child's efforts that you are not giving feedback about whether the child's responses are correct. Encouragement should be given throughout administration of the items, not only when a child is struggling or giving incorrect responses.

Some children may require more than verbal and nonverbal praise to maintain motivation. In these cases, it may be useful to develop a reward system. For example, an agreement may be reached that the child can play with certain toys after a required number of tasks have been completed. Sometimes a small snack may be used as a reward, but you should always discuss this with the parent ahead of time (some parents disapprove of certain types of foods, don't want dinner spoiled, or will need to warn you about their child's food allergies).

CAUTION

Appropriate Feedback and Encouragement

- Praise frequently but don't be repetitive, which lessens the reinforcement value.
- Be aware that encouragement/feedback may be verbal or nonverbal:
  - Smile
  - Give a pat on the hand
  - Say "Good job," "You sure are working hard," etc.
- Praise and encourage the child's level of effort.
- Be careful *not* to give feedback on whether a particular response is right or wrong.
- Give encouragement *throughout* items, not just when the child is struggling.

Source: From A. S. Kaufman & E. O. Lichtenberger, *Essentials of WISC-III and WPPSI-R Assessment.* Copyright © 2000 John Wiley & Sons, Inc. This material is used by permission of John Wiley & Sons, Inc.

Maintaining the child's motivational level requires consistent effort on the examiner's part. It is important to be able to remove materials skillfully and present the next task quickly, which creates a smooth and rapid transition between subtests. It is wise to continue small-talk while recording behavioral observations between subtests, as this helps maintain a child's attention, but it is important to limit such conversation to the time between subtests. Frequent eye contact also helps maintain rapport; thus, it is crucial to be familiar enough with the standardized instructions so that you do not have to read them word for word with your head buried in the manual during administration.

Children may occasionally refuse to cooperate, be easily fatigued, or become too nervous to continue. In such situations it is appropriate to give several breaks throughout the testing or to reschedule the testing for another day. However, you should be aware that many children are skilled in "testing" examiners and may try to distract an examiner from the task at hand. Being alert to such behavior helps to keep the testing flowing. When children indicate that they do not want to continue with a subtest (perhaps a challenging subtest), it is advisable to provide encouragement such as "Just try your best" or "Give it your best shot." To prevent undue frustration during timed subtests, it may be useful to allow the child to work past the time limit if he or she is actively involved in the task. Although any response given on timed tests after the time limit has expired is not counted toward the score, al-

DON'T FORGET

Keys to Maintaining Rapport

- Provide frequent praise and encouragement.
- Praise examinees for their effort rather than the correctness of their responses.
- Record all responses, not just incorrect responses.
- Set up a reward system if necessary.
- Give frequent breaks if necessary.
- Reschedule testing if the child is too tired, anxious, or uncooperative.
- Make eye contact; don't bury your head in the manual.
- Make smooth and rapid transitions *between* subtests.
- Use small talk *between* subtests but not *during* subtests.
- Familiarize yourself ahead of time with test directions and test materials.
- Be subtle, not distracting, when using a stopwatch.

Source: From A. S. Kaufman & E. O. Lichtenberger, *Essentials of WISC-III and WPPSI-R Assessment.* Copyright © 2000 John Wiley & Sons, Inc. This material is used by permission of John Wiley & Sons, Inc.

lowing extra time under these circumstances may lessen discouragement. The Don't Forget box on page 50 summarizes various ways to maintain rapport.

TESTING INDIVIDUALS WITH SPECIAL NEEDS

Children with special needs—including those with speech, language, or hearing deficits, visual impairments, mental retardation, neurological impairments, physical disabilities, or behavioral disorders—may require certain modifications during an evaluation to ensure that the assessment results reflect their abilities accurately. Therefore, it is crucial to obtain thorough information about any disability from the caregiver prior to beginning the assessment. The caregiver may be able to provide suggestions about the best way to elicit a response from the child when he or she is presented with both verbal and nonverbal stimuli. This information is likely to lead to the most appropriate modifications or accommodations during an evaluation for a child with special needs. Examiners should be prepared to be flexible with regard to the types of accommodations that may need to be implemented for children with specific impairments or disabilities, and should be aware of conditions that may occur earlier than is typical, such as fatigue. In short, the examiner must understand the specific needs of any child; make appropriate modifications or accommodations as necessary; and pay close attention to signs of inattention, tiredness, fatigue, and the like to make sure that the evaluation constitutes a fair assessment of a child's cognitive capabilities.

Notwithstanding, when modifications are made to the standardized testing procedures for any reason, test scores may be altered in an unknown way and use of the test's norms may be invalid. Clinical judgment must be exercised in determining whether modifications to the test or the impact of the specific impairment itself prevent the calculation of standard scores. Modifications may include, but are not limited to, the following:

1. Administer only the VCI and WMI subtests to a child with a visual impairment. However, for Vocabulary (a core VCI subtest) the first four items (pictorial stimuli) cannot be given to visually impaired children who do not earn perfect scores on Items 5 and 6; also, the printed words in the Stimulus Book, which are shown to children aged 9–16 as each item is presented, is a procedure that cannot be followed for children with a visual impairment. For Arithmetic (a supplemental WMI subtest), the first five items, which include pictorial stimuli, cannot be administered. Children aged 6–7 start the Arithmetic subtest with Item 3, so this supplemental subtest is not recommended for children aged 6 or 7 with a visual impairment.

2. For children who are deaf or hard of hearing, administer the test in the child's preferred mode of communication (e.g., American Sign Language) or allow the child to lip-read if he or she is able. Examiners who are skilled in testing children who are deaf or hard of hearing are encouraged to study Tables 1.4 and 1.5 and the associated text in the *WISC-IV Administration and Scoring Manual* (Wechsler, 2003, pp. 12–18). Testing this population with the WISC-IV is also discussed in Chapter 6.

3. Provide an appropriate translation for a child who is an English-language learner by using an interpreter, administering the test bilingually or in the child's native language, or using an adapted or translated version of the test.

4. Consider administering only the VCI subtests, WMI subtests, and those PRI subtests that require minimal or no motor skills (i.e., Picture Concepts, Matrix Reasoning, and Picture Completion) to children with motor impairments. Cancellation, which involves less-fine motor skill, may serve as a substitute for Coding in deriving the PSI.

5. Extend testing over more than one session for children with special needs, as necessary.

It is important to realize that successful evaluation of a child with special needs, indeed of any child, may require the use of supplemental measures or another instrument altogether. Careful consideration of the child's needs, coupled with astute observations of his or her range of verbal and nonverbal capabilities, will help to determine what types of modifications are best.

CAUTION

Modifying Standardized Procedures

- Modification of the standardized procedures to accommodate a child's special needs may invalidate the scores on the test.
- Clinical judgment is key in determining what quantitative and qualitative data are interpretable from the test administration.
- Translating the test into another language through the use of a translator or administering the test bilingually may cause problems in interpreting scores (e.g., word meanings are not equivalent across all languages).

Source: From A. S. Kaufman & E. O. Lichtenberger, *Essentials of WISC-III and WPPSI-R Assessment.* Copyright © 2000 John Wiley & Sons, Inc. This material is used by permission of John Wiley & Sons, Inc.

ADMINISTRATION CONSIDERATIONS

Special Considerations for Testing Children at the Extreme Ends of the Age Range

The WISC-IV may be administered to children as young as age 6 years 0 months and as old as age 16 years 11 months. When testing children at these lower and upper limits of the WISC-IV age range, examiners must decide whether this instrument is the most appropriate or whether, for example, the WPPSI-III or WAIS-III, respectively, may be preferable. When making this determination, it is recommended that you use the WISC-IV with 6-year-olds whom you consider to be of average intelligence (or higher). Otherwise, the WPPSI-III or another instrument with norms for children aged 6 and younger should be used as deemed appropriate. Likewise, it is recommended that you use the WISC-IV with 16-year-olds whom you consider to be within the average range or below. Otherwise, the WAIS-III or another instrument with norms for adolescents and adults should be used. That is, to ensure the availability of a sufficient number of items to assess a child's ability adequately, the WPPSI-III should be used with 6-year-olds who are below the average range because it provides significantly easier items than the WISC-IV, and the WAIS-III should be used with 16-year-olds who are above the average range because it provides significantly more difficult items than the WISC-IV. These recommendations are summarized in Table 2.1.

Table 2.1 Deciding on the WISC-IV vs. Another Battery for 6- and 16-Year-Olds

Age	Estimated Level of Ability	Battery to Administer
6	Below Average	WPPSI-III or an appropriate alternative battery
	Average Range	WISC-IV
	Above Average	WISC-IV
16	Below Average	WISC-IV
	Average Range	WISC-IV
	Above Average	WAIS-III or an appropriate alternative battery

Source: From A. S. Kaufman & E. O. Lichtenberger, *Essentials of WISC-III and WPPSI-R Assessment.* Copyright © 2000 John Wiley & Sons, Inc. This material is used by permission of John Wiley & Sons, Inc.

Note: WPPSI-III = Wechsler Preschool and Primary Scale of Intelligence–Third Edition; WAIS-III = Wechsler Adult Intelligence Scale–Third Edition.

RULES FOR STARTING AND DISCONTINUING SUBTESTS

The administration rules of the WISC-IV are detailed in the *WISC-IV Administration and Scoring Manual* (Wechsler, 2003) and are also located on the Record Form. In this section we highlight the general administration rules. Some of the WISC-IV subtests start at predetermined items according to the child's age, whereas other subtests begin at Item 1 regardless of age. Rapid Reference 2.1 identifies which subtests have age-based starting points (denoted by checkmarks) and re-

≋Rapid Reference 2.1

Starting Points and Reverse Rules of Subtests

Subtest	Age-Based Starting Point (reverse rules)	Age and Starting Point
1. Block Design	✓ (Yes)	6–7: Item 1 8–16: Item 3
2. Similarities	✓ (Yes)	6–8: sample, then Item 1 9–11: sample, then Item 3 12–16: sample, then Item 5
3. Digit Span	(No)	6–16: Forward, Item 1; Backward, sample, then Item 1
4. Picture Concepts	✓ (Yes)	6–8: Samples A and B, then Item 1 9–11: Samples A and B, then Item 5 12–16: Samples A and B, then Item 7
5. Coding	(No)	6–7: Coding A, sample items, then test items 8–16: Coding B, sample items, then test items
6. Vocabulary	✓ (Yes)	6–8: Item 5 9–11: Item 7 12–16: Item 9
7. Letter-Number Sequencing	(No)	6–7: qualifying items, sample item, then Item 1 8–16: sample item, then Item 1
8. Matrix Reasoning	✓ (Yes)	6–8: Samples A–C, then Item 4 9–11: Samples A–C, then Item 7 12–16: Samples A–C, then Item 11
9. Comprehension	✓ (Yes)	6–8: Item 1 9–11: Item 3 12–16: Item 5

10. Symbol Search	(No)	6–7: Symbol Search A, sample items, practice items, then test items 8–16: Symbol Search B, sample items, practice items, then test items
11. Picture Completion	✓ (Yes)	6–8: sample, then Item 1 9–11: sample, then Item 5 12–16: sample, then Item 10
12. Cancellation	(No)	6–16: sample, practice, then Item 1
13. Information	✓ (Yes)	6–8: Item 5 9–11: Item 10 12–16: Item 12
14. Arithmetic	✓ (Yes)	6–7: Item 3 8–9: Item 9 10–16: Item 12
15. Word Reasoning	✓ (Yes)	6–9: Samples A and B, then Item 1 10–16: Samples A and B, then Item 5

Source: From the Administration and Scoring Manual of the Wechsler Intelligence Scale for Children–Fourth Edition. Copyright © 2003 The Psychological Corporation. Adapted and reproduced by permission. All rights reserved.

Note: Children suspected of developmental delay or cognitive impairment may begin subtests at earlier items.

verse rules and also provides the starting points for specific age categories throughout the entire age range of the battery.

On subtests with age-based starting points (later than item 1), examinees must establish a *basal* or perfect score on the first two items administered to receive full credit for all previous items (called "reversal items"). When the examinee does not achieve an initial basal on a subtest with an age-based starting point, the examiner must give the reversal items in reverse sequence until perfect scores are achieved on two consecutive items. The *WISC-IV Administration and Scoring Manual* (Wechsler, 2003) includes specific instructions for examiners when the first set of items administered is too difficult for the child. These instructions are referred to as *reverse rules.* Table 2.2 provides the reverse rules for each subtest, and the Don't Forget boxes on pages 55 and 57 contain important information relating to these rules.

At times, an examiner may administer items prior to the recommended start point for a child suspected of

DON'T FORGET

When the examinee receives full credit on the first item administered but not the second item, on a subtest with age-based starting points, the first item is used to meet the reversal criterion of two consecutive perfect scores.

Table 2.2 Summary of Reverse Rules

Subtest	Reverse Rule
1. Block Design	Ages 8–16: Score of 0 or 1 on *either* of the first two items given, administer preceding items in reverse order until two consecutive perfect scores are obtained.
2. Similarities	Ages 9–16: Score of 0 or 1 on *either* of the first two items given, administer preceding items in reverse order until two consecutive perfect scores are obtained.
3. Digit Span	None
4. Picture Concepts	Ages 9–16: Score of 0 on *either* of the first two items given, administer preceding items in reverse order until two consecutive perfect scores are obtained.
5. Coding	None
6. Vocabulary	Ages 6–16: Score of 0 or 1 on *either* of the first two items given, administer preceding items in reverse order until two consecutive perfect scores are obtained.
7. Letter-Number Sequencing	None
8. Matrix Reasoning	Ages 6–16: Score of 0 on *either* of the first two items given, administer preceding items in reverse order until two consecutive perfect scores are obtained.
9. Comprehension	Ages 9–16: Score of 0 or 1 on *either* of the first two items given, administer preceding items in reverse order until two consecutive perfect scores are obtained.
10. Symbol Search	None
11. Picture Completion	Ages 9–16: Score of 0 on *either* of the first two items given, administer preceding items in reverse order until two consecutive perfect scores are obtained.
12. Cancellation	None
13. Information	Ages 6–16: Score of 0 on *either* of the first two items given, administer preceding items in reverse order until two consecutive perfect scores are obtained.
14. Arithmetic	Ages 6–16: Score of 0 on *either* of the first two items given, administer preceding items in reverse order until two consecutive perfect scores are obtained.
15. Word Reasoning	Ages 10–16: Score of 0 on *either* of the first two items given, administer preceding items in reverse order until two consecutive perfect scores are obtained.

Source: From the Administration and Scoring Manual of the Wechsler Intelligence Scale for Children–Fourth Edition. Copyright © 2003 The Psychological Corporation. Adapted and reproduced by permission. All rights reserved.

developmental delay or cognitive impairment. Although this is an acceptable practice, it is important to remember that if the child receives full credit on the first two items of his or her age-appropriate start point, full

DON'T FORGET

Scores obtained on reverse items are included in the discontinue criteria.

credit must be given to all previous items even when one or more of these items were answered incorrectly. The Caution box on pages 88–92 lists common general errors in administration.

In addition to starting points and reverse rules, subtests also have *discontinue rules*. Starting and discontinue rules were developed to minimize testing time. Similar to starting rules, discontinue rules differ across subtests. These rules typically require that a certain number of consecutive zero-point responses be obtained prior to discontinuing the subtest. Table 2.3 lists the discontinue rules for the WISC-IV subtests.

When administering a subtest, you may occasionally find that you are unsure of how to score a response and, therefore, of whether a subtest should be discontinued. Most often this uncertainty may arise during Verbal Comprehension subtests that have some subjectivity in scoring, most notably Vocabulary, Similarities, and Comprehension. If it is not possible to quickly determine whether a response is correct, it is best to continue administering further items until you are certain that the discontinue rule has been met. This procedure is the safest because the scores can always be reviewed later and items that are passed after the discontinue criterion has been met can be excluded from the child's raw score on the subtest. However, the information obtained on the items that were accidentally administered beyond the discontinue criterion may provide valuable *clinical* information. If you do not follow the procedure just described, and note later that you did not administer enough items to meet the discontinue rule, then the subtest should be considered spoiled. You should *not* go back and administer the items in an attempt to meet the discontinue rule. If you need to derive a scaled score based on the subtest raw score on this test, you would need to explain that the score most likely underestimates the child's ability.

RECORDING RESPONSES

The manner in which responses are recorded during administration of the WISC-IV is very important. Examiners should be careful to write down responses verbatim for all items administered or attempted. This recording is especially important for Vocabulary, Similarities, Comprehension, and Information (i.e.,

Table 2.3 Summary of Discontinue Rules

Subtest	Discontinue Rule
1. Block Design	After 3 consecutive scores of 0
2. Similarities	After 5 consecutive scores of 0
3. Digit Span	Digit Span Forward: After scores of 0 on *both trials* of an item Digit Span Backward: After scores of 0 on *both trials* of an item
4. Picture Concepts	After 5 consecutive scores of 0
5. Coding	Coding A and B: After 120 seconds have elapsed (or sooner if the child finishes in less than 120 seconds)
6. Vocabulary	After 5 consecutive scores of 0
7. Letter-Number Sequencing	If a child aged 6–7 is unable to respond correctly to either qualifying item *or* if a child receives scores of 0 on *all three trials* of an item
8. Matrix Reasoning	After 4 consecutive scores of 0 *or* 4 scores of 0 on *five* consecutive items
9. Comprehension	After 4 consecutive scores of 0
10. Symbol Search	Symbol Search A and B: After 120 seconds have elapsed (or sooner if the child finishes in less than 120 seconds)
11. Picture Completion	After 6 consecutive scores of 0
12. Cancellation	After 45 seconds have elapsed for each item (or sooner if the child finishes in less than 45 seconds)
13. Information	After 5 consecutive scores of 0
14. Arithmetic	After 4 consecutive scores of 0
15. Word Reasoning	After 5 consecutive scores of 0

Source: From the Administration and Scoring Manual of the Wechsler Intelligence Scale for Children–Fourth Edition. Copyright © 2003 The Psychological Corporation. Adapted and reproduced by permission. All rights reserved.

subtests that tend to elicit a good amount of verbiage). However, even when only brief verbal responses are given, such as during the Arithmetic and Digit Span subtests, they should be recorded, as they may prove useful in the interpretation process. It is tempting for some examiners to write down only a child's score, rather than the child's exact response, but this practice is discouraged. If only a 0, 1, or 2 is recorded on the Record Form, then irretrievable clinical information may be lost. Recording all responses affords the examiner an opportunity to note patterns in responding that may be useful in interpretation. For these same reasons, it is crucial to attempt to capture most of what is said verbatim. This can be quite a challenge with extremely verbose children. The use of abbreviations can make the process of recording information easier, and can also help to balance the maintenance of rapport with the gathering of essential information. Rapid Reference 2.2 shows a list of commonly used abbreviations.

In addition to recording what a child says, you may need to also record your own statements. For example, if you probed to clarify an answer by saying, "Tell me more about it," you should always record the letter "Q" in parentheses on the Record Form directly after the response that you queried. During the process of interpretation of a child's performance, it may be of clinical interest to note whether many of the child's responses were elicited by querying or whether the

≡Rapid Reference 2.2

Abbreviations for Recording Responses

@	at
B	both
DK	don't know
EO	everyone
INC	incomplete (response wasn't completed within the time limit)
LL	looks like
NR	no response
P	prompt
PC	points correctly
PPL	people
PX	points incorrectly
Q	question or query
R	repeated
Shd	should
SO	someone
ST	something
↓	decrease
↑	increase
U	you
w/	with
w/o	without
W/d	would

Source: From A. S. Kaufman & E. O. Lichtenberger, Essentials of WISC-III and WPPSI-R Assessment. Copyright © 2000 John Wiley & Sons, Inc. This material is used by permission of John Wiley & Sons, Inc.

child produced most responses spontaneously. Beyond noting the level of querying typically required for a child, it may be useful to determine whether the quality of response improved after the child was queried. Some children may tend not to add anything to their first responses (e.g., they may respond to most queries with "I don't know"); others may elaborate a great deal after a query but may not necessarily improve their scores; and some children will improve their scores most of the time when queried.

TIMING

Precision is necessary for administration of subtests that require timing. The examiner must be prepared to utilize his or her stopwatch for 6 out of the 15 WISC-IV subtests.

The use of a stopwatch should be unobtrusive so that it is not distracting to the child. If possible, use a stopwatch that does not make beeping sounds. If children ask whether they are being timed, you may want to respond, "Yes, but you don't need to worry about that." The WISC-IV Record Form contains a picture of a clock at the beginning of each timed subtest as a reminder to examiners that a stopwatch is required.

As you are giving the directions to the timed subtests, you should already have your stopwatch out and ready for use. This is especially helpful when testing children who are impulsive and may want to begin testing earlier than you expected. Rapid Reference 2.3 lists some important points to remember when timing a child.

DON'T FORGET

The six timed subtests on the WISC-IV include the following:
- Block Design
- Coding
- Symbol Search
- Picture Completion
- Cancellation
- Arithmetic

QUERYING

Examiner judgment often comes into play during subtests that allow a wide variety of responses, such as many of the Verbal Comprehension subtests. If a child's response appears too vague or ambiguous to score, examiners must decide whether to query or prompt the child for clarification. The administration manual of the WISC-IV lists responses to Vocabulary, Similarities, Comprehension, and Information items that should be queried. However, the responses in the manual are only illustrative, leaving the examiner to decide whether to query

≋ Rapid Reference 2.3

Important Points to Remember When Using a Stopwatch on Timed Tests

1. If a child asks for clarification or repetition of an item after timing has begun, continue timing while you repeat the item.
2. When a child appears to have completed a timed item but does not pro-vide you with a clear indication that he or she is finished, ask "Are you done?"
3. If you stop timing because a child appears to have completed an item, restart the stopwatch immediately upon recognizing that the child is still working and record the entire time that he or she worked on that item. Estimate the number of seconds that the stopwatch was off and add that to the total completion time.

other responses that are not presented in the manual's scoring system. The key to deciding whether to query a response is its ambiguity or incompleteness.

The manner in which children are queried may impact how they respond. Therefore, it is crucial that querying be done with neutral, non-leading questions. Good queries include, "Tell me more about it" or "Explain what you mean." The examiner should avoid providing any hints or clues to the answer and should use only the queries listed in the manual. Be careful not to ask, "Can you tell me more?" because a likely response is "No."

DON'T FORGET

- Whenever you query a child, place a "Q" in parentheses on the Record Form next to the response you queried.
- Do not query a child if he or she spontaneously produced an incorrect or zero-point response, unless a "Q" appears in parentheses next to the same or a similar response in the manual.

REPEATING ITEMS

Occasionally, a child you are testing may not completely hear the instructions or understand the instructions or a question that was read. In some cases, the child may ask you to repeat the question. Generally, it is okay to repeat a question or set of instructions; however, for the WISC-IV Digit Span and Letter-Number Sequencing subtests, a number or number-and-letter sequence, respectively, may not be repeated. When a child requests to have instructions or an item repeated, you must repeat the entire set of instructions or the entire item, not just a portion of it.

Another situation that may warrant a repetition of items is a pattern of responding in which the child provides correct answers to difficult items and incorrect or "I don't know" responses to easier items. That is, if you believe that a child may have known the answers to earlier, easier items, then it is acceptable and desirable to readminister these items, as responses to these testing-of-the-limits procedures may prove useful in interpretation. A child may have received a zero on initial items due to anxiety or insecurity, leading to an incorrect response. Testing the limits may reveal that the child actually knew the answers to these questions. Although you are not permitted to change 0-point responses to 1- or 2-point responses in this situation, information from the testing-of-the-limits procedure may be used, for example, to support an interpretation of a subtest score's reflecting an underestimate of ability due to anxiety. It is important to note, however, that an incorrect response that is *spontaneously* corrected at any time during the evaluation session should be changed from a raw score of 0 to a raw score of 1 or 2 as appropriate.

SUBTEST-BY-SUBTEST RULES OF ADMINISTRATION OF THE WISC-IV CORE SUBTESTS

I. Block Design (PRI, Core)

The WISC-IV Block Design subtest requires the examinee to replicate a set of modeled or printed two-dimensional geometric patterns using red-and-white blocks within a specified time limit. The stimulus materials for the Block Design subtest include nine cubes, each having two red sides, two white sides, and two red-and-white sides. A stopwatch, the *WISC-IV Administration and Scoring Manual* (Wechsler, 2003), the Stimulus Book, and the Record Form are needed for this subtest.

The WISC-IV Block Design subtest administration is based on age-based starting points. A child aged 6–7 begins at Item 1; a child aged 8–16 begins at Item 3. If a child aged 8–16 does not receive credit on either trial of Item 3, the examiner should administer Items 1 and 2 in reverse sequence until the child obtains a perfect score on two consecutive items. The Block Design subtest is discontinued after three consecutive zero-point responses.

The WISC-IV Block Design subtest, like the WISC-III Block Design subtest, provides two trials for Items 1, 2, and 3. The child works directly from models constructed by the examiner on Items 1 and 2 and constructs the remaining designs based on the pictorial models presented in the Stimulus Book. If the child attempts to duplicate the sides of the model, the examiner should tell the child to match only the tops of the blocks. Demonstrations are provided by the examiner on both trials of Items 1–3. The second trials of each of these three items are administered only if the child is unable to assemble the blocks correctly within the time limit. Item 1 has a 30-second time limit, Items 2–5 have a 45-second time limit, Items 6–10 have a 75-second time limit, and Items 11–14 have a 120-second time limit. Item 1 utilizes two blocks, Items 2–10 utilize four blocks, and the remaining items include all nine blocks.

Similar to the rotation rules on the WISC-III Block Design subtest, any rotation of 30 degrees or more is considered a failure. The examiner is allowed to correct only the first rotation. All incorrect responses, including rotations, should be recorded on the Record Form by sketching the design constructed by the child. Correct responses are indicated by placing a checkmark over the grid of stimulus blocks associated with those items on the Record Form. Table 2.4 provides a description of the changes in the administration of the Block Design subtest from WISC-III to WISC-IV. The Don't Forget box on page 64 provides a description of behaviors that the examiner should note during the administration of the Block Design subtest. It is important to note that the behaviors outlined in this Don't Forget box (and in subsequent Don't Forget boxes outlining "behaviors" to note for each WISC-IV subtest) are meant to provide examiners with information that may aid in hypothesis generation. Any hypotheses that are generated from this list, however, must be tested with other methods and data sources. Consistent findings from multiple data sources are necessary to either retain or reject hypotheses.

Table 2.4 Changes in Administration: Subtest 1, Block Design (PRI, Core)

WISC-III	WISC-IV
Administered in the middle of the test sequence (Subtest 7)	Administered as the first subtest in the test sequence
Reverse in normal sequence, i.e., Design 1, then Design 2	Reverse in reverse sequence, i.e., Design 2, then Design 1
No diagram explaining setup for right-handed vs. left-handed children	Diagram explaining setup for right-handed vs. left-handed children
12 test designs	14 test designs: 10 retained designs, 4 new designs
All ages begin with Design 1	Aged-based starting points: • Ages 6–7 begin with Design 1 • Ages 8–16 begin with Design 3

DON'T FORGET

Behaviors to Note on Block Design

- Observe problem-solving styles while the child is manipulating the blocks. Some children use a trial-and-error approach, whereas others appear to approach the construction of a design haphazardly, seemingly without learning from earlier errors. Other children develop a strategy and use it consistently throughout the subtest.

- Consider the level of planning involved. Does the child examine the problem systematically and appear to plan carefully before arranging the blocks, or does the child approach the task impulsively?

- Observe how the child arranges the blocks to form a correct response. For example, does the child work from the outside in, constructing the corners first and then the center of the design, or vice versa? Such approaches may provide information about the child's visual analytic style.

- Be aware that motor coordination and hand preference may be apparent during this task. Note whether children seem clumsy in their manipulation of the blocks, have hands that are noticeably trembling, or move very quickly and steadily.

- Look to see whether children refer back to the model while they are working. This could indicate a visual memory difficulty, cautiousness, or other factors.

- Examine whether children tend to be obsessively concerned with details (e.g., lining up the blocks perfectly). Such behaviors may negatively impact the child's speed.

- Observe how well children persist, especially when the task becomes more difficult. Note how well they tolerate frustration. Do they persist past the time limit, or do they give up with time to spare?

- Look to see whether children lose the square shape of some designs (violation of the matrix), even if they have managed to recreate the overall pattern. This kind of response may indicate figure-ground problems.

- Note whether children are noticeably twisting their bodies to obtain a different perspective on the model or are rotating their own designs. Such behaviors may indicate visual-perceptual difficulties.

- Note whether children fail to recognize that their designs look different from the model, as this may indicate visual-perceptual difficulties.

Source: From A. S. Kaufman & E. O. Lichtenberger, *Essentials of WISC-III and WPPSI-R Assessment.* Copyright © 2000 John Wiley & Sons, Inc. This material is used by permission of John Wiley & Sons, Inc.

A noteworthy change from WISC-III to WISC-IV is that the Block Design subtest is administered as the first, as opposed to the seventh, subtest. The changes in administration order from WISC-III to WISC-IV may affect examinees' performance. By its being positioned as the first subtest administered, children might perform differently on Block Design than they would have if it remained in the middle of the sequence. Thompson's research (Thompson, 1987;

Thompson, Howard, & Anderson, 1986) suggests that its position is a significant variable in the scores the child earns. Although scores for Block Design on the WISC-IV are normed as the first WISC-IV subtest administered, for the clinician it is important to note that this variable may be important for test interpretation. If a child performs surprisingly low on Block Design (relative to other PRI subtests or to the remainder of subtests in general), that weakness might be related to a slow establishment of rapport, emotional content of the child, metacognitive issues of the child, or cognitive issues of the child. It is also possible that examinees will perform *better* on Block Design, as the first subtest administered (when they are "fresh"), than they would have performed had the subtest been embedded in the middle of the sequence. That finding was supported for a sample of adults tested on the WAIS-R in the research conducted by Thompson and his colleagues.

In working with brain-injured children it is important to note that difficulties with Block Design may be observed. By virtue of its being the first administered subtest, poor performance may have a negative effect on rapport, which may lead to an adverse impact on subsequent subtests. Picture Completion, the first subtest administered on the WISC-III, was, and is, seen as a nonthreatening, low-*Gf*, easy-to-respond-to task. As a result, Picture Completion, rather than Block Design, appears to be a better fit as the first subtest in the battery. WISC-IV Picture Completion is a supplemental subtest and was, therefore, not a legitimate contender to be administered first. However, examiners who are testing brain-injured individuals—or anyone who is believed to need a more gradual introduction to the cognitive assessment—would be wise to administer the supplemental Picture Completion subtest before administering Block Design.

Similarly, whenever a child performs poorly on the last couple of tasks administered during a test session, examiners need to consider factors such as fatigue or boredom. This topic is pertinent for Digit Span, which was moved to the beginning of the WISC-IV, whereas it was administered near the end of the WISC-III. By approaching testing from a clinical perspective, the examiner is advised to be cognizant of the fact that children with attentional problems are likely to do better on WISC-IV Digit Span (administered as Subtest 3) than they would have done on WISC-III Digit Span (Subtest 12).

Given these caveats, the examiner is reminded that the WISC-IV was intended to be administered in the order presented in the manual. Although there are times when this is not advisable (e.g., using a substitution), most times the subtests are administered in the suggested sequence. It is important that rapport be established and maintained throughout the evaluation. To establish rapport, the examiner may wish to give a task that is viewed by most children as mildly interesting, nonthreatening, and without excessive demands prior to administering the first subtest on the

CAUTION

Seating Arrangement for the Block Design subtest

When administering the WISC-IV Block Design subtest, the examiner should sit in a position (e.g., directly opposite the child) that maximizes his or her ability to recognize any rotations to the child's designs.

Source: From A. S. Kaufman & E. O. Lichtenberger, *Essentials of WISC-III and WPPSI-R Assessment.* Copyright © 2000. John Wiley & Sons, Inc. This material is used by permission of John Wiley & Sons, Inc.

WISC-IV (Block Design). As noted, administering Picture Completion first should accomplish that goal.

2. Similarities (VCI, Core)

The WISC-IV Similarities subtest requires the examinee to describe how two words that represent common objects or concepts are similar. Unlike for Block Design and many other WISC-IV subtests, there is no separate stimulus material for the Similarities subtest. The *WISC-IV Administration and Scoring Manual* (Wechsler, 2003) and Record Form are the only items needed for this subtest.

The WISC-IV Similarities subtest item administration is based on age-based starting points. A child aged 6–8 begins with the sample item, then Item 1; a child

DON'T FORGET

Behaviors to Note on Similarities

- Observe whether the child benefits from feedback (if it is given) on items that allow the examiner to provide an example. Children who learn from the example may have flexibility, whereas those who do not may be more rigid or concrete.

- Be aware that length of verbal responses gives important behavioral clues. Overly elaborate responses *may* suggest obsessiveness. Of course, data from other sources are necessary to support or rule out this hypothesis.

- Be aware that quick responses or abstract responses to easy items *may* indicate overlearned associations rather than higher-level abstract reasoning.

- Note how the child handles frustration on this test. For example, some children may give up when faced with frustration by repeatedly responding, "I don't know," or stating that the two items are not alike. While these responses may indicate difficulty with conceptualization or categorization, they may also indicate defensiveness or avoidance, especially when seen in older children.

- Note spontaneous corrections during the administration of this test and remember to give credit for them.

Source: From A. S. Kaufman & E. O. Lichtenberger, *Essentials of WISC-III and WPPSI-R Assessment.* Copyright © 2000. John Wiley & Sons, Inc. This material is used by permission of John Wiley & Sons, Inc.

Table 2.5 Changes in Administration: Subtest 2, Similarities (VCI, Core)

WISC-III	WISC-IV
All ages begin with sample item, then Item 1	All ages begin with sample item, then age-based starting points • Ages 6–8 begin with Item 1 • Ages 9–11 begin with Item 3 • Ages 12–16 begin with Item 5
No reverse rules	Reverse rules for ages 9–16 if either of the scores for the first two items is not perfect
Discontinue after 4 consecutive scores of 0	Discontinue after 5 consecutive scores of 0
The examiner is not allowed to repeat the test items	The examiner may repeat the test items as often as necessary
19 test items	23 test items: 11 retained items, 1 modified item, 11 new items

aged 9–11 begins with the sample item, then Item 3; and a child aged 12–16 begins with the sample item, then Item 5. If a child aged 9–16 does not obtain a perfect score on either of the first two administered items, the preceding items should be administered in reverse sequence until a perfect score on two consecutive items is obtained. The Similarities subtest is discontinued after five consecutive zero-point responses.

Items 1 and 2 on the Similarities subtest are teaching items. Thus, if the child does not respond or provides an incorrect response to either Item 1 or Item 2, the examiner provides the correct response. However, if a child fails to provide a correct response on the remaining items (i.e., Items 3–23), no further assistance is provided. Neutral queries may be given throughout the subtest to clarify vague or ambiguous responses. Table 2.5 provides a description of the changes in the administration of the Similarities subtest from WISC-III to WISC-IV. The Don't Forget box on page 66 provides a description of behaviors that the examiner should note during the administration of the Similarities subtest.

3. Digit Span (WMI, Core)

The WISC-IV Digit Span subtest consists of two parts: Digit Span Forward and Digit Span Backward. Digit Span Forward requires the examinee to repeat numbers verbatim as they were stated by the examiner. Digit Span Backward requires the examinee to repeat numbers in the reverse order as they were stated by the examiner. There are no stimulus materials for the WISC-IV Digit Span subtest. The only materials needed to administer the WISC-IV Digit Span subtest are the *WISC-IV Administration and Scoring Manual* (Wechsler, 2003) and Record Form.

There are no age-based starting points for the WISC-IV Digit Span subtest; all children begin with Digits Forward, Item 1. Each item has two trials. If an examinee fails both trials of a Digits Forward item, testing is discontinued and the examiner proceeds to the sample of Digits Backward. If the child can correctly complete the first trial of the Digits Backward sample, then the second trial of the sample item is administered. However, if the child does not respond correctly to the first trial of the Digits Backwards sample, then the examiner tells the child the correct answer and readministers the trial before administering the second trial of the Digits Backward sample. If the child responds incorrectly to the second trial of the Digits Backward sample, the examiner tells the child the correct answer and readministers the trial before beginning Trial 1 of the first Digits Backward item. The Digits Backward task should be discontinued after a score of zero is obtained on both trials of an item.

The rate and intonation of the examiner's speech are important during this subtest. Each of the numbers is to be read at a rate of one per second, and at the end of the sequence of numbers, the examiner's voice should drop slightly, indicating the end of a sequence. It is crucial not to inadvertently "chunk" the numbers into small groups while reading them, as this may provide extra help. Table 2.6 provides

Table 2.6 Changes in Administration: Subtest 3, Digit Span (WMI, Core)

WISC-III	WISC-IV
Digits Forward includes 8 items, each with 2 trials	Digits Forward (called Digit Span Forward on the WISC-IV) includes 8 items, each with 2 trials; Trial 1 of Item 7 was slightly modified (an "8" was substituted for a "6")
Digits Backward includes 7 items, each with 2 trials; only Item 1 requires repetition of *two* digits	Digits Backward (called Digit Span Backward on the WISC-IV) includes 8 items, each with 2 trials; Items 1 and 2 *both* require repetition of two digits. Also, there were slight modifications in 4 trials (both trials of Item 2, Trial 1 of Item 7, and Trial 1 of Item 8)
No process scores available	Process scores able to be calculated to more clearly describe the child's Digit Span performance
Feedback was given for only one of the two sample items on Digits Backward	Feedback is given for *both* of the sample items on Digit Span Backward
Administered near the end of the battery (Subtest 12) when children might be bored, tired, or distractible	Administered near the beginning of the battery (Subtest 3) when children are more likely to be attentive

DON'T FORGET

Behaviors to Note on Digit Span

- Note whether children are attempting to use a problem-solving strategy such as "chunking." Some children use such a strategy from the beginning; others learn a strategy as they progress through the task.
- Note whether errors are due simply to transposing numbers or to completely forgetting numbers.
- Be aware that inattention, a hearing impairment, or anxiety can influence performance on this test; therefore, such difficulties should be noted if present. Clinical judgment must be exercised in determining whether one or more of these factors is responsible for a spuriously low score.
- Interference with the quality of the testing conditions (e.g., noise outside the testing room) should be noted. Such interference may spoil the subtest, rendering it uninterpretable.
- Watch for rapid repetition of digits or beginning to repeat the digits before the examiner has completed the series. Such behavior may indicate impulsivity.
- Observe whether there is a pattern of failing the first trial and then correctly responding to the second trial. Such a pattern may indicate learning or may simply be a warm-up effect.
- Note spontaneous corrections during the administration of this test and remember to give credit for them.

Source: From A. S. Kaufman & E. O. Lichtenberger, Essentials of WISC-III and WPPSI-R Assessment. Copyright © 2000 John Wiley & Sons, Inc. This material is used by permission of John Wiley & Sons, Inc.

a description of the changes in the administration of the Digit Span subtest from WISC-III to WISC-IV. The Don't Forget box on page above provides a description of behaviors that the examiner should note during the administration of the Digit Span subtest.

4. Picture Concepts (PRI, Core)

The new WISC-IV Picture Concepts subtest requires the examinee to choose one picture from each of the two or three rows of pictures presented, to form a group with a common characteristic. The materials necessary for the administration of WISC-IV Picture Concepts include the *WISC-IV Administration and Scoring Manual* (Wechsler, 2003), the Stimulus Book, and the Record Form.

The WISC-IV Picture Concepts subtest administration is based on age-based starting points. A child aged 6–8 begins with Sample Items A and B and then Item

1; a child aged 9–11 begins with Sample Items A and B and then Item 5; and a child aged 12–16 begins with Sample Items A and B and then Item 7. If a child aged 9–16 fails to obtain a perfect score on either of the first two items administered, the preceding items should be administered in reverse order until a perfect score on two consecutive items is obtained. The Picture Concepts subtest is discontinued after five consecutive zero-point responses.

For Sample Items A and B, if the child provides a correct response the examiner should inquire as to the reason the child chose the items. If the child fails to provide a response, the examiner provides a reason. If the child provides an incorrect response, the examiner should provide the correct response as well as the reason the items go together. Items 1–12 of the WISC-IV Picture Concepts subtest are two-row items; Items 13–28 are three-row items. The Don't Forget box below provides a description of behaviors that the examiner should note during the administration of the Picture Concepts subtest.

5. Coding (PSI, Core)

The WISC-IV Coding subtest requires the examinee to copy symbols that are paired with either geometric shapes or numbers using a key within a specified time limit. The stimulus material for the Coding subtest is the Response Booklet. A stopwatch, the *WISC-IV Administration and Scoring Manual* (Wechsler, 2003), the

---

DON'T FORGET

Behaviors to Note on Picture Concepts

- Be aware that quick responses to easy items may indicate overlearned associations rather than higher-level abstract reasoning.
- Note how the child handles frustration on this test. For example, the child may respond by saying "Nothing is alike," indicating defensiveness or avoidance. Other children may give up when faced with frustration by repeatedly responding, "I don't know."
- Note whether the child studies the pictures for a few seconds prior to answering. Such behavior may indicate a reflective style.
- Observe whether there is verbalization during problem solving.
- Note any behaviors that give clues to whether errors relate to social or cultural misinterpretation, as opposed to visual-perceptual difficulties.
- Note spontaneous corrections during the administration of this test and remember to give credit for them.

Record Form, and a pencil without an eraser are also needed to administer this subtest.

The WISC-IV has two different Coding forms: Form A for children aged 6–7 and Form B for children aged 8–16. The different Coding forms have their own separate pages in the Response Booklet. If the child is left-handed, an extra Coding response key should be placed to the right of the child's Response Booklet so that he or she may have an unobstructed view of the Coding key (some left-handers' hand positions obstruct the key on the Record Form). There are no reverse rules for the Coding subtest. The subtest is discontinued after 120 seconds.

The directions for Coding are very lengthy and contain a lot of important detail. Examiners must be prepared to look up from reading the directions to check that the child is following what is being said. Therefore, the directions should be rehearsed and read carefully to each child. During administration of the sample items, if the child makes any mistake it should be corrected immediately. If the child does not appear to understand the task after the sample items have been completed, further instruction should be given until the child clearly understands the task.

Once the subtest has begun, examiners should be astute observers. Children are not permitted to omit any item or to complete all items of one type at a time; if they are observed doing this they need to be told, "Do them in order. Don't skip any." Some children appear to stop midway through the task; the examiner should remind them to continue until told to stop. Occasionally, children appear frustrated at the end of the test because they are able to complete only a few lines. If this behavior is observed, you may want to reassure the child that most children are not able to complete the entire sheet. Any of the above-mentioned behaviors are worthy of noting. Table 2.7 provides a description of the changes in the administration of the Coding subtest from WISC-III to WISC-IV. The Don't For-

Table 2.7 Changes in Administration: Subtest 5, Coding (PSI, Core)

WISC-III	WISC-IV
Response sheet attached to protocol	Separate Response Booklet
Specific print (i.e., designs to be copied and the word "sample" with the accompanying right angle) appears in teal-colored ink	All print appears in black ink; item content remains unchanged
	Directions to child have been shortened to be more age appropriate and reduce excess verbiage

DON'T FORGET

Behaviors to Note on Coding

- Be aware that the eye movements of children taking the subtest can be informative. Frequent use of the Coding key may indicate poor memory or insecurity. In contrast, a child who uses the key infrequently may have a good memory span, visual memory, and/or associative memory. Check to see where on the key the child's eyes focus, especially with older children. Failing to recognize that the key is numerically ordered (i.e., from 1 through 9) not only suggests poor visual memory, but may also suggest difficulty with number concepts.
- Note whether the child quickly but carelessly fills in symbols across the rows. This behavior may suggest impulsivity.
- Note whether a child attempts to fill in the symbol for the number 1s first, followed by the symbol for the number 2s. This behavior may suggest good planning ability.
- Watch for shaking hands, a tight grip on the pencil, or pressure on the paper when writing. These behaviors may indicate anxiety.
- Observe signs of fatigue, boredom, or inattention as the subtest progresses. Noting the number of symbols copied during 3-second intervals provides helpful behavioral information in this regard.
- Note whether children spend a significant amount of time trying to perfect each of the symbols that are drawn. This behavior may suggest obsessiveness, excessive attention to detail, or perfectionism.

Source: From A. S. Kaufman & E. O. Lichtenberger, Essentials of WISC-III and WPPSI-R Assessment. Copyright © 2000 John Wiley & Sons, Inc. This material is used by permission of John Wiley & Sons, Inc.

get box above provides a description of additional behaviors that the examiner should note during the administration of the Coding subtest.

6. Vocabulary (VCI, Core)

The WISC-IV Vocabulary subtest requires the examinee to name pictures or provide definitions for words. Administration of the Vocabulary subtest requires the *WISC-IV Administration and Scoring Manual* (Wechsler, 2003), the Record Form, and the Stimulus Book. Items 1–4 are picture items and are administered only if necessary, as reversal items. Items 5–36 are verbal items; the examiner reads the word printed in the Stimulus Book aloud and asks the child to provide a definition. The printed words in the Stimulus Book must be used for children aged 9–16, with the examiner pointing to each word as the word is pronounced. One exception to this rule is that the Stimulus Book is not presented to nonreaders above age 8, and can be removed from view when the examiner realizes that the child cannot read. The Stimulus Book is not used for children aged 6–8.

The WISC-IV Vocabulary subtest administration is based on age-based starting points. A child aged 6–8 begins with Item 5, a child aged 9–11 begins with Item 7, and a child aged 12–16 begins with Item 9. If a child aged 6–16 fails to obtain a perfect score on either of the first two items administered, the preceding items should be administered in reverse order until a perfect score on two consecutive items is obtained. It is important to note that the first two verbal items (i.e., Items 5 and 6) on the WISC-IV Vocabulary subtest require the examiner to provide an example of a 2-point response if the child does not spontaneously give a 2-point response. The Vocabulary subtest is discontinued after five consecutive zero-point responses.

Children sometimes respond by defining a homonym of a word, which is not given credit, and the examiner should query the response. Sometimes a child may

DON'T FORGET

Behaviors to Note on Vocabulary

- Note whether children have difficulties pronouncing words or whether they seem uncertain about how to express what they think.
- Some children supplement what they say with gesturing; others rely on verbal expression more than nonverbal communication.
- Make note of "I don't know" responses or the "tip of the tongue" phenomenon, as these responses and behaviors may indicate word retrieval problems. A lack of rapidity and efficiency in retrieving words from the lexicon can influence test performance negatively, leading to an underestimate of the child's actual word knowledge.
- Note that hearing difficulties may be apparent on this test. The Vocabulary words are not presented in a meaningful context. Note behaviors such as leaning forward during administration to hear better, as well as indications of auditory discrimination problems (e.g., defining "confine" rather than "confide").
- Note verbosity in childrens' responses. They may be attempting to compensate for insecurity about their ability, or they may be obsessive or inefficient in their verbal expression.
- Note spontaneous corrections during the administration of this test and remember to give credit for them.

Source: From A. S. Kaufman & E. O. Lichtenberger, Essentials of WISC-III and WPPSI-R Assessment. Copyright © 2000 John Wiley & Sons, Inc. This material is used by permission of John Wiley & Sons, Inc.

Table 2.8 Changes in Administration: Subtest 6, Vocabulary (VCI, Core)

WISC-III	WISC-IV
Four age-based starting points • Ages 6–8 begin with Item 1 • Ages 9–10 begin with Item 3 • Ages 11–13 begin with Item 5 • Ages 14–16 begin with Item 7	Three age-based starting points • Ages 6–8 begin with Item 5 • Ages 9–11 begin with Item 7 • Ages 12–16 begin with Item 9
Discontinue after 4 consecutive scores of 0	Discontinue after 5 consecutive scores of 0
No reverse rules for ages 6–8	Reverse rules for all ages if either of the scores on the first two items is not perfect
Corrective feedback is provided for Item 1	Corrective feedback is provided for Items 5 and 6
No Stimulus Book	Stimulus Book is used for ages 9–16 (Vocabulary words are not shown to non-readers)
No picture items	Items 1–4 are picture items that are used as reversal items only (e.g., if a child aged 6–8 fails to provide a 2-point response on either of the first two items administered)
30 test items	36 test items: 27 retained items, 4 new picture items, 5 new verbal items

provide a slang response that is not found in the dictionary, and the examiner should inquire for another response. Children never receive credit for simply pointing to an object, so if a child responds nonverbally he or she should be encouraged to give a verbal response. Occasionally, it is apparent that children have mis-heard the word you asked them to define; in such a case, the examiner should repeat the word. However, the examiner should never spell the word presented to the child. Table 2.8 provides a description of the changes in the administration of the Vocabulary subtest from WISC-III to WISC-IV. The Don't Forget box on page 73 provides a description of behaviors that the examiner should note during the administration of the Vocabulary subtest.

7. Letter-Number Sequencing (WMI, Core)

The new WISC-IV Letter-Number Sequencing subtest requires the examinee to listen to a sequence of numbers and letters presented orally by the examiner and to recall the numbers in ascending order and the letters in alphabetical order. Administration materials include the *WISC-IV Administration and Scoring Manual* (Wechsler, 2003) and the Record Form.

The WISC-IV Letter-Number Sequencing subtest administration is based on age-based starting points. A child aged 6–7 is presented with the qualifying items (counting numbers and reciting the alphabet), sample item, and then Item 1. A child aged 8–16 is presented with the sample item, then Item 1. If the child provides an incorrect response on either trial of the sample item, the examiner should provide the correct response and readminister the trial. Each item is composed of three trials and each trial is presented only one time. The Letter-Number Sequencing subtest is discontinued if a child aged 6–7 is unable to respond correctly to either qualifying item, or if a child obtains three zero-point responses are obtained on all three trials of an item. Standard prompts are allowable on Items 1, 4, and 5. If a standard prompt is needed for any of these items, the examiner should provide the prompt and place a "P" on the Record Form to indicate that a prompt was given. The Don't Forget box below provides a description of be-

DON'T FORGET

Behaviors to Note on Letter-Number Sequencing

- Note whether children are attempting to use a problem-solving strategy such as "chunking." Some children use such a strategy from the beginning; others learn a strategy as they progress through the task.
- Note whether errors are due to the failure to reorder the letter-number sequence, with the sequence being repeated verbatim (which is still credited as correct on certain items) versus the sequence's having been forgotten (which is scored "0").
- Be aware that inattention, a hearing impairment, or anxiety can influence performance on this test.
- Interference with the quality of the testing conditions (e.g., noise outside the testing room) should be noted. Such interference may spoil the subtest, rendering it uninterpretable.
- Observe how well children persist, noting how well they tolerate frustration.
- Observe whether there is a pattern of failing the first trial and then correctly responding to the second trial. Such a pattern may indicate learning or may simply be a warm-up effect.
- Note whether the child treats the task as digits forward or digits backward. Approaching the task in such a manner, although not consistent with examiner instructions, may lead to an adequate score, especially at the younger ages. Remember that when a child gives only verbatim responses (as opposed to the appropriate reordered responses), you cannot draw valid inferences about his or her working memory.
- Note spontaneous corrections during the administration of this test and remember to give credit for them.

haviors that the examiner should note during the administration of the Letter-Number Sequencing subtest.

8. Matrix Reasoning (PRI, Core)

The new WISC-IV Matrix Reasoning subtest requires the child to complete the missing portion of a picture matrix by selecting one of five response options. Administration materials used for the Matrix Reasoning subtest include the *WISC-IV Administration and Scoring Manual* (Wechsler, 2003), the Record Form, and the Stimulus Book.

The WISC-IV Matrix Reasoning subtest administration is based on age-based starting points. A child aged 6–8 is administered Samples A–C, then Item 4; a child aged 9–11 is administered Samples A–C, then Item 7; and a child aged 12–16 is administered Samples A–C, then Item 11. If the child does not obtain a perfect score on either of the first two items, the preceding items should be administered in reverse order until a perfect score on two consecutive items is obtained. The Matrix Reasoning subtest is discontinued after four consecutive zero-point responses or after four zero-point responses on five consecutive items.

The examiner may provide assistance on the sample items only. The child should indicate his or her response by pointing to the picture in the Stimulus Book or by stating the number associated with the desired answer. The Don't Forget box below provides a description of behaviors that the examiner should note during the administration of the Matrix Reasoning subtest.

DON'T FORGET

Behaviors to Note on Matrix Reasoning

- Observe the level of planning involved. Does the child systematically examine the problem and appear to carefully plan before providing an answer, or does the child appear to be impulsive?
- Be aware that the eye movements of children taking the subtest may be informative, providing information about a systematic versus random approach to problem solving.
- Note whether the child appears to give up easily on more difficult items by stating "I don't know" before examining the item. This type of behavior may indicate that the child has become frustrated with the task.
- Note spontaneous corrections during the administration of this test and remember to give credit for them.

9. Comprehension (VCI, Core)

The WISC-IV Comprehension subtest requires the examinee to answer a series of questions based on his or her understanding of general principles and social situations. The *WISC-IV Administration and Scoring Manual* (Wechsler, 2003) and Record Form are the only items needed for the administration of this subtest.

Unlike the WISC-III, the WISC-IV Comprehension subtest has age-based starting points. A child aged 6–8 begins with Item 1; a child aged 9–11 begins with Item 3, and a child aged 12–16 begins with Item 5. If a child aged 9–16 does not obtain a perfect score on either of the first two items, the preceding items should be administered in reverse order until a perfect score on two consecutive items is obtained. The Comprehension subtest is discontinued after four consecutive zero-point responses.

The WISC-IV Comprehension subtest questions should be read at such a pace that children find it easy to follow the examiner but do not become distracted because of the speed. The questions may be repeated as many times as necessary without changing the wording. It is important to note that the first item on the WISC-IV Comprehension subtest requires the examiner to provide an example of a 2-point response if the child does not spontaneously give a 2-point response. This is done in order to teach the child the type of response expected for each item. On Items 4, 9, 11, 13, 14, and 18–21, the child is required to give two general concepts in response to the question in order to receive full credit (i.e., 2 points). On these items, the examiner is required to prompt the child for another response if only one general concept is reflected in the child's response. If the

DON'T FORGET

Behaviors to Note on Comprehension

- Observe whether unusually long verbal responses are an attempt to cover up for not actually knowing the correct response, or an indication that the child tends to be obsessive about details.

- Be aware that Comprehension requires a good amount of verbal expression; therefore word-finding difficulties, articulation problems, circumstantiality, tangentiality, or circumlocutions (e.g., verbal discourse that is overly detailed, irrelevant, or convoluted, respectively) may be apparent during this subtest.

- Be aware that some Comprehension questions have rather long verbal stimuli; note whether inattention is influencing the child's responses to such items. For example, only part of the question may be answered.

(continued)

- Note whether defensiveness is occurring in responses to some Comprehension items. For example, when asked about seat belts, if the child's response does not really answer the question and is something like, "We shouldn't have to wear seat belts," this may be defensive responding. Although such responses are scored "0," it is recommended that you follow up if you believe that the child knows the answer.
- Note whether children need consistent prompting when a second response is required or whether they spontaneously provide enough information in their initial answer.
- Observe children's responses carefully to determine whether incorrect responses are a result of poor verbal ability or poor social judgment.
- Note how children respond to queries and requests for elaboration (e.g., "Give me another reason"). Some may be threatened or frustrated by the interruptions, and others may seem comfortable with the added structure. Some children, when asked for "another reason," simply restate the first reason in different words or otherwise do not give a second idea.
- Note spontaneous corrections during the administration of this test and remember to give credit for them.

Source: From A. S. Kaufman & E. O. Lichtenberger, *Essentials of WISC-III and WPPSI-R Assessment.* Copyright © 2000 John Wiley & Sons, Inc. This material is used by permission of John Wiley & Sons, Inc.

child's response replicates the same general concept, the examiner should prompt once more. If the child's first spontaneous response is incorrect, however, examiners should not prompt for a second response. Table 2.9 provides a description of the changes in the administration of the Comprehension subtest from WISC-III to WISC-IV. The Don't Forget box on pages 77–78 provides a description of

Table 2.9 Changes in Administration: Subtest 9, Comprehension (VCI, Core)

WISC-III	WISC-IV
All children begin with Item 1	Age-based starting points • Ages 6–8 begin with Item 1 • Ages 9–11 begin with Item 3 • Ages 12–16 begin with Item 5
No reverse rules	Reverse rules for ages 9–16 if either of the scores on the first two items is not perfect
Examiner may ask for a second response *once* on items requiring the examinee's response to reflect two (or more) general concepts	Examiner may ask for a second response *twice* (not including a query) if the child's response to the examiner's initial re-questioning reflects the same general concept as his or her first response
18 test items	21 test items: 10 retained items with few or no wording changes, 11 new items

behaviors that the examiner should note during the administration of the Comprehension subtest.

10. Symbol Search (PSI, Core)

The WISC-IV Symbol Search subtest requires the examinee to scan a search group and indicate the presence or absence of a target symbol or symbols within a specified time limit. The stimulus material for the Symbol Search subtest is the Response Booklet. A stopwatch, the *WISC-IV Administration and Scoring Manual* (Wechsler, 2003), the Record Form, and a pencil without an eraser are also needed to administer this subtest.

The Symbol Search subtest has one Response Booklet with two forms: Symbol Search A for children aged 6–7 and Symbol Search B for children aged 8–16. There are no reverse rules for the Symbol Search subtest. The subtest is discontinued after 120 seconds.

Although the Symbol Search subtest has a time limit of 120 seconds, prior to beginning the subtest children must go through sample items and practice items that are not timed. It is important not to skip any of the demonstration, even if the child appears to readily understand the task. The directions to the sample, practice, and test items are lengthy and require multiple rehearsals in order to be able to communicate them while maintaining rapport with the child. A minimum of paraphrasing is acceptable while reading the directions; however, every attempt should be made to state them verbatim from the manual. The task should not begin until it is clear that the child understands what is required.

The timing of 120 seconds should be exact. Some children may purposefully or inadvertently skip items, and they should be reminded to complete items in order and to not skip any. Other children may appear to stop the task before the 120-second time limit expires and should be reminded to continue. Table 2.10 provides a description of the changes in the administration of the Symbol Search

Table 2.10 Changes in Administration: Subtest 10, Symbol Search (PSI, Core)

WISC-III	WISC-IV
Symbol Search B: 45 test items	Symbol Search B: 60 test items—45 retained, 15 new
	Directions to child have been shortened to be more age appropriate and reduce excess verbiage

DON'T FORGET

Behaviors to Note on Symbol Search

- Watch for shaking hands, a tight pencil grip, or pressure on the paper when writing. These behaviors may indicate anxiety.
- Observe attention and concentration. Is the child's focus consistent throughout the task, or does it wane as the task progresses?
- Observe whether children check each row of symbols only once, or whether they recheck the row of symbols in an item more than once. Obsessive concern with detail may be noted.
- Note whether the child quickly but carelessly identifies a symbol as present or absent in a row. This behavior may suggest impulsivity.
- Be aware that eye movements of children taking the subtest can be informative. Consistent glancing back and forth between the target and search groups before making a choice may indicate poor memory. In contrast, a child who refers to the target symbol infrequently may have a good memory span and/or visual memory.
- Watch for signs of fatigue, boredom, or inattention as the subtest progresses, as this subtest is one of the last administered. Noting the number of items answered during each of the four 30-second intervals with the 120-second time limit may provide helpful behavioral information in this regard.

Source: From A. S. Kaufman & E. O. Lichtenberger, Essentials of WISC-III and WPPSI-R Assessment. Copyright © 2000 John Wiley & Sons, Inc. This material is used by permission of John Wiley & Sons, Inc.

subtest from WISC-III to WISC-IV. The Don't Forget box above provides a description of behaviors that the examiner should note during the administration of the Symbol Search subtest.

SUBTEST-BY-SUBTEST RULES OF ADMINISTRATION OF THE WISC-IV SUPPLEMENTAL SUBTESTS

11. Picture Completion (PRI, Supplemental)

The WISC-IV Picture Completion subtest requires the examinee to view a picture and name the essential missing part of the picture within a specified time limit. To administer this subtest, the examiner needs the *WISC-IV Administration and Scoring Manual* (Wechsler, 2003), the Stimulus Book, the Record Form, and a stopwatch.

The WISC-IV Picture Completion subtest administration is based on age-based starting points. A child aged 6–8 begins with the sample item, then Item 1; a child aged 9–11 begins with the sample item, then Item 5; and a child aged 12–16 begins with the sample item, then Item 10. If a child aged 9–16 does not obtain a perfect score on either of the first two items administered, the preceding items should be administered in reverse order until a perfect score on two consecutive items is obtained. The Picture Completion subtest is discontinued after six consecutive zero-point responses.

It is important to note that the first two items on the WISC-IV Picture Completion subtest require the examiner to provide corrective feedback if the child provides an incorrect answer. This is done in order to teach the child the type of response expected from each item.

Because each item on the Picture Completion subtest is timed, the examiner should be exact about his or her timing and begin timing immediately after the item is presented to the child. Timing stops when the child provides an answer or when 20 seconds have elapsed.

Most children find this subtest fun, making it easy to administer. Examiners most frequently make errors on the queries that may be given during the subtest (e.g., forgetting to say the queries altogether or using them more frequently than allowed). Other errors may occur when a child produces an unclear verbal response. In some cases, verbal or nonverbal responses are considered acceptable answers. In other cases, a child must provide a nonverbal response to receive credit for an initial verbal response. If a child provides verbal and nonverbal responses that differ (i.e., one is correct and one is not), the response is considered spoiled and no credit is given. It is noteworthy if a child consistently provides only nonverbal responses (e.g., pointing). Table 2.11 provides a description of the

Table 2.11 Changes in Administration: Subtest 11, Picture Completion (PRI, Supplemental)

WISC-III	WISC-IV
Four age-based starting points	Three age-based starting points
• Ages 6–7 begin with sample, then Item 1	• Ages 6–8 begin with sample, then Item 1
• Ages 8–9 begin with sample, then Item 5	• Ages 9–11 begin with sample, then Item 5
• Ages 10–13 begin with sample, then Item 7	• Ages 12–16 begin with sample, then Item 10
• Ages 14–16 begin with sample, then Item 11	
Discontinue after 5 consecutive scores of 0	Discontinue after 6 consecutive scores of 0
30 test items	38 test items: 27 modified items, 11 new items

DON'T FORGET

Behaviors to Note on Picture Completion

- Note the speed with which the child responds. A reflective individual may take more time in responding (but most likely can respond within the time limit), whereas an impulsive individual may respond very quickly but incorrectly.

- Note whether the child is persistent in stating that nothing is missing from the picture (rather than responding, "I don't know"), as it may reflect oppositional-ity or inflexibility.

- Note that consistent nonverbal responses (e.g., pointing) may be evidence of word retrieval problems in children. Although it is acceptable to give a nonverbal response, it is far more common to give a verbal response.

- Be aware that verbal responses that are imprecise ("the thingy on the door") or overly elaborate ("the small piece of metal which forms a connection between the molding around the door frame and the door itself, allowing it to open easily") are also noteworthy.

- Be aware that after individuals have been redirected (e.g., "Yes, but what is the *most important* part that is missing?"), it is important to note whether they continue to respond with the same quality of response. This persistence in approach may indicate inability to understand the task or inflexibility in thinking.

Source: From A. S. Kaufman & E. O. Lichtenberger, *Essentials of WISC-III and WPPSI-R Assessment.* Copyright © 2000 John Wiley & Sons, Inc. This material is used by permission of John Wiley & Sons, Inc.

changes in the administration of the Picture Completion subtest from WISC-III to WISC-IV. The Don't Forget box above provides a description of behaviors that the examiner should note during the administration of the Picture Completion subtest.

12. Cancellation (PSI, Supplemental)

The new WISC-IV Cancellation subtest requires the examinee to scan both a random and a structured arrangement of pictures and mark target pictures within a specified time limit. The stimulus material for the Cancellation subtest is the Response Booklet. A stopwatch, the *WISC-IV Administration and Scoring Manual* (Wechsler, 2003), the Record Form, and a red pencil without an eraser are also needed to administer this subtest.

There are no age-based starting points for the WISC-IV Cancellation subtest; all children begin with the sample item, continue to the practice items, and then begin Item 1. There are no reverse rules on this subtest. The subtest items are discontinued after 45 seconds have elapsed.

DON'T FORGET

Behaviors to Note on Cancellation

- Watch for shaking hands, a tight grip on the pencil, or pressure on the paper when writing. These behaviors may indicate anxiety.
- Note whether children have difficulty understanding that they are expected to work quickly. This behavior may relate to immaturity.
- Observe attention and concentration. Is the child's focus consistent throughout the task, or does it wane as the task progresses?
- Observe signs of fatigue, boredom, or inattention as the subtest progresses. Noting the number of responses produced during each of the 45-second item intervals may provide helpful behavioral information in this regard.
- Observe whether the child's response rate is consistent throughout the subtest.
- Note whether the child quickly but carelessly circles responses. This behavior may suggest impulsivity.
- Note the effect of distractors on the child's performance. Remember that the target items are identically placed on both the randomized and nonrandomized forms.

There are two types of items contained within the Response Booklet: random (i.e., the distractors are scattered across the page) and structured (i.e., the target items and distractors are arranged in rows). Each target item is an animal. If the child fails to mark a target or marks a distractor item during the practice items, the examiner should provide corrective feedback. It is important not to proceed to Item 1 until the child fully understands the task. Spontaneous corrections should not be discouraged, unless such corrections occur frequently enough to impede performance. The Don't Forget box above provides a description of behaviors that the examiner should note during the administration of the Cancellation subtest.

13. Information (VCI, Supplemental)

The WISC-IV Information subtest requires the examinee to answer questions that address a wide range of general-knowledge topics. To administer this subtest, the examiner needs only the *WISC-IV Administration and Scoring Manual* (Wechsler, 2003) and the Record Form.

The WISC-IV Information subtest administration is based on age-based starting points. A child aged 6–8 begins with Item 5, a child aged 9–11 begins with Item 10, and a child aged 12–16 begins with Item 12. If the child does not obtain a perfect score

Table 2.12 Changes in Administration: Subtest 13, Information (VCI, Supplemental)

WISC-III	WISC-IV
Four age-based starting points	Three age-based starting points
• Ages 6–7 begin with Item 1	• Ages 6–8 begin with Item 5
• Ages 8–10 begin with Item 5	• Ages 9–11 begin with Item 10
• Ages 11–13 begin with Item 8	• Ages 12–16 begin with Item 12
• Ages 14–16 begin with Item 11	
30 test items	33 test items: 22 retained items with few or no wording changes, 11 new items

on either of the first two items administered, the preceding items should be administered in reverse order until a perfect score on two consecutive items is obtained. The Information subtest is discontinued after five consecutive zero-point responses.

It is important to note that the first two items on the WISC-IV Information subtest require the examiner to provide corrective feedback if the child provides an incorrect answer. This is done in order to teach the child the type of response expected from each item. In terms of item repetition, each item may be repeated as often as necessary, as long as the examiner does not reword the original item in any manner. If the child mis-hears a word and provides an incorrect answer, the examiner should repeat the entire item with emphasis on the mis-heard word. This pertains especially to Items 4 and 15. Table 2.12 provides a description of the changes in the administration of the Information subtest from WISC-III to WISC-IV. The Don't Forget box below provides a description of behaviors that the examiner should note during the administration of the Information subtest.

DON'T FORGET

Behaviors to Note on Information

- Note any observable patterns in a child's responses. Patterns of responding such as missing early, easy items and having success on harder items may suggest anxiety, poor motivation, or retrieval difficulties.
- Consider whether incorrect responses are related to the child's cultural background (e.g., on questions about a character in U.S. history at a certain time or about the geography of a specific location). Such observations should be incorporated into interpretation.
- Note whether children provide unnecessarily long responses. Long responses filled with excessive detail may be indicative of obsessiveness, a desire to impress the examiner, or an attempt to cover up for not knowing the correct response.

- Note whether the content of failed items consistently owes to lack of knowledge in a specific area (e.g., numerical information, history, or geography); an error analysis may be useful in this regard.
- Note spontaneous corrections during the administration of this test and remember to give credit for them.

14. Arithmetic (WMI, Supplemental)

The WISC-IV Arithmetic subtest requires the examinee to mentally solve a variety of orally presented arithmetic problems within a specified time limit. The materials necessary for the administration of the WISC-IV Arithmetic subtest include the *WISC-IV Administration and Scoring Manual* (Wechsler, 2003), the Record Form, the Stimulus Book, and a stopwatch.

The WISC-IV Arithmetic subtest administration is based on age-based starting points. A child aged 6–7 begins with Item 3, a child aged 8–9 begins with Item 9, and a child aged 10–16 begins with Item 12. If the child does not obtain a perfect score on either of the first two items administered, the preceding items should be administered in reverse order until a perfect score on two consecutive items is obtained. If a child provides an incorrect answer or does not respond within 30 seconds to Items 1–3, the examiner should provide corrective feedback. The Arithmetic subtest is discontinued after four consecutive zero-point responses.

It is important to note that the Arithmetic items are timed. The examiner should begin timing immediately after each item presentation and stop timing immediately after a child responds or 30 seconds have elapsed. In terms of item repetition, the examiner may repeat each item only once under two conditions (i.e., at the child's request or when it is apparent that the child failed to understand the item); however, timing continues throughout the repetition. There are corresponding pictures in the Stimulus Book for Items 1–5, while Items 6–34 are presented orally to the child. The child should not use a pencil or paper for this subtest. If the child provides a spontaneous second answer within the 30-second time limit, score the second response. Table 2.13 provides a description of the changes in the administration of the Arithmetic subtest from WISC-III to WISC-IV. The Don't Forget box on page 86 provides a description of behaviors that the examiner should note during the administration of the Arithmetic subtest.

Table 2.13 Changes in Administration: Subtest 14, Arithmetic (WMI, Supplemental)

WISC-III	WISC-IV
Four age-based starting points	Three age-based starting points
• Age 6 begins with Item 1	• Ages 6–7 begin with Item 3
• Ages 7–8 begin with Item 6	• Ages 8–9 begin with Item 9
• Ages 9–12 begin with Item 12	• Ages 10–16 begin with Item 12
• Ages 13–16 begin with Item 14	
Discontinue after 3 consecutive scores of 0	Discontinue after 4 consecutive scores of 0
No corrective feedback	Corrective feedback is provided for Items 1–3
Time limits vary depending on the item	Every item has a 30-second time limit
24 test items	34 test items: 7 retained items, 16 new items, 11 modified items

DON'T FORGET

Behaviors to Note on Arithmetic

- Observe children for signs of anxiety. Some children who view themselves as "poor at math" may be anxious during this task. Be aware of statements such as, "I was never taught that in school" or "I can't do math in my head."
- Note whether the child appears to be focusing on the stopwatch. This may be a sign of anxiety, distractibility, or competitiveness. Watch for statements such as, "How long did that take me?"
- Watch for signs of distractibility or poor concentration.
- Be aware that finger counting may occur in children of any age. This may be indicative of insecurity about math skills or may be an adaptive problem-solving tool for younger children. Note if the child attempts to hide finger counting from the examiner, is brazen about finger counting, or is nonchalant about finger counting.
- Note when the child asks for repetition of a question, as it may indicate several things, including poor hearing, inattention, or stalling.
- Observe the child's response style. Does he or she respond quickly, or is he or she methodical and careful in his or her responding?

Source: From A. S. Kaufman & E. O. Lichtenberger, *Essentials of WISC-III and WPPSI-R Assessment*. Copyright © 2000 John Wiley & Sons, Inc. This material is used by permission of John Wiley & Sons, Inc.

15. Word Reasoning (VCI, Supplemental)

The new WISC-IV Word Reasoning subtest requires the examinee to identify a common concept being described by a series of clues. To administer this subtest, the examiner needs only the *WISC-IV Administration and Scoring Manual* (Wechsler, 2003) and the Record Form.

The WISC-IV Word Reasoning subtest administration is based on two age-based starting points. A child aged 6–9 begins with Sample Items A and B, then Item 1; and a child aged 10–16 begins with Sample Items A and B, then Item 5. If a child aged 10–16 does not obtain a perfect score on either of the first two items administered, the preceding items should be administered in reverse order until a perfect score on two consecutive items is obtained. The Word Reasoning subtest is discontinued after five consecutive zero-point responses.

When administering the Word Reasoning subtest, the examiner reads each item clue verbatim and gives the child 5 seconds to respond. If the child does not respond within the 5-second time limit, or if the child requests repetition, the examiner should repeat the clue only once and wait 5 seconds more. If the child still fails to respond, or provides an incorrect response, the examiner should present the next clue or item as long as the discontinue rule has not been met. Beginning with Item 7, each item has two clues, and beginning with Item 16, each item has three clues. It is important to remember that when presenting items with two or three clues, the examiner must provide any clues that were already stated (e.g., restate the first and second clue before presenting the third and final clue). If the child provides a correct response before all clues for an item have been presented, the examiner should score 1 point for the item and continue to the next item. The examiner may provide assistance only with the sample items. The Don't Forget box below provides a description of behaviors that the examinee should note during the administration of the Word Reasoning subtest.

DON'T FORGET

Behaviors to Note on Word Reasoning

- Note when the child asks for repetition of a question, as it may indicate several things, including poor hearing, inattention, or stalling.
- Take note of whether children respond quickly, are impulsive, or are methodical and careful in their processing of the information.
- Be aware that because children will almost always respond incorrectly before subsequent clues are given, they may become frustrated or insecure about responding.
- Note spontaneous corrections during the administration of this test and remember to give credit for them.

CAUTION

Common Errors in WISC-IV Subtest Administration

Verbal Subtests

Common errors on the Similarities subtest

- Forgetting to provide the correct response if the child fails to respond or the response is incorrect on Items 1 and 2
- Forgetting to administer previous items in *reverse sequence* if a child aged 9–16 does not obtain a perfect score on either of the first two items administered
- Over-querying or under-querying vague responses

Common errors on the Vocabulary subtest

- Forgetting to give an example of a 2-point response if the child's response to Item 5 or 6 is not perfect
- Forgetting to administer previous items in *reverse sequence* if the child does not obtain a perfect score on either of the first two items administered
- Not correcting the child if he or she mis-hears items, especially Items 11, 23, 32, 33
- Not recording verbal responses verbatim
- Not querying vague or incomplete responses as indicated in the *WISC-IV Administration and Scoring Manual* (Wechsler, 2003)
- Forgetting to use the stimulus book for children aged 9–16 (excluding non-readers)

Common errors on the Comprehension subtest

- Forgetting to give an example of a 2-point response if the child's response to Item 1 is not perfect
- Forgetting to administer previous items in *reverse sequence* if a child aged 9–16 does not obtain a perfect score on either of the first two items administered
- Forgetting to query for a second response if necessary on Items 4, 9, 11, 13, 14, and 18–21
- Not recording verbal responses verbatim
- Defining words if asked by child

Common errors on the Information subtest

- Forgetting to provide the correct response if the child fails to respond or responds incorrectly to Items 1 or 2
- Forgetting to administer previous items in *reverse sequence* if the child does not obtain a perfect score on either of the first two items administered
- Not correcting the child if he or she mis-hears items, especially Items 4 and 15
- Defining words if asked by the child

- Forgetting to query an incomplete answer as indicated in the *WISC-IV Administration and Scoring Manual* (Wechsler, 2003)
- Being unaware that neutral queries may be given to responses that are incomplete or ambiguous

Common errors on the Word Reasoning subtest

- Forgetting to administer previous items in *reverse sequence* if a child aged 9–16 does not obtain a perfect score on either of the first two items administered
- Forgetting to repeat the clue once after the child fails to respond in the first 5 seconds
- Forgetting to restate first clues when presenting second and third clues
- Repeating a clue more than once (each entire clue may be repeated *one time only*)
- Forgetting the 5-second response-time rules, namely, allowing a child approximately 5 seconds to respond, allowing an additional 5 seconds if a child asks for a clue to be repeated, and crediting responses given in more than 5 seconds
- Forgetting to say "Let's try another one" before *every* new item that is administered

Perceptual Reasoning Subtests

Common errors on the Block Design subtest

- Forgetting to time the child
- Forgetting to administer previous items in *reverse sequence* if a child aged 8–16 fails the second trial of Item 3 or provides an incorrect response to Item 4
- Neglecting to make sure that the proper variety of block faces is showing before an item has been started
- Neglecting to give the five extra blocks on Items 11 through 14
- Placing the model or stimulus book in an incorrect position
- Correcting block rotations more than once
- Forgetting to leave the examiner's manual intact when the child constructs his or her designs for Items 1 and 2
- Forgetting to disassemble the examiner's model when the child constructs his or her design for Item 3

Common errors on the Picture Concepts subtest

- Forgetting to provide the correct response and point to the corresponding pictures in Sample Items A and B if the child responds incorrectly
- Forgetting to administer previous items in *reverse sequence* if a child aged 9–16 does not obtain a perfect score on either of the first two items administered
- Forgetting to point across the first and second row of pictures when providing instructions for completing two-row items

(continued)

- Forgetting to point across the first, second, and third rows of pictures when providing instructions for completing three-row items
- Forgetting to provide the standard prompts listed in the WISC-IV Administration and Scoring Manual (Wechsler, 2003), as often as necessary, when a child does not select a picture in each row or selects more than one picture in a single row

Common errors on the Matrix Reasoning subtest
- Forgetting to provide the correct response and point to the correct corresponding pictures in Sample Items A, B, and C
- Forgetting to administer previous items in reverse sequence if the child does not obtain a perfect score on either of the first two items administered
- Forgetting to point to the pictured responses and the box with the question mark as often as needed when presenting test items

Common errors on the Picture Completion subtest
- Forgetting to time the items (i.e., 20 seconds per item)
- Forgetting to give the correct response to Items 1 and 2 if the child does not respond within 20 seconds or responds incorrectly
- Forgetting to administer previous items in reverse sequence if a child aged 9–16 does not obtain a perfect score on either of the first two items administered
- Forgetting to query when the child does not spontaneously point when providing a response from the right-hand column items (which require pointing in addition to a verbal response)
- Giving specific queries listed in the WISC-IV Administration and Scoring Manual (Wechsler, 2003) more than once
- Asking, "Which one is your answer?" when a child points to the correct place in the picture, but provides a verbal elaboration that spoils the response
- Forgetting to query ambiguous or incomplete verbal responses by asking "Show me where you mean" as often as necessary

Working Memory
Common errors on the Digit Span subtest
- Reading the sequence of digits too quickly
- Inadvertently "chunking" the numbers when reading them
- Repeating a digit sequence if asked
- Giving extra help beyond the sample item on Digits Backward
- Forgetting to administer Digits Backward to a child who receives 0 points on Digits Forward
- Forgetting to administer both trials of an item

Common errors on the Letter-Number Sequencing subtest
- Administering the subtest if a child aged 6–7 fails the qualifying items

- Forgetting to remind the child of the correct order on Item 1, Trial 1; Item 4, Trial 2; and Item 5, Trial 1
- Forgetting to acknowledge responses repeated verbatim as correct on Items 1.1, 1.2, 1.3, 2.1, 2.2, 2.3, 3.1, 3.2, and 4.1
- Repeating a letter-number sequence if asked
- Forgetting to administer all three trials of an item

Common errors on the Arithmetic subtest
- Forgetting to time the child
- Stopping the stopwatch when a question is repeated
- Repeating an item more than one time
- Allowing paper and pencil to be used
- Forgetting to provide the correct response to Items 1, 2, and 3 if the child does not respond within 30 seconds or responds incorrectly
- Forgetting to administer previous items in *reverse sequence* if the child does not obtain a perfect score on either of the first two items administered
- Forgetting to remove the Stimulus Booklet after administering Item 5
- Forgetting to give credit for spontaneous corrections within the time limit

Processing Speed
Common errors on the Coding subtest
- Forgetting to administer the correct form, based on the examinee's age (e.g., Coding A: 6–7; Coding B: 8–16)
- Forgetting to time the child
- Forgetting to correct errors on sample items immediately
- Not paying attention to the child and allowing him or her to skip over items or complete a row in reverse order

Common errors on the Symbol Search subtest
- Forgetting to administer the correct form, based on the examinee's age (e.g., Symbol Search A: 6–7; Symbol Search B: 8–16)
- Forgetting to time the child
- Proceeding with the task before the child clearly understands what is required
- Burying your head in the manual while reading directions
- Not paying attention to the child and allowing him or her to skip over items

Common errors on the Cancellation subtest
- Forgetting to time the child
- Forgetting to discontinue after a 45-second interval
- Forgetting to provide corrective feedback when the child marks incorrect responses during the practice items

(continued)

- Forgetting to provide further explanation as needed when presenting Items 1 and 2

Source: From A. S. Kaufman & E. O. Lichtenberger, Essentials of WISC-III and WPPSI-R Assessment. Copyright © 2000 John Wiley & Sons, Inc. This material is used by permission of John Wiley & Sons, Inc.

Note: The WISC-IV allows examinees to spontaneously correct responses at any time during the administration of the entire test and receive the appropriate credit on any subtest with the exception of memory tasks, processing-speed tasks, and timed tasks (i.e., Block Design, Arithmetic, Coding, Symbol Search, Picture Completion, Cancellation), which allows for spontaneous correction only during the specified time limits of each subtest. The WISC-IV also allows for the examiner to return to a previously given item and readminister it, if the examiner believes that the child knows the answer. The only exception to this, of course, is if the answer to that item is addressed elsewhere on the test.

FREQUENTLY ASKED QUESTIONS: SUBTEST ADMINISTRATION

The Psychological Corporation® has provided information on their Web site (http://marketplace.psychcorp.com/PsychCorp.com/Cultures/en-US/dotCom/WISC-IV .com/WISC-IV+Frequently+Asked+Questions.htm) to respond to frequently asked questions (FAQs) regarding the WISC-IV. One category on this Web site reflects FAQs related to subtest administration. The information contained in this category has been reproduced for the benefit of practitioners and is presented in Rapid Reference 2.4.

≡ Rapid Reference 2.4

Frequently Asked Questions: Subtest Administration

Why does WISC-IV start with Block Design?

Although Picture Completion has traditionally been the first subtest administered, it is not a core subtest in the WISC–IV. Block Design was chosen as the first subtest because it is an engaging task that allows the examiner additional opportunity to establish rapport. This is consistent with a recent revision of another Wechsler product, the WPPSI–III, where the initial subtest of Block Design has been well-received by examiners. When testing children with motor difficulties, examiners may decide to begin with a different subtest in the interest of rapport.

Why is Digit Span placed so early in the subtest order?

In order to avoid interference effects between Digit Span and Letter-Number Sequencing, these subtests were widely separated in the order of administration.

Why have picture items been added to the Vocabulary subtest?

These items were added to improve the floor, providing a more effective way to assess very low functioning children.

On Picture Concepts, why do some children seem to lose track of the task when three rows are first introduced?

Typically, if children lose the instructional set when three rows are introduced, they have reached the upper limit of their ability on this subtest; they lose track of the instructions and are drawn to the distracters included in each row of items. Children should be prompted as instructed each time this loss of set occurs.

What does it mean if a child guesses right on the first clue of Word Reasoning?

Children are more likely to guess correctly on the easier items such as those that appear in the first half of the item set, especially Item 9. The more difficult items found in the second half of the item set show a very low percentage of correct responses to the first clue. In order to respond correctly, even on the first clue, the child must use deductive reasoning; that is, on the first clue the child has to narrow the potential responses to those that fit a search set defined by the clue and then make a reasoned guess from the range of responses within the set. It is possible that a child who consistently guesses correctly on the first clue may have taken the test recently, or may have been coached on the correct responses.

Is color-blindness a factor in performance on the Cancellation subtest?

Color-blindness is not a factor in performance on the Cancellation subtest. The Cancellation task utilizes color as a visual distracter; it is possible that children who are color blind will be less distracted by the bright colors or will have greater difficulty differentiating objects of various colors. However, it is recognition of the shapes of the objects that is required to place them in categories properly.

🐟 TEST YOURSELF 🐟

1. **Which of the following subtests require the use of a stopwatch?**

    (a) Block Design, Picture Concepts, Coding, Symbol Search, Cancellation

    (b) Cancellation, Coding, Symbol Search

    (c) Block Design, Cancellation, Coding, Symbol Search

    (d) Block Design, Coding, Picture Completion, Symbol Search, Cancellation, Arithmetic

(continued)

2. **On a subtest with age-based starting points, when the examinee receives full credit on the first item administered but not the second, the first item is used to meet the reversal criteria of two consecutive perfect scores.** True or False?

3. **Which of the following subtests listed does not have reverse rules?**

    (a) Digit Span

    (b) Picture Concepts

    (c) Block Design

    (d) Similarities

4. **Which of the following subtests listed requires the use of a separate Response Booklet?**

    (a) Matrix Reasoning

    (b) Coding

    (c) Arithmetic

    (d) Block Design

5. **If a child asks for clarification or repetition of an item after timing has begun, the examiner should discontinue timing.** True or False?

6. **When a child requests to have instructions or an item repeated, the examiner must**

    (a) repeat the entire set of instructions or item, not just a portion of it.

    (b) repeat only the portion of instructions that the child requested repetition for.

    (c) tell the examinee that you are unable to repeat any instructions.

    (d) repeat the entire set of instructions or item, with the exception of items on Letter-Number Sequencing and Digit Span.

7. **Which of the following subtests can serve as a substitute for Digit Span?**

    (a) Arithmetic

    (b) Coding

    (c) Symbol Search

    (d) Letter-Number Sequencing

8. **Which of the following subtests can serve as a substitute for Coding?**

    (a) Arithmetic

    (b) Symbol Search

    (c) Information

    (d) Cancellation

9. **When administering the Word Reasoning test, the examiner must repeat preceding clues as more clues are added.** True or False?

10. **Block Design, Digit Span, and Cancellation require a modified administration if the examiner wishes to calculate process scores at a later time.** True or False?

11. **You are advising a parent how to describe testing to her 6-year-old child; which of the following is a good example of what the parent might say?**

   (a) "You are going to take a test with a lot of questions, just try your best."

   (b) "You are going to play with some blocks, look at books with pictures and words, complete some puzzles, and answer some questions."

   (c) "The doctor is going to test you for about 2 or 3 hours to try to find out why you have problems in school."

   (d) "You are going to play with the doctor for a while; it will be a lot of fun."

12. **When assessing a child with a visual impairment, it may be advisable to administer subtests from the VCI and WMI only.** True or False?

13. **In which of the following situations can an examiner query a response?**

   (a) The response is vague.

   (b) The response is ambiguous.

   (c) The response is incomplete.

   (d) All of the above.

14. **If an examiner finds that he or she did not administer enough items to meet the discontinue rule for a subtest, the subtest should be considered spoiled.** True or False?

15. **Which of the following can aid in establishing rapport with an examinee?**

   (a) Telling the examinee your name

   (b) Addressing the examinee by his or her name

   (c) Spending a reasonable amount of time interacting with the examinee prior to testing

   (d) All of the above

Answers: 1. d; 2. True; 3. a; 4. b; 5. False; 6. d; 7. a; 8. d; 9. True; 10. False; 11. b; 12. True; 13. d; 14. True; 15. d

Three

HOW TO SCORE THE WISC-IV

TYPES OF SCORES

Administration of the WISC-IV results in three types of scores: raw scores, scaled scores (standard scores with mean = 10 and SD = 3), and Indexes/Full Scale IQ (standard scores with mean = 100 and SD = 15). The first score calculated by the examiner is the *raw score,* which is simply the total number of points earned on a single subtest. The raw score by itself is meaningless because it is not norm-referenced. That is, it has no meaning with respect to level of functioning compared to the general population. To interpret an examinee's performance on a subtest, relative to the general population (and more specifically, to same-age peers), raw scores must be converted to *standard scores* (i.e., a scaled score, process score, Index, or IQ). The metrics for the various Wechsler standard scores are listed in Rapid Reference 3.1. Each subtest produces a scaled score (ranging from 1 to 19) having a mean of 10 and a standard deviation of 3. The factor indexes and IQ (also referred to as "Composite Scores") have a mean of 100 and a standard deviation of 15. The Verbal Comprehension Index (VCI) and the Perceptual Reasoning Index (PRI) have a standard score range of 45 to 155, the Working Memory Index (WMI) and the Processing Speed Index (PSI) have a standard score range of 50 to 150, and the Full Scale IQ (FSIQ) has a standard score range of 40 to 160.

Intellectual abilities are distributed along the normal probability curve in the general population. Most children score within 1 SD below and above the mean on measures of these abilities. That is, about 68 out of every 100 children tested obtain IQ or Index scores between 85 and 115. A greater number of children, about 96 %, obtain scores ranging from 70 to 130 (2 SDs below and above the mean, respectively). The number of children earning extremely high scores (i.e., above 130) is about 2%, and the number earning very low scores (i.e., less than 70) is about 2%.

≡Rapid Reference 3.1

Metrics for WISC-IV Standard Scores

Type of Standard Score	Mean	Standard Deviation	Range of Values
Scaled score	10	3	1–19
VCI and PRI	100	15	45–155
WMI and PSI	100	15	50–150
FSIQ	100	15	40–160

STEP-BY-STEP: HOW THE WISC-IV IS SCORED

Raw Scores

Each of the items of a subtest contributes directly to the raw score. Three subtests (Block Design, Digit Span, and Cancellation) also allow for the calculation of process scores. *Process scores* involve calculating raw scores for specific items or portions of a subtest (process scores will be discussed later in this chapter and in Chapter 6). The scoring of most subtests is not complicated. Simple arithmetic is all that is necessary to calculate the subtests' raw scores. There are a few subtests, however, in which some element of subjectivity presents a challenge to the examiner during the scoring process. Tips for scoring responses that clearly involve subjectivity are discussed later in this chapter. The Caution box at the top of page 98 presents common errors that examiners make in calculating the raw scores.

Scaled Scores

After the raw scores have been transferred from the inside of the Record Form to the front cover, they are converted to scaled scores. To convert the child's raw score to a scaled score the examiner needs the following: (1) the child's chronological age at the time of testing, (2) the child's raw scores on all subtests, and (3) Table A.1 from the *WISC-IV Administration and Scoring Manual* (Wechsler, 2003). In the section of Table A.1 that encompasses the child's chronological age, find the child's raw score for each subtest and the corresponding scaled score. Record the scaled score equivalents in the appropriate boxes in two separate places on the front cover of the Record Form, one labeled "Total Raw Score to Scaled

CAUTION

Common Errors in Raw Score Calculation

- Neglecting to include points from the items below the basal (i.e., items that were not administered) to the total raw score
- Neglecting to add the points recorded on one page of the Record Form to the points recorded on the next (e.g., Similarities lists the first 18 items on one page and the last 5 items on the next page; Vocabulary lists the first 17 items on one page and the last 19 items on the next page; Comprehension lists the first 6 items on one page and last 15 items on the next page; and Word Reasoning lists the first 15 items on one page and the last 9 items on the next page)
- Forgetting to subtract the number of incorrect responses from the number of correct responses on Symbol Search and Cancellation
- Transferring total raw scores incorrectly from inside the Record Form to the front page of the Record Form
- Miscalculating the raw score sum
- Including points earned on items that were presented after the discontinue criterion was met
- Forgetting to attend closely to items that are scored 0, 1, or 2 rather than 0 or 1 only

Source: From A. S. Kaufman & E. O. Lichtenberger, Essentials of WISC-III and WPPSI-R Assessment. Copyright © 2000 John Wiley & Sons, Inc. This material is used by permission of John Wiley & Sons, Inc.

CAUTION

Most Frequent Errors in Obtaining Scaled Scores

- Using a score conversion table that references the wrong age group
- Misreading across the rows of the score conversion tables
- Transferring scaled scores incorrectly from the conversion table to the Record Form

Note. From A. S. Kaufman & E. O. Lichtenberger, Essentials of WISC-III and WPPSI-R Assessment. Copyright © 2000 John Wiley & Sons, Inc. This material is used by permission of John Wiley & Sons, Inc.

Score Conversions," and another labeled "Subtest Scaled Score Profile." The Caution box at left lists the most frequent errors that examiners make in obtaining scaled scores.

Indexes and FSIQ

Converting scaled scores to Indexes and the FSIQ is the next step in the WISC-IV scoring process. The following is a list of steps necessary to convert scaled scores to Index scores and FSIQ. (The Don't Forget box on page 99 lists the subtests that make up the WISC-IV Indexes and FSIQ.)

DON'T FORGET

Subtests Making Up WISC-IV Indexes

VCI	PRI	WMI	PSI
Similarities	Block Design	Digit Span	Coding
Vocabulary	Picture Concepts	Letter-Number	Symbol Search
Comprehension	Matrix Reasoning	Sequencing	(Cancellation)
(Information)	(Picture Completion)	(Arithmetic)	
(Word Reasoning)			

Note: Subtests in parentheses are supplemental tests. All other subtests compose the core battery. The FSIQ is made up of the 10 core battery subtests unless a substitution has been made. See Table 3.1 for allowable substitutions of supplemental tests for core battery tests.

1. Calculate the sum of the appropriate subtests' scaled scores for each of the four Indexes and the FSIQ. Note that Information, Word Reasoning, Picture Completion, Arithmetic, and Cancellation are not used in the sum of scaled scores *unless* they are replacing another subtest. Subtest substitutions are discussed later in this chapter and are presented in Table 3.1. It is important to note that only *one* substitution per scale is allowed.

2. Record the "Sums of Scaled Scores" in the appropriate boxes on the front of the Record Form in the sections labeled "Total Raw Score to Scaled Score Conversions" and "Sum of Scaled Scores to Composite Score Conversions." In both these sections, the boxes in which the sums of scaled scores are placed are shaded light green.

3. Convert the sum of scaled scores to VCI, PRI, WMI, PSI, and FSIQ using Tables A.2, A.3, A.4, A.5, and A.6, respectively, in the *WISC-IV Administration and Scoring Manual* (Wechsler, 2003).

4. Record the Index scores and FSIQ (referred to as "Composite Scores" on the Record Form) in two places, one labeled "Sum of Scaled Scores to Composite Score Conversions" and another labeled "Composite Score Profile." Note that, in the former section, examiners should also record the percentile ranks and confidence intervals for the Index scores and FSIQ, which may also be found in Tables A.2–A.6 in the *WISC-IV Administration and Scoring Manual* (Wechsler, 2003).

5. Plot scaled scores and composite scores on "Subtest Scaled Score Profile" and "Composite Score Profile," respectively.

Table 3.1 Guidelines for Substituting Supplemental Subtests for Core Battery Subtests

Core Subtest	Acceptable Substitution
Similarities	Information, Word Reasoning
Vocabulary	Information, Word Reasoning
Comprehension	Information, Word Reasoning
Block Design	Picture Completion
Picture Concepts	Picture Completion
Matrix Reasoning	Picture Completion
Digit Span	Arithmetic
Letter-Number Sequencing	Arithmetic
Coding	Cancellation
Symbol Search	Cancellation

Source: From the Administration and Scoring Manual of the Wechsler Intelligence Scale for Children–Fourth Edition. Copyright © 2003 The Psychological Corporation. Adapted and reproduced by permission. All rights reserved.

Special Considerations for Calculating WISC-IV Index Scores and FSIQ Using Supplemental Subtests

According to the *WISC-IV Administration and Scoring Manual* (Wechsler, 2003), supplemental subtests can be substituted for core battery tests under certain conditions. For example, an examiner may choose to substitute the Cancellation subtest for the Coding subtest for an individual with fine motor difficulties because, like the Symbol Search test, Cancellation requires making slash-marks rather than drawing specific shapes. Likewise, the examiner may choose to substitute the Picture Completion subtest for Block Design for the same examinee because Picture Completion requires either a verbal or a pointing response rather than the manual manipulation of objects. Another situation in which a substitution may be warranted is when a core battery subtest is spoiled or invalidated for some reason. For example, when a child clearly misunderstands the directions for the Coding subtest, rendering the results uninterpretable, the Cancellation test may be used along with Symbol Search to calculate a PSI.

An examiner may also choose to calculate an Index using a supplemental test, even when no core battery tests have been spoiled, in order to allow for the most meaningful and accurate interpretation of findings. For example, recently one of the authors supervised the evaluation of a student aged 6 years 10 months who was referred because he had not acquired basic reading skills. This student did not know the alphabet and recognized only a few letters of the alphabet (including A–C). Alternatively, he was able to count to 20 and recognized numbers 1–10 readily. He earned a Digit Span scaled score of 11, an Arithmetic scaled score of 10, and a Letter-Number Sequencing scaled score of 5. The examiner reasoned that because of this student's lack of facility with letters, his score on the Letter-Number Sequencing subtest and the WMI (88) was an underestimate of his working memory ability. Substituting Arithmetic for Letter-Number Sequencing resulted in a WMI of 102, which was considered a more accurate representation of his working memory ability. Finally, using a supplemental test for a core battery test may be done when the child earns a raw score of zero on one core battery test *only* and earns credit for items on an appropriate supplemental test. Table 3.1 provides a list of acceptable substitutions for the WISC-IV core battery tests.

In general, although there may be many situations in which substitutions of supplemental subtests for core battery subtests is judged appropriate, they should be done cautiously and in accordance with the guidelines established by the test publisher. The Don't Forget box below lists the guidelines that should be followed by examiners who choose to substitute a core battery test with a supplemental test.

DON'T FORGET

1. One substitution is allowed for each Index score.
   a. Information or Word Reasoning may substitute for one core VCI subtest.
   b. Picture Completion may substitute for one core PRI subtest.
   c. Arithmetic may substitute for either WMI subtest.
   d. Cancellation may substitute for either PSI subtest.
2. When deriving the FSIQ, no more than two substitutions from different Indexes may be made.
3. A supplemental subtest may replace only one subtest in an Index, not two. For example, Picture Completion may replace either Block Design or Matrix Reasoning, but may not replace both Block Design *and* Matrix Reasoning.
4. The standard subtest administration order should be followed even when substituting supplemental tests for core battery tests. For example, if Cancellation is being used to replace Coding, then Cancellation should be administered in the order in which it is intended to be administered in the battery. That is, if Coding was not administered, then Cancellation would be administered as the 10th subtest in the core battery or as the 11th subtest when all supplemental tests are administered.

It is important to remember that when supplemental subtests are used to replace core battery subtests, the underlying construct intended to be measured by the Index may change. For example, the subtests that compose the VCI (i.e., Similarities, Vocabulary, and Comprehension) measure qualitatively different aspects of mainly Crystallized Intelligence *(Gc)*. That is, Similarities measures Lexical Knowledge (VL), Language Development (LD), and, to some extent, Fluid Reasoning *(Gf;* Induction); Vocabulary measures VL and LD; and Comprehension measures LD and General Information (K0) and may require general sequential reasoning or deductive reasoning *(Gf*-RG) for some items. Despite our belief that *Gf* is involved in responding to VCI items, the common or most robust portion of the variance among the VCI core battery subtests is *Gc*. However, when Word Reasoning is substituted for Vocabulary, for example, the composition of the VCI changes, consisting of items that rely more substantially on *Gf.* The extent to which the underlying constructs of Indexes change as a result of substitutions was discussed in Chapter 1 and will be addressed again in the next chapter.

Special Considerations for Indexes and IQ with Subtest Raw Scores of Zero

Subtest raw scores of zero deserve special consideration when being converted to scaled scores, Index scores, and IQ. The problem with a raw score of zero is that you cannot determine the child's true ability to perform on the test. A zero raw score does not mean that a child lacks a certain ability. Rather, it means that the particular subtest did not have enough low-level (or easy) items (called *floor items*) to adequately assess the child's skills. The Don't Forget box on page 103 lists the only situations in which we believe it is appropriate to calculate Index scores and a FSIQ when one or more raw scores of zero are obtained.

Prorating on the WISC-IV

Prorating the sums of scaled scores to derive composites is allowed in specific instances. However, due to the multitude of problems associated with this technique, examiners are advised to avoid it whenever possible (see *WISC-IV Administration and Scoring Manual,* Wechsler, 2003, pp. 49–50). If an examiner determines through his or her sound clinical judgment that prorating is required, the following should be noted:

1. The sum of scaled scores for the Verbal Comprehension and Perceptual Reasoning Indexes may be prorated only when two of the three contributing subtest scaled scores are valid. Table A.7 in the *WISC-IV*

DON'T FORGET

Appropriate Situations for Calculating Index Scores and a Full Scale IQ When Raw Scores of Zero Are Obtained

The FSIQ may be calculated when no more than two raw scores of zero are included in its derivation.
Subtest raw scores of zero must be from different Indexes.

The VCI may be calculated when no more than one raw score of zero is included in its derivation.
If a child obtains one or more raw scores of zero on the subtests that contribute to the VCI, then the supplemental tests (i.e., Information or Word Reasoning) should be administered. A supplemental test on which the child earns a basal should substitute for the core battery subtest having a raw score of zero. Remember, no more than one substitution is permissible.

The PRI may be calculated when no more than one raw score of zero is included in its derivation.
If a child obtains one or more raw scores of zero on the subtests that contribute to the PRI, then the Picture Completion subtest should be administered. If the child earns a basal on Picture Completion, then this subtest should substitute for one of the core battery subtests having a raw score of zero.

The WMI should not be calculated when a raw score of zero is obtained on any subtest that will be included in its derivation.
If a child obtains a raw score of zero on one of the two core subtests that contribute to the WMI, then Arithmetic should be administered. If the child earns a basal on Arithmetic, then this subtest should substitute for the core battery subtest having a raw score of zero.

The PSI should not be calculated when a raw score of zero is obtained on any subtest that will be included in its derivation.
If a child obtains one raw score of zero on one of the two core subtests that contribute to the PSI, then Cancellation should be administered. If the child achieves a basal on Cancellation, then this subtest should substitute for the core battery subtest having a raw score of zero.

Administration and Scoring Manual (Wechsler, 2003) provides prorated sums of scaled scores for deriving the VCI and PRI.

2. The sum of scaled scores for the Working Memory and Processing Speed Indexes cannot be prorated unless an appropriate *and* valid supplemental subtest scaled score is available for either scale (i.e., Arithmetic and Cancellation, respectively).

3. The examiner should always record the term "PRORATED" next to

any Index that was prorated. This term should be marked clearly on the front page of the Record Form and explained fully in the psychological report.

Scoring Subtests Requiring Judgment

While administering the WISC-IV you will likely find that the verbal subtests elicit many more responses than listed in the manual. The multitude of responses given by an examinee, although interesting, may cause frustration for the examiner during the scoring process because of the need to rely on one's judgment. The general scoring criteria are found on pages 40–44 in the *WISC-IV Administration and Scoring Manual* (Wechsler, 2003).

In addition to these criteria, there are some basic rules to consider when scoring verbal subtests. First, a child must not be penalized for poor grammar or improper pronunciation. Although grammar and pronunciation are important to note for clinical reasons, it is the *content* of what the child says that is most important for scoring a response. Second, long and elaborate answers are not necessarily worth more points than short, concise ones. Some children have a tendency to respond in paragraph form, which may lead to two or three answers' being given within the context of a single response. If this occurs, either spontaneously or after a query, it is the examiner's responsibility to determine two things, namely, (1) which part of the response was intended as the final response, and (2) whether the response has been spoiled. If a child's response contains many answers but none that spoil the response, further querying may be necessary. Sometimes it is clear that in a series of responses, the last answer is the final response. In that case, the final response should be the one scored. At other times it is unclear whether the second or third response is intended as the actual response. For clarification purposes you may ask, "You said, 'we wear bicycle helmets because our parents want us to wear them, they look cool, and they protect you.' Which one was your answer?" In some instances children say that their *entire* long response was what they intended the answer to be, and embedded in that long response are 0-, 1-, and 2-point answers. In such a case, if no response spoils part of the long response, then simply score the *best* response (i.e., the response that would allow the maximum number of points to be awarded to the child).

Subtest-by-Subtest Scoring Keys

The following sections provide important points to remember when scoring the respective subtests on the WISC-IV. We do not review all of the nuances of scoring each part of the subtests here, but we do cover areas that commonly cause difficulty for examiners. Additionally, tables outlining the most salient scoring revisions from the WISC-III to the WISC-IV are presented after each subtest, where applicable.

It is important to note that in addition to the subtest raw score calculations, three WISC-IV subtests presented in this section (i.e., Block Design, Digit Span, and Cancellation) allow for the calculation of *process scores*. According to the test authors, "process scores are designed to provide more detailed information on the cognitive abilities that contribute to a child's subtest performance" (*WISC-IV Technical and Interpretive Manual,* Wechsler, 2003, pp. 107–108). The procedures for calculating process scores for the Block Design, Digit Span, and Cancellation subtests appear in the sections that follow.

1. Block Design (PRI, Core)
- For Items 1–3, successful completion on Trial 1 earns 2 points, successful completion on Trial 2 earns 1 point.
- For Items 4–8, successful completion of the designs (within the time limit) earns 4 points.
- For Items 9–14, bonus points (either 4, 5, 6, or 7 bonus points) are awarded for successfully completed designs on the basis of completion time.
- It is possible to calculate a process score for this subtest (Block Design No Time Bonus [BDN]). This may be accomplished by scoring 0, 1, or 2 on Items 1–3, and 4 points for *correct* designs completed within the time limit with no rotation errors on Items 4–14.
- Rotated designs of 30 degrees or more are scored 0 points. Circle "Y" or "N" in the "Correct Design" column to indicate whether the child constructed the design correctly, irrespective of rotation.
- Partially complete or incorrect designs are scored 0 points. Incorrect or partially complete designs should be drawn in the "Constructed Design" column of the protocol, and the "N" in the "Correct Design" column should be circled.
- If a child correctly completes a design after the time limit has expired, then no points are awarded (although a note should be made of the child's performance by circling "Y" in the "Correct Design" column of the protocol to indicate that the child constructed the design correctly).
- Include early unadministered items (as correct) and reversal items when calculating the total raw score.

- A maximum of 68 raw score points for standard administration (with bonus points) may be obtained.
- The maximum "Block Design No Time Bonus" raw score is 50 points.

See Table 3.2 for Block Design scoring revisions from the WISC-III to the WISC-IV.

Table 3.2 Changes in Scoring: Subtest 1, Block Design (PRI, Core)

WISC-III	WISC-IV
Scoring includes the time bonus points for Items 4–12.	Use of time bonus points restricted to last 6 items.
Block Design No Time Bonus process score unavailable.	Block Design No Time Bonus process score available.
Maximum raw score 69 points.	Maximum raw score 68 points.

2. Similarities (VCI, Core)

- For all Similarities items, use the general 0-, 1-, or 2-point scoring criteria and specific sample responses as a guide (see *WISC-IV Administration and Scoring Manual,* Wechsler, 2003, p. 71).
- Responses listed in the manual are not all-inclusive. Give credit for responses that are of the same caliber as those in the manual.
- The key to scoring Similarities items is the *degree of abstraction* evident in the response. Responses that reflect a relevant general categorization earn 2 points, whereas responses that reflect only one or more common properties or functions of the members of an item pair earn 0 or 1 point.
- Items 1 and 2 are scored either 0 or 1 point and Items 3–23 are scored either 0, 1, or 2 points.
- For multiple responses, score the best response as long as no portion of the child's answer spoils the response.
- Include early unadministered items (as correct) and reversal items when calculating the total raw score.
- A maximum of 44 raw score points may be obtained.

See Table 3.3 for Similarities scoring revisions from the WISC-III to the WISC-IV.

Table 3.3 Changes in Scoring: Subtest 2, Similarities (VCI, Core)

WISC-III	WISC-IV
Corrective feedback provided on first 2-point item.	Sample item revised to require a creditable response from child before beginning subtest.
Items 1–5 score 0 or 1 point, 6–19 score 0, 1, or 2 points.	Items 1–2 score 0 or 1 point, 3–23 score 0, 1, or 2 points.
Maximum raw score 33 points.	Maximum raw score 44 points.
	Spontaneous correction and readministration of item(s) with correct answer achieves a score.

3. Digit Span (WMI, Core)
- For each trial, score 1 point for correct responses and 0 points for incorrect responses (or no response).
- The item score is the sum of the two *trial scores* for each item.
- The Digit Span raw score is equivalent to the sum of the item scores for Digits Forward and Digits Backward.
- The Digit Span Forward (DSF) process score is obtained by summing all item scores on DSF.
- The Digit Span Backward (DSB) process score is obtained by summing all item scores on DSB, excluding the sample.
- The Longest Digit Span Forward (LDSF) and the Longest Digit Span Backward (LDSB) process scores both indicate the number of digits recalled on the last Digit Span trial (Forward or Backward, respectively) with a score of 1. For instance, if a child correctly recalls five digits forward once and misses both trials of six digits forward, the LDSF is 5.
- A maximum of 32 raw score points may be obtained.

See Table 3.4 for Digit Span scoring revisions from the WISC-III to the WISC-IV.

Table 3.4 Changes in Scoring: Subtest 3, Digit Span (WMI, Core)

WISC-III	WISC-IV
No score indicating the longest number of digits recalled correctly.	LDSF and LDSB indicate the longest number of digits recalled correctly.
No scaled scores available for Digit Span Forward or Digit Span Backward.	Scaled scores available for Digit Span Forward and Digit Span Backward.
Maximum raw score 30 points.	Maximum raw score 32 points.

4. Picture Concepts (PRI, Core)

- Circle the numbers that correspond to the child's responses for each item on the Record Form. Correct answers are printed in color. Circle "DK" if the child does not respond or states that he or she does not know the answer.
- One point is awarded *only* if the child chooses the correct pictures from *all* rows of an item; 0 points are earned for incorrect responses or no response.
- Score 1 point if a child responds correctly after being given one or more of the following three standardized prompts listed in the *WISC-IV Administration and Scoring Manual* (Wechsler, 2003, p. 91):
  - For two-row items: "Pick one picture from each row, one here (point across first row), and one here (point across second row)."
  - For three-row items: "Pick one picture from each row, one here (point across first row), one here (point across second row), and one here (point across third row)."
  - If a child offers more than one combination of selected pictures as a response, say, "You can give only one answer. Just choose the best one."
- Include early unadministered items (as correct) and reversal items when calculating the total raw score.
- A maximum of 28 raw score points may be obtained.

5. Coding (PSI, Core)

- When 120 seconds has elapsed, tell the child to stop working and record the completion time as 120 seconds, even if the child has not completed all of the items. Do not score any items that may have been completed beyond the time limit (e.g., if the child attempts to finish an item after he or she has been told to stop, or if an examiner allows a child to continue working on a nearly finished item in the interest of maintaining rapport). If the child completes all of the items before the 120-second time limit, stop timing and record the time in seconds on the Record Form. Award appropriate bonus points for Coding A.
- Careful placement of the Coding template is necessary for accurate scoring. Be sure to use the appropriate side of the scoring key depending on the form (A or B) administered.
- Score 1 point for each symbol drawn correctly within the 120-second time limit.
- Do not penalize a child for an imperfectly drawn symbol. Symbols do not have to be perfectly drawn to obtain credit, but they must be recognizable.
- If a child spontaneously corrects his or her drawing, give credit to the corrected drawing.

- Items that a child did not attempt (e.g., skipped or did not reach before the time limit expired) should not be counted in the total score.
- Do not count sample items toward the final score.
- On Coding A, if a child completed all items correctly before the time limit has expired, he or she receives bonus points based on the total completion time.
- On Coding B, there are no time bonus points awarded for items completed correctly before the time limit.
- A maximum of 65 raw score points may be obtained with time bonus for Coding A; a maximum of 119 raw score points for Coding B may be obtained.

6. Vocabulary (VCI, Core)

- Picture Items 1–4 are scored either 0 or 1 point and Verbal Items 5–36 are scored either 0, 1, or 2 points.
- Responses listed in the manual are not all-inclusive. Give credit for responses that are of the same caliber as those in the manual.
- On Picture Items 1–4, score 0 points for the following responses:
  - Inappropriate marginal responses (e.g., saying "engine" for a pictured fire truck)
  - Generalized responses (e.g., saying "drink" for a pictured milk container)
  - Functional responses (e.g., saying "it's a money holder" for a pictured wallet)
  - Hand gestures (e.g., pretending to pedal in response to a pictured bicycle)
  - Personalized responses (e.g., saying "I have one in front of my house" when shown a picture of a tree)
- Do not penalize a child for articulation errors or poor grammar if it is clear that the child knows the correct name of an object or is able to define it.
- In general, any recognized word meaning is acceptable, but a response that lacks significant content should be penalized (e.g., a response that indicates only a vague knowledge of the word's meaning).
- For multiple responses, score the best response as long as no portion of the child's answer spoils the response.
- Include early unadministered items (as correct) and reversal items when calculating the total raw score.
- A maximum of 68 raw score points may be obtained.

See Table 3.5 for Vocabulary scoring revisions from the WISC-III to the WISC-IV.

Table 3.5 Changes in Scoring: Subtest 6, Vocabulary (VCI, Core)

WISC-III	WISC-IV
Items 1–30 score 0, 1, or 2 points.	Items 1–4 (picture items) score 0 or 1 point; items 5–36 (verbal items) score 0, 1, or 2 points.
Maximum raw score 60 points.	Maximum raw score 68 points.
	Spontaneous correction and readministration of item(s) with correct answer achieves a score.

7. Letter-Number Sequencing (WMI, Core)

- For the qualifying items, circle "Y" or "N" on the Record Form to indicate whether the child aged 6–7 years correctly counted to *at least* three or recited *at least* the first three letters of the alphabet.
- For each trial, score 1 point if the child recalls all the numbers and letters in their correct sequence, *even if the child recalls the letters before the numbers.* Score 0 points for incorrect items.
- If standardized prompts are given on specific trials of Items 1, 4, or 5 and the child subsequently corrects his or her previous answer, do not award credit. Record a "P" on the Record Form for any prompt given. The *WISC-IV Administration and Scoring Manual* marks with an asterisk those trials that should be prompted (Wechsler, 2003, pp. 129–130). The following prompts should be used:
  - Item 1 (Trial 1): "Remember to say the numbers first, in order. Then say the letters in alphabetical order. Let's try another one."
  - Item 4 (Trial 2): "Remember to say the letters in order."
  - Item 5 (Trial 1): "Remember to say the numbers in order."
- Sum the scores on the three trials for each item to calculate the item score. A child can score up to 3 points (i.e., all three trials correct) on each item.
- A maximum of 30 raw score points may be obtained.

8. Matrix Reasoning (PRI, Core)

- Circle the numbers that correspond to the child's responses for each item on the Record Form. Correct answers are printed in color.
- Score 1 point for a correct response and 0 points for either an incorrect response or no response.

- Circle "DK" on the Record Form when the child does not respond or states that he or she does not know the answer.
- Include early unadministered items (as correct) and reversal items when calculating the total raw score.
- A maximum of 35 raw score points may be obtained.

9. Comprehension (VCI, Core)

- For all Comprehension items, use the general 0-, 1-, or 2-point scoring criteria and specific sample responses as a guide (see *WISC-IV Administration and Scoring Manual,* Wechsler, 2003, pp. 135–136).
- Responses listed in the manual are not all-inclusive. Give credit for responses that are of the same caliber as those in the manual.
- For items that contain more than one general concept, the child's response must reflect at least two different concepts to earn 2 points. If the child's response reflects only one concept, score the item 1 point and prompt for another concept. If the child's second response reflects the same concept as his or her first response, prompt once more. If the initial response is repeated, or a second concept is not provided, the item score remains 1.
- If a child improves an answer spontaneously or after a query, give credit for the improvement (e.g., when asked why children should drink milk, the child responds, "It's good for you" [1-point response requiring a query] and then, when queried, says "It keeps you healthy" [2-point response]).
- If a child provides several responses that vary in quality, but nevertheless do not spoil his or her response, then score the best response (i.e., the response that will result in the maximum number of score points' being awarded).
- Include early unadministered items (as correct) and reversal items when calculating the total raw score.
- A maximum of 42 raw score points may be obtained.

See Table 3.6 for Comprehension scoring revisions from the WISC-III to the WISC-IV.

Table 3.6 Changes in Scoring: Subtest 9, Comprehension (VCI, Core)

WISC-III	WISC-IV
Maximum raw score 36 points.	Maximum raw score 42 points. Spontaneous correction and readministration of item(s) with correct answer achieves a score.

10. Symbol Search (PSI, Core)

- When 120 seconds have elapsed, tell the child to stop working and record the completion time as 120 seconds, even if the child has not completed all of the items. Do not score any items that may have been completed beyond the time limit (e.g., if the child attempts to finish an item after he or she has been told to stop, or if an examiner allows a child to continue working on a nearly finished item in the interest of maintaining rapport). If the child completes all of the items before the 120-second time limit, stop timing and record the time on the Record Form.
- Careful placement of the Symbol Search template is necessary for accurate scoring. Be sure to use the appropriate side of the scoring key depending on the form (A or B) administered.
- Score 0 points if a child marks both "Yes" and "No" for the response to one item.
- On items where there is a clear indication of self-correction (e.g., the child crossed out one answer and endorsed another), score the latter response.
- Sum the number of correct items and the number of incorrect items separately.
- Unanswered items (i.e., skipped or not reached before the time limit) do count toward either the correct or the incorrect total.
- Calculate the raw score by subtracting the number of incorrect items from the number correct.
- A maximum of 45 raw score points may be obtained for Symbol Search A; a maximum of 60 raw score points may be obtained for Symbol Search B.

See Table 3.7 for Symbol Search scoring revisions from the WISC-III to the WISC-IV.

Table 3.7 Changes in Scoring: Subtest 10, Symbol Search (PSI, Core)

WISC-III	WISC-IV
Maximum raw score 45 points on Symbol Search B.	Maximum raw score 60 points on Symbol Search B.

11. Picture Completion (PRI, Supplemental)

- If the child responds with an appropriate synonym for the missing part of the picture (e.g., says "door opener" for "door knob"), score 1 point.
- If the child points correctly to the missing part of the picture, but then provides a verbal elaboration that spoils the response (e.g., points correctly to a missing part of a car door, but then says "horn"), score 0 points.
- If the child responds correctly within 20 seconds, score 1 point.
- If the child responds incorrectly or fails to respond within 20 seconds, score 0 points.
- Responses found in the left-hand column of the *WISC-IV Administration and Scoring Manual* (Wechsler, 2003, pp. 166–169) are scored 1 regardless of whether the child points; responses in the right-hand column of the manual are scored 1 *only if* the child points correctly in addition to providing the indicated verbal response.
- The sample responses in the manual are not an exhaustive list. Award credit for any response that is of the same caliber as the samples.
- If a child responds by pointing, record "PC" on the Record Form if the child pointed correctly or "PX" if the child pointed incorrectly.
- Include early unadministered items (as correct) and reversal items when calculating the total raw score.
- A maximum of 38 raw score points may be obtained.

See Table 3.8 for Picture Completion scoring revisions from the WISC-III to the WISC-IV.

Table 3.8 Changes in Scoring: Subtest 11, Picture Completion (PRI, Supplemental)

WISC-III	WISC-IV
No distinctions made between verbal responses that require pointing and those that should be scored 1 point without pointing.	Distinctions are made between verbal responses that require pointing and those that should be scored 1 point without pointing.
Strict 20-second time limit for each item.	20-second time limit for each item can be flexibly applied, based on the examiner's clinical judgment.
No indication to be made on protocol of whether the child's response was verbal or indicated by pointing.	Indicate "PC" on protocol when child points correctly, "PX" when child points incorrectly.
Maximum raw score 30 points.	Maximum raw score 38 points.

12. Cancellation (PSI, Supplemental)

- When 45 seconds have elapsed, tell the child to stop working and record the completion time as 45 seconds, even if the child has not completed the item. Do not score any item that may have been completed beyond the time limit (e.g., if the child attempts to finish an item after he or she has been told to stop, or if an examiner allows a child to continue working on a nearly finished item in the interest of maintaining rapport). If the child completes the item before the 45-second time limit, stop timing and record the time on the Record Form. Award appropriate bonus points.
- Careful placement of the Cancellation Scoring Template is essential for accurate scoring.
- When using the scoring template, marks on target objects are scored as correct; marks on nontarget objects are scored as incorrect. Consider objects as marked *only* if it is clear that the child intended to mark them (see *WISC-IV Administration and Scoring Manual,* Wechsler, 2003, pp. 171–172).
- Add the total number of correct and incorrect responses separately.
- Calculate the total raw score by subtracting the total number of incorrect responses from the total number of correct responses. The total raw score for Cancellation is the sum of the item raw scores for *both* Items 1 and 2.
- It is also possible to obtain process scores for this subtest. The total raw score for Cancellation Random (CAR) and Cancellation Structured (CAS) are the total raw scores (including any applicable time-bonus points) for Items 1 and 2, respectively.
- A maximum of 136 raw score points may be obtained.

13. Information (VCI, Supplemental)

- Score 1 point for a correct response and score 0 points for either an incorrect response or no response.
- Responses listed in the manual are not all-inclusive. Give credit for responses that are of the same caliber as those in the manual.
- For multiple responses, score the best response as long as no portion of the child's answer spoils the response.
- Include early unadministered items (as correct) and reversal items when calculating the total raw score.
- A maximum of 33 raw score points may be obtained.

See Table 3.9 for Information scoring revisions from the WISC-III to the WISC-IV.

Table 3.9 Changes in Scoring: Subtest 13, Information (VCI, Supplemental)

WISC-III	WISC-IV
Maximum raw score 30 points.	Maximum raw score 33 points.
	Spontaneous correction and readministration of item(s) with correct answer achieves a score.

14. Arithmetic (WMI, Supplemental)

- Score 1 point for a correct response given within the 30-second time limit; score 0 points for either an incorrect response, no response, or a response given after the time limit has expired.
- If the child provides a numerically correct response but leaves out the units (or states the units incorrectly) that appeared in the question (e.g., says "five" rather than "five *crayons*" or "six" rather than "six *minutes*"), score the response correct. The only exception to this is on items where money or time is the unit; on such items, *alternate* numerical responses must be accompanied by the correct unit (e.g., if the answer is "one dollar," saying "one" is correct; however, if the child transforms the units to quarters, they must say "four quarters," rather than just "four" to receive credit).
- If the child spontaneously provides a correct response in place of an incorrect response within the time limit, score 1 point.
- Include early unadministered items (as correct) and reversal items when calculating the total raw score.
- A maximum of 34 raw score points may be obtained.

See Table 3.10 for Arithmetic scoring revisions from the WISC-III to the WISC-IV.

Table 3.10 Changes in Scoring: Subtest 14, Arithmetic (WMI, Supplemental)

WISC-III	WISC-IV
Point bonus awarded if the answer was given within 10 seconds on items 19–24.	No point bonus for answers provided quickly.
Maximum raw score 30 points.	Maximum raw score 34 points.
	Spontaneous correction and readministration of item(s) with correct answer achieves a score.

15. Word Reasoning (VCI, Supplemental)

- For each clue presented, circle the letter "Y" for a correct response or circle the letter "N" for either an incorrect response or no response.
- If a clue is repeated, record "R" on the Record Form.
- Score 1 point for a correct response or score 0 points for an incorrect response.
- The sample responses provided in the manual are not all-inclusive. Score a response as correct if the response provided is of the same caliber as the listed sample responses.
- Include early unadministered items (as correct) and reversal items when calculating the total raw score.
- A maximum of 24 raw score points may be obtained.

Frequently Asked Questions: Scoring

The Psychological Corporation has provided information on its Web site (http://marketplace.psychcorp.com/PsychCorp.com/Cultures/en-US/dotCom/WISC-IV.com/WISC-IV+Frequently+Asked+Questions.htm) to respond to frequently asked questions (FAQs) regarding the WISC-IV. One category on this Web site reflects FAQs related to the scoring of WISC-IV subtests. The information contained in this category has been reproduced for the benefit of practitioners and is presented in Rapid Reference 3.2.

≡Rapid Reference 3.2

Frequently Asked Questions: Scoring

Why are there separate norms for Block Design with and without time bonuses?

Practitioners have suspected that children who emphasize accuracy over speed of performance may score lower on Block Design because of time bonuses, and some believe that faster performance reflects a higher level of the ability being measured and is therefore deserving of a higher score. The separate scores allow practitioners to evaluate these hypotheses with individual children. Practitioners should be aware that most children in the standardization sample achieve very similar scores on Block Design and Block Design No Time Bonus. In fact, a difference as small as two points is considered rare.

If you wanted to reduce the effects of speeded performance, why not completely eliminate a time bonus from Block Design?

In general, higher ability children tend to perform the task faster. Without time bonuses, Block Design is not as good of a measure of high ability.

On Letter-Number Sequencing, the examinee is instructed to give the numbers in order first and then the letters in order. Why is credit awarded if the examinee gives the letters first in order and then the numbers in order?

There is a distinction between reordering and sequencing: Reordering involves placing the numbers as a group prior to the letters as a group, and sequencing involves placing the numbers in numerical order and the letters in alphabetical order—regardless of which grouping comes first. This distinction is reflected in the prompt given and relates directly to how a trial is scored. If a child states the letter first on Item 1, the child is prompted to *reorder* the group. However, despite the prompt, the child still receives credit for his or her original answer because the response is one of the two correct responses listed. Items 4 and 5 prompt the child to place the numbers or letters in sequential order. On these items no credit is awarded if the child has to be prompted because, unlike Item 1, the original sequence is not one of the correct responses listed for these items. You may prompt the child once for Items 1, 4, and 5; you cannot prompt a child on any of the other items for this subtest. Regardless of how the child reorders the numbers and letters, he or she is using working memory in order to place the numbers in sequence and the letters in sequence. Data analyses of the standardization sample showed that the task is equally difficult when either numbers or letters are given first. The reason for instructing examinees to give the numbers first is to provide them with a set or structured way of approaching the task, which is especially helpful for young children or children who have difficulty structuring their own work. This is the same scoring method used for Letter-Number Sequencing on WAIS-III.

On Letter-Number Sequencing, a child can simply mimic the examiner and earn credit on the first 10 trials. Is this really working memory?

The early items measure short-term auditory memory, which is a precursor skill to working memory. The 6–7 year old norms demonstrate that children scoring 10 raw score points obtain above average scaled scores; this reflects the developmentally appropriate use of short-term memory prior to the exhibition of working memory. Thus, for younger children, Letter-Number Sequencing may assess short-term memory, a prerequisite skill for the development of working memory. The item set and norms reflect this change as children develop working memory. This is analogous to the difference between Digit Span Forward and Backward, which assesses short-term memory and working memory, respectively. Performance on the early items of Letter-Number Sequencing in younger children may be related to performance on Digit Span Forward with any differences potentially attributable to automaticity of letters as compared to numbers.

On Letter-Number Sequencing, how do I score a child's response after a prompt is given on Items 1, 4, and 5?

As noted in the third bullet under General Directions on page 126 of the Administration and Scoring Manual, certain responses to specific trials on Items 1, 4, and 5 require a prompt to remind the child of the task. The prompt for Trial 1 of Item 1 is designed to remind the child to say the numbers first and then the letters. If the child forgets to say the numbers first, award credit for the trial as indicated and provide the prompt. Because the child received credit for his or her initial response to this trial, it is not necessary to award additional credit if the child attempts to correct his or her initial response after the prompt. Trial 2 of Item 4 is the first trial in

(continued)

which the child is required to alphabetically sequence the letters to produce a correct response. If the child provides either of the specified incorrect responses by forgetting to alphabetically sequence the letters, provide the prompt as indicated. If the child provides a correct response to the trial after the prompt, do not award credit for the trial. Similarly, Trial 1 of Item 5 is the first trial in which the child is required to sequence the numbers to produce a correct response. If the child forgets to sequence the numbers and provides either of the designated incorrect responses, provide the prompt as indicated. If the child provides a correct response to the trial after the prompt, do not award credit for the trial.

Why does there seem to be multiple responses for some of the items on Picture Concepts?

The Picture Concepts subtest is scored with either 0 or 1 point. The keyed response represents the best single response in terms of the level of reasoning involved. For example, on more difficult items, credit is not given for categories involving color or shape; emphasis is placed on underlying function. The keyed response was determined through years of research in Pilot, Tryout, and Standardization phases of development. The categories children provided, the ability level of children choosing specific responses, and relationships to performance on Similarities and Matrix Reasoning were all used to determine the keyed response.

The answer to Matrix Reasoning item #26 does not appear to be the only possible answer. Why wasn't "2" given credit?

Item #26 is the second 3 × 3 item. On the first 3 × 3 item (#24), children learn to apply the same transformation from cell #1 across to cell #2, and again from cell #2 to cell #3. If the child follows the pattern from #24, they answer correctly (1) on item #26. Children can arrive at a different answer (2) if they use one transformation rule from cell #1 to cell #2, and a different one from cell #2 to cell #3. This is not the most parsimonious solution, and analyses indicated that children who arrived at the correct response (1) had higher ability levels.

Some of the responses I get on Word Reasoning seem correct to me, but are listed as incorrect. What was the rationale for determining correct and incorrect responses?

Some of these responses may have been given 1 point in a 0, 1, 2 point scoring rubric. Such responses may be correct, or partially correct, but do not represent a high level of abstract reasoning. They also tended to be given by children with lower ability. Not all possible responses are included in the examples, however, and the examiner may give credit for a response not listed if she or he determines that it is at the same level of abstraction as the credited responses.

What should I do if a child writes too lightly to be seen through the Cancellation scoring template?

You do not need the scoring template to score the subtest. If necessary, remove the template and simply count each animal with a mark through it and each nonanimal with a mark through it, being sure to double-check your work.

TEST YOURSELF

1. **Which subtests allow for the calculation of a "process score"?**
   (a) Block Design, Digit Span, and Cancellation
   (b) Block Design, Digit Span, and Symbol Search
   (c) Coding, Symbol Search, and Digit Span
   (d) Arithmetic, Symbol Search, and Coding

2. **On a Similarities subtest item, Jessica, age 7, provides several responses that vary greatly in quality, but do not spoil her response. You should**
   (a) score Jessica's best response.
   (b) score the last response given by Jessica.
   (c) score the first response given by Jessica.
   (d) query Jessica for further information.

3. **If a child obtains total raw scores of 0 on two of the three subtests that compose the Verbal Comprehension scale, including potential substitutes, no VCI or FSIQ can be derived.** True or False?

4. **Susan, age 12, attempts to self-correct an item on the Coding subtest. You should**
   (a) score the last response given by Susan within the time limit.
   (b) score Susan's first response, ignoring her self-correction attempt.
   (c) query Susan as to which response is her intended response.
   (d) score Susan's best response.

5. **A *poor* response is an elaboration that does not improve the child's spontaneous response, whereas a *spoiled* response is an elaboration that reveals a fundamental misconception about the item.** True or False?

6. **If an examiner administered additional items to a child beyond the point at which testing should have discontinued, the examiner should**
   (a) include all additional items in the total raw score.
   (b) include the additional items in the total raw score only if they are correctly answered.
   (c) award no points for items beyond the correct discontinue point.
   (d) include the additional items in the total raw score by deducting points for incorrect responses committed after the discontinue point.

(continued)

7. **Samuel, age 10, is suspected to be intellectually deficient. Hence, you administer him items prior to his age-appropriate start point. Samuel answered these items incorrectly, but obtained perfect scores on his age-appropriate start point and subsequent item. In this case, you should**

    (a) consider the subtest spoiled and do not calculate a raw score.

    (b) include the incorrect responses in the calculation of the total raw score.

    (c) award partial credit (i.e., _____ point) for each incorrect item that precedes the age-appropriate start point.

    (d) award full credit for all items preceding the age-appropriate start point.

8. **Although prorating sum of scaled scores is allowed in some situations, it should be avoided when possible.** True or False?

9. **Information should be included in the calculation of which WISC-IV Index:**

    (a) VCI

    (b) PRI

    (c) PSI

    (d) WMI

    (e) None of the above, unless it is used to substitute for another test contributing to the VCI.

10. **When scoring the Symbol Search subtest, you notice that Angela, age 9, skipped some items. You should count the items that she skipped in the incorrect total.** True or False?

Answers: 1. a; 2. a; 3. True; 4. a; 5. True; 6. c; 7. d; 8. True; 9. e; 10. False

Four

HOW TO INTERPRET THE WISC-IV

This chapter is designed to simplify the daunting task of generating psychometrically sound and clinically meaningful interpretations of performance on the WISC-IV. A series of steps is provided that will allow the practitioner to organize WISC-IV data in meaningful ways and interpret performance within the context of contemporary theory and research. Our systematic method of interpretation begins with an analysis of the WISC-IV Indexes to determine the best way to summarize a child's overall intellectual ability. Next, both Normative and Personal Strengths and Weaknesses among the Indexes are identified. Interpretation of fluctuations in the child's Index profile offers the most reliable and meaningful information about WISC-IV performance because it identifies strong and weak areas of cognitive functioning relative to both same-age peers from the normal population (interindividual or normative approach) and the child's own overall ability level (intra-individual or ipsative approach). Finally, we offer optional interpretive steps involving *new* WISC-IV composites (called Clinical Clusters) for examiners who choose to go beyond the FSIQ and Index profile in an attempt to uncover additional information about the child's cognitive capabilities as well as generate potentially meaningful hypotheses about areas of integrity or dysfunction.

As discussed in Chapter 1, our interpretive approach reflects numerous modifications of and enhancements to prior methods of Wechsler test interpretation, including our own (Alfonso, Flanagan, & Radwan, in press; Flanagan et al., 2000; Flanagan & Ortiz, 2001; Flanagan et al., 2002; Kaufman, 1979, 1994; Kaufman & Lichtenberger, 1999, 2000, 2002). Previously, Kaufman (1979, 1994) stressed ipsative methods for identifying areas of strength and weakness, whereas Flanagan and colleagues emphasized normative approaches (e.g., Flanagan & Ortiz, 2001; Flanagan et al., 2002). Our new method links ipsative analysis with normative analysis, rather than focusing exclusively on either one or the other. In addition, our method (1) excludes individual subtest interpretation; (2) uses base rate data to evaluate the clinical meaningfulness of score variability; (3) grounds interpretation firmly in the CHC theory of cognitive abilities; and (4) provides guidance on the use of supplemental measures to test hypotheses about significant subtest variation or outlier scores.

In addition to a *quantitative* analysis of WISC-IV data, we also encourage practitioners to consider a variety of *qualitative* factors that may help to explain a child's test performance. This information is discussed in terms of its utility in interpreting WISC-IV performance and in selecting supplemental measures to augment the WISC-IV when deemed necessary. *In the end, any and all interpretations of test performance gain diagnostic meaning when they are corroborated by other data sources and when they are empirically or logically related to the area or areas of difficulty specified in the referral.*

The interpretive steps described here are illustrated using a WISC-IV profile of Ryan J., a 10-year-old boy referred for a possible reading disability. In addition, a comprehensive worksheet that walks the examiner through our interpretation method is included in Appendix F and is used throughout this chapter to illustrate each step.

REQUIRED INTERPRETIVE STEPS: *ANALYZE THE FSIQ AND THE INDEX PROFILE WHEN ALL CORE WISC-IV SUBTESTS ARE ADMINISTERED*[1]

STEP 1. Report the Child's WISC-IV Standard Scores (FSIQ and Indexes) and Subtest Scaled Scores

Create a table of the child's standard scores (FSIQ and four Indexes) as well as the child's scaled scores from all subtests administered. Report the name of each Index and subtest along with the child's obtained score on each one. For the FSIQ and Indexes *only,* report the confidence interval, percentile rank, and descriptive category associated with the child's obtained standard scores. For subtests, report only the percentile rank associated with the child's obtained scaled scores. Rapid Reference 4.1 provides a handy guide to locate the tables in the *WISC-IV Administration and Scoring Manual* (Wechsler, 2003) and the *WISC-IV Technical and Interpretive Manual* (The Psychological Corporation, 2003), which the examiner will need to convert raw scores to scaled scores and standard scores, to convert sums of scaled scores to the FSIQ and Indexes, and to obtain confidence intervals and percentile ranks.

Examiners need to select either the 90% or the 95% confidence interval for standard scores, namely the FSIQ and the four Indexes. Note that the confidence intervals reported in Tables A.2–A.6 in Appendix A of the *WISC-IV Administra-*

---

[1]These steps may also be used when supplemental tests are used to replace core battery tests in a manner consistent with the publisher's guidelines.

≡ Rapid Reference 4.1

Location of Information in *WISC-IV Administration and Scoring Manual* and *WISC-IV Technical and Interpretive Manual* Needed for Score Conversions

Conversion Type	Manual	Location	Page(s)
Total Raw Scores to Scaled Scores	A & S	Appendix A, Table A.1	204–236
Sum of Scaled Scores to VCI	A & S	Appendix A, Table A.2	237
Sum of Scaled Scores to PRI	A & S	Appendix A, Table A.3	237
Sum of Scaled Scores to WMI	A & S	Appendix A, Table A.4	238
Sum of Scaled Scores to PSI	A & S	Appendix A, Table A.5	238
Sum of Scaled Scores to FSIQ	A & S	Appendix A, Table A.6	239
Scaled Scores to Percentile Ranks	T & I	Chapter 6, Table 6.1	100

Note: A & S = *WISC-IV Administration and Scoring Manual* (Wechsler, 2003); T & I = *WISC-IV Technical and Interpretive Manual* (The Psychological Corporation, 2003). Percentile ranks and 90% and 95% confidence intervals for the WISC-IV Indexes (VCI, PRI, WMI, PSI, and FSIQ) are provided in Tables A.2 through A.6 (pp. 237–240) in the *WISC-IV Administration and Scoring Manual*.

tion and Scoring Manual (The Psychological Corporation, 2003, pp. 237–240) take regression toward the mean into account and, therefore, are more asymmetrical at the extremes of the distribution than at the center of the distribution. For example, a PRI of 73 is associated with a 95% confidence interval of +10/−5 (i.e., 68–83); a PRI of 100 is associated with a 95% confidence interval of ±8 (i.e., 92–108); and a PRI of 127 is associated with a 95% confidence interval of +5/−10 (i.e., 117–132). Examiners should always report standard scores with their associated confidence intervals. Although we recommend using a confidence interval of 95%, examiners have the option of using the 90% confidence interval, which is also included in Tables A.2–A.6 of the *WISC-IV Technical and Interpretive Manual.*

Three descriptive category systems are reported in Rapid References 4.2–4.4. The WISC-IV system, located in Rapid Reference 4.2, is the most traditional of the three and is recommended by the test's publisher (see The Psychological Corporation, 2003, Table 6.3, p. 101). The normative descriptive system, reported in Rapid Reference 4.3, is commonly used by neuropsychologists and is becoming more widespread among clinical and school psychologists (Flanagan & Ortiz, 2001; Flanagan et al., 2002; Kaufman & Kaufman, 2004). Although either system may be used, of the two, we prefer the latter. Nonetheless, some practitioners may prefer using a system with both descriptive categories (similar to the traditional ones presented in Rapid Reference 4.2) *and* normative categories (similar to those

≡ Rapid Reference 4.2

Traditional Descriptive System for the WISC-IV

Standard Score Range	Description of Performance
130 and above	Very Superior
120 to 129	Superior
110 to 119	High Average
90 to 109	Average
80 to 89	Low Average
70 to 79	Borderline
69 and below	Extremely Low

Source: This descriptive system is reported in Table 6.3 in the *WISC-IV Technical and Interpretive Manual* (The Psychological Corporation, 2003, p. 101).

≡ Rapid Reference 4.3

Normative Descriptive System

Standard Score Range	Descriptive Classification	Description of Performance
131+	Upper Extreme	**Normative Strength**
116 to 130	Above Average	> +1 SD (top 16% of the population) ≥ 116 (85th percentile)
85 to 115	Average Range	**Within Normal Limits** ±1 SD, inclusive (68% of the population) 115 (84th percentile)–85 (16th percentile)
70 to 84	Below Average	**Normative Weakness**
≤ 69	Lower Extreme	< −1 SD (bottom 16% of the population) ≤ 84 (15th percentile)

presented in Rapid Reference 4.3). An alternative categorical system of this nature is provided in Rapid Reference 4.4. For example, according to the information presented in Rapid Reference 4.4, an obtained score of 119 is both Above Average and a Normative Strength. Therefore, an examiner may choose to describe this score as "Above Average/Normative Strength." This alternative categorical system will be used in our interpretive approach.

≡Rapid Reference 4.4

Alternative Descriptive System for the WISC-IV

Standard Score Range	Alternative Description of Performance[a]
131+	Upper Extreme/Normative Strength
116 to 130	Above Average/Normative Strength
85 to 115	Average Range/Within Normal Limits
70 to 84	Below Average/Normative Weakness
≤ 69	Lower Extreme/Normative Weakness

[a] This classification system is preferred by the authors and is used in this book.

Figure 4.1 provides a snapshot of the WISC-IV interpretive worksheet that includes the scores for Ryan, who was administered all 15 WISC-IV subtests. Ryan's examiner used the 95% confidence interval. Although most of the information contained in this figure is found on the cover of the WISC-IV Record Form, examiners may choose to create a similar table for inclusion in a psychological report. Table 4.1 provides a similar summary for Mark, age 7, who was referred because of attentional problems.

STEP 2. Determine the Best Way to Summarize Overall Intellectual Ability

Two composites for summarizing a child's overall intellectual ability were available for the WISC-III: (1) the FSIQ, composed of the subtests that made up the Verbal IQ and Performance IQ; and (2) the General Ability Index (GAI), composed of the subtests that made up the Verbal Comprehension Index (VCI) and Perceptual Organization Index (POI; Prifitera, Weiss, & Saklofske, 1998). Prifitera and colleagues recommended the GAI when Arithmetic differed significantly from the mean of the Verbal subtests or when Coding differed significantly from the mean of the Performance subtests. In other words, the GAI was considered the best estimate of overall intellectual ability when the Verbal and Performance IQs were abandoned in favor of the Verbal Comprehension and Perceptual Organization Indexes (Prifitera et al.). Following similar logic, we recommend the following steps for determining the best way to summarize overall intellectual ability.

Step 2a. Consider the four WISC-IV Indexes. Subtract the lowest Index from

STEP 1. Report the Child's WISC-IV Standard Scores (FSIQ and Indexes) and Subtest Scaled Scores

For IQ and Indexes, report standard score, confidence interval, percentile rank, and descriptive category. For subtests, report scaled scores and percentile ranks only. (See Rapid Reference 4.1, "Location of Information in *WISC-IV Administration and Scoring Manual* and *WISC-IV Technical and Interpretive Manual* Needed for Score Conversions;" see Rapid Reference 4.4 for descriptive categories.)

Index/Subtest	Score	95% CI	Percentile Rank	Descriptive Category
Verbal Comprehension	**98**	**[91–105]**	**45th**	**Average Range/Normal Limits**
Similarities	9		37th	
Vocabulary	7		16th	
Comprehension	13		84th	
(Information)	12		75th	
(Word Reasoning)	6		9th	
Perceptual Reasoning	**90**	**[83–98]**	**25th**	**Average Range/Normal Limits**
Block Design	6		9th	
Picture Concepts	10		50th	
Matrix Reasoning	9		37th	
(Picture Completion)	8		25th	
Working Memory	**83**	**[77–92]**	**13th**	**Below Average/Normative Weakness**
Digit Span	7		16th	
Letter-Number Sequencing	7		16th	
(Arithmetic)	11		63rd	
Processing Speed	**70**	**[65–83]**	**2nd**	**Below Average/Normative Weakness**
Coding	5		5th	
Symbol Search	4		2nd	
(Cancellation)	5		5th	
Full Scale IQ	**83**	**[79–88]**	**13th**	**Below Average/Normative Weakness**

Note: Tests appearing in parentheses are supplemental measures. CI = Confidence Interval.

Figure 4.1 WISC-IV Interpretive Worksheet: STEP 1, Illustrated for Ryan, Age 10

Table 4.1 Summary of WISC-IV Scores for Mark, Age 7

Index/Subtest	Score	95% CI	Percentile Rank	Descriptive Category
Verbal Comprehension	112	[105–118]	79th	Average Range/Within Normal Limits
Similarities	10		50th	
Vocabulary	14		91st	
Comprehension	13		84th	
(Information)	10		50th	
Perceptual Reasoning	110	[102–117]	75th	Average Range/Within Normal Limits
Block Design	12		75th	
Picture Concepts	10		50th	
Matrix Reasoning	13		84th	
Working Memory	107	[99–114]	68th	Average Range/Within Normal Limits
Digit Span	11		63rd	
Letter-Number Sequencing	12		75th	
(Arithmetic)	11		63rd	
Processing Speed	103	[94–112]	58th	Average Range/Within Normal Limits
Coding	9		37th	
Symbol Search	12		75th	
(Cancellation)	8		25th	
Full Scale IQ	112	[107–117]	79th	Average Range/Within Normal Limits

Note: Tests appearing in parentheses are supplemental measures. CI = Confidence Interval.

the highest Index. Answer the following question: *Is the size of the standard score difference less than 1.5 SDs (< 23 points)?*

- If YES, then the FSIQ may be interpreted as a reliable and valid estimate of a child's global intellectual ability. Rapid Reference 4.5 provides an example of how to describe this finding. Proceed directly to Step 3.
- If NO, then the variation in the Indexes that compose the FSIQ is considered too great (i.e., ≥ 23 points) for the purpose of summarizing global intellectual ability in a single score (i.e., the FSIQ). Proceed to Step 2b.

Step 2b. When the FSIQ is not interpretable, determine whether an abbreviated GAI may be used to describe overall intellectual ability. Answer the following question: *Is the size of the standard score difference between the VCI and the PRI less than 1.5 SDs (< 23 points)?*

- If YES, then the GAI may be calculated and interpreted as a reliable and valid estimate of a child's global intellectual ability. Because The Psychological Corporation did not provide GAI norms in the *WISC-IV Technical and Interpretive Manual* (The Psychological Corporation, 2003), we developed a table for converting the VCI and PRI sums of scaled scores to a GAI having a mean of 100 and a standard deviation of 15. This conversion table (located in Appendix F) was based on data provided in the *WISC-IV Technical and Interpretive Manual* (Table 5.1, p. 51)

≡ *Rapid Reference 4.5*

Example of How to Describe an Interpretable FSIQ in a Psychological Report

An interpretable FSIQ means that the size of the difference between the highest and lowest Indexes does not equal or exceed 1.5 SDs (23 points). In the case of Mark (see Table 4.1), the difference between his highest Index (112 on the VCI) and his lowest Index (103 on the PSI) = 9 points. This value is less than 23 points, so his FSIQ is interpretable

Mark earned a FSIQ of 112, classifying his overall intellectual ability, as measured by the WISC-IV, as Average Range/Within Normal Limits. The chances are good (95%) that Mark's true FSIQ is somewhere within the range of 108 to 115. His FSIQ is ranked at the 79th percentile, indicating that he scored higher than 79% of other children of the same age in the standardization sample.

and on a statistical technique for linear equating provided by Tellegen
and Briggs (1967, Formula 4). We included percentile ranks and 95%
confidence intervals for the GAI in Appendix G. We also calculated the
reliability and standard error of measurement (SEM) for the GAI by
age and overall WISC-IV standardization sample and included this information in Table 4.2. This table shows that the reliability estimates
for the GAI (range = .94–.96) are high and very similar to those reported for the FSIQ (range = .96–.97; *WISC-IV Technical and Interpretive
Manual,* Table 4.1, p. 34).

To calculate the GAI, simply sum the VCI and PRI standard scores
and locate the GAI that corresponds to this sum in Appendix F. For
example, the sum of Ryan's VCI (98) and PRI (90) is 188. Appendix F
shows that the sum of 188 corresponds to a GAI of 93, a percentile
rank of 33, and a 95% confidence interval of 87 to 99. Rapid Reference
4.6 provides an example of how to describe the GAI. Proceed to
Step 3.

- If NO, then the variation in the Indexes that compose the GAI is too
  great (≥ 23 points) for the purpose of summarizing global ability in a

**Table 4.2 General Ability Index Reliabilities and SEMs based on Age and
Overall WISC-IV Sample**

Age	Reliability	SEM
6	.94	3.58
7	.95	3.32
8	.95	3.25
9	.96	2.96
10	.96	3.00
11	.96	3.11
12	.96	2.85
13	.96	3.00
14	.96	3.03
15	.96	2.96
16	.96	3.11
All	**.96**	**3.11**

Note: Internal consistency reliability coefficients are reported in this table. SEM = Standard Error of Measurement.

≡ Rapid Reference 4.6

Example of How to Describe the GAI in a Psychological Report

Ryan's WISC-IV Full Scale IQ (FSIQ) could not be interpreted because he demon- strated too much variability in his performance across the four Indexes that make up this score, namely, the Verbal Comprehension, Perceptual Reasoning, Working Memory, and Processing Speed Indexes. However, because Ryan's performance on the Verbal Comprehension (98) and Perceptual Reasoning (90) Indexes was similar, these In- dexes can be combined to yield a General Ability Index (GAI). The GAI differs from the FSIQ in that it is not influenced directly by Ryan's performance on working memory and processing-speed tasks.

Ryan earned a GAI of 93, classifying his general level of intellectual ability as Aver- age Range/Within Normal Limits. The chances are good (95%) that Ryan's true GAI is somewhere within the range of 87 to 99. His GAI is ranked at the 33rd percentile, indicating that he scored higher than 33% of other children of the same age in the standardization sample.

single score (i.e., GAI). Rapid Reference 4.7 provides an example of how to describe the finding of both a noninterpretable FSIQ and a noninterpretable GAI. Proceed to Step 3.

Figure 4.2 provides a snapshot of Step 2 of the WISC-IV interpretive work- sheet for Ryan. In this step, it was determined that Ryan's overall intellectual abil- ity was best described by the GAI.

STEP 3. Determine Whether Each of the Four Indexes Is Unitary and Thus Interpretable

When the variability among subtest scaled scores within an Index is unusually large, then the Index does not provide a good estimate of the ability it is intended to measure and, therefore, is not interpretable. In other words, when a substan- tial difference between the scaled scores composing an Index is found, the Index cannot be interpreted as representing a unitary ability.

Step 3a. Determine whether the size of the difference among subtest scaled scores within the VCI (comprising three subtests) is unusually large. Subtract the lowest subtest scaled score from the highest subtest scaled score. Answer the fol- lowing question: *Is the size of the difference less than 1.5 SDs (< 5 points)?*

- If YES, then the ability presumed to underlie the VCI is unitary and may be interpreted.

≡Rapid Reference 4.7

Example of How to Describe in a Psychological Report the Finding of *Both* a Noninterpretable FSIQ and a Noninterpretable GAI

A noninterpretable FSIQ means that the size of the difference between the highest and lowest Indexes equals or exceeds 1.5 SDs (23 points). A noninterpretable GAI means that the size of the difference between the VCI and PRI equals or exceeds 1.5 SDs (23 points). In the case of Susan, the difference between her highest Index (98 on the VCI) and her lowest Index (70 on the PSI) = 28 points. This value is more than 23 points, so her FSIQ is noninterpretable. In addition, the difference of 25 points between Susan's VCI (98) and PRI (73) equals or exceeds 1.5 SDs (23 points). Consequently, her GAI is also noninterpretable.

Susan earned a Full Scale IQ (FSIQ) of 76, but this estimate of her overall intellectual ability cannot be interpreted meaningfully because she displayed too much variability in the four Indexes that compose this full scale score. Therefore, Susan's intelligence is best understood by her performance on the separate WISC-IV Indexes, namely, Verbal Comprehension, Perceptual Reasoning, Working Memory, and Processing Speed.

DON'T FORGET

Definition of a Unitary Ability

A *unitary ability* is an ability (such as Crystallized Intelligence or Processing Speed) that is represented by a cohesive set of scaled scores, each reflecting slightly different or unique aspects of the ability. Thus, when the variability among the subtest scaled scores that compose a WISC-IV Index is not unusually large, then the ability presumed to underlie the Index is considered unitary and may be interpreted. For example, a child obtaining scaled scores of 9, 5, and 8 on Comprehension, Similarities, and Vocabulary, respectively, has a difference score of 4 associated with the VCI (9 − 5 = 4). A difference of less than 1.5 SDs (i.e., less than 5 points) between the highest and lowest subtest scaled score is needed for an Index to be considered as representing a unitary ability. Therefore, in this example, the VCI represents a unitary ability and may be interpreted as a reliable and valid estimate of Crystallized Intelligence *(Gc)*.

- If NO, then the difference is too large (5 points or greater) and the VCI cannot be interpreted as representing a unitary ability.

Step 3b. Follow the same procedure as in Step 3a to determine the interpretability of the PRI (also comprising three subtests).

Step 3c. Determine whether the size of the difference between the subtest

STEP 2. Determine the Best Way to Summarize Overall Intellectual Ability

Step 2a. To determine whether the FSIQ is interpretable, subtract the lowest Index from the highest Index.

Index names: VCI   PSI
Index standard scores: $\underline{98}$ − $\underline{70}$ = $\underline{28}$
  (Highest) (Lowest) (Difference)

Is the size of the difference less than 1.5 SDs (i.e., < 23 points)?   Yes   (No)

- If YES, then the FSIQ may be interpreted as a reliable and valid estimate of a child's overall intellectual ability.
- If NO, then proceed to Step 2b.

See Rapid Reference 4.5 for an example of how to describe the FSIQ in a psychological report.

Step 2b. To determine whether the General Ability Index (GAI) may be used to summarize overall intellectual ability, calculate the difference between the VCI and PRI.

Index standard scores: $\underline{98}$ − $\underline{90}$ = $\underline{8}$
  (VCI) (PRI) (Difference)

Is the size of the difference less than 1.5 SDs (i.e., < 23 points)?   (Yes)   No

- If YES, then the GAI can be calculated and interpreted as a reliable and valid estimate of the child's overall intellectual ability.
- If NO, then proceed to Step 3.

To calculate the GAI, sum the VCI and PRI standard scores and locate the GAI that corresponds to this sum in Appendix G.

Index standard scores: $\underline{98}$ + $\underline{90}$ = $\underline{188}$ = $\underline{93}$
  (VCI) (PRI) (Sum of Standard Scores) (GAI)

See Rapid Reference 4.6 for an example of how to describe the GAI in a psychological report. Proceed to Step 3.

Figure 4.2 WISC-IV Interpretive Worksheet: STEP 2, Illustrated for Ryan, Age 10

scaled scores that compose the two-subtest Working Memory Index (WMI) is too large. Subtract the lower scaled score from the higher one. Answer the following question: *Is the size of the difference less than 1.5 SDs (< 5 points)?*

- If YES, then the ability presumed to underlie the WMI is unitary and may be interpreted.
- If NO, then the difference is too large (5 points or greater) and the WMI cannot be interpreted as representing a unitary ability.

Step 3d. Follow this same procedure as in step 3c to determine the interpretability of the Processing Speed Index (PSI, also comprising two subtests).

For example, the difference between Ryan's subtest scaled scores that compose the PSI is 1 point (i.e., a Coding scaled score of 5 minus a Symbol Search scaled score of 4 equals 1; see Figure 4.1). Ryan's 1-point difference between the scaled scores for the PSI is less than the value needed to render the PSI uninterpretable (i.e., it is less than 5). Therefore, Ryan's PSI represents a unitary ability and may be interpreted. Figure 4.3 illustrates the decision process regarding the interpretability of all four of Ryan's Indexes. Rapid Reference 4.8 provides an example of how to interpret a unitary (interpretable) Index. Rapid Reference 4.9 provides an example of how to describe a nonunitary (noninterpretable) Index.

It is important to note that we opted to use the critical value of 5 points for determining the interpretability of all four WISC-IV Indexes instead of using the "base rate < 10% criterion." Our rationale for selecting this criterion was based on the results of the base rate analyses, which indicated that 6 or more points (2 SDs or more) were needed to identify a noninterpretable VCI, WMI, or PSI; and 7 or more points were needed to identify a noninterpretable PRI. These differences seemed too extreme, in our clinical judgment. It would mean, for example, that a child who earned a scaled score of 3 on Coding and 8 on Symbol Search would have an interpretable PSI. Therefore, we opted to use 5 or more points to denote a noninterpretable Index. The value of 5 points was not arbitrary, however. It corresponds to 1.5 SDs (4.5 scaled score points, rounded up), the same rule used to determine interpretability of the FSIQ and GAI.

Although an Index is considered uninterpretable when the variability among the subtests it comprises is unusually large, in some instances it makes sense to look at the normative classifications of the scaled scores to determine whether a general conclusion may be made about a child's range of observed functioning in the ability presumed to underlie the Index. Specifically, when *all* subtest scaled scores within an Index are either ≤ 8 or ≥ 12, we believe that a statement may be made about performance. For example:

1. If the variability among subtest scaled scores composing an Index is unusually large and all scaled scores are ≥ 12, then describe the child's range of observed functioning in the ability presumed to underlie the Index as a notable integrity as follows: *The Perceptual Reasoning Index (PRI), a measure of Fluid Reasoning and Visual Processing (Gf/Gv), represents Amy's ability to reason using visual stimuli. Amy's Gf/Gv was assessed by tasks that required her to recreate a series of modeled or pictured designs using blocks (Block Design), identify the missing portion of an incomplete visual matrix from one of five response options*

STEP 3. Determine Whether Each of the Four Indexes is Unitary and Thus Interpretable

Step 3a. Calculate the difference between the highest and lowest VCI subtest scaled scores.

VCI subtest scaled scores: $\underline{13}$ – $\underline{7}$ = $\underline{6}$

(Highest)   (Lowest)   (Difference)

Is the difference between the highest and lowest VCI subtest scaled scores < 5?   Yes

- If YES, interpret the VCI as representing a unitary Index.
- If NO, do not interpret the VCI as representing a unitary Index.

Proceed to Step 3b.

Step 3b. Calculate the difference between the highest and lowest PRI subtest scaled scores.

PRI subtest scaled scores: $\underline{10}$ – $\underline{6}$ = $\underline{4}$

(Highest)   (Lowest)   (Difference)

Is the difference between the highest and lowest PRI subtest scaled scores < 5?   No

- If YES, interpret the PRI as representing a unitary Index.
- If NO, do not interpret the PRI as representing a unitary Index.

Proceed to Step 3c.

Step 3c. Calculate the difference between the WMI subtest scaled scores.

WMI subtest scaled scores: $\underline{7}$ – $\underline{7}$ = $\underline{0}$

(Highest)   (Lowest)   (Difference)

Is the difference between the highest and lowest WMI subtest scaled scores < 5?   Yes   No

- If YES, interpret the WMI as representing a unitary Index.
- If NO, do not interpret the WMI as representing a unitary Index.

Proceed to Step 3d.

Step 3d. Calculate the difference between the PSI subtest scaled scores.

PSI subtest scaled scores: $\underline{5}$ – $\underline{4}$ = $\underline{1}$

(Highest)   (Lowest)   (Difference)

Is the difference between the highest and lowest PSI subtest scaled scores < 5?   No

- If YES, interpret the PSI as representing a unitary Index.
- If NO, do not interpret the PSI as representing a unitary Index.

Proceed to Step 4. If all four Indexes are not interpretable, refer to pages 133, 135, 136, and Step 7 for additional interpretive options.

Figure 4.3 WISC-IV Interpretive Worksheet: STEP 3, Illustrated for Ryan, Age 10

≡Rapid Reference 4.8

Example of How to Interpret a Unitary Index in a Psychological Report

The Processing Speed Index (PSI), a measure of Processing Speed (Gs), represents Ryan's ability to perform simple, clerical-type tasks quickly. Ryan's Gs ability was assessed with two tasks—one required Ryan to quickly copy symbols that were paired with numbers according to a key (Coding), and the other required him to identify the presence or absence of a target symbol in a row of symbols (Symbol Search). The difference between Ryan's performances on these two tasks (Coding scaled score of 5 minus Symbol Search scaled score of 4 equals 1) was not unusually large (i.e., was not ≥ 5 points), indicating that his PSI is a good estimate of his processing speed. Ryan obtained a PSI of 70 (65–83), which is ranked at the 2nd percentile and is classified as Below Average/Normative Weakness.

≡Rapid Reference 4.9

Example of How to Describe a Nonunitary Index in a Psychological Report

The Verbal Comprehension Index (VCI), a measure of Crystallized Intelligence (Gc), represents Ryan's ability to reason with previously learned information. Gc ability develops largely as a function of both formal and informal educational opportunities and experiences and is highly dependent on exposure to mainstream U.S. culture. Ryan's Gc was assessed by tasks that required him to define words (Vocabulary, scaled score = 7), draw conceptual similarities between words (Similarities, scaled score = 9), and answer questions involving knowledge of general principles and social situations (Comprehension, scaled score = 13). The variability among Ryan's performances on these tasks was unusually large (i.e., the scaled score range was greater than or equal to 5 points), indicating that his overall Gc ability cannot be summarized in a single score (i.e., the VCI).

Note: Subsequent steps (i.e., Steps 4–7) may be used to provide additional information about Ryan's Gc performance.

(Matrix Reasoning), and select one picture from each of two or three rows of pictures to form a group with a common characteristic (Picture Concepts). The variability among Amy's performances on these tasks was unusually large, indicating that her overall Gf/Gv ability cannot be summarized in a single score (i.e., the PRI). However, it is clear that Amy's Gf/Gv ability is a notable integrity for her because her performance on the tasks that compose the PRI ranged from Average Range/Within Normal Limits to Upper Extreme/Normative Strength.

2. If the variability among subtest scaled scores composing an Index is unusually large and all scaled scores are ≤ 8, then describe the child's range

of observed functioning in the ability presumed to underlie the Index as a notable limitation, as follows: *The Working Memory Index (WMI), a measure of Short-Term Memory* (Gsm), *represents Amy's ability to apprehend and hold information in immediate awareness. Amy's* Gsm *was assessed by tasks that required her to repeat numbers verbatim or in reverse order as presented by the examiner (Digit Span); and to listen to a sequence of numbers and letters and repeat the numbers in ascending order, followed by the letters in alphabetical order (Letter-Number Sequencing). The variability among Amy's performances on these tasks was unusually large, indicating that her overall* Gsm *ability cannot be summarized in a single score (i.e., the WMI). However, Amy's* Gsm *ability is a notable limitation for her because her performance on the tasks that compose the WMI ranged from Below Average/Normative Weakness to Lower Extreme/Normative Weakness.*

In the rare instance in which all four Indexes are not interpretable, then you should proceed to Step 7.

STEP 4. Determine Normative Strengths and Normative Weaknesses in the Index Profile

Only unitary Indexes identified in the previous step are included in this analysis. For example, in the case of Ryan, only his PRI, WMI, and PSI would be considered at this step. To determine Normative Strengths and Normative Weaknesses in a child's Index profile, review the child's scores and consider the exact value of the interpretable Indexes. If the Index standard score is greater than 115, then the ability measured by the Index is a *Normative Strength*. If the Index standard score is less than 85, then the ability measured by the Index is a *Normative Weakness*. If the Index standard score is between 85 and 115 (inclusive), then the ability measured by the Index is *Within Normal Limits*. Although Ryan's PRI of 90 is Within Normal Limits, his WMI and PSI of 83 and 70, respectively, are Normative Weaknesses. Figure 4.4 provides a snapshot of Step 4 of the WISC-IV interpretive worksheet for Ryan.

DON'T FORGET

What Do I Do with a Noninterpretable Index?

When an Index is found to be noninterpretable at Step 3, this means that the variability among the subtest scaled scores composing the Index is unusually large to allow for the interpretation of a single ability. For example, when the variability among the VCI subtest scaled scores is unusually large, then the VCI cannot be interpreted as representing the ability of Crystallized Intelligence (Gc). However, the subtests composing the noninterpretable Index may be combined with other subtests in different ways to allow for meaningful interpretations of more specific abilities at later steps in the interpretive process (e.g., Step 7).

STEP 4. Determine Normative Strengths and Normative Weaknesses in the Index Profile

Enter the name of each interpretable Index in the table below. Record the standard score for each interpretable Index. Place a checkmark in the box corresponding to the appropriate normative category for each Index.

Interpretable Index	Standard Score	Normative Weakness < 85	Within Normal Limits 85–115	Normative Strength > 115
PRI	90		✓	
WMI	83	✓		
PSI	70	✓		

Figure 4.4 WISC-IV Interpretive Worksheet: STEP 4, Illustrated for Ryan, Age 10

STEP 5. Determine Personal Strengths and Personal Weaknesses in the Index Profile

Step 5a. Compute the mean of the child's Index standard scores and round to the nearest 10th of a point. Note that all Indexes (interpretable and noninterpretable) are included in the computation of the mean for practical reasons. Excluding any Index would result in the need for numerous tables for determining both statistical significance and uncommon Index variation (i.e., mean Indexes based on two-, three-, and four-Index combinations).

Step 5b. Subtract the mean of all Index standard scores from each *interpretable* Index standard score. Using the values reported in Table 4.3, determine whether the size of the difference between an interpretable Index and the mean of all Indexes is significant. This table includes differences required for statistical significance at both the .05 and .01 levels. We recommend using the values that correspond to the .05 level, which appear in the shaded rows of Table 4.3. To be considered statistically significant, the difference must be equal to or greater than the value reported in Table 4.3. Because some of the values for specific age levels differ from those reported for the total sample, we recommend using the differences reported by age. Use the following criteria for identifying personal strengths and weaknesses:

1. If the difference is significant and the interpretable Index is higher than the mean, then the Index is a *Personal Strength* for the child.
2. If the difference is significant and the interpretable Index is lower than the mean, then the Index is a *Personal Weakness* for the child.

Step 5c. Determine whether Personal Strengths and Personal Weaknesses are uncommon using the < 10% base rate criterion. Because *statistical significance* means only that an observed difference is "real" (i.e., not due to chance), it is necessary to determine whether the difference is also unusually large or uncommon.

Table 4.3 Differences Required for Statistical Significance (at $p < .05$ and $p < .01$) between an Index and the Mean of all Four Indexes, by Age and Overall Sample

Age	p value	Verbal Comprehension	Perceptual Reasoning	Working Memory	Processing Speed
6	.05	7.9	7.9	7.6	9.8
	.01	10.4	10.4	10.0	12.9
7	.05	7.7	7.7	8.2	10.3
	.01	10.1	10.1	10.8	13.6
8	.05	7.3	7.1	7.6	8.4
	.01	9.7	9.3	10.0	11.1
9	.05	7.1	10.9	7.7	8.5
	.01	9.4	14.3	10.2	11.2
10	.05	7.1	10.9	7.7	8.2
	.01	9.3	14.3	10.1	10.8
11	.05	6.9	6.9	7.2	7.8
	.01	9.1	9.1	9.5	10.2
12	.05	6.1	6.8	6.8	8.0
	.01	8.1	9.0	9.0	10.5
13	.05	6.6	6.9	7.5	8.1
	.01	8.7	9.1	9.9	10.6
14	.05	6.2	7.2	6.9	8.0
	.01	8.1	9.4	9.0	10.5
15	.05	6.2	7.2	7.2	7.7
	.01	8.1	9.4	9.4	10.2
16	.05	6.2	7.5	6.9	8.0
	.01	8.2	9.8	9.1	10.6

Table 4.3 (Continued)

Age	*p* value	Verbal Comprehension	Perceptual Reasoning	Working Memory	Processing Speed
All[a]	.05	6.8	7.2	7.3	8.4
	.01	8.9	9.4	9.6	11.0

Source: Information in this table was provided by Jack A. Naglieri (personal communication, January 28, 2004).

Note: Enter this table only with *interpretable* Indexes. To use this table, calculate the mean of all four Indexes (rounded to the nearest 10th). Subtract this mean value from each interpretable Index and obtain difference scores. Select a significance level (.05 or .01). We recommend using .05 (the shaded portions of the table). Compare the difference score to the value in the appropriate row (.01 or .05) and the appropriate Index column. If the difference score is equal to or greater than this value, then the difference is statistically significant. If the difference score is less than this value, then the difference is not statistically significant. For example, if a 7-year-old obtained an interpretable WMI of 85 and the mean of all four Indexes was 93.2, then you would subtract the mean of all four Indexes from the WMI. The difference score of 8.2 (85 − 93.2 = −8.2) is compared to the value for the WMI at the .05 level for a 7-year-old (i.e., 8.2). Because the difference score equals the value listed in the table, you would interpret the difference as statistically significant. Additionally, because the WMI was lower than the mean, it is considered a Personal Weakness.

[a] All = overall WISC-IV standardization sample (ages 6–16).

Differences among Indexes that occur infrequently in the standardization sample may be valuable in making diagnoses and generating educational recommendations when corroborated by other data. Table 4.4 includes the information necessary to determine whether the differences between a child's interpretable Indexes and the mean of all Indexes occur less than 10% of the time in the standardization sample. The shaded row in Table 4.4 contains values reflecting differences that occur less than 10% of the time in the WISC-IV

DON'T FORGET

Identifying Personal Strengths and Weaknesses

When determining the child's Personal Strengths and Personal Weaknesses, compare only *interpretable* Indexes to the child's mean Index. *Noninterpretable* Indexes ARE included in the computation of the child's mean Index, but they ARE NOT compared to that mean or interpreted.

Table 4.4 The Size of the Difference Between Each Index and the Mean of All Four Indexes That Is Needed to be Considered Unusually Large or Uncommon

Base Rates	Verbal Comprehension	Perceptual Reasoning	Working Memory	Processing Speed
.01	22.3	21.1	25.0	25.6
.02	20.8	19.3	22.5	23.3
.05	16.8	16.3	18.8	20.0
.10	14.0	13.5	15.0	17.0

Source: Wechsler Intelligence Scale for Children–Fourth Edition. Copyright © 2003 by Harcourt Assessment, Inc. Reproduced by permission of the publisher. All rights reserved. *Wechsler Intelligence Scale for Children* and *WISC* are trademarks of Harcourt Assessment, Inc., registered in the United States of America and/or other jurisdictions.

Note: "Unusually large or uncommon" denotes difference values that occur infrequently within the WISC-IV standardization sample. Enter this table only with *interpretable* Indexes. To use this table, calculate the mean of all four Indexes (rounded to the nearest 10th). Subtract this mean value from each interpretable Index and obtain difference scores. Select a base rate value (i.e., .01, .02, .05, or .10). We recommend using .10 (the shaded portion of the table). Compare the difference score to the value listed in the table for each interpretable Index. If the difference score is equal to or greater than the value listed in the table, then the difference is uncommon. If the difference score is less than the value listed in the table, then the difference is not uncommon. For example, if the mean of all four Indexes is 90.5 and the VCI standard score is 104, then the difference score for VCI is 13.5 (i.e., 104 – 90.5 = 13.5). A 14-point difference between the VCI and the mean of all Indexes is needed to be considered uncommon using the 10% base rate criterion. Thus, the difference score of 13.5 for VCI is considered common in the normal population. The values provided in this table are based on the overall WISC-IV standardization sample (ages 6–16).

standardization sample. Although we recommend a .10 base rate, Table 4.4 also includes base rates of .01, .02, and .05. If the magnitude of the observed difference between an interpretable Index and the mean of all Indexes is equal to or greater than the value reported for the comparison in the shaded row of Table 4.4, then the difference is uncommon; otherwise, the difference is not uncommon.

Step 5d. Identify Key Assets and High-Priority Concerns in the child's profile using the following criteria to identify Personal Strengths and Weaknesses that are of greatest importance, diagnostically and educationally.

1. Personal Strengths that are also uncommon and greater than 115 are labeled *Key Assets.*

2. Personal Weaknesses that are also uncommon and less than 85 are labeled *High-Priority Concerns*.

Once the previous steps (Steps 5a–5d) have been completed with the aid of the worksheet (see Figure 4.5), summarize the results of all Index analyses (Steps 3, 4, and 5) using the table provided in Appendix G. An example of a completed table for Ryan is provided in Figure 4.6. This figure includes a section called "Clinical Impressions and Suggested (Post Hoc) Clinical Comparisons." After reflecting on the findings generated from Steps 3–5, you should record your clinical impressions. In addition, you should specify whether any Planned Clinical Comparisons might be useful to conduct in order to gain a better understanding of the child's cognitive capabilities. When an Index is uninterpretable due to too much variability among its component scaled scores, and when all the scaled scores within the Index are neither ≤ 8 nor ≥ 12, then it is likely that additional assessment is warranted to gain a better understanding of the ability or abilities that underlie the Index. For example, Jill obtained scaled scores of 5, 10, and 9 on the Block Design, Matrix Reasoning, and Picture Concepts subtests, respectively. The 5-point difference between Jill's highest and lowest scaled scores within this Index (Matrix Reasoning scaled score of 10 minus Block Design scaled score of 5 equals 5) is unusually large, rendering the PRI uninterpretable. However, because the primary ability measured by Block Design is Visual Processing *(Gv)* and

DON'T FORGET

Size of Difference Needed Between an Interpretable Index and the Mean of All Indexes to Be Considered Statistically Significant ($p < .05$) and Unusually Large or Uncommon

Index	Difference Required for Statistical Significance	Difference Required for an Uncommon Difference
Verbal Comprehension	6.8	14.0
Perceptual Reasoning	7.2	13.5
Working Memory	7.3	15.0
Processing Speed	8.4	17.0

Note: Differences required for statistical significance are reported for the overall WISC-IV sample. "Unusually large or uncommon" denotes difference sizes occurring less than 10% of the time in the WISC-IV standardization sample.

STEP 5. Determine Personal Strengths and Personal Weaknesses in the Index Profile

Step 5a. Compute the mean of the child's Indexes and round to the nearest 10th of a point. Note that all Indexes (interpretable and noninterpretable) are included in the computation of the mean.

$$\underset{\text{(VCI)}}{98} + \underset{\text{(PRI)}}{90} + \underset{\text{(WMI)}}{83} + \underset{\text{(PSI)}}{70} = \underset{\text{(Sum)}}{341} \div 4 = \underset{\text{(Index Mean)}}{85.25}$$

Step 5b. Fill in the table below as follows:

- Record the name of each interpretable Index in Column (1).
- Record each interpretable Index standard score in Column (2).
- Record the rounded mean of all Indexes (from Step 5a) in Column (3).
- Record the difference score (i.e., standard score minus mean) in Column (4).
- Record the critical value needed for the difference score to be considered significant in Column (5) (these values are included in the "Personal Strength/Weakness Table for Ages 6 through 16").
- If difference score equals or exceeds the critical value, record a "PS" for a postive (+) difference score or a "PW" for a negative (−) difference score.

Interpretable Index (1)	Standard Score (2)	Rounded Mean of All Indexes (3)	Difference Score (4)	Critical Value Needed for Significance (5)	Personal Strength or Personal Weakness (PS or PW) (6)
PRI	90	85.3	+ 4.7	10.9	
WMI	83	85.3	−2.3	7.7	
PSI	70	85.3	−15.3	8.2	PW

Personal Strength/Weakness Table for Ages 6 through 16

	6	7	8	9	10	11	12	13	14	15	16
VCI	7.9	7.7	7.3	7.1	7.1	6.9	6.1	6.6	6.2	6.2	6.2
PRI	7.9	7.7	7.1	10.9	10.9	6.9	6.8	6.9	7.2	7.2	7.5
WMI	7.6	8.2	7.6	7.7	7.7	7.2	6.8	7.5	6.9	7.2	6.9
PSI	9.8	10.3	8.4	8.5	8.2	7.8	8.0	8.1	8.0	7.7	8.0

Note: The critical values listed in this table are at the $p < .05$ level of significance. For critical values at the $p < .01$ level of significance, see Table 4.3.

Figure 4.5 WISC-IV Interpretive Worksheet: STEP 5, Illustrated for Ryan, Age 10

Are there any Personal Strengths or Weaknesses evident in the child's Index profile?   No

- If YES, go to Step 5c.
- If NO, proceed directly to Step 6.

Step 5c. **Determine whether the Personal Strength/Weakness is uncommon (base rate < 10%) in the general population.**

Index	Difference Score (from Step 5b)	PS or PW (from Step 5b)	Critical Value	Uncommon (U) or Not Uncommon (NU)
VCI			≥14	
PRI			≥13.5	
WMI			≥15	
PSI	−15.3	PW	≥17	NU

Note: Difference scores are entered into this table only for *unitary* Indexes that were identified as Personal Strengths or Personal Weaknesses in Step 5b. Difference scores that are equal to or exceed the critical value listed in the fourth column of this table should be denoted Uncommon (U). Difference scores that are less than the critical value should be denoted Not Uncommon (NU).

Are there any uncommon personal strengths or weaknesses evident in the child's Index profile?   Yes

- If YES, go to Step 5d.
- If NO, proceed directly to Step 6.

Step 5d. **Determine whether any of the Interpretable Indexes are Key Assets or High-Priority Concerns.**

Review your findings from Steps 4, 5b, and 5c. In the following table, for each relevant Index place a checkmark in the column that accurately describes the findings for that Index. An Index that is both a Normative Strength and an Uncommon Personal Strength should be identified as a "Key Asset." An Index that is both a Normative Weakness and an Uncommon Personal Weakness should be identified as a "High-Priority Concern."

Index	NS (Step 4)	NW (Step 4)	PS (Step 5b)	PW (Step 5b)	Uncommon (Step 5c)	Key Asset	High-Priority Concern
VCI							
PRI							
WMI		✔					
PSI		✔		✔			

Note: NS = Normative Strength; NW = Normative Weakness; PS = Personal Strength; PW = Personal Weakness.

Proceed to Step 6.

Figure 4.5 (Continued)

Name: Ryan Date of testing: 2/26/04 Age: 10		INTERPRETIVE STEP				
WISC-IV Index	Standard Score	(STEP 3) Is Index Standard Score Interpretable?	(STEP 4) Normative Strength (NS) or Normative Weakness (NW)?	(STEP 5b) Personal Strength (PS) or Personal Weakness (PW)?	(STEP 5c) Is PS or PW Uncommon?	(STEP 5d) Key Asset (KA) or High-Priority Concern (HPC)?
VCI	98	NO	N/A	N/A	N/A	N/A
PRI	90	YES	NO	NO	N/A	N/A
WMI	83	YES	YES-NW	NO	NO	NO
PSI	70	YES	YES-NW	YES-PW	NO	NO

Clinical Impressions and Suggested (Post Hoc) Clinical Comparisons:

1. Although VCI is the highest standard score in the profile, analysis of its components seems warranted. Examination of the influence of Gf-nonverbal on VCI tasks may be informative (e.g., examine the Verbal Fluid Reasoning Cluster vs. Nonverbal Fluid Reasoning Cluster Clinical Comparison). Certain aspects of Gc should play a prominent role in educational planning.

2. Although PRI is Average/Within Normal Limits, analyses of its components and of Gf-nonverbal versus Gv difference are warranted (e.g., examine the Nonverbal Fluid Reasoning [Gf-nonverbal] Cluster vs. Visual Processing Cluster Planned Clinical Comparison).

3. Comparison of WMI to information stored in Long-Term Memory (LTM) may be informative (e.g., examine the LTM vs. WM Planned Clinical Comparison).

4. Processing Speed is a notable weakness and suggests a disorder in this basic psychological process, a finding that should play an essential role for developing educational interventions (e.g., minimizing the extent to which this process is featured in educational and learning activities).

Figure 4.6 Summary of Analyses of WISC-IV Indexes for Ryan

the primary ability measured by Matrix Reasoning and Picture Concepts is Fluid Reasoning *(Gf)*, conducting the Planned Clinical Comparison of *Gv* (Block Design + Picture Completion) versus *Gf* (Matrix Reasoning + Picture Concepts) may reveal important information about Jill's abilities. Planned clinical comparisons were described in Chapter 1 and will be discussed in further detail in Step 7.

STEP 6. Interpret Fluctuations in the Child's Index Profile

Interpreting the child's Index profile provides reliable and useful information for making diagnostic and educational decisions. Because many of the descriptions that are used to classify Indexes (e.g., High-Priority Concerns, Key Assets) are new to the examiner and other professionals and laypersons who read psychological reports, you should include a paragraph in (or appendix to) your report that defines these terms. To avoid confusion, only provide descriptions of the terms that are actually used in your report. For example, if the child did not have any High Priority Concerns, then you do not need to define this term in your report. Rapid Reference 4.10 provides a description of all the terms that are used to classify Indexes.

Interpret each Index in a separate paragraph. Begin with strengths (including Key Assets), followed by weaknesses (including High-Priority Concerns). Next, indicate the Index or Indexes that are neither strengths nor weaknesses. Finally, describe the Index or Indexes that are noninterpretable. Figure 4.6 shows that Ryan has a Personal Weakness, PSI, that is also a Normative Weakness; a Normative Weakness (WMI); one Index that is interpretable and Within Normal Limits (PRI); and one Index (VCI) that is not interpretable. Rapid Reference 4.11 provides examples of how to interpret fluctuations in a child's Index profile. This Rapid Reference shows that Indexes may be classified in 1 of 12 ways following the analyses outlined in Steps 3–5, each having a different interpretation.

OPTIONAL INTERPRETIVE STEP: ANALYZE PLANNED CLINICAL COMPARISONS WHEN SUPPLEMENTAL WISC-IV SUBTESTS ARE ADMINISTERED

STEP 7. Conduct Planned Clinical Comparisons

Based on our knowledge of the abilities measured by the WISC-IV, CHC theory, and relevant research on the relations between specific cognitive abilities and learning/achievement, we offer a select number of additional comparisons that we believe may provide potentially meaningful hypotheses about a child's cognitive capabilities—beyond the information generated from the Index Profile Analysis.

In this step, comparisons are made between pairs of clinical clusters. Each *clin-*

≡ Rapid Reference 4.10

Terms Used to Describe Fluctuations in a Child's WISC-IV Index Profile

Term (Abbreviation)	Definition
Index	A standard score with a mean of 100 and standard deviation of 15.
Normative Strength (NS)	An Index that is above 115.
Normative Weakness (NW)	An Index that is below 85.
Within Normal Limits (WNL)	An Index ranging from 85 to 115 (inclusive).
Personal Strength (PS)	An Index that is significantly higher than the child's own mean Index, using the .05 level of significance.
Personal Weakness (PW)	An Index that is significantly lower than the child's own mean Index, using the .05 level of significance.
Uncommon Personal Strength (PS/Uncommon)	A Personal Strength that is also substantially different from the child's own mean. That is, the size of the difference between the Index and the mean of all four Indexes is unusually large, occurring less than 10% of the time in the WISC-IV standardization sample.
Uncommon Personal Weakness (PW/Uncommon)	A Personal Weakness that is also substantially different from the child's own mean. That is, the size of the difference between the Index and the mean of all four Indexes is unusually large, occurring less than 10% of the time in the WISC-IV standardization sample.
Key Asset (KA)	An Index that is an uncommon Personal Strength and a Normative Strength.
High-Priority Concern (HPC)	An Index that is an uncommon Personal Weakness and a Normative Weakness.

ical cluster comprises two or three subtests. Examiners may decide a priori to conduct one or more of these comparisons, in which case the comparisons would be referred to as *Planned Clinical Comparisons*. Alternatively, examiners may decide to conduct one or more of these comparisons *after* they have evaluated a child's performance on the core battery, in which case the comparisons would be referred to as *Post Hoc Clinical Comparisons*.

Rapid Reference 4.12 lists the clinical clusters and the subtests they comprise.

≡ Rapid Reference 4.11

Classification and Interpretation of Index Fluctuations Based
on the Index Profile Analyses Described in Steps 3–5

INDEX SCORES THAT ARE CLASSIFIED AS A STRENGTH

1. **Key Asset (Normative Strength and Personal Strength/ Uncommon)**
   Interpretation: Jessica's processing speed is considered a significant strength as compared to other individuals her age in the normal population. In addition, her ability in this area is significantly higher than her abilities in other areas. In fact, the difference between Jessica's processing speed and her abilities in other areas is so large that it is not commonly achieved by other children her age in the normal population. Therefore, Jessica's processing speed is a Key Asset and a notable integrity, a finding that should play an essential role in developing educational interventions. Note that the latter part of this interpretive statement may be germane only when other abilities (cognitive or academic) are either in the lower end of the Average range or lower, suggesting that intervention is indeed warranted.

2. **Normative Strength and Personal Strength/Not Uncommon**
   Interpretation: Jessica's processing speed is considered a significant strength as compared to other individuals her age in the normal population. In addition, her ability in this area is significantly higher than her abilities in other areas. Therefore, Jessica's processing speed is a notable integrity, a finding that may play an essential role in developing educational interventions. Note that the latter part of this interpretive statement may be germane only when other abilities (cognitive or academic) are either in the lower end of the Average range or lower, suggesting that intervention is indeed warranted.

3. **Personal Strength/Uncommon but not a Normative Strength**
   Interpretation: Jessica's processing speed is considered a significant strength compared to her abilities in other areas. In fact, the difference between her processing speed and her abilities in other areas is so large that it is not commonly achieved by other children her age in the normal population. Therefore, Jessica's processing speed is a notable Personal Strength, a finding that should play an essential role in developing educational interventions. Note that the latter part of this interpretive statement may be germane only when other abilities (cognitive or academic) are either in the lower end of the Average range or lower, suggesting that intervention is indeed warranted. Also, in this scenario, Jessica's processing speed may be considered a "notable integrity," as it was in the first two scenarios, if her Processing Speed standard score is at the upper end of the Average Range (i.e., 110 to 115). Finally, it is also possible for Jessica's processing speed to be a Personal Strength/Uncommon but a Normative Weakness (i.e., if the Personal Strength/Uncommon is associated with a standard score of < 85).

4. **Normative Strength but not a Personal Strength**
   Interpretation: Jessica's processing speed is considered a significant strength compared to other children her age in the normal population. Her processing

(continued)

speed is a notable integrity, a finding that may play an essential role in developing educational interventions. Note that the latter part of this interpretive statement may be germane only when other abilities (cognitive or academic) are either in the lower end of the Average Range or lower, suggesting that intervention is indeed warranted.

5. **Personal Strength/Not Uncommon but not a Normative Strength**
   Interpretation: Jessica's processing speed is considered a significant strength compared to her abilities in other areas. Her processing speed is a notable Personal Strength, a finding that should play an essential role in developing educational interventions. Note that the latter part of this interpretive statement may be germane only when other abilities (cognitive or academic) are either in the lower end of the Average Range or lower, suggesting that intervention is indeed warranted. Also, it is possible for Jessica's processing speed to be a Personal Strength/Not Uncommon but a Normative Weakness (i.e., if the Personal Strength/Not Uncommon is associated with a standard score of < 85).

INDEX SCORES THAT ARE CLASSIFIED AS A WEAKNESS

6. **High-Priority Concern (Normative Weakness and Personal Weakness/Uncommon)**
   Interpretation: Jessica's processing speed is considered a significant weakness as compared to other individuals her age in the normal population. In addition, her ability in this area is significantly lower than her abilities in other areas. In fact, the difference between her processing speed and her abilities in other areas is so large that it is not commonly found in the normal population. Therefore, Jessica's processing speed is a High-Priority Concern and suggests that she has a disorder in this basic psychological process, a finding that should play an essential role in developing educational interventions.

7. **Normative Weakness and Personal Weakness/Not Uncommon**
   Interpretation: Jessica's processing speed is considered a significant weakness as compared to other individuals her age in the normal population. In addition, her ability in this area is significantly lower than her abilities in other areas. Therefore, Jessica's processing speed is a notable weakness and suggests that she has a disorder in this basic psychological process, a finding that should play an essential role in developing educational interventions.

8. **Personal Weakness/Uncommon but not a Normative Weakness**
   Interpretation: Jessica's processing speed is considered a significant weakness compared to her abilities in other areas. In fact, the difference between her processing speed and her abilities in other areas is so large that it is not commonly found in the normal population. Therefore, Jessica's processing speed is a notable Personal Weakness, a finding that may play an essential role in developing educational interventions. Note that the latter part of this interpretive statement may be germane only when the actual Processing Speed standard score is in the lower end of the Average Range (i.e., 85–90, suggesting that intervention may indeed be warranted. The finding of a Personal Weakness that is uncommon in the normal population does not provide *de facto* evidence of a processing disorder. It is feasible for a child to have a Personal Weakness/Uncommon that is associated with a standard score that falls in either the Average/Within Normal Limits range or the Above Average/Normative Strength Range.

9. **Normative Weakness but not a Personal Weakness**

Interpretation: Jessica's processing speed is considered a significant weakness compared to other children her age in the normal population. Her processing speed is a notable weakness and suggests that she has a disorder in this basic psychological process, a finding that should play an essential role in developing educational interventions.

10. **Personal Weakness/Not Uncommon but not a Normative Weakness**

Interpretation: Jessica's processing speed is considered a significant weakness compared to her abilities in other areas. Her processing speed is a notable Personal Weakness, a finding that may play an essential role in developing educational interventions. Note that the finding of a Personal Weakness, in and of itself, does not provide *de facto* evidence of a processing disorder. A Personal Weakness that is associated with a standard score that falls Within Normal Limits or higher does not, in and of itself, provide evidence of a disorder. Also, it is feasible for a child to have a Personal Weakness/Not Uncommon that is associated with a standard score that falls in the Above Average/ Normative Strength range.

OTHER

11. **Index is not interpretable as a unitary construct**

Description: The Processing Speed Index (PSI), a measure of Processing Speed (Gs), represents Jessica's ability to fluently and automatically perform cognitive tasks, especially when under pressure to maintain focused attention and concentration. Jessica's Gs was assessed by tasks that required her to copy a series of symbols that are paired with numbers using a key (Coding) and indicate the presence or absence of a target symbol within a search group (Symbol Search). The variability among Jessica's performances on these tasks was unusually large, indicating that her overall Gs ability cannot be summarized in a single score (i.e., the PSI).

12. **Index is unitary but is neither a strength nor a weakness**

Interpretation: The Processing Speed Index (PSI), a measure of Processing Speed (Gs), represents Jessica's ability to fluently and automatically perform cognitive tasks, especially when under pressure to maintain focused attention and concentration. Jessica's Gs was assessed by tasks that required her to copy a series of symbols that are paired with numbers using a key (Coding) and indicate the presence or absence of a target symbol within a search group (Symbol Search). Jessica obtained a PSI standard score of 100, which is ranked at the 50th percentile and is classified as Average Range/Within Normal Limits.

Table 4.5 provides internal consistency reliability coefficients and SEMs for each clinical cluster by age and overall WISC-IV standardization sample.

Step 7a. Prior to conducting clinical comparisons, you must first determine whether the clusters in the comparison represent unitary abilities. To do this, compute the difference between the highest and lowest scaled scores that make

≡Rapid Reference 4.12

Composition of CHC Clinical Clusters

Clinical Comparison

Clinical Cluster: Subtests Composing Cluster

1. Fluid Reasoning vs. Visual Processing

Fluid Reasoning (Gf) Cluster:
Matrix Reasoning + Picture Concepts + Arithmetic
Definition: The Fluid Reasoning (Gf) Cluster consists of three subtests that measure the broad Gf ability in CHC theory. Gf is defined as encompassing the mental operations that an individual uses when faced with a novel task that cannot be performed automatically. These mental operations include forming and recognizing concepts, perceiving relationships among patterns, drawing inferences, problem solving, and so forth. Matrix Reasoning and Arithmetic primarily measure the narrow Gf ability of *General Sequential Reasoning (Deduction)*, which is defined as the ability to start with stated rules, premises, or conditions and to engage in one or more steps to reach a solution to a novel problem. Matrix Reasoning also involves Induction (I). Arithmetic also measures Math Achievement (A3) and Quantitative Reasoning (RQ). Its primary classification as a measure of Gf is based on Keith and colleagues (2004). Picture Concepts primarily measures the narrow Gf ability of *Induction,* which is defined as the ability to discover the underlying characteristic (e.g., rule, concept, process, trend, class membership) that governs a problem or set of materials. Matrix Reasoning appears to measure both Deduction and Induction about equally. Although the tests this cluster comprises may involve CHC abilities other than Gf (e.g., Visual Processing, Crystallized Intelligence, Quantitative Knowledge, and Short-Term Memory), the label "Fluid Reasoning" reflects the *primary* ability measured by these tests.

Visual Processing (Gv) Cluster:
Block Design + Picture Completion
Definition: The Visual Processing (Gv) Cluster consists of two subtests that measure the broad Gv ability in CHC theory. Gv is defined as the ability to generate, perceive, analyze, synthesize, store, retrieve, manipulate, and transform visual patterns and stimuli. Block Design primarily measures the narrow Gv ability of *Spatial Relations,* which is defined as the ability to perceive and manipulate visual patterns rapidly, or to maintain orientation with respect to objects in space. Picture Completion primarily measures the narrow Gv ability of *Flexibility of Closure,* which is defined as the ability to find, apprehend, and identify a visual figure or pattern embedded in a complex visual array, *when knowing in advance* what the pattern is. Although Picture Completion may also involve specific Gc abilities (e.g., General Information), the label "Visual Processing" reflects the primary ability measured by this test.

2. Nonverbal Fluid Reasoning vs. Visual Processing

Nonverbal Fluid Reasoning (*Gf*-nonverbal) Cluster:
Matrix Reasoning + Picture Concepts

Definition: The Nonverbal Fluid Reasoning (*Gf*-nonverbal) Cluster consists of two subtests that measure the broad *Gf* ability in CHC theory. *Gf* was defined in Comparison 1. The *Gf*-nonverbal Cluster is less broad than the *Gf* Cluster in Comparison 1 and deemphasizes language demands. Also, because both Matrix Reasoning and Picture Concepts involve the use of visual stimuli and do not require expressive language, the *Gf* ability underlying this cluster was qualified with the term "nonverbal."

Visual Processing (*Gv*) Cluster:
Block Design + Picture Completion

Definition: The Visual Processing (*Gv*) Cluster was defined in Comparison 1.

3. Nonverbal Fluid Reasoning vs. Verbal Fluid Reasoning

Nonverbal Fluid Reasoning (*Gf*-nonverbal) Cluster:
Matrix Reasoning + Picture Concepts

Definition: The Nonverbal Fluid Reasoning (*Gf*-nonverbal) Cluster was defined in Comparison 2.

Verbal Fluid Reasoning (*Gf*-verbal) Cluster:
Similarities + Word Reasoning

Definition: The Verbal Fluid Reasoning (*Gf*-verbal) Cluster consists of two subtests that primarily measure the broad *Gc* ability in CHC theory but also involves reasoning (*Gf*). *Gc* is defined as the breadth and depth of a person's accumulated knowledge of a culture and the effective use of that knowledge. Similarities measures the narrow *Gc* ability of *Language Development,* which is defined as the general development of—or the understanding of words, sentences, and paragraphs (*not* requiring reading) in—spoken native language skills. Word Reasoning measures the narrow *Gc* ability of *Lexical Knowledge,* which is defined as the extent of vocabulary that can be understood in terms of correct word meanings. Because Similarities and Word Reasoning (although primarily verbal or *Gc* subtests) both require the ability to reason (inductively) with verbal stimuli we chose to label this cluster *Verbal* Fluid Reasoning.

4. Lexical Knowledge vs. General Information

Lexical Knowledge (*Gc*-VL) Cluster:
Word Reasoning + Vocabulary

Definition: The Lexical Knowledge (*Gc*-VL) Cluster consists of two subtests that primarily measure the broad *Gc* ability in CHC theory. *Gc* was defined in Comparison 3. These subtests, Word Reasoning and Vocabulary, primarily measure the narrow *Gc* ability of *Lexical Knowledge,* which is defined as the extent of vocabulary that can be understood in terms of correct word meanings. Therefore, we chose to label this cluster "Lexical Knowledge."

(continued)

General Information (Gc-K0) Cluster: Comprehension + Information

Definition: The General Information (Gc-K0) Cluster consists of two subtests that primarily measure the broad Gc ability in CHC theory. Gc was defined in Comparison 3. These subtests, Comprehension and Information, primarily measure the narrow Gc ability of *General Information,* which is defined as an individual's range of general knowledge. Therefore, we chose to label this cluster "General Information."

5. Long-Term Memory vs. Short-Term Memory

Long-Term Memory (Gc-LTM) Cluster: Information + Vocabulary

Definition: The Long-Term Memory (Gc-LTM) Cluster consists of two subtests that measure the broad Gc ability in CHC theory. Gc was defined in Comparison 3. These subtests, Information and Vocabulary, measure to a greater or lesser extent the narrow Gc ability of General Information. Vocabulary also measures the narrow Gc ability of Lexical Knowledge. However, because both Information and Vocabulary represent knowledge that is typically stored in long-term memory, we chose to label this cluster "Long-Term Memory." Note that "Long-Term Memory" is not a CHC label per se and therefore should not be confused with the broad Long-Term Retrieval *(Glr)* ability in CHC theory.

Short-Term Memory (Gsm-WM) Cluster[a]: Letter-Number Sequencing + Digit Span

Definition: The Short-Term Memory (Gsm-WM) Cluster consists of two subtests that measure the broad Gsm ability in CHC theory. Gsm is defined as the ability to apprehend and hold information in immediate awareness and to use it within a few seconds. Letter-Number Sequencing and Digit Span (Backward) measure the narrow Gsm ability of *Working Memory,* which is defined as the ability to temporarily store and perform a set of cognitive operations on information that requires divided attention and the management of the limited capacity of short-term memory. Digit Span also measures the narrow Gsm ability of *Memory Span,* which is defined as the ability to attend to and immediately recall temporally ordered elements in the correct order after a single presentation.

6. Long-Term Memory vs. Verbal Fluid Reasoning

Long-Term Memory (Gc-LTM) Cluster: Vocabulary + Information

Definition: The Long-Term Memory (Gc-LTM) Cluster was defined in Comparison 5.

Verbal Fluid Reasoning (Gf-verbal) Cluster: Similarities + Word Reasoning

Definition: The Verbal Fluid Reasoning (Gf-verbal) Cluster was defined in Comparison 3.

[a] The Short-Term Memory (Gsm-WM) Cluster is identical to the WISC-IV Working Memory Index (WMI).

Table 4.5 Internal Consistency Reliability Coefficients and SEMs for the New WISC-IV Clinical Clusters, by Age and Overall Sample

Cluster	6	7	8	9	10	11	12	13	14	15	16	All
Age												
Gf												
Reliability	.92	.94	.93	.94	.94	.93	.93	.92	.92	.92	.92	**.93**
SEM	4.24	3.67	3.97	3.67	3.67	3.97	3.97	4.24	4.24	4.24	4.24	**4.02**
Gv												
Reliability	.88	.89	.90	.89	.90	.92	.91	.91	.89	.91	.91	**.90**
SEM	5.20	4.97	4.74	4.97	4.74	4.24	4.50	4.50	4.97	4.50	4.50	**4.72**
Gf-nonverbal												
Reliability	.90	.91	.91	.92	.91	.90	.91	.89	.90	.88	.88	**.90**
SEM	4.74	4.50	4.50	4.24	4.50	4.74	4.50	4.97	4.74	5.20	5.20	**4.72**
Gf-verbal												
Reliability	.87	.89	.90	.90	.90	.87	.89	.89	.91	.92	.89	**.89**
SEM	5.41	4.97	4.74	4.74	4.74	5.41	4.97	4.97	4.50	4.24	4.97	**4.89**
Gc-VL												
Reliability	.88	.89	.91	.91	.91	.90	.90	.91	.92	.94	.91	**.91**
SEM	5.20	4.97	4.50	4.50	4.50	4.74	4.74	4.50	4.24	3.67	4.50	**4.57**

(continued)

Table 4.5 (Continued)

Cluster						Age						
	6	7	8	9	10	11	12	13	14	15	16	All
Gc-K0												
Reliability	.88	.85	.87	.89	.88	.89	.92	.90	.91	.92	.93	.90
SEM	5.20	5.81	5.41	4.97	5.20	4.97	4.24	4.74	4.50	4.24	3.97	4.87
Gc-LTM												
Reliability	.89	.89	.91	.92	.93	.92	.94	.94	.94	.96	.95	.93
SEM	4.97	4.97	4.50	4.24	3.97	4.24	3.67	3.67	3.67	3.00	3.35	4.07
Gsm-WM												
Reliability	.92	.90	.91	.92	.92	.92	.93	.91	.93	.92	.93	.92
SEM	4.24	4.74	4.50	4.24	4.24	4.24	3.97	4.50	3.97	4.24	3.97	4.27

Note: The Short-Term Memory (*Gsm*-WM) Cluster is identical to the WISC-IV Working Memory Index (WMI). SEM = standard error of measurement. *Gf* = Fluid Reasoning; *Gv* = Visual Processing; *Gf*-nonverbal = Nonverbal Fluid Reasoning; *Gf*-verbal = Verbal Fluid Reasoning; *Gc*-VL = Lexical Knowledge; *Gc*-K0 = General Information; *Gc*-LTM = Long-Term Memory; and *Gsm*-WM = Working Memory.

up the clinical cluster. Answer the following question: *Is the size of the scaled score difference less than 5?*

- If YES, then the clinical cluster represents a unitary ability and the clinical comparison that includes this cluster may be made *only* if the other cluster in the comparison also represents a unitary ability. Proceed to Step 7b.

> ### DON'T FORGET
>
> **When Can I Make a Planned or Post Hoc Clinical Comparison?**
>
> Clinical Comparisons can be made only when both clusters in the comparison represent unitary abilities.

- If NO, then the clinical cluster does not represent a unitary ability and the clinical comparison that includes this cluster should not be made.

Step 7b. Calculate the clinical cluster by summing the scaled scores for the subtests that compose the clinical cluster and converting the sum to a standard score using Appendix H.

Step 7c. Determine whether the size of the difference between the clusters in the comparison is unusually large or uncommon, occurring less than 10% of the time in the WISC-IV standardization sample. To do this, calculate the difference between the clusters in the comparison. If the size of the difference is equal to or greater than the value reported for the comparison in Table 4.6, then the difference is uncommon. If the size of the difference between the two clusters in the comparison is less than the table value, then the difference is not uncommon. Rapid Reference 4.13 provides examples of interpretive statements that may be used in psychological reports to describe the findings of Planned and Post Hoc Clinical Comparisons. Specifically, a comparison between two interpretable clinical clusters can have either one of two outcomes:

1. The size of the difference between the two interpretable clinical clusters is uncommon in the normative population.
2. The size of the difference between the two interpretable clinical clusters is not uncommon in the normative population.

Step 7d. Regardless of the outcome of Step 7c, review Rapid Reference 4.13 to identify an example of an interpretive statement that most appropriately describes the results of the child's clinical cluster comparison. If the child demonstrated a Normative Weakness in any clinical cluster, refer to Rapid Reference 4.14 for hypotheses about the meaning of such findings. Rapid Reference 4.14 also provides suggestions for educational interventions and instructional strate-

Table 4.6 Size of Difference between Pairs of Clinical Clusters Needed to be Considered Unusually Large or Uncommon

Cluster Comparison	Amount of Difference
Fluid Reasoning *(Gf)*—Visual Processing *(Gv)*	21
Nonverbal Fluid Reasoning (*Gf*-nonverbal)—Visual Processing *(Gv)*	24
Verbal Fluid Reasoning (*Gf*-verbal)—Nonverbal Fluid Reasoning (*Gf*-nonverbal)	24
Lexical Knowledge (*Gc*-VL)—General Information (*Gc*-K0)	17
Long-Term Memory (*Gc*-LTM)—Short-Term Memory (*Gsm*-WM)[a]	24
Long-Term Memory (*Gc*-LTM)—Verbal Fluid Reasoning (*Gf*-verbal)	17

Source: Wechsler Intelligence Scale for Children–Fourth Edition. Copyright © 2003 by Harcourt Assessment, Inc. Reproduced by permission of the publisher. All rights reserved. *Wechsler Intelligence Scale for Children* and *WISC* are trademarks of Harcourt Assessment, Inc., registered in the United States of America and/or other jurisdictions.

Note: "Unusually large or uncommon" denotes differences occurring less than 10% of the time in the WISC-IV Standardization Sample.

[a] The Short-Term Memory (*Gsm*-WM) Cluster is identical to the WISC-IV Working Memory Index (WMI).

gies that may be useful for children who demonstrate uncommon patterns of performance on the WISC-IV clinical clusters. An example of how to use Rapid References 4.13 and 4.14 follows. Figure 4.7 provides a snapshot of Step 7 of the WISC-IV interpretive worksheet for Ryan.

Ryan demonstrated an uncommon difference between his Lexical Knowledge (*Gc*-VL) Cluster of 81 and his General Information (*Gc*-K0) Cluster of 114. An interpretive statement that can be used to describe Ryan's specific performance pattern on the *Gc*-VL and *Gc*-K0 Post Hoc Clinical Comparison is found in Rapid Reference 4.13. This Rapid Reference shows that Ryan's *Gc*-VL versus *Gc*-K0 pattern corresponds to Interpretive Statement 7. This interpretive statement provides an example of how to describe a pattern of performance wherein one Index is < 85 and the other is ≥ 85 and the difference between them is uncommon. Using Ryan's *Gc*-VL versus *Gc*-K0 pattern of performance, the following interpretive statement may be made: *The difference between Ryan's General Information (Gc-K0) Cluster of 114 (83rd percentile; Average Range/Within Normal Limits) and his Lexical Knowledge (Gc-VL) Cluster of 81 (11th percentile; Below Average/Normative Weakness) is unusually large (differences as large as Ryan's discrepancy of 33 points occur less*

Examples of How to Describe the Findings of Planned and Post Hoc Clinical Comparisons in a Psychological Report

Planned Clinical Comparison Finding	Both SS ≤ 85	One SS < 85 One SS ≥ 85	Both SS 85–115 (inclusive)	One SS < 115 One SS ≥ 115	Both SS ≥ 115
Difference Not Uncommon	*Interpretive Statement 1*	*Interpretive Statement 2*	*Interpretive Statement 3*	*Interpretive Statement 4*	*Interpretive Statement 5*
Difference Uncommon	*Interpretive Statement 6*	*Interpretive Statement 7*	*Interpretive Statement 8*	*Interpretive Statement 9*	*Interpretive Statement 10*

Note: SS = Standard Score.

INTERPRETIVE STATEMENT (numbers below correspond to numbers in table)

1. Example: *Verbal Fluid Reasoning (Gf-verbal) Cluster = 80; Nonverbal Fluid Reasoning (Gf-nonverbal) Cluster = 75. The difference between Bob's Gf-verbal Cluster of 80 (9th percentile) and his Gf-nonverbal Cluster of 75 (5th percentile) was not unusually large, indicating that it is not uncommon to find a difference of this magnitude in the normative population. Nevertheless, it is important to recognize that Bob's abilities to reason with both verbal and nonverbal information are Below Average and therefore represent Normative Weaknesses relative to his age mates.*

2. Example: *Long-Term Memory (Gc-LTM) Cluster = 90; Verbal Fluid Reasoning (Gf-verbal) Cluster = 84. The difference between Bob's Gc-LTM Cluster of 90 (25th percentile) and his Gf-verbal Cluster of 84 (14th percentile) was not unusually large, indicating that it is not uncommon to find a difference of this magnitude in the normative population. Nevertheless, it is important to recognize that Bob's ability to reason with knowledge (Gf-verbal) fell within the Below Average range of functioning and represents a Normative Weakness relative to his age mates.*

(continued)

3. Example: Long-Term Memory (Gc-LTM) Cluster = 106; Short-Term Memory (Gsm-WM) Cluster = 100. The difference between Bob's Gc-LTM Cluster of 106 (65th percentile) and his Gsm-WM Cluster of 100 (50th percentile) was not unusually large, indicating that it is not uncommon to find a difference of this magnitude in the normative population. Relative to his age mates, Bob's performances in these areas are within the Average Range of functioning or Within Normal Limits.

4. Example: Nonverbal Fluid Reasoning (Gf-nonverbal) Cluster = 118; Visual Processing (Gv) Cluster = 112. The difference between Bob's Gf-nonverbal Cluster of 118 (88th percentile) and his Gv Cluster of 112 (79th percentile) was not unusually large, indicating that it is not uncommon to find a difference of this magnitude in the normative population. Relative to his age mates, Bob's Gv ability is within the Average Range of functioning, and his Gf-nonverbal ability is Above Average and therefore represents a Normative Strength.

5. Example: Lexical Knowledge (Gc-VL) Cluster = 125; General Information (Gc-K0) Cluster = 120. The difference between Bob's Gc-VL Cluster of 125 (95th percentile) and his Gc-K0 Cluster of 120 (91st percentile) was not unusually large, indicating that it is not uncommon to find a difference of this magnitude in the normative population. Relative to his age mates, Bob's lexical knowledge and general information abilities are Above Average (or if scores are > 130, then "in the Upper Extreme") and therefore represent Normative Strengths.

6. Example: Visual Processing (Gv) Cluster = 84; Nonverbal Fluid Reasoning (Gf-nonverbal) Cluster = 60. The difference between Bob's Gv Cluster of 84 (14th percentile; Below Average/Normative Weakness) and his Gf-nonverbal Cluster of 60 (< 1st percentile; Lower Extreme/Normative Weakness) is unusually large (differences as large as Bob's discrepancy of 24 points occur less than 10% of the time in the normative population). Higher standard scores on Gv than Gf-nonverbal can occur for many reasons. For example, some children might have a better ability to analyze or manipulate isolated aspects of visual stimuli than to reason with such stimuli. Although Bob's visual processing is better developed than his fluid reasoning, it is important to recognize that Bob demonstrated Normative Weaknesses in both domains. Note that Bob's Gf-nonverbal ability, in particular, represents a disorder in a basic psychological process—but only when this Lower Extreme performance is corroborated by other data sources.

7. Example: Verbal Fluid Reasoning (Gf-verbal) Cluster = 110; Nonverbal Fluid Reasoning (Gf-nonverbal) Cluster = 83. The difference between Bob's Gf-verbal Cluster of 110 (75th percentile; Average Range/Within Normal Limits) and his Gf-nonverbal Cluster of 83 (13th percentile; Below Average/Normative Weakness) is unusually large (differences as large as Bob's discrepancy of 27 points occur less than 10% of the time in the normative population). Higher standard scores on Gf-verbal than Gf-nonverbal can occur for many reasons. For example, some children might have the ability to reason with verbal information but have difficulty applying their reasoning skills in a similar manner when the stimuli are visual in nature. Not only is Bob's nonverbal fluid reasoning ability less well developed than his verbal fluid reasoning ability, it is also Below Average relative to his age mates and therefore is a Normative Weakness.

8. Example: Long-Term Memory (Gc-LTM) Cluster = 115; Verbal Fluid Reasoning (Gf-verbal) Cluster = 85. The difference between Bob's Gc-LTM Cluster of 115 (84th percentile; Average Range/Within Normal Limits) and his Gf-verbal Cluster of 85 (16th percentile; Average Range/Within Normal Limits) is unusually large (differences as large as Bob's discrepancy of 30 points occur less than 10% of the time in the normative population). Higher standard scores on Gc-LTM than Gf-verbal can occur for many reasons. For example, some children might have a well-developed fund of information but are unable to reason well with this information. Although Bob's performance in both domains falls Within Normal Limits relative to his age mates, it would not be unusual for Bob to become easily frustrated when required to reason with general information (e.g., drawing inferences from text).

9. Example: Short-Term Memory (Gsm-WM) Cluster = 116; Long-Term Memory (Gc-LTM) Cluster = 86. The difference between Bob's Gsm-WM Cluster of 116 (86th percentile; Above Average/Normative Strength) and his Gc-LTM Cluster of 86 (17th percentile; Average Range/Within Normal Limits) is unusually large (differences as large as Bob's discrepancy of 30 points occur less than 10% of the time in the normative population). Higher standard scores on Gsm-WM than Gc-LTM can occur for many reasons. For example, some children might have the ability to encode information in immediate awareness long enough to manipulate or transform it but have difficulty retrieving this information. Although Bob's performance in long-term memory falls within Normal Limits relative to his age mates, he may benefit from strategies designed to facilitate information storage and retrieval (e.g., use of mnemonics). (Note: When the standard score on the lower cluster in the comparison is < 85, then replace last sentence with "Not only is Bob's long-term memory ability less well developed than his short-term memory ability, but it is also in the Below Average [or Lower Extreme, depending on the score] range of functioning relative to his age mates and therefore represents a Normative Weakness." Also note that Bob's Below Average [or Lower Extreme] performance in long-term memory represents a disorder in a basic psychological process—but only when such performance is corroborated by other data sources.)

10. Example: Verbal Fluid Reasoning (Gf-verbal) Cluster = 146; Nonverbal Fluid Reasoning (Gf-nonverbal) Cluster = 116. The difference between Bob's Gf-verbal Cluster of 146 (>99th percentile; Upper Extreme/Normative Strength) and his Gf-nonverbal Cluster of 116 (86th percentile; Above Average/Normative Strength) is unusually large (differences as large as Bob's discrepancy of 30 points occur less than 10% of the time in the normative population). Nevertheless, it is important to recognize that Bob's abilities to reason with both verbal and nonverbal information are very well developed, falling in the Upper Extreme and Above Average ranges, respectively, compared to his age mates and therefore represent Normative Strengths.

≡Rapid Reference 4.14

Hypotheses for Observed Differences Between Clinical Clusters and Suggestions for Intervention

Fluid Reasoning (Gf) Cluster > Visual Processing (Gv) Cluster or Nonverbal Fluid Reasoning (Gf-nonverbal) Cluster

Hypotheses for Observed Difference: May indicate that the child's overall reasoning ability is good and that, despite difficulty with visual processing, the child can solve problems by focusing on characteristics that are less visual in nature. For example, on Matrix Reasoning, the child may not focus on the spatial aspects of the pattern to arrive at an answer (e.g., the pattern shifts from top to bottom, then left to right, then back to the top), but rather, may focus on the *number* of dots in a pattern to complete the matrix. Also, a child with a Fluid Reasoning *(Gf)* Cluster higher than his or her Visual Processing *(Gv)* Cluster may do well when he or she uses a strategy such as verbal mediation to solve problems with substantial visual information. That is, a child may be able to solve a problem involving visual stimuli only after translating the visual information into verbal information.

Suggestions for Intervention: Instructional strategies that may be useful for a child with this pattern of performance include (1) avoiding excessive reliance on visual models, diagrams, and demonstrations; (2) accompanying visual demonstrations with oral explanations; and (3) breaking down spatial tasks into component parts (e.g., providing a set of verbal instructions to match each part). Additionally, because the child may have trouble forming a visual representation of a concept in his or her mind (e.g., a mental image), manipulatives or hands-on, concrete learning experiences may be beneficial when learning about an abstract concept that is visual in nature (e.g., the rotation of the planets in the solar system). Concrete or hands-on experiences should also be supplemented with verbal information.

Visual Processing (Gv) Cluster > Fluid Reasoning (Gf) Cluster or Nonverbal Fluid Reasoning (Gf-nonverbal) Cluster

Hypotheses for Observed Difference: May indicate that the child has good concrete visual skills, but experiences difficulty when asked to *reason* with visual information. Implications may include difficulty with mathematical application tasks, such as making predictions based on visual stimuli (e.g., graphs, charts). A child with this pattern of performance may also have difficulty *interpreting* visual information. That is, a child with higher visual processing skills than visual reasoning skills may be able to see specific details in visual information but may have difficulty integrating visual information to solve problems.

Suggestions for Intervention: Instructional strategies that may be useful for a child with this pattern of performance include (1) providing step-by-step instructions for mathematical applications tasks that include if-then statements (e.g., "First, look at the slope of the line; next, determine the direction of the gradient; if the slope is positive, then interpret as follows," and so forth); (2) highlighting key visual information that must be integrated in some way to arrive at a solution to the problem.

Nonverbal Fluid Reasoning (Gf-nonverbal) Cluster > Verbal Fluid Reasoning (Gf-verbal) Cluster

Hypotheses for Observed Difference: May indicate that the child can reason better with visually based stimuli as compared to verbal stimuli. A child with this pattern of performance may learn best when new information is presented visually.

Suggestions for Intervention: Instructional strategies that may be useful for a child with this pattern of performance include (1) allowing the child to sketch drawings or diagrams when learning new information or (2) providing visual adjuncts (e.g., graphs, charts, tables) when teaching verbal concepts.

Verbal Fluid Reasoning (Gf-verbal) Cluster > Nonverbal Fluid Reasoning (Gf-nonverbal) Cluster

Hypotheses for Observed Difference: May indicate that the child can reason better with verbally based stimuli as compared to visual stimuli. A child with this pattern of performance may learn best when new information is presented verbally. Moreover, a child with this pattern of performance may do well with lecture formats that are primarily verbal in nature but may "get lost" when too many visual aids are used (e.g., graphs, diagrams) to teach a new concept.

Suggestions for Intervention: Instructional strategies that may be useful for a child with this pattern of performance are similar to those used with the Nonverbal Fluid Reasoning (*Gf*-nonverbal) Cluster > Visual Processing (*Gv*) Cluster pattern of performance described above.

Lexical Knowledge (Gc-VL) Cluster > General Information (Gc-K0) Cluster

Hypotheses for Observed Difference: May indicate that the child has facility with words and can reason with words, but has minimal knowledge of factual information or has difficulty applying knowledge in specific situations. A child with this pattern of performance may have difficulty with written expression, in terms of breadth and depth of content, despite an appropriate vocabulary. On reading tasks, the child may be able to read (decode) well and generally comprehend what he or she is reading but may not be able to make meaningful connections or draw inferences due to a lack of background knowledge.

Suggestions for Intervention: Instructional strategies that may be useful for a child with this pattern of performance include (1) providing advanced organizers (outline of material to be discussed in a lecture); (2) teaching the student previewing strategies (e.g., skimming, scanning); (3) highlighting key information; (4) using a method of "what we know, what we don't know" to activate prior knowledge in the student before presenting new topics; and (4) having the student engage in prewriting activities (e.g., brainstorming about the ideas, words, etc. that the child plans to use in written work and assisting the child in "fleshing out" these ideas) when completing writing assignments.

(*continued*)

General Information (Gc-K0) Cluster > Lexical Knowledge (Gc-VL) Cluster

Hypotheses for Observed Difference: May indicate that the child has good knowledge of factual information, but lacks facility with words and may have difficulty reasoning with words. On writing assignments, a child with this pattern of performance may have good content but may be unable to communicate his or her thoughts well. That is, the child's writing may appear immature (e.g., writing is bland, lacks variety with regard to adjectives, and so forth). On reading tasks, a child with this pattern of performance may have good comprehension when reading about familiar topics, but may have poor comprehension when reading about topics that are novel or that contain several unknown words. Thus, it is not unusual for a child with this pattern of performance to be described as having "inconsistent" comprehension skills.

Suggestions for Intervention: Instructional strategies that may be useful for a child with this pattern of performance include (1) providing a word bank for written expression tasks; (2) providing a glossary of terms that a child can refer to when completing reading assignments; (3) ensuring that test questions do not include vocabulary terms that are unknown; (4) reviewing or teaching vocabulary words when the child is asked to read from content-area texts; (5) writing key words and terms on the board when lecturing on new content areas; (6) ensuring that instructions contain words that the child knows; (7) simplifying instructions by extending upon unknown words with words that are familiar to the child or defining terms when initially presenting them (e.g., "The *composition* of igneous rock, that is, *what it is made up of*, is. . . ."); and (8) teaching the child to use a thesaurus when completing writing tasks.

Long-Term Memory (Gc-LTM) Cluster > Short-Term Memory (Gsm-WM) Cluster

Hypotheses for Observed Difference: May indicate that the child can retrieve information but has trouble encoding the information. In other words, the child's stores of knowledge are likely the result of repeated practice using a number of meaningful associations. On reading and writing tasks, a child with this pattern of performance may do well with known topics but poorly on new ones. Additionally, due to difficulty with holding information in immediate awareness long enough to use it, a child with this pattern of performance may have difficulty efficiently copying information from written material or recording information from a lecture or from the board. Finally, a child with this pattern of performance may have difficulty with a "bottom-up" teaching approach where the component parts of a general concept are presented separately and sequentially. This teaching approach may cause particular difficulty for the child primarily because he or she cannot hold the component parts in memory long enough to be able to synthesize them into the whole concept.

Suggestions for Intervention: Instructional strategies that may be useful for a child with this pattern of performance include (1) providing succinct directions; (2) ensuring that the child has retained sufficient information from a set of instructions to work independently; (3) providing written directions to supplement oral directions; (4) supplementing oral presentations and lectures by writing important information on the board; (5) repeating important information often; (6) using intonation in your voice to emphasize key points or words; (7) allowing for multiple exposures to new material using different instructional techniques; (8) underlining or highlighting key words in text so that the child has a quick visual aid when attempting to locate information that he or she may have forgotten; (9) encouraging the child to immediately record key information, new vocabulary words, and concepts presented in a lecture or in reading materials; (10) encouraging the child to develop a picture dictionary/encyclopedia that can serve as a word and concept bank to be used for completing assignments; (11) providing the child with a lecture outline in a cloze (fill-in-the-blank) format that allows him or her to record key words and concepts; (12) reducing copying tasks; (13) allowing extra time for copying information; (14) breaking instruction into parts; and (15) using a top-down approach for presenting new concepts, in which the entire concept is presented first, followed by the component parts.

Short-Term Memory (Gsm-WM Cluster) > Long-Term Memory (Gc-LTM) Cluster

Hypotheses for Observed Difference: May indicate that the child can encode information but has trouble retrieving it. Children with this pattern may do well with new topics in the short term, but if there is a delay between their learning of information and the need to demonstrate their knowledge, they may demonstrate a poor outcome. A classic example of this is when a parent or teacher indicates that the child demonstrated an understanding of a particular topic while it was being presented but did not remember it later in the day. Also, a child with this pattern of performance is often described as knowing information shortly after studying it, but not being able to demonstrate that knowledge later (e.g., on a cumulative exam). It is likely that these children are not forgetting information per se; rather, they are not encoding information at a level that is necessary for efficient retrieval.

Suggestions for Intervention: Instructional strategies that may be useful for a child with this pattern of performance include (1) employing test formats that require recognition (multiple choice, matching, true/false, and fill in the blank with an associated word bank) in favor of test formats that require recall (essay, fill in the blank without a word bank, writing definitions); and (2) introducing "key words" to the child to facilitate learning and retrieval.

Long-Term Memory (Gc-LTM) Cluster > Verbal Fluid Reasoning (Gf-verbal) Cluster

Hypotheses for Observed Difference: May indicate that the child has an adequate fund of knowledge, but cannot reason well with that knowledge.

Suggestions for Intervention: Instructional strategies that may be useful for a child with this pattern of performance include (1) using specific aids that make the reasoning process more concrete—for instance, if asked to make a prediction based on a reading passage, the child may benefit from a "guided questions" list that aids in the use of inductive strategies for arriving at the answer; (2) when working with math problems that involve reasoning, providing a "guided steps" list that aids in externalizing the reasoning process for the child. Examples of guided steps include: determine known facts; determine what you are being asked to do; identify what operations should be used to solve a problem; (3) demonstrating the deductive reasoning process by providing various examples of how a rule can

(continued)

be applied across situations; (4) using study guides that contain facts and general information about a topic that can aid the child in completing reading and writing tasks; and (5) making abstract concepts more meaningful by using known information to teach the concept.

Verbal Fluid Reasoning (Gf-verbal) Cluster > Long-Term Memory (Gc-LTM) Cluster

Hypotheses for Observed Difference: May indicate that the child can reason well, but that he or she has an insufficient amount of information to reason with.

Suggestions for Intervention: A general instructional strategy that may be useful for children with this pattern of performance is to ensure that they have the relevant information that is required to complete assignments; this may require providing them with a glossary of terms, study guides containing key facts about a specific topic, and so forth. The general goal is to ensure that a lack of foundational knowledge does not interfere with the student's ability to fully demonstrate his or her ability to reason with information (e.g., make predictions and inferences, draw conclusions).

Source: The interventions recommended above were based primarily on Mather and Jaffe (2002) and Shapiro (1996).

than 10% of the time in the normative population). Higher standard scores on Gc-K0 than Gc-VL can occur for many reasons. For example, some children might have an adequate fund of information but lack a strong vocabulary knowledge base and the ability to reason well with words. Not only is Ryan's lexical knowledge ability less well developed than his general information ability, but it is also in the Below Average range of functioning relative to his age mates and therefore is a Normative Weakness.

Based on information provided in Rapid Reference 4.14, Ryan's pattern of performance (i.e., Gc-K0 > Gc-VL) may indicate that he has good knowledge of factual information, but may lack facility with words and may have difficulty reasoning with words. Hence, Ryan may demonstrate difficulty communicating his thoughts well in writing, despite good content. More specifically, Ryan's writing may appear immature (e.g., bland, lacking variety with regard to adjectives, and so forth). Although Ryan may demonstrate adequate comprehension when reading about familiar topics, he may have poor comprehension when reading about topics that are novel or that contain several unknown words. Thus, it would not be unusual for Ryan's reading comprehension skills to appear "inconsistent."

In addition to providing information related to academic implications of specific performance patterns on the WISC-IV clinical clusters, Rapid Reference 4.14 also provides suggestions for intervention based on these patterns. In Ryan's case it may be beneficial to (1) provide him with a word bank for written

STEP 7. (Optional) Conduct Select Clinical Comparisons

There are six possible clinical comparisons. Select which of the six (if any) make sense to compare based on either the referral question(s) or assessment results (see Rapid Reference 4.12).

Step 7a. Determine whether each clinical cluster is unitary. Using the table below (at left), record the scaled score (SS) for each relevant subtest. On the lines to the right of the table, subtract the lowest from the highest scaled scores to compute the differences. If a difference equals or exceeds 5 points (i.e., 1.5 SDs), the related clinical cluster is not unitary and cannot be used to conduct clinical comparisons. If a difference is less than 5 points, then the clinical cluster is unitary. Clinical comparisons may be made *only* when both clusters that make up the comparison are unitary.

Subtest	SS
MR	9
PCn	10
AR	11
BD	6
PCm	8
SI	9
WR	6
VO	7
CO	13
IN	12
LNS	7
DS	7

Fluid Reasoning (*Gf*) Cluster
Matrix Reasoning + Picture Concepts + Arithmetic
$\underline{11}$ (Highest) $-$ $\underline{9}$ (Lowest) $=$ $\underline{2}$ (Difference)

Visual Processing (*Gv*) Cluster
Block Design + Picture Completion
$\underline{8}$ (Highest) $-$ $\underline{6}$ (Lowest) $=$ $\underline{2}$ (Difference)

Nonverbal Fluid Reasoning (*Gf*-nonverbal) Cluster
Matrix Reasoning + Picture Concepts
$\underline{10}$ (Highest) $-$ $\underline{9}$ (Lowest) $=$ $\underline{1}$ (Difference)

Verbal Fluid Reasoning (*Gf*-verbal) Cluster
Similarities + Word Reasoning
$\underline{9}$ (Highest) $-$ $\underline{6}$ (Lowest) $=$ $\underline{3}$ (Difference)

Lexical Knowledge (*Gc*-VL) Cluster
Word Reasoning + Vocabulary
$\underline{7}$ (Highest) $-$ $\underline{6}$ (Lowest) $=$ $\underline{1}$ (Difference)

General Information (*Gc*-K0) Cluster
Comprehension + Information
$\underline{13}$ (Highest) $-$ $\underline{12}$ (Lowest) $=$ $\underline{1}$ (Difference)

Long-Term Memory (*Gc*-LTM) Cluster
Vocabulary + Information
$\underline{12}$ (Highest) $-$ $\underline{7}$ (Lowest) $=$ $\underline{5}$ (Difference)

Short-Term Memory (*Gsm*-MW) Cluster
Letter-Number Sequencing + Digit Span
$\underline{7}$ (Highest) $-$ $\underline{7}$ (Lowest) $=$ $\underline{0}$ (Difference)

Figure 4.7 WISC-IV Interpretive Worksheet: STEP 7, Illustrated from Ryan, Age 10

Step 7b. For unitary clusters only, sum the scaled scores for the subtests that compose the cluster. Convert the sums of scaled scores to clinical clusters (i.e., standard scores having a mean of 100 and SD of 15) using Appendix H.

Subtest	SS
MR	9
PCn	10
AR	11
BD	6
PCm	8
SI	9
WR	6
VO	7
CO	13
IN	12
LNS	7
DS	7

$$\frac{9}{\text{(MR)}} + \frac{10}{\text{(PCn)}} + \frac{11}{\text{(AR)}} = \frac{30}{\text{(Sum of Scaled Scores)}} = 100 \quad \textit{Gf}\ \text{Cluster}$$

$$\frac{6}{\text{(BD)}} + \frac{8}{\text{(PCm)}} = \frac{14}{\text{(Sum of Scaled Scores)}} = 83 \quad \textit{Gv}\ \text{Cluster}$$

$$\frac{9}{\text{(MR)}} + \frac{10}{\text{(PCn)}} = \frac{19}{\text{(Sum of Scaled Scores)}} = 97 \quad \textit{Gf}\text{-nonverbal Cluster}$$

$$\frac{9}{\text{(SI)}} + \frac{6}{\text{(WR)}} = \frac{15}{\text{(Sum of Scaled Scores)}} = 86 \quad \textit{Gf}\text{-verbal Cluster}$$

$$\frac{6}{\text{(WR)}} + \frac{7}{\text{(VO)}} = \frac{13}{\text{(Sum of Scaled Scores)}} = 81 \quad \textit{Gc}\text{-VL Cluster}$$

$$\frac{13}{\text{(CO)}} + \frac{12}{\text{(IN)}} = \frac{25}{\text{(Sum of Scaled Scores)}} = 114 \quad \textit{Gc}\text{-K0 Cluster}$$

$$\frac{}{\text{(VO)}} + \frac{}{\text{(IN)}} = \frac{}{\text{(Sum of Scaled Scores)}} = \quad \textit{Gc}\text{-LTM Cluster}$$

$$\frac{7}{\text{(LNS)}} + \frac{7}{\text{(DS)}} = \frac{14}{\text{(Sum of Scaled Scores)}} = 83 \quad \textit{Gsm}\text{-MW Cluster}$$

Figure 4.7 (Continued)

Note: For Ryan, the Gc-LTM Cluster is not interpretable. Therefore, no standard score is computed for that cluster.

Step 7c. Conduct Planned Clinical Comparisons.

Calculate the difference between the clusters in the comparison. If the size of the difference is equal to or greater than the value reported in the following table, then the difference is uncommon. If the size of the difference is less than the table value, then the difference is not uncommon.

Clinical Comparison	Difference Score (use values from Step 7b to calculate difference score)	Critical Value	Uncommon (U) or Not Uncommon (NU)
Gf versus *Gv*	100 − 83 = 17	≥ 21	NU
Gf-nonverbal versus *Gv*	97 − 83 = 14	≥ 24	NU
Gf-nonverbal versus *Gf*-verbal	97 − 86 = 11	≥ 24	NU
Gc-VL versus *Gc*-K0	114 − 81 = 33	≥ 17	U
Gc-LTM versus *Gsm*-MW		≥ 24	
Gc-LTM versus *Gf*-verbal		≥ 17	

Note: Difference scores that are equal to or exceed the critical values listed in the third column of this table should be denoted Uncommon (U). Difference scores that are less than these critical values should be denoted Not Uncommon (NU).

Step 7d. Describe results of Planned Clinical Comparisons.

Regardless of the outcome of Step 7c, review Rapid Reference 4.13 to identify an example of an interpretive statement that most appropriately describes the results of the child's clinical cluster comparison. If the child demonstrated a Normative Weakness in any clinical cluster, refer to Rapid Reference 4.14 for hypotheses about the meaning of such findings. Rapid Reference 4.14 also provides suggestions for educational interventions and instructional strategies that may be useful for children who demonstrate uncommon patterns of performance on the WISC-IV clinical clusters.

Note: MR = Matrix Reasoning; PCn = Picture Concepts; AR = Arithmetic; BD = Block Design; PCm = Picture Completion; SI = Similarities; WR = Word Reasoning; VO = Vocabulary; CO = Comprehension; IN = Information; LNS = Letter-Number Sequencing; DS = Digit Span.

Figure 4.7 (Continued)

expression tasks; (2) provide a glossary of terms that he can refer to when completing reading assignments; (3) ensure that test questions do not include vocabulary terms that he does not know; and so forth. See Rapid Reference 4.14 for additional suggestions.

It is also possible that uncommon differences between clinical clusters are due to factors other than true differences in ability. A child may demonstrate an uncommon difference between two clinical clusters, *suggesting* a true difference in ability; but further investigation may reveal that the uncommon difference is more appropriately attributable to factors that are external to the child. For example, a child who obtains a Nonverbal Fluid Reasoning (*Gf*-nonverbal) Cluster of 109 and a Visual Processing *(Gv)* Cluster of 80 is considered to have a true (and uncommon) difference between the abilities presumed to underlie these clusters (i.e., Table 4.6 shows that a 24-point difference in the *Gf*-nonverbal > *Gv* comparison is needed to be considered uncommon). Although each cluster in the comparison is unitary, in some cases it makes sense to examine the subtest scaled scores composing each cluster to determine whether external, rather than internal (cognitive), factors are the primary cause for the observed difference. For instance, suppose a child's scores on the subtests that make up the Nonverbal Fluid Reasoning (*Gf*-nonverbal) Cluster were both within the Average Range (e.g., Matrix Reasoning scaled score of 12 and Picture Concepts scaled score of 11), and the child's scores on the subtests making up the Visual Processing *(Gv)* Cluster were in the Below Average to Average Range (e.g., Block Design scaled score of 5 and Picture Completion scaled score of 8). Before concluding that the child's *Gv* ability is a Normative Weakness and less well developed than his or her *Gf*-nonverbal ability, it makes sense to examine the differences between the task demands of the three subtests on which the child obtained scaled scores in the Average Range and the subtest on which the child earned a Below Average scaled score.

Consider the *response formats* for each subtest in the above example. Of these four subtests, Block Design is the only one that *requires* a motor response. Although a pointing response, for example, is acceptable on the Matrix Reasoning and Picture Concepts subtests, the primary response format for these subtests is oral. Furthermore, consideration of the *item formats* for each of the four subtests reveals that Block Design is the only test with strict time limits. Based on these qualitative subtest characteristics, the examiner may hypothesize that the nature of the response format and item format of the Block Design subtest—namely, a timed task requiring a motor response—resulted in a low Block Design score, which attenuated the Visual Processing *(Gv)* Cluster, leading to a spurious finding of an uncommon difference between the Visual Processing *(Gv)* and Nonverbal

Fluid Reasoning (*Gf*-nonverbal) Clusters. To test this hypothesis, you may identify other WISC-IV tasks that are timed and require a motor response (i.e., Coding, Symbol Search, and Cancellation) to determine whether the child's performance on these additional measures is also hindered by the same qualitative characteristics. To test this hypothesis further, you may administer tests from other batteries that measure visual processing in a manner that does not require a motor response under timed conditions. For example, the WJ III includes tests of visual processing (e.g., Spatial Relations and Picture Recognition) that are not timed and that do not require a motor response. If performance on these visual processing tests is within the Average Range or higher, then the hypothesis that the score on Block Design is spuriously low due to qualitative factors and not underlying ability is supported and the uncommon Visual Processing *(Gv)* Cluster < Nonverbal Fluid Reasoning (*Gf*-nonverbal) Cluster difference is best explained using qualitative information regarding task characteristics rather than true differences in ability.

 TEST YOURSELF

1. **John obtained scaled scores of 8 and 9 on the WISC-IV Digit Span and Letter-Number Sequencing tasks, respectively. When interpreting his WMI of 89, you should consider the Index as representing**

   (a) a unitary ability.

   (b) a nonunitary ability.

   (c) a normative strength.

   (d) a key asset.

2. **The approach to test interpretation presented in this chapter emphasizes the importance of featuring the**

   (a) subtest profile.

   (b) Index profile.

   (c) Verbal-Performance discrepancy.

   (d) FSIQ.

3. **A noninterpretable Index should be used when calculating the mean of all Indexes for use in person-relative (ipsative) analyses.** True or False?

4. **Using the normative descriptive system to describe WISC-IV Index scores, a score of 119 should be described as**

   (a) a Normative Strength.

   (b) Within Normal Limits.

   (c) a Normative Weakness.

   (d) none of the above.

(continued)

5. Mary obtained a VCI of 122, which is significantly higher than her other Indexes and is uncommon in the normal population. Mary's VCI is *best* described as a

   (a) Key Asset.

   (b) Personal Strength.

   (c) noninterpretable Index.

   (d) Normative Strength.

6. **An Index that is an uncommon Personal Weakness and a Normative Weakness should be considered a High-Priority Concern.** True or False?

7. **The difference between Joseph's highest and lowest Indexes was 26 standard score points. Therefore, Joseph's FSIQ is**

   (a) noninterpretable.

   (b) interpretable.

   (c) interpretable if you have reason to believe that his lowest Index is invalid.

   (d) a High-Priority Concern.

8. **The new WISC-IV Clinical Clusters can be used in Planned Clinical Comparisons only when they represent unitary abilities.** True or False?

9. **Which of the following is *not true* of the interpretive method presented in this book:**

   (a) Individual subtest interpretation is featured.

   (b) Base rate data are used to evaluate the clinical meaningfulness of score variability.

   (c) Interpretation is grounded firmly in the CHC theory of cognitive abilities.

   (d) Guidance regarding the use of supplemental measures to test hypotheses about significant subtest variation or outlier scores is provided.

10. **The variability among Anna's subtest scaled scores composing the VCI is uncommon, but all her scaled scores are > 12. Anna's range of observed functioning in the area of Crystallized Intelligence can be described as a notable integrity.** True or False?

Answers: 1. a; 2. b; 3. True; 4. a; 5. a; 6. True; 7. a; 8. True; 9. a; 10. True

Five

STRENGTHS AND WEAKNESSES OF THE WISC-IV

Many additions and modifications have been made to the latest version of the WISC. This chapter provides a brief summary of the strengths and weaknesses of the WISC-IV in terms of its development and content, administration and scoring, reliability and validity, interpretation guidelines, and standardization procedures.

The WISC-IV has several strengths and represents the most substantial revision of any Wechsler scale to date. Some of the WISC-IV's most salient strengths include (1) a robust four-factor structure across the age range of the test; (2) increased developmental appropriateness (e.g., via modified instructions, the addition of specific teaching items); (3) a deemphasis on time; (4) improved psychometric properties; and (5) an exemplary standardization sample.

Many of the ways in which the instrument has been altered and restructured are considered strengths, including (1) the addition of fluid reasoning tasks; (2) better representation of short-term memory (viz., Working Memory); (3) elimination of factorially complex composites (i.e., VIQ, PIQ, Freedom from Distractibility); and (4) emphasis on psychological constructs consistent with contemporary psychometric theory and research.

Although the WISC-IV, like all major intelligence batteries, has weaknesses, we do not consider any of them major. For example, although we have included several ways in which the validity data reported in the *WISC-IV Technical and Interpretive Manual* (The Psychological Corporation, 2003) do not fully meet some of the criteria set forth in the joint standards for educational and psychological tests (American Educational Research Association, American Psychological Association, National Council on Measurement in Education, 1999), these standards are new and most current intelligence tests fall short for the same reasons cited here (for a detailed discussion, see Braden & Niebling, 2004). Rapid References 5.1–5.5 include the strengths and weaknesses of the WISC-IV that we consider most important for examiners to know. These strengths and weaknesses are organized in five categories: (1) test development and content (Rapid Reference

5.1), (2) administration and scoring (Rapid Reference 5.2), (3) reliability and validity (Rapid Reference 5.3), (4) interpretation (Rapid Reference 5.4), and (5) standardization (Rapid Reference 5.5).

≡Rapid Reference 5.1

Strengths and Weaknesses of the WISC-IV: Test Development and Content

Strengths	Weaknesses
• The WISC-IV is the first revision of the WISC that represents a *substantial improvement over its predecessors,* mainly because it adheres more closely to theory (Flanagan, Kaufman, & Mascolo, 2004). • The FSIQ is based on four Indexes that yield a broader representation of general intellectual functioning than the WISC-III FSIQ. • The VIQ and PIQ were eliminated, presumably because they were factorially complex and, therefore, difficult to interpret (Flanagan et al., 2004). • A Working Memory Index is included. The Index formerly-known-as Freedom from Distractibility has been renamed and restructured. Digit Span is now paired with Letter-Number Sequencing, a good measure of working memory. The factorially complex Arithmetic subtest has been relegated to supplemental status—a good decision by the publisher—and the new scale name (Working Memory Index) corresponds to a well-researched aspect of executive functioning. Eliminating the label "Freedom from Distractibility" (FD)—a label first recommended by Cohen (1952) and perpetuated by Kaufman (1975)—was sensible because it had long outlived its usefulness. The FD factor (often	• Long-Term Retrieval *(Glr)*[a] and Auditory Processing *(Ga)* are not represented, although *Glr* is measured by the Children's Memory Scale (CMS; Cohen, 1997), for example, and *Ga* is measured to some extent by the Wechsler Individual Achievement Test–Second Edition (WIAT-II; The Psychological Corporation, 2002), both of which are linked to the WISC-IV through a common sample (Flanagan et al., 2004). • Test items were developed and reviewed by expert panels to ensure that they reflected their intended constructs. However, details regarding the selection and composition of the panels are lacking (Braden & Niebling, 2004). • Results of item bias analyses were used to modify or eliminate items that evidenced bias. However, a summary of findings (e.g., item bias index means, variances) was not provided (Braden & Niebling, 2004). • Reduction of manipulatives, through the elimination of Picture Arrangement and Object Assembly, seemingly reduces the "engaging" quality of the WISC-IV as compared to the WISC-III, WISC-R, and WISC. Apart from its use of manipulatives, many examiners found Picture Arrangement to be a valuable sub-

composed of Arithmetic, Digit Span, and Coding/Digit Symbol) was an artifact of the factor analyses of a limited battery of subtests (those composing a variety of Wechsler batteries, starting with the Wechsler-Bellevue, and including the WISC-R and WISC-III) and should not be considered a valid psychological construct (Carroll, 1993).

- The VCI, WMI, and PSI include qualitatively different measures of the constructs they are presumed to measure (Crystallized Intelligence [Gc], Short-Term Memory [Gsm], and Processing Speed [Gs], respectively), making interpretation of these broad cognitive abilities psychometrically sound under certain circumstances (e.g., when the construct is considered a unitary ability; see Chapter 4 of the present volume, as well as Flanagan et al., 2004).

- Items were added at the lower and upper levels of subtests to increase their floors and ceilings, respectively (see Chapter 1 and Appendix D for details).

- Because the WISC-III Information subtest seemed more highly correlated with knowledge acquired in school as compared to other VCI tests, its inclusion as a supplemental VCI subtest on the WISC-IV ensures that the core VCI scale has a reduced dependence on exposure to formal schooling.

- Dropping some of the original 11 subtests, moving others to supplemental status, and adding new ones strengthened the factor structure (though some confounds remain; see Chapter 1 as well as Flanagan et al., 2004, and Keith et al., 2004).

- Mixed measures of ability were either dropped (e.g., Picture Arrange-

ment clinically. Indeed, it was the only WISC-III subtest that depicted interpersonal situations. There are no such subtests on the WISC-IV, a test structure that Wechsler—the consummate clinician—never would have approved. The structure of the WISC-IV would have permitted the inclusion of Picture Arrangement as a supplemental subtest.

- The WISC-IV, like its predecessors, does not include controlled learning tests, or tests that allow corrective feedback throughout. These types of tests are useful because they allow examiners to observe the learning process more directly and determine whether a child benefits from feedback.

- Substituting a supplemental test for a core battery test may alter the underlying cognitive construct intended to be measured by the Index (e.g., when Picture Completion is substituted for Matrix Reasoning, the resultant PRI will represent a Visual Processing/Crystallized Intelligence [Gv/Gc] blend much more so than a Visual Processing/Fluid Reasoning [Gv/Gf] blend; Flanagan et al., 2004).

- Separate norms tables for Visual Processing (Gv) and Fluid Reasoning (Gf) were not made available in the WISC-IV Administration and Scoring Manual. (Wechsler, 2003). However, The Psychological Corporation provided us with the data necessary to calculate separate Gv and Gf Indexes (see Chapter 4 and Appendix H).

- Matrix Reasoning appears to be the only relatively pure measure of Fluid Reasoning (Gf), although a combination of Matrix Reasoning and Picture Concepts provides an adequate Gf-nonverbal cluster (see Chapter 4). Alternatively, a combination of

(continued)

ment) or moved to supplemental status (e.g., Picture Completion).

- Picture Concepts appears to be a good visual analog to Similarities (a "verbal concepts" test).
- The developmental appropriateness of the instrument was improved through the modification of instructions and addition of sample and practice items.
- Updated artwork makes the instrument more attractive and engaging to children.

Matrix Reasoning, Picture Concepts, and Arithmetic may be used to represent a broad *Gf* cluster (Keith et al., 2004; see also Chapter 4).

- The colors on some Matrix Reasoning items may be distracting and potentially unfair to colorblind individuals.

ª Long-Term Retrieval is the ability to store information in and fluently retrieve new or previously acquired information from long-term memory. While the WISC-IV measures *what* is stored in long-term memory (e.g., Information, Vocabulary), it does not measure the *efficiency* by which this information is initially stored in and later retrieved from long-term memory.

≡ *Rapid Reference 5.2*

Strengths and Weaknesses of the WISC-IV: Administration and Scoring

Strengths	Weaknesses
• The WISC-IV places considerably less emphasis on time as compared to its predecessors. With the addition of a "no time bonus" option for Block Design and the allowance of more flexible timing for Picture Completion, the latest edition of the WISC can be administered using time limits only for those tests that were designed to measure speed directly (i.e., Coding, Symbol Search, and Cancellation). • The WISC-IV has good subtest *floors*, meaning that it contains a sufficient number of easy items to reliably distinguish between individuals functioning in the average, below average, and lower extreme ranges of ability.	• Sections of the protocol or Record Form are confusing. For example, the analysis page includes three subtest-level discrepancy comparisons with no rationale as to why these particular comparisons were selected. Subsequent to the publication of the WISC-IV, however, The Psychological Corporation provided a rationale for the Similarities–Picture Concepts comparison. Specifically, The Psychological Corporation stated that while the task demands of the two subtests are similar (i.e., understanding the common concept among two or more things), the stimuli and response modalities of the two subtests differ—Similarities uses verbal stimuli

- The WISC-IV has good subtest *ceilings,* meaning that it contains a sufficient number of difficult items to reliably distinguish between individuals functioning in the average, above average, and upper extreme ranges of ability.

- The WISC-IV has good *item gradients,* meaning that subtest items are approximately equally spaced in difficulty along the entire subtest scale, and the spacing between items is small enough to allow for reliable discrimination between individuals of different ability ranges on the construct measured by the subtest.

- Scoring criteria were revised to be more straightforward.

- A Block Design No Time Bonus (BDN) process score can be calculated. This feature may be useful for a child who has physical limitations, lacks problem-solving strategies, or has personality characteristics that are believed to affect performance on timed tasks (e.g., perfectionism).

- Process scores are available for the Cancellation Random (CAR) and Cancellation Structured (CAS) items, which allow the child's visual selective attention and speed of processing to be evaluated using two modes of presentation.

- Digits Forward and Digits Backward may be scored separately, allowing for a comparison between Memory Span (Digits Forward) and Working Memory (Digits Backward).

- The WISC-IV allows for the calculation of two digit span process scores, namely Longest Digit Span Forward (LDSF) and Longest

- and requires a verbal response, whereas the Picture Concepts subtest uses visual stimuli and requires a motor response (see The Psychological Corporation's Web site). Based on this rationale, it appears that differences in subtest stimuli may also be the rationale for the other subtest comparisons listed on the analysis page (i.e., Coding–Symbol Search and Digit Span–Letter-Number Sequencing).

- Because the reliability of the separate Digit Span Forward and Digit Span Backward scores is lower than the combined score (Digit Span), when meaningful differences are found, they should be corroborated with other data sources.

- The directions for the Letter-Number Sequencing subtest indicate that the examinee must first recall the numbers followed by the letters. However, if the opposite occurs, the examinee is given credit. The Psychological Corporation, however, maintains that regardless of how the child reorders the numbers and letters, he or she is using working memory in order to place the numbers in sequence followed by the letters in sequence (see The Psychological Corporation's Web site). Moreover, data analyses of the standardization sample showed that the task is equally difficult when either numbers or letters are given first. The purported reason for instructing examinees to give the numbers first is to provide them with a set or structured way of approaching the task, which is primarily intended to help young children or children who have difficulty structuring their own work.

- Some items on the Letter-Number Sequencing subtest allow credit to

(continued)

Digit Span Backward (LDSB). Evaluation of these process scores may help examiners evaluate a child's memory capacity further when considerable variability in terms of correct and incorrect responses was demonstrated throughout either the Digits Forward or Digits Backward (or both) components of the Digit Span subtest. For example, when variability on the Digit Span subtest leads to a spuriously low Digit Span scaled score (e.g., as a result of a child's tendency to respond impulsively), LDSF and LDSB will likely provide a better estimate of actual memory capacity.

- The WISC-IV requires examiners to record examinees' responses verbatim, which encourages item analysis and, therefore, adds to the clinical utility of the WISC-IV. For example, examiners may review a child's verbal responses and discover certain patterns (e.g., word-finding difficulties, verbosity).

be given for verbatim responses. Although this is counterintuitive to the task demands of a working memory task (i.e., transforming information), The Psychological Corporation explained that the early items on the Letter-Number Sequencing subtest measure short-term auditory memory (or memory span) which is a precursor skill to working memory. Thus, for younger children, the Letter-Number Sequencing test may assess memory span only, a prerequisite skill for the development of working memory. According to The Psychological Corporation, item set and norms purportedly reflect this change as children develop working memory (see The Psychological Corporation's Web site).

- Some correct and incorrect responses to items on Matrix Reasoning and Picture Completion are not explained—therefore, it is not clear to many examiners why certain responses are given (or not given) credit. The Psychological Corporation, however, has been quick to respond to inquiries of this nature. For example, on their Web site, they stated that for specific Matrix Reasoning items, children can arrive at correct answers other than those specified in the manual; however, when these answers do not represent the most parsimonious solution, they are not awarded credit.

- Audiotapes are not used for memory tests, which would have provided a more reliable means of administering the Digit Span and Letter-Number Sequencing subtests, in particular.

- Examiner training activities are not included in the WISC-IV Administration and Scoring Manual (Wechsler, 2003).

≋ *Rapid Reference 5.3*

Strengths and Weaknesses of the WISC-IV: Reliability and Validity

Strengths	Weaknesses
• Reliabilities of the FSIQ and four Indexes are generally high (i.e., .90+) across the age range; reliabilities of subtests are generally medium (i.e., .80–.89) across the age range.	• Invariance of the factor structure across the age range of the WISC-IV was not investigated by The Psychological Corporation. However, Keith and colleagues (2004) found that the four factors that underlie the WISC-IV are stable across the entire age range of the test. This study was summarized in Chapter 1.
• Test-retest reliability (mean interval = 32 days) was provided for 243 children and adolescents aged 6–16 years. Coefficients for the FSIQ and the four Indexes were high to medium for each of the five age groups studied (ranging from .96 for the FSIQ at ages 12–13 to .84 for the WMI at ages 8–9).	• Correlational studies are provided between the WISC-IV and nine other instruments, *eight* of which are also published by The Psychological Corporation, including five Wechsler scales. It would have been desirable for The Psychological Corporation to report correlations with a more diverse group of cognitive and achievement tests, including measures from other publishers (such as the Woodcock-Johnson III Tests of Cognitive Abilities and Tests of Achievement [WJ III COG, WJ III ACH; Woodcock, McGrew, & Mather, 2001]; the Stanford-Binet Intelligence Scales, Fifth Edition [SB5; Roid, 2003]; and the Cognitive Assessment System [CAS; Das & Naglieri, 1997]), to name a few.
• Construct validity of the four Indexes is supported by *exploratory factor analysis* (EFA). These analyses support the structure for core subtests and for a combination of core and supplemental subtests. Only Picture Concepts, at ages 6–7, fails to load substantially on its designated factor (i.e., PRI).	
• Construct validity of the four Indexes also appears to be supported by *confirmatory factor analysis* (CFA), although the support is stronger when only core subtests are included in the analyses. In the analyses of core subtests, goodness-of-fit (GFI) statistics ranged from .96 to .98; when supplemental subtests were added to the analyses, GFI values for four factors dropped to .90–.95. Similarly, root mean square error of approximation (RMSEA) values were excellent for the core analyses (.03–.05) and good when all	• The WISC-IV FSIQ correlated .87 with Total Achievement on the Wechsler Individual Achievement Test–Second Edition [WIAT-II; The Psychological Corporation, 2001]. This coefficient is comparable in magnitude to the correlations between the FSIQ on the WISC-IV and the FSIQ on other Wechsler scales (i.e., WPPSI-III, WISC-III,

(continued)

subtests were analyzed (.04–.06). Nevertheless, in order to evaluate the CFA studies sufficiently, an examination of factor loadings is necessary. These values were not reported in the *WISC-IV Technical and Interpretive Manual* (The Psychological Corporation, 2003).

- The WISC-IV FSIQ correlated substantially with the FSIQ on the WISC-III (.89), WPPSI-III (.89), WAIS-III (.89), and WASI (.86), supporting the criterion-related validity of the WISC-IV global cognitive score. The validity of the VCI was also given strong support because it correlated in the .80s (.83–.87) with verbal measures on the other four Wechsler scales.

- The *WISC-IV Technical and Interpretive Manual* (The Psychological Corporation, 2003) provides initial clinical validity data by offering Index and subtest profiles for 16 clinical groups: Intellectually Gifted; mild and moderate Mental Retardation; Learning Disorders (four separate groups with disorders in "reading," "reading and written expression," "mathematics," and "reading, written expression, and mathematics"); Attention-Deficit/Hyperactivity Disorder (one ADHD group with learning disorders, one without); Language-Impaired (one group with expressive disorders, one with mixed receptive-expressive); Traumatic Brain Injury (one group with open head injuries, one with closed head injuries); Autistic; Asperger's Syndrome; and Motor Impairment.

WAIS-III, and WASI; mean = .88). This curious finding suggests that the WISC-IV and WIAT-II may be *measuring constructs that are more similar than they are different.*

- It was assumed that each subtest would correlate highest with subtests on its own scale, but that was not always the case. At least 40% of all intersubtest correlations represented a violation of this assumption (Flanagan et al., 2004).

- No empirical support is provided for specific claims regarding the development of treatment plans and their presumed correlates to neuropsychological foundations (Braden & Niebling, 2004).

- Although g-loadings were used to explain inconsistencies in the expected pattern of intercorrelations among subtests, they were not reported in the *WISC-IV Technical and Interpretive Manual* (The Psychological Corporation, 2003). However, we obtained g-loadings from The Psychological Corporation and independent researchers who derived them through different methods (Keith et al., 2004). Both sets of g-loadings are reported in Chapter 1 (Appendix C).

- Most of the cited evidence that Indexes and subtests elicit specific psychological processes is based on studies with previous versions of the WISC; however, because common item content was subjectively identified and processes that explain interitem correlations were inferred, no direct evidence is currently available to substantiate claims that examinees actually use those processes (Braden & Niebling, 2004).

- Interview evidence regarding examinees' response processes was obtained and analyzed for two new subtests, but not for other subtests, indicating that validity claims with respect to these processes are based on insufficient data (Braden & Niebling, 2004).[a]

- The use of the term "process score" implies that the score reflects a neuropsychological process, but no direct evidence is available to support this implication (Braden & Niebling, 2004).

- Score differences between groups defined by ethnic, gender, and socioeconomic status are not mentioned. This omission is curious, given the debate that was sparked by research on ethnic group differences with previous editions of the WISC (Braden & Niebling, 2004).

[a] The *response processes standard* refers to evidence that supports the contention that examinees use intended psychological processes when responding to test items (e.g., a reasoning test elicits reasoning rather than recall; Braden & Niebling, 2004).

≡Rapid Reference 5.4

Strengths and Weaknesses of the WISC-IV: Interpretation

Strengths	Weaknesses
• Differences between Indexes required for statistical significance (critical values) are available as well as the cumulative percentages of the standardization sample (base rates)[a] obtaining various Index differences. • Critical values and base rates are available for all process score comparisons.	• The *WISC-IV Technical and Interpretive Manual* (The Psychological Corporation, 2003) provides limited information and guidance on test interpretation (Flanagan et al., 2004). • There are continued reliance and emphasis on subtest-level pairwise comparisons (i.e., comparing subtest pairs, such as Block Design and Matrix Reasoning) and subtest-level ipsative analysis (e.g., comparing one subtest to the mean of the 10 core battery subtests). • Critical values are provided for 105 subtest-level comparisons in the *WISC-IV Administration and Scoring Manual* (Wechsler, 2003, Appendix B.3) with no guidance on how to use this information, and no consideration for the "statistical significance" errors that occur when many comparisons are made simultaneously. • Interpretive steps and interpretive tables are not presented sequentially, which detracts from the user-friendliness of the manual. For example, early steps correspond to high-numbered tables and later steps correspond to low-numbered tables. • Although an interpretive step for process analysis of performance on certain subtests was included, there is little to no guidance on how to interpret the findings of this type of analysis. • Although Chapter 6 of the *WISC-IV Technical and Interpretive Manual* (The Psychological Corporation,

2003) provides a lengthy description of how examiners may use test findings to identify strengths and weaknesses in a child's scaled score profile, implying that there is value in the method with regard to clinical and educational interventions, no evidence is cited in direct support of this claim (Braden & Niebling, 2004).

- Discussion related to the identification of person-relative strengths and weaknesses using Index, subtest, and within-subtest responses does not include mention of the limitations of these methods that have been cited in the literature over the past decade.

[a] *Base rate* refers to the prevalence or frequency of an observed score difference in the normal population. Typically, score differences that occur in less than 10% of the population are considered uncommon and therefore may be clinically meaningful.

≡Rapid Reference 5.5

Strengths and Weaknesses of the WISC-IV: Standardization

Strengths	Weaknesses
• The WISC-IV was stratified according to a broad base of variables closely matching March 2000 U.S. Census data.	• No major weaknesses.
• The WISC-IV is co-equated with the WIAT-II, based on a linking sample of 550 participants aged 6–16. However, no information is available regarding the representativeness of the sample.	

TEST YOURSELF

1. **The WISC-IV is the first revision of the WISC that represents a *substantial improvement over its predecessors*, mainly because it adheres more closely to theory.** True or False?

2. **The Block Design No Time Bonus process score can be useful in which of the following situations?**
   (a) When a child has physical limitations
   (b) When a child lacks problem-solving strategies
   (c) When a child has personality characteristics believed to affect performance on timed tests
   (d) All of the above

3. **The WISC-IV requires examiners to record examinees' responses verbatim, which facilitates later item analysis (e.g., error analysis) and, therefore, adds to the clinical utility of the WISC-IV.** True or False?

4. **Which of the following statements is true regarding the construct validity of the four WISC-IV Indexes:**
   (a) The construct validity of the four WISC-IV Indexes is supported by confirmatory factor analysis only.
   (b) The construct validity of the four WISC-IV Indexes is supported by exploratory factor analysis only.
   (c) The construct validity of the four WISC-IV Indexes has not yet been supported because the battery is too new.
   (d) The construct validity of the four WISC-IV indexes is supported by both confirmatory and exploratory factor analysis.

5. **Which of the following cognitive abilities is not represented on the WISC-IV?**
   (a) Crystallized Intelligence *(Gc)*
   (b) Fluid Intelligence *(Gf)*
   (c) Auditory Processing *(Ga)*
   (d) Short-Term Memory *(Gsm)*

6. **Which of the following WISC-III VCI subtests has been dropped to supplemental status on the WISC-IV?**
   (a) Information
   (b) Similarities
   (c) Comprehension
   (d) Vocabulary

7. **Because the reliability of the separate Digit Span Forward and Digit Span Backward scores is lower than that of the combined score (Digit Span), when meaningful differences are found between these scores, they should be corroborated with other data sources.** True or False?

Answers: 1. True; 2. d; 3. True; 4. d; 5. c; 6. a; 7. True

Six

CLINICAL APPLICATIONS
A Review of Special Group Studies with the WISC-IV
and Assessment of Low-Incidence Populations

REVIEW OF SPECIAL GROUP STUDIES AND UTILITY OF THE PROCESS APPROACH WITH THE WISC-IV

Nancy Hebben

Special Group Studies

WISC-IV test score results for several special groups are included in the *WISC-IV Technical and Interpretive Manual* (The Psychological Corporation, 2003) to help provide information about the test's specificity and its clinical utility for diagnostic assessment. The special groups studied included children with Autistic Disorder, children with Asperger's Disorder, children with Expressive Language Disorder, children with Mixed Receptive-Expressive Language Disorder, intellectually gifted children, children with mild or moderate Mental Retardation, children with Attention-Deficit/Hyperactivity Disorder (ADHD), children with learning disorders, children with learning disorders and ADHD, children with Traumatic Brain Injury (TBI), and children with Motor Impairment. The specific composition of each group is available in the manual.

Caution must be exercised when generalizing from these data for several reasons. The samples for these studies did not consist of randomly selected subjects and generally were based on small numbers, ranging from as few as 19 to as many as 89 subjects. In most cases, data are included from a number of independent clinical settings that did not guarantee that the same criteria and procedures were used for diagnosis. In a number of cases, the groups consisted of participants with a heterogeneous and diverse set of diagnoses. For example, the "children with learning disorders" group included children with reading, written expression, and mathematics disorders. The "children with TBI" group included children with both open and closed head injuries, as well as different causes and severities of brain injury.

It is crucial to remember that these are group data and are not necessarily representative of a whole diagnostic class, and in many cases, are not specific to the

---

The sections that make up Chapter 6 were written by invited contributors. Dawn Flanagan and Alan Kaufman edited the text and developed Rapid References 6.1–6.12.

diagnostic class. Though these data may be useful in describing individual children in terms of patterns of cognitive performance, they should not be used to make differential diagnoses. As Kaufman and Lichtenberger (2000) point out with regard to learning disability: "Many variables—including performance on standardized measures of achievement, academic history, developmental history, medical history, family history, and behavioral observations—must be combined to properly evaluate a child with a potential learning disability"(p. 205). This caution should be applied to each of the groups listed previously.

Children with Autistic Disorder and Asperger's Disorder

Rapid Reference 6.1 details the highest and lowest mean WISC-IV subtest scaled scores for children with Autistic Disorder and Asperger's Disorder. Given that children with Asperger's Disorder are unlike children with Autistic Disorder because they do not show clinically significant delays in language, it not surprising that two of three of their highest scores are on tasks dependent on language (i.e., Similarities and Information). In contrast, for children with Autistic Disorder, whose difficulties include Language Disorder, one of their three lowest scores was

≡Rapid Reference 6.1

Highest and Lowest Mean WISC-IV Subtest Scaled Scores of Children with Autistic Disorder and Asperger's Disorder

Autistic Disorder (FSIQ = 76.4) (N = 19)		Asperger's Disorder (FSIQ = 99.2) (N = 27)	
Highest Subtests	**Scaled Score**	**Highest Subtests**	**Scaled Score**
Block Design	7.9	Similarities	12.1
Matrix Reasoning	7.7	Information	12.0
Picture Concepts	7.4	Picture Completion	11.5
Lowest Subtests	**Scaled Score**	**Lowest Subtests**	**Scaled Score**
Comprehension	5.3	Symbol Search	8.2
Symbol Search	5.2	Cancellation	8.0
Coding	4.0	Coding	6.7

Source: Mean FSIQs and scaled scores are from the WISC-IV Technical and Interpretive Manual (The Psychological Corporation, 2003, Tables 5.35 and 5.36).

Note: The Arithmetic subtest is excluded because of very small sample sizes.

on a language-based task (e.g., Comprehension). Picture Completion, which was a high score for the children with Asperger's Disorder, might reflect the fact that this subtest requires attention to detail without the sensitivity to social interaction required by Picture Arrangement. One might speculate that Block Design was the highest score for the children with Autistic Disorder because this task is not related in any substantial way to Crystallized Intelligence and, therefore, has minimal language demands. Like many of the special groups, the lowest performances were on subtests that make up the PSI, which likely reflects the sensitivity of these measures to generalized cognitive impairment. See the section by Elizabeth O. Lichtenberger on pages 199–205 for a more thorough treatment of Autistic-Spectrum Disorders.

Children with Expressive Language Disorders and Mixed Receptive-Expressive Language Disorders

As expected, and as can be seen in Rapid Reference 6.2, children with language disorders show their best performances on tasks that make little demand on lan-

≡Rapid Reference 6.2

Highest and Lowest Mean WISC-IV Subtest Scaled Scores of Children with Expressive Language Disorders

Expressive Language Disorder (FSIQ = 83.0) (N = 27)		Mixed Receptive-Expressive Language Disorder (FSIQ = 77.3) (N = 40)	
Highest Subtests	**Scaled Score**	**Highest Subtests**	**Scaled Score**
Block Design	9.6	Cancellation	8.4
Cancellation	9.4	Block Design	8.3
Picture Completion	8.4	Picture Completion	8.0
Matrix Reasoning	8.4		
Lowest Subtests	**Scaled Score**	**Lowest Subtests**	**Scaled Score**
Comprehension	6.8	Vocabulary	6.2
Vocabulary	6.8	Comprehension	6.2
Arithmetic	6.8	Coding	6.0

Source: Mean FSIQs and scaled scores are from the WISC-IV Technical and Interpretive Manual (The Psychological Corporation, 2003, Tables 5.31 and 5.32).

Note: Sample sizes for Arithmetic are 18 (Expressive) and 25 (Mixed).

guage and they do most poorly on tasks reliant on language skills, particularly ones that require complex verbal expression (i.e., Comprehension and Vocabulary). In addition, Coding, though technically a performance test, is a language-like task that requires a written code and the use of symbols, both areas of difficulty for children with language disorders, and an area of weakness for the children with Mixed Receptive-Expressive Language Disorder.

Children Who Are Intellectually Gifted or Mentally Retarded

Rapid Reference 6.3 indicates that the intellectually gifted child does best on conceptually based tasks, but interestingly does not show a strength on tasks dependent on speeded processing. This is particularly important because clinicians are sometimes tempted to infer the presence of acquired deficits in bright individuals who do not show Above Average or better performances across all subtest scores. Intellectual giftedness may reflect Superior conceptual ability without Superior performance on speeded tasks. It is possible that this pattern of performance in children who are intellectually gifted reveals a response set reflecting that they are more interested in optimal performance and accuracy than speed. For a more comprehensive discussion of gifted students, see the section by Martin A. Volker and Le Adelle Phelps in Chapter 7.

It is very difficult to analyze the pattern of strengths and weaknesses for the children with Mental Retardation because this group combines multiple etiologies. Mental Retardation may result from acquired brain damage as well as a variety of genetic and congenital conditions, each potentially affecting the brain and the development of intelligence in a different way. The pattern of strengths and weaknesses for children with Mild or Moderate Mental Retardation appears to be one of best performance on Cancellation, a task that requires simple processing and scanning with minimal reliance on conceptualization. Their poorest performances are generally on those tasks that rely heavily on acquired knowledge (i.e., Vocabulary and Arithmetic). See the section by Elizabeth O. Lichtenberger on pages 205–208 for a more thorough treatment of Mental Retardation.

Children with Attention-Deficit/Hyperactivity Disorder with and without Learning Disorders

Rapid Reference 6.4 shows the highest and lowest scores for a sample of children with ADHD and no Learning Disorder compared with a sample of children with ADHD and Learning Disorder. Though this study contains the largest sample sizes among the special group studies, the data need to be interpreted with special caution because of the heterogeneity of learning disorders included in the sample. It is very likely that children with Mathematics Disorder will have a different pattern of strengths and weaknesses than children with Reading Disorder. In cases where one group's strength is the other's weakness, the mean score of the

≡ Rapid Reference 6.3

Highest and Lowest Mean WISC-IV Subtest Scaled Scores of Children Who Are Intellectually Gifted or Have Mental Retardation

Intellectually Gifted (FSIQ = 123.5) (N = 63)		Mild Mental Retardation (FSIQ = 60.5) (N = 63)		Moderate Mental Retardation (FSIQ = 46.4) (N = 57)	
Highest Subtests	**Scaled Score**	**Highest Subtests**	**Scaled Score**	**Highest Subtests**	**Scaled Score**
Vocabulary	14.6	Cancellation	6.2	Cancellation	4.4
Arithmetic	14.2	Word Reasoning	5.5	Word Reasoning	3.0
Similarities	14.1	Symbol Search	5.2	Similarities	2.7
Comprehension	14.1				
Lowest Subtests	**Scaled Score**	**Lowest Subtests**	**Scaled Score**	**Lowest Subtests**	**Scaled Score**
Digit Span	12.0	Vocabulary	4.1	Arithmetic	1.8
Coding	11.5	Matrix Reasoning	4.0	Comprehension	1.8
Cancellation	11.0	Arithmetic	3.8	Vocabulary	1.7

Source: Mean FSIQs and scaled scores are from the *WISC-IV Technical and Interpretive Manual* (The Psychological Corporation, 2003, Tables 5.22, 5.23, and 5.24).

Note: Sample sizes for Arithmetic are 24 (gifted), 25 (mild Mental Retardation), and 30 (moderate Mental Retardation).

Rapid Reference 6.4

Highest and Lowest Mean WISC-IV Subtest Scaled Scores of Children with Attention-Deficit/Hyperactivity Disorder (ADHD)

ADHD (FSIQ = 97.6) (*N* = 89)		Learning Disorder/ADHD (FSIQ = 88.1) (*N* = 45)	
Highest Subtests	**Scaled Score**	**Highest Subtests**	**Scaled Score**
Picture Concepts	10.5	Picture Completion	10.3
Picture Completion	10.4	Block Design	9.5
Word Reasoning	10.1	Word Reasoning	9.4
Similarities	10.1		
Lowest Subtests	**Scaled Score**	**Lowest Subtests**	**Scaled Score**
Cancellation	9.1	Arithmetic	7.7
Arithmetic	8.7	Letter-Number Sequencing	7.7
Coding	8.3	Coding	7.5

Source: Mean FSIQs and scaled scores are from *WISC-IV Technical and Interpretive Manual* (The Psychological Corporation, 2003, Tables 5.29 and 5.30).

Note: Sample sizes for Arithmetic are 45 (ADHD) and 27 (Learning Disorder/ADHD).

collapsed group for these subtests might literally cancel out the appearance of subtest patterns that are group specific.

Children with ADHD would be expected to show strengths in verbal and perceptual reasoning areas (as long as their attentional problems are not so great as to interfere with test-taking itself). Poor performance on Arithmetic, Cancellation, and Coding is likely related to the premium these tasks place on attention, concentration, and speed, all critical areas of concern in this population.

Children with Reading or Mathematics Disorders

In Rapid Reference 6.5 the highest and lowest subtest scores for children with Reading Disorder compared to children with Mathematics Disorder can be seen. These groups show somewhat different patterns of strengths and weaknesses. The children with Reading Disorder do best on tasks that are not language based (e.g., Cancellation), while the children with Mathematics Disorder do poorest on the Arithmetic subtest. The Arithmetic subtest is among the lowest scores for the

≡Rapid Reference 6.5

Highest and Lowest Mean WISC-IV Subtest Scaled Scores of Children with Reading or Math Disorder

Reading Disorder (FSIQ = 89.1) (N = 56)		Math Disorder (FSIQ = 88.7) (N = 33)	
Highest Subtests	**Scaled Score**	**Highest Subtests**	**Scaled Score**
Cancellation	10.1	Cancellation	8.9
Picture Concepts	9.3	Vocabulary	8.9
Symbol Search	9.2	Digit Span	8.9
Lowest Subtests	**Scaled Score**	**Lowest Subtests**	**Scaled Score**
Digit Span	8.0	Coding	7.8
Letter-Number Sequencing	7.7	Information	7.5
Arithmetic	7.7	Arithmetic	6.5

Source: Mean FSIQs and scaled scores are from the WISC-IV Technical and Interpretive Manual (The Psychological Corporation, 2003, Tables 5.25 and 5.27).

Note: Sample sizes for Arithmetic are 35 (Reading) and 22 (Math).

children with Reading Disorder as well, suggesting that this subtest measures a wider range of processes than arithmetic ability alone.

It is interesting that Cancellation is among the strengths for each group, but in the previous Rapid Reference was among the poorest performances for children with ADHD with or without learning disorders. This indicates that poor scanning and motor speed are not necessary prerequisites for learning disorders per se.

Children with Reading and Written Expression Disorders Compared to Children with Reading, Written Expression, and Mathematics Disorders

Rapid Reference 6.6 displays the patterns of highest and lowest subtest scores for two somewhat heterogeneous groups: one that included children with reading and written expression disorders and another that included children with reading, written expression, and mathematics disorders. Again, results based on such heterogeneous groups must be interpreted cautiously for the reasons previously noted. The WISC-IV Technical and Interpretive Manual (The Psychological Corporation, 2003) also points out the need for studies containing more homogeneous clinical groups. Though both groups would be expected to show weaknesses on

≡≡*Rapid Reference 6.6*

Highest and Lowest Mean WISC-IV Subtest Scaled Scores of Children with Reading and Written Expression Disorders

Reading and Written Expression Disorders (FSIQ = 92.5) (N = 35)		Reading, Written Expression, and Math Disorders (FSIQ = 87.6) (N = 42)	
Highest Subtests	**Scaled Score**	**Highest Subtests**	**Scaled Score**
Block Design	10.3	Cancellation	9.8
Picture Completion	9.7	Word Reasoning	9.0
Word Reasoning	9.7	Picture Concepts	8.7
		Comprehension	8.7
Lowest Subtests	**Scaled Score**	**Lowest Subtests**	**Scaled Score**
Arithmetic	8.5	Similarities	7.9
Digit Span	8.1	Digit Span	7.9
Coding	7.7	Information	7.7
		Arithmetic	7.0

Source: Mean FSIQs and scaled scores are from the *WISC-IV Technical and Interpretive Manual* (The Psychological Corporation, 2003, Tables 5.26 and 5.28).

Note: Sample sizes for Arithmetic are 23 (reading and writing) and 32 (reading, writing, and math).

tasks that are primarily based on language, Word Reasoning was among their strengths. Closer inspection of the data also revealed only small difference between the highest and lowest scores for both groups. Had the children with specific learning disabilities been grouped separately and their data analyzed separately, very different patterns might have emerged.

Children with Traumatic Brain Injury and Motor Impairment

Rapid Reference 6.7 contains the highest and lowest subtest scores for children with Traumatic Brain Injury (TBI) and Motor Impairment. These groups are also heterogeneous with respect to the localization and severity of their brain damage.

≣ Rapid Reference 6.7

Highest and Lowest Mean WISC-IV Subtest Scaled Scores of Children with Traumatic Brain Injury and Motor Impairment

Open Head Injury (FSIQ = 92.4) (N = 16)		Closed Head Injury (FSIQ = 90.0) (N = 27)		Motor Impairment (FSIQ = 85.7) (N = 21)	
Highest Subtests	**Scaled Score**	**Highest Subtests**	**Scaled Score**	**Highest Subtests**	**Scaled Score**
Picture Concepts	9.8	Digit Span	9.7	Word Reasoning	9.3
Digit Span	9.8	Picture Concepts	9.4	Vocabulary	9.1
Matrix Reasoning	9.3	Picture Completion	9.4	Digit Span	8.8
		Similarities	9.4		
		Information	9.4		
Lowest Subtests	**Scaled Score**	**Lowest Subtests**	**Scaled Score**	**Lowest Subtests**	**Scaled Score**
Letter-Number Sequencing	7.9	Cancellation	7.9	Symbol Search	6.2
Block Design	7.9	Coding	7.4	Cancellation	5.9
Coding	7.3	Symbol Search	7.2	Coding	5.9
Symbol Search	6.8				

Source: Mean FSIQs and scaled scores are from the WISC-IV Technical and Interpretive Manual (The Psychological Corporation, 2003, Tables 5.33, 5.34, and 5.37).

Note: Sample sizes for Arithmetic are 12 (open), 22 (closed), and 11 (Motor).

The highest subtest scores are in areas known to be fairly well preserved in TBI, while the lowest would be consistent with the conventional wisdom that TBIs impact working memory (i.e., attention and concentration) and speed of processing. This pattern likely reflects the diffuse cortical and subcortical pathology in many TBIs, rather than focal or localized damage. As expected, the lowest subtest scores for children with motor impairment are on paper and pencil tasks that are speeded.

A Comparison of the Verbal Conceptual Index and the Perceptual Reasoning Index for the Clinical Samples

The *WISC-IV Technical and Interpretive Manual* (The Psychological Corporation, 2003) suggests that the basic profile analysis begin with an evaluation of discrepancies among the Indexes and that this may be used to "help the practitioner identify potentially meaningful patterns of strengths and weaknesses" (pp. 102–103). Rapid Reference 6.8 presents notable differences between the VCI and PRI composite scores for the special study groups. A *notable discrepancy* is defined in the manual as a difference between Indexes that is ≥ 0.20 SDs (i.e., 3 standard score points or greater). The clinician should be careful in drawing conclusions based on this criterion because a 3-point difference between Indexes does not reflect functional or clinically significant differences in individual children. The discrepancies shown in Rapid Reference 6.8 do make some intuitive sense. For example, children with language disorders have a higher PRI than VCI, while children with Motor Impairment have a higher VCI than PRI. Nevertheless, it is recommended that you follow the interpretive steps outlined in Chapter 4 of this book.

Clinical Samples with Relatively Low Scores on the Processing Speed Index

Rapid Reference 6.9 compares the PSI composite scores relative to the combined mean of the VCI, PRI, and WMI composite scores for the special study groups. As defined before, a notable discrepancy is a difference of ≥ 0.20 SD or 3 standard score points between the two scores. It is important to notice that every group, including the intellectually gifted, show some degree of "deficit" on the PSI relative to the mean index on the VCI, PRI, and WMI. The lack of specificity of this Index, therefore, does not make it suitable for differential diagnosis. These data provide another instance where children who are intellectually gifted appear to have a deficit in a function—in this case, processing speed—relative to general intellectual abilities. A more parsimonious explanation is that superior intelligence is not necessarily accompanied by superior processing speed.

Utility of the Process Approach

The *WISC-IV Technical and Interpretive Manual* (The Psychological Corporation, 2003) advises the clinician that "the final step in a profile analysis is the qualita-

≡ Rapid Reference 6.8

Verbal-Perceptual Discrepancies: Clinical Samples with Notable VCI-PRI Differences

Clinical Sample	Mean VCI	Mean PRI	VCI-PRI Discrepancy
VCI > PRI			
Motor Impairment	95.5	83.8	+11.7
Math Disorder	93.2	87.7	+5.5
Asperger's Disorder	105.6	101.2	+4.4
Intellectually Gifted	124.7	120.4	+4.3
VCI < PRI			
Expressive Language Disorder	82.7	91.6	−8.9
Mixed Receptive-Expressive Language Disorder	78.2	86.7	−8.5
Autistic Disorder	80.2	85.7	−5.5
Reading and Writing Disorders	94.8	98.0	−3.2

Source: Data are from the WISC-IV Technical and Interpretive Manual (The Psychological Corporation, 2003, Chapter 5).

Note: Discrepancy = VCI minus PRI. Notable differences are defined in the WISC-IV Technical and Interpretive Manual as ≥ 0.20 SD (3 standard score points or greater).

tive analysis of individual responses" (p. 107). The *process approach* (Kaplan, 1988)—or the Boston Process Approach, as it was originally called (Milberg, Hebben, & Kaplan, 1986, 1996)—focuses on the various processes an individual might use to correctly solve a problem and the processes that might lead to the failure to solve a problem (Hebben & Milberg, 2002).

Though the process approach is intellectually and intuitively appealing, with its emphasis on breaking performance down into elements with potential relevance to rehabilitation and education, its empirical basis is not sufficiently well developed to allow for scientifically supportable clinical predictions by all clinicians. Without precise norms and a clearly spelled out blueprint of how and when these procedures should be used, there is likely to be tremendous variation in the skill and accuracy with which this approach is applied. The process scores provided in the *WISC-IV Administration and Scoring Manual* (Wechsler, 2003) provide a relatively limited but quantitative picture of some of the processes that may be involved in the performance of several subtests, but as with other data derived

≡≡Rapid Reference 6.9

Processing Speed Deficits: Clinical Samples with Relatively Low Scores on the PSI

Clinical Sample	Mean Index on VCI, PRI, and WMI	Mean PSI	PSI Deficit
Asperger's Disorder	100.7	86.5	−14.2
Autistic Disorder	80.9	70.2	−10.7
Open head injury	93.9	84.1	−9.8
Closed head injury	93.9	85.0	−8.9
Intellectually gifted	119.2	110.6	−8.6
Motor Impairment	90.4	83.8	−6.6
Learning Disorder/ADHD	91.4	88.2	−3.2

Source: Data are from the WISC-IV Technical and Interpretive Manual (Chapter 5).

Note: PSI Deficit = mean of VCI, PRI, and WMI minus mean PSI. Notable differences are defined in the WISC-IV Technical and Interpretive Manual as ≥ 0.20 SD (3 standard score points or greater).

from the clinical samples, these analyses cannot typically be used for differential diagnosis.

Clinical Samples with Notable Differences between Scaled Scores on Digits Forward and Digits Backward

The scaled score differences between Digits Forward and Digits Backward shown in Rapid Reference 6.10 range from 0.7 to 2.9. With the exception of the latter difference, obtained by the children with Motor Impairment, the small differences obtained by the other groups are not likely to be clinically significant and may not even be specific to the clinical samples. Table B.9 in the *WISC-IV Administration and Scoring Manual* (Wechsler, 2003) indicates that children must show a greater than 3.62 scaled score difference between Digits Forward and Digits Backward for the difference to be statistically significant at the .05 level. Digit Span Backward is more difficult than Digit Span Forward, so it is not surprising that Digits Forward is better than Digits Backward for most groups.

It is difficult to explain why children with expressive language disorders para-

≡ Rapid Reference 6.10

WISC-IV Process Scores: Clinical Samples with Notable Differences between Scaled Scores on Digits Forward and Digits Backward

Clinical Sample	Mean Digits Forward	Mean Digits Backward	Difference
Forward > Backward			
Motor Impairment	10.3	7.4	+2.9
Learning Disorder/ADHD	9.4	8.0	+1.4
Moderate Mental Retardation	3.9	2.6	+1.3
Math Disorder	9.6	8.6	+1.0
Reading, written expression, and math disorders	8.8	7.9	+0.9
Backward > Forward			
Expressive Language Disorder	7.9	8.6	−0.7

Source: Data are from the *WISC-IV Technical and Interpretive Manual* (The Psychological Corporation, 2003, Chapter 5).

Note: Difference = mean of Digits Forward minus mean of Digits Backward. Notable differences are defined in the *WISC-IV Technical and Interpretive Manual* as ≥ 0.20 SD (0.6 of a scaled score point or greater).

doxically seemed to have more difficulty with Digits Forward than Digits Backward, but these data are derived from a single small sample of children and may not be generalizable to other children with similar diagnostic labels. One explanation for this finding is that it is possible that the requirement to actively manipulate numbers in the backward condition may have engaged these children more than passively reciting them in the forward condition, but a hypothesis such as this requires testing before it can be applied to clinical practice.

Clinical Samples with Notable Differences between Scaled Scores on Cancellation Random and Cancellation Structured

As can be seen in Rapid Reference 6.11 there is a general advantage for performance on the Random versus the Structured Cancellation conditions. This difference is typically less than 1 scaled-score point between the two conditions for most of the special study groups, however, with only the children with Mental Retardation exhibiting greater than 1–scaled score point difference between Random and Structured Cancellation. This finding is probably due, in part, to practice effects because the random condition follows the structured condition. However, the matched controls in the majority of these special group studies demonstrated no notable difference between the random and structured conditions.

Rapid Reference 6.11 indicates that the children with ADHD show a slight advantage for the structured condition over the random condition. Though it is not clear how consistent this pattern is for the individuals in this group, the finding suggests that children with ADHD may benefit from the alignment of the stimuli in the structured condition.

≡Rapid Reference 6.11

WISC-IV Process Scores: Clinical Samples with Notable Differences between Scaled Scores on Cancellation Random and Cancellation Structured

Clinical Sample	Mean Cancellation Random	Mean Cancellation Structured	Difference
Random > Structured			
Moderate Mental Retardation	5.7	4.3	+1.4
Mild Mental Retardation	7.1	6.0	+1.1
Asperger's Disorder	8.4	7.5	+0.9
Motor Impairment	6.7	5.9	+0.8
Reading Disorder	10.3	9.6	+0.7
Reading and written expression disorders	9.7	9.1	+0.6
Mixed Receptive-Expressive Language Disorder	9.0	8.4	+0.6
Structured > Random			
ADHD	8.7	9.5	−0.8

Source: Data are from the WISC-IV Technical and Interpretive Manual (The Psychological Corporation, 2003, Chapter 5).

Note: Difference = mean of Cancellation Random minus mean of Cancellation Structured. Notable differences are defined in the WISC-IV Technical and Interpretive Manual as ≥ 0.20 SD (0.6 of a scaled score point or greater).

Interesting Facts about the WISC-IV Profiles of Select Clinical Samples
Rapid Reference 6.12 summarizes a number of notable characteristics of the performances of the special study groups on the WISC-IV. A number of cautions should be observed, however, before using these data clinically.

Children with reading, written expression, and mathematics disorders earned virtually the same mean Index on the VCI, PRI, WMI, and PSI. As noted previously, this grouping is very heterogeneous and collapsing these groups may be obscuring significant differences and meaningful findings between the various subgroups.

None of the 16 clinical samples studied scored very differently on the Block

≡Rapid Reference 6.12

Interesting Facts about the WISC-IV Profiles of Select Clinical Samples

- Children with reading, written expression, and math disorders earned virtually the same mean Index on all four scales (89.7 to 90.5).
- None of the 16 clinical samples included in the WISC-IV manual scored very differently on the Block Design process scaled score (no bonus points) when compared to their regular Block Design scaled score (largest difference was 0.3 of a scaled score point, or 0.1 SD).
- Children with Motor Impairment had great difficulty reversing digits even though they performed at an average level on Digits Forward (see Rapid Reference 6.10).
- Intellectually gifted children averaged 122.6 on VCI and PRI, but only 111.6 on WMI and PSI.
- Children classified as having Motor Impairment averaged 93.8 on VCI and WMI, but only 81.0 on PRI and PSI.
- Children with reading disorders displayed a relative weakness in working memory (their mean WMI of 87 was about 6 points lower than their average Index on the other three scales).
- Children with math disorders (including those who had other learning disorders) displayed a relative weakness in reversing digits (see Rapid Reference 6.10), perhaps because Digits Backward requires manipulation of numbers.
- Children with Traumatic Brain Injury (TBI)—both closed and open head injuries—had a notable relative weakness in processing speed (see Rapid Reference 6.9).
- Children with Autistic Disorder and Asperger's Disorder each had a striking relative weakness in processing speed, even larger than that of children with TBI (see Rapid Reference 6.9).

Design process scaled score (i.e., no additional time bonus points for rapid completion) when compared to their Block Design scaled score. This finding suggests that this particular process score does not add any information above and beyond the standard score, although additional studies of the measure are needed to see if this reduced emphasis on speed benefits particular children (e.g., children with physical limitations).

Children with Motor Impairment had great difficulty reversing Digits Backward, but scored normally reciting Digits Forward. Motor Impairment in this group is not clearly defined, however. One could speculate that at least some of the motor impairments that were included reflected deficits in frontal lobe functioning, and that Digit Span Backward, a task sensitive to working memory, may also be reflecting deficits in frontal lobe functioning. This does not necessarily mean that the motor impairment and weakness in Digit Span Backward are caused by the same underlying problem, but rather that they are reflections of different functions attributable to the same structure or neural system.

Children classified as intellectually gifted scored in the Superior range on VCI and PRI but in the average range on WMI and PSI. As previously noted, intellectually gifted children who are superior at accumulating and manipulating knowledge do not necessarily show superiority in working memory and motor speed.

Children with Motor Impairment scored in the Average range on VCI and WMI, but in the Low Average range on PRI and PSI. Children with Motor Impairment are at a disadvantage on speeded tasks requiring motor movement; thus it is not surprising that they obtain lower scores on PRI and PSI. Their motor impairments can prevent them from successfully completing tasks within time limits. It appears that reducing the motor demands on the WISC-IV relative to the WISC-III did not entirely eliminate the motor demands from this instrument.

Children with Reading Disorder displayed a relative deficit in working memory. Their mean WMI was about 6 points lower than their average Index on VCI, PRI, and PSI. This pattern is consistent with other evidence that children with reading disorders often have working memory problems (Gathercole, Hitch, Service, & Martin, 1997; Swanson & Howell, 2001). It is by no means clear, though, whether this pattern is due to problems with mental sequencing, auditory processing, mental manipulation, or some other factor.

Children with Mathematics Disorder showed a weakness in their ability to reverse digits for backward recall relative to forward recall. This finding underlines the lack of specificity of this measure. Children with Math Disorder may be hampered on this task because Digit Span Backward requires mental manipulation of numbers. Other groups without specific problems with numbers, however, showed a larger difference between Digits Forward and Digits Backward than did children with Math Disorder.

Children with TBI, whether closed head injury or open head injury (i.e., skull fracture), displayed a notable weakness in processing speed. In adults, TBI is more often associated with lower PSIs and WMIs than VCIs and PRIs. This finding probably reflects the diffuse axonal injury common to those who have sustained TBI. Because so many groups, including the intellectually gifted, show larger VCIs and PRIs than PSIs, this pattern may not be helpful for diagnosis. Clinically this pattern may be meaningful, though, because slowed processing speed can affect learning in general.

Children with Autistic Disorder and Asperger's Disorder had a weakness in PSI that was even larger than that seen in children with TBI. The *Diagnostic and Statistical Manual of Mental Disorders–Fourth Edition, Text Revision* (*DSM-IV-TR*; American Psychiatric Association, 2000) relates that motor clumsiness is an associated feature of Asperger's Syndrome. It also relates that Autistic Disorder is often accompanied by stereotyped body movements, abnormalities of posture, and various nonspecific neurological symptoms, such as delayed hand dominance. Perhaps these factors influence processing speed, or perhaps there is an interaction between the attentional problems associated with Autistic Disorder and Asperger's Disorder and the difficulties that these children have with motor speed and coordination. This finding needs to be replicated to be considered a reliable feature of these disorders. A more detailed discussion of these disorders is found in the next section of this chapter.

AUTISTIC-SPECTRUM DISORDERS

Elizabeth O. Lichtenberger

In order to further describe the research on the cognitive profiles of autistic-spectrum disorders, it is important to first review the controversy that has increasingly been brought to light in the literature about the clinical diagnoses of Autistic and Asperger's disorders. Numerous papers have questioned whether Asperger's Disorder and high-functioning autism are indeed separate and distinct disorders. Some researchers definitively state that the *DSM-IV* diagnosis of Asperger's Disorder is "unlikely or impossible" (e.g., Eisenmajer et al., 1996; Ghaziuddin, Tsai, & Ghaziuddin, 1992b; Manjiviona & Prior, 1995; Mayes, Calhoun, & Crites, 2001; Miller & Ozonoff, 1997; Szatmari, Archer, Fisman, Streiner, & Wilson, 1995). Many authors agree that the symptoms of Asperger's Disorder differ only in degree from autism, and thereby place Asperger's simply at another point on the autism spectrum (e.g., Attwood, 1998; Eisenmajer et al.; Manjiviona & Prior; Mayes et al.; Miller & Ozonoff; Myhr, 1998; Schopler, 1996; Szatmari et al.; Wing, 1998). However, other researchers support differentiating Asperger's syndrome and high-functioning autism as distinct disorders (e.g., Klin, 1994; Klin, Volkmar, Sparrow, Cicchetti, & Rourke, 1995; McLaughlin-Cheng, 1998; Ozonoff, Rogers, & Pennington, 1991).

Asperger's Disorder and Autistic Disorder have similar diagnostic criteria in the *DSM-IV,* but have key diagnostic differences. According to the *DSM-IV-TR* (American Psychiatric Association, 2000), children with Asperger's do not have communication deficits (including delay of language, inability to initiate or sustain a conversation, repetitive use of language, and lack of symbolic play), and they do not typically show delays in cognitive development. Also, children with Asperger's Disorder are not generally attracted to inanimate objects, as is typical of children with Autism. Table 6.1 reviews the differences between Asperger's

Table 6.1 Differences between Asperger's Disorder and Autistic Disorder, According to *DSM-IV-TR* Diagnostic Criteria

DSM-IV-TR characteristic	Asperger's Disorder	Autistic Disorder
Impairment in social interaction		
Impaired nonverbal behavior	Yes	Yes
Impaired ability to develop peer friendships	Yes	Yes
Impaired ability to seek and share interests	Yes	Yes
Impaired ability in social and emotional reciprocity	Yes	Yes
Restricted, repetitive behaviors		
Preoccupation with restricted interests	Yes	Yes
Stereotypic, repetitive motor interests	Yes	Yes
Restricted range of interests	Yes	Yes
Interests in nonfunctional activities	Yes	Yes
Interests in inanimate objects	No	Yes
Impairments in communication		
Delay in or lack of spoken language	No	Yes
Impaired ability to initiate or sustain conversation	No	Yes
Stereotypic, repetitive use of language	No	Yes
Impaired or lack of symbolic play	No	Yes
Onset		
Delays must be present prior to age 3	No	Yes
Comorbidity		
No delay in cognitive development or adaptive functioning (except in social interaction)	Yes	No

Disorder and Autistic Disorder according to *DMS-IV-TR* diagnostic criteria. A final key factor in making a differential diagnosis for autistic-spectrum disorders is that "Asperger's disorder is not diagnosed if the criteria are met for Autistic disorder" (American Psychiatric Association, 2000).

Because of the controversy surrounding the diagnosis of Asperger's Disorder and Autistic Disorder, researchers have repeatedly investigated whether specific patterns of performance on cognitive measures are useful in distinguishing the two disorders. However, the large number of research studies on the topic has not allowed a consensus about cognitive patterns to be reached, partly because of methodological issues involved in analyzing the different studies. The following issues exemplify why comparing various studies is difficult:

- Some studies use participants with high-functioning autism, whereas others use individuals with classic autism (who generally have more developmental disabilities and less-intact speech and language skills).
- Some researchers strictly adhere to diagnoses based on *DSM-IV* criteria, but others use modified criteria.
- Age differences between groups exist in many studies, bringing into question whether age is a critical factor affecting the dependent variables.
- The dependent measures vary across studies, as well (e.g., WISC, WISC-R, WISC-III, WAIS-R).
- Sample sizes are generally small, which limits the conclusions that can be drawn.

Cognitive Performance Patterns of Individuals with Asperger's and Autistic Disorders

Bearing in mind the methodological issues involved in researching autistic-spectrum disorders, some of the key findings in the literature on cognitive functioning in children with these disorders is summarized here. Research has focused mainly on verbal versus nonverbal functioning, and patterns of specific high and low subtests.

Verbal versus Nonverbal Performance   Although the research of a decade or so ago on children with autism (e.g., Lincoln, Courschesne, Kilman, Elmasian, & Allen, 1988; Rumsey, 1992; Yirmiya & Sigman, 1991) typically reported a consistent pattern of higher nonverbal (Wechsler PIQ) than verbal (VIQ) ability, more recent research indicates that autistic-spectrum disorders vary extensively with regard to Verbal-Performance IQ discrepancies. Most of the available research analyzes the WISC-R and WAIS-R, with a handful of WISC-III studies available, as well as other instruments such as the Kaufman Assessment Battery for Children (K-ABC) or Stanford-Binet Intelligence Scale, Fourth Edition (SB-IV). Some studies report Verbal-Performance IQ discrepancies based on the mean group performance whereas others report the percentage of subjects who showed a Verbal > Performance or Performance > Verbal discrepancy. In the various research studies, the discrepancy size needed to be considered significant is often based on normative data from a test's manual, but other times a Verbal-Performance difference of any size is reported simply if one score is larger than another.

The recent literature shows that, in groups of children with autism (most labeled as having high-functioning autism), the greatest proportion of subjects appear to have Verbal and Performance IQs that are not significantly different from one another. For example, Mayes and Calhoun (2003) found no significant differences in WISC-III Verbal and Performance IQs in autistic subjects with either high or low FSIQs. This finding was further supported by Miller and Ozonoff's (2000) mean WISC-III data. Other studies have found that 56% (Manjiviona & Prior, 1995) to 62% (Siegel, Minshew, & Goldstein, 1996) to 77% (Gilchrist, Green, Cox, Burton, Rutter, & Le Couteur, 2001) of autistic samples had nonsignificant Verbal-Performance differences. A Performance > Verbal pattern was the next most commonly reported finding, ranging from 15% to 33% of the subjects with autism (Gilchrist et al.; Manjiviona & Prior; Siegel et al.).

For children diagnosed with Asperger's Disorder some studies also report a large percentage (50–67%) of subjects with a nonsignificant discrepancy between their Verbal and Performance IQs (Gilchrist et al., 2001; Manjiviona & Prior, 1995), but others indicate that only a small percentage (3%) of their subjects have this pattern (Barnhill, Hagiwara, Myles, & Simpson, 2000). Some studies indicate that 17% to 64% of their subjects with Asperger's display a significant Verbal > Performance pattern (Barnhill et al.; Gilchrist et al.; Manjiviona & Prior). Yet others report some percentage of subjects with Asperger's (17–33%) with the opposite pattern (Performance > Verbal).

High and Low Subtests   Although patterns of verbal and nonverbal performance have not consistently been shown in either Autistic or Asperger's Disorder samples, two Wechsler subtests have repeatedly been shown to be the highest and lowest in the profiles of these populations. Specifically, Block Design has been reported in numerous studies to be the highest for individuals with autism. Barnhill et al. (2000) reviewed 20 studies with this population and found high Block Design present in 19 of them. The Comprehension subtest is commonly reported as the low subtest in profiles of autistic individuals. Barnhill's review of 20 studies found low Comprehension in 18 of them. Subsequent studies have also validated these Wechsler high and low subtests with autistic populations (e.g., Goldstein, Beers, Siegel, & Minshew, 2001; Goldstein, Minshew, Allen, & Seaton, 2002).

As summarized by Kaufman and Lichtenberger (2002), the Autistic Disorder and Asperger's Disorder populations can vary extensively with regard to the Verbal-Nonverbal discrepancy. Despite the fact that high Block Design–low Comprehension remains prevalent across samples of individuals with autistic-spectrum disorders, general patterns on the Wechsler tests or other tests measuring verbal and nonverbal ability have not been shown to differentially diagnosis autistic-spectrum disorders reliably. However, intellectual evaluations of individuals with autism or Asperger's Disorder are nonetheless valuable for educational planning.

WISC-IV Findings for Individuals with Autism and Asperger's Disorder

The WISC-IV manual reports findings from a sample of 19 children with Autistic Disorder and 27 children with Asperger's Disorder. The mean ages for the autistic and Asperger's groups were 11.7 and 12.5, respectively. The mean WISC-IV composite scores for each of these groups are shown in Figure 6.1. Globally, the cognitive functioning of the Asperger's group was higher than that of the autistic group across all domains. The largest discrepancy (25 points) between the autistic and Asperger's groups was on the VCI, which is consistent with some recent research (e.g., Gilchrist et al., 2001; Miller & Ozonoff, 2000).

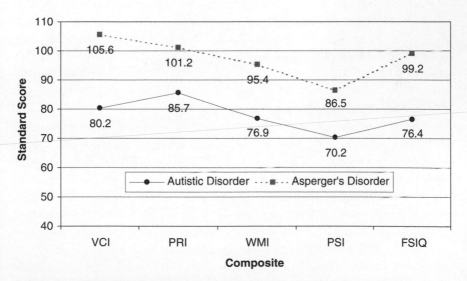

Figure 6.1 Mean WISC-IV Composite Scores for Children with Autistic Disorder (N = 19) and Asperger's Disorder (N = 27)

Both groups showed their poorest performance on the PSI (70.2 for the autistic group and 86.5 for the Asperger's group). These deficits are also evident from an examination of the lowest WISC-IV subtest scores (refer back to Rapid Reference 6.1). For both the Autistic group and the Asperger's group, Symbol Search and Coding were two of the three lowest scaled scores. Similar findings were reported by Mayes and Calhoun (2003), who found a low WISC-III PSI relative to both VCI and POI in children with autism.

In addition to the low PSI subtests, the children with Autistic Disorder also had Comprehension as one of their lowest WISC-IV subtests. This finding is consistent with the vast majority of studies previously cited (e.g., Barnhill et al., 2000). The relatively weaker verbal abilities of the autistic group in comparison to the group with Asperger's Disorder helps to explain why Comprehension is one of the three lowest subtests for the autistic group, but not for the Asperger's group. Most researchers purport that poor performance of autistic groups on Comprehension is related to poor social judgment and perception, as well as poor verbal expression.

Also similar to previously cited research on subtest patterns is the finding that Block Design is the highest subtest for children with Autistic Disorder (see Rapid Reference 6.1). The triad of the highest subtests for the autistic group are from the PRI. In contrast, two of the three highest subtests in the Asperger's group are from the VCI. Picture Completion (a supplemental PRI subtest) is the third-highest subtest for those with Asperger's Disorder. Thus, there are some similarities between WISC-IV findings with the autism-spectrum disorders and findings reported in the literature. Future studies are needed to test the validity of the data reported in the *WISC-IV Technical and Interpretive Manual* (The Psychological Corporation, 2003).

Clinical Implications for Testing These Populations
The controversy surrounding differentially diagnosing children with autism from those with Asperger's Disorder may make clinicians and researchers lose sight of what is truly important during assessment: helping individual children. Klin, Sparrow, Marans, Carter, and Volkmar (2000) eloquently state: "Clinicians should also be aware that by simply associating a name to a complex clinical presentation, the understanding of a child's individualized profile of challenges is not necessarily advanced" (p. 310). Thus, although research has not shown a definitive pattern of scores on Wechsler tests to help distinguish children with Asperger's from those with autism, as clinicians, we can certainly use individuals' test data to help develop the most appropriate recommendations for treating the deficits of autism-spectrum disorders.

Some of the consistent research findings have implications for educational interventions for children with autism. For example, the consistently poor performance on Wechsler's Comprehension subtest implies problems with language and social reasoning, which could be addressed by social skills training and adaptations to help compensate for poor language development. Developing keyboarding and word-processing skills on the computer can help some of the visual-motor or graphomotor difficulties found in children with autism. In addition, educational accommodations developed for children with ADHD may also be useful for children with autism who have difficulties with executive functioning or attentional deficits.

Mental Retardation

Unlike the diagnosis of autistic-spectrum disorders, the diagnosis of Mental Retardation has historically been fairly clear-cut. The key criteria for diagnosis of Mental Retardation are twofold: deficits in overall cognitive functioning and impairment in adaptive functioning. Both the *DSM-IV-TR* (American Psychiatric Association, 2000) and the American Association on Mental Retardation (AAMR; Luckasson et al., 2002) require that symptoms of Mental Retardation be present before age 18. The criterion of subaverage intellectual functioning is defined as an FSIQ (or other global ability score) of approximately 70 or below. The criterion of deficits in adaptive functioning requires impairment in two or more of the following areas: communication, self-care, home living, social interaction, functional academic skills, work, leisure, health, and safety. Both the *DSM-IV-TR* and the AAMR criteria emphasize that standardized tests include measurement error that should be considered in the diagnostic process, along with using careful clinical judgment.

Research with children who are mentally retarded has generally found equally depressed performance on Wechsler Verbal and Performance scales (Slate, 1995; Spruill, 1998; The Psychological Corporation, 2002; Wechsler, 1991). Children assessed with other tests of cognitive ability also typically reveal little variability between scales. For example, the SB-IV Verbal Reasoning and Abstract/Visual Reasoning Area Scores are often equally depressed (Bower & Hayes, 1995), and on the SB5, mean Verbal and Nonverbal IQs were virtually identical for a sample of 119 individuals with documented diagnoses of Mental Retardation (ages 3–25 years, no mean or median age reported; Roid, 2003, Table 4.12). On the second edition of the K-ABC (KABC-II; Kaufman & Kaufman, 2004a), scores on the composite measuring Visual Processing (Simultaneous/*Gv* mean of 64.5) were similar to scores on the composite measuring Crystallized Intelligence (Knowledge/*Gc* mean of 69.1) for 41 children with Mental Retardation. In addition, discrepancies between language and cognitive performance in young children with Mental Retardation do not usually add prognostic information beyond that contained in the global measure of cognitive ability (Vig, Kaminer, & Jedrysek, 1987).

No characteristic Wechsler profiles for children with Mental Retardation have been consistently reported (Spruill, 1998). In an analysis of 10 WISC-R studies, Harrison (1990) reported that children with Mental Retardation have the most difficulty (i.e., score the lowest) on tests of crystallized intelligence, including Vocabulary, Information, Arithmetic, and Similarities. In contrast, these children have their highest scores on Picture Completion and Object Assembly. The occasional slight trend for some groups of children with very low ability to perform better on Performance than Verbal subtests is not something that can be used as a diagnostic characteristic of the population. Indeed, that pattern did not consistently characterize samples of children with Mental Retardation on the WISC-III or WPPSI-III (Bolen, 1998; Canivez & Watkins, 2001; Lichtenberger & Kaufman, 2004). Further, although the FSIQ has been shown to be adequately stable in mentally retarded populations, subtest stability and stability of Verbal-Performance discrepancies have been reported as inadequate (Canivez & Watkins).

WISC-IV Findings on Mental Retardation

The *WISC-IV Technical and Interpretive Manual* (The Psychological Corporation, 2003) reports the results of a study of 63 children diagnosed with mild Mental Retardation and 57 diagnosed with moderate Mental Retardation. The mean ages of the groups were 11.9 and 12.2 for the mild and moderate groups, respectively. As commonly found in mentally retarded populations, there was very little variability in the subjects' performance. The standard deviations of the composite scores ranged from 9 to 11 points in the mildly retarded group and from 7 to 11 points in the moderately retarded group (a 15-point standard deviation is typical for the nonretarded general population).

The small discrepancies between verbal and nonverbal abilities typically shown on Wechsler tests for samples of children with Mental Retardation was also found in the WISC-IV samples. The mean differences between the WISC-IV VCI and PRI were 1.6 points and 0.2 points for the mild and moderate groups, respectively. Figure 6.2 shows the mean performance of the groups with mild and moderate retardation on all four of the WISC-IV Indexes. The highest Index scores for both groups were noted on the PSI (73 for the mild group and 58 for the moderate group). These PSI scores were about 6 to 7.5 points higher than the VCI and PRI scores for both the mild and moderate groups, indicating again a rather small amount of variability between the In-

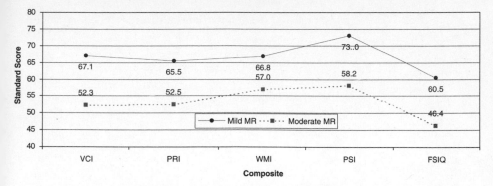

Figure 6.2 Mean WISC-IV Composite Scores for Children with Mild (N = 63) and Moderate (N = 57) Mental Retardation (MR)

dexes. The WMI was nearly identical to the PSI in the group with moderate retardation, and the WMI was about 6 points lower than the PSI in the group with mild retardation.

Although specific subtest patterns on Wechsler tests have not historically been able to characterize the performance of children with Mental Retardation, the highest and lowest WISC-IV subtest scores for these children were examined nonetheless. The patterns of high and low subtests were slightly different for the mild and moderate groups (refer back to Rapid Reference 6.3). Both groups had Cancellation and Word Reasoning among their three highest subtests, and also had Vocabulary and Arithmetic among their lowest three subtests. For the group with mild Mental Retardation, the third highest subtest was Symbol Search, but for the group with moderate Mental Retardation it was Similarities. Further, Matrix Reasoning was among the three lowest subtests for the mild group, but Comprehension was among the three lowest for the moderate group. Thus, poor acquired knowledge, crystallized abilities, and school-learned knowledge are reflected in the lowest subtests. In contrast, relatively stronger visual attention is one of the skills reflected in the highest subtests. However, these high and low patterns of subtests in and of themselves should not be considered indicative of Mental Retardation.

Finding Subtests with Adequate Floors

Young children with Mental Retardation sometimes have difficulty achieving a floor on tests of cognitive ability. For example, a 6-year-old with moderate Mental Retardation may not be able to get enough items correct on the WISC-IV to determine where the bottom level of his cognitive functioning truly is. Thus, for children with low levels of cognitive functioning from ages 6:0 to 7:3, the WPPSI-III (The Psychological Corporation, 2002) may be a better measure to administer than the WISC-IV. The WPPSI-III has a larger number of low-level items than the WISC-IV, which allows children referred for suspected retardation to achieve a floor if they are functioning at very low levels of ability. For example, consider the scaled scores that children will obtain at ages 6:0 to 6:3 if they earn raw scores of 2 points. On the WISC-IV, raw scores of 2 translate to scaled scores as high as 5 (on Letter-Number Sequencing), with Similarities, Picture Concepts, Matrix Reasoning, and Symbol Search yielding scaled scores of 4. In contrast, at ages 6:0 to 6:3 on the WPPSI-III, raw scores of 2 yield scaled scores as high as 4 only on Comprehension and Similarities.

The findings from the WISC-IV samples of children with Mental Retardation indicate that the test will provide an adequate measure of cognitive ability for most individuals with Mental Retardation (except perhaps for the youngest age). That fact notwithstanding, a diagnosis of Mental Retardation should be made based only on the results of appropriate measures of both IQ and adaptive functioning. The findings from cognitive testing and measures of adaptive functioning need to be considered within the context of relevant clinical data from a child's background (developmental, educational, medical) history and behavioral observations before making a differential diagnosis of Mental Retardation.

USING THE WISC-IV WITH DEAF OR HARD-OF-HEARING STUDENTS

Steven T. Hardy-Braz

Historical Overview

The WISC-IV is the latest edition of an intellectual testing instrument with a long tradition of use with deaf and hard-of-hearing populations. This is due primarily to the historical practice of providing a composite that was based on an examinee's ability to manipulate objects in order to solve novel problems or respond with answers that could be communicated with little to no formal language demands (i.e., the Wechsler PIQ). The PIQ, rather than the FSIQ, was considered the best estimate of ability in deaf and hard-of-hearing populations because it did not reflect verbal abilities in any substantial way. Use of the VIQ or FSIQ with these populations often resulted in their being misclassified as Mentally Retarded. Since there were virtually no alternative instruments that assessed intelligence nonverbally or in a reduced-language format back in the days of the WISC and WISC-R, the Wechsler Performance Scale was (and still is) the most widely used scale with these populations (Brauer, Braden, Pollard, & Hardy-Braz, 1998).

WISC-IV Administration Guidelines for Deaf and Hard-of-Hearing Populations

The *WISC-IV Administration and Scoring Manual* (Wechsler, 2003) provides extensive (six pages of the manual) administration guidelines for using this instrument with deaf and hard-of-hearing populations as compared to the WISC-III (Hardy-Braz, 2003b). These guidelines mention essential variables that are often overlooked in these groups (see Rapid Reference 6.13), discuss the modes of communication often used with members of these groups, and formally rate each subtest and scale on its administration appropriateness for each of four categories of different communication modalities commonly used by members of these populations (see Rapid Reference 6.14). These guidelines were developed as the results of extensive research, feedback, and back translations of every item on every subtest/scale of the WISC-IV.

While the guidelines are very helpful in the selection of subtests and scales that are most appropriate for different individuals, they do not by themselves provide evidence of validity for use of the WISC-IV with members of deaf or hard-of-hearing

---

≡Rapid Reference 6.13

Variables to Consider When Assessing Deaf or Hard-of-Hearing Examinees

- Mode(s) of communication
- Age of onset
- Degree of loss
- Type of loss
- Stability of loss
- Age of identification
- Sound frequencies affected
- Educational/communication history
- Historical use of assistive listening devices (ALDs)
- Etiology
- Comorbid conditions
- Parental communication skills

≡Rapid Reference 6.14

Communication Modalities/ Languages Used by Deaf or Hard-of-Hearing Examinees

- American Sign Language (ASL)
- Simultaneous communication
- Manually coded English
- Signed exact English
- Other native sign languages (e.g., British Sign Language)
- Contact signs or Pidgin signed English
- Cued speech
- Aural/oral

populations. Therefore, examiners should either wait for such evidence to be published or use professional judgment with regard to the utility of the WISC-IV with deaf and hard-of-hearing populations in accordance with ethical codes.

Use of the WISC-IV Verbal Subtests with Deaf and Hard-of-Hearing Populations

The changes from the WISC-III to the WISC-IV were extensive and therefore warrant close inspection with regard to the appropriateness of the WISC-IV in deaf and hard-of-hearing populations. The commonly practiced preassessment decision not to administer sections of the full test (e.g., the Verbal Scale) to these populations was always a compromise with consequences. While the Verbal Scale was shown to be a better predictor of academic achievement than the Performance Scale (Kelly & Braden, 1990), the latter scale was most often used. Through the sole use of the PIQ, predictive validity was sacrificed, but the misclassification of deaf and hard-of-hearing individuals as Mentally Retarded was substantially reduced.

Some researchers suggested the careful use of the Verbal Scale with different groups of deaf students with strong warnings about the potential dangers for misuse (see Maller, 2003, for an overview). While this recommendation made sense to specialists with the fluent and direct communication skills needed to translate items into signs and cues, no standard administration guidelines or procedures in American Sign Language (ASL) were ever published; thus, no standardized signed administration procedures with appropriate norms exist. The recommendation to use the Verbal Scale with caution does not work for the vast majority of examiners who are monolingual and untrained either in working with deaf and hard-of-hearing populations or in the proper use of interpreters.

Use of the WISC-IV Perceptual Reasoning Subtests with Deaf and Hard-of-Hearing Populations

While the publisher of the WISC-IV states that the PRI can be used in situations wherein the PIQ formerly was used, examiners should consider the composition of the WISC-III PIQ versus the WISC-IV PRI. The WISC-III PIQ was composed of five core subtests (Picture Completion, Coding, Picture Arrangement, Block Design, and Object Assembly) and two supplemental subtests (Symbol Search and Mazes). The WISC-IV's PRI is composed of three subtests (Block Design, Picture Concepts, and Matrix Reasoning), two of which are new. Picture Completion is now a supplemental subtest. Coding and Symbol Search now form the PSI. Picture Arrangement and Object Assembly have been eliminated. Thus, the only core subtest retained from the PIQ on the WISC-III is Block Design. In addition, the cognitive abilities measured by the WISC-III PIQ and the motor skills required to perform the PIQ tasks are different than those measured by the WISC-IV PRI. Therefore, the WISC-IV PRI is not equivalent to the WISC-III PIQ with members of deaf and hard-of-hearing populations. Data are needed before decisions can be made regarding the relationship between the WISC-IV PRI and the WISC-III PIQ with these populations. Until such data are available, examiners should consider using other instruments that have been studied more extensively with regard to their use with deaf and hard-of-hearing populations.

Examinee Variables to Consider in the Assessment of Deaf and Hard-of-Hearing Populations

The questions an examiner should consider when selecting or planning for an assessment with the WISC-IV as well as when interpreting results obtained from administration of this instrument are

- How does the examinee match the characteristics of other individuals with hearing losses?
- How well does the examinee communicate in different modalities?

Deaf and hard-of-hearing individuals vary greatly in terms of developmental history, etiology, presence of comorbid conditions, degree of loss, stability of loss, type of loss, sound frequencies affected, age of onset of the loss, age of identification of the loss, effective use of ALDs, educational placement, and the communication skills of family members (see the annual demographic studies from the Gallaudet Research Institute for more information). Each of these variables should be considered in planning a proper psychological assessment (Sattler & Hardy-Braz, 2002). Nevertheless, the most important one to consider when using the WISC-IV is that of the communication modality or language used by the examinee.

Many deaf or hard-of-hearing examinees need to have the assessment session communicated in different fashions (e.g., via signs or cues or with the aid of an ALD). For example, examinees may communicate in more than one modality and in different modalities depending on whether their communication is receptive or expressive, and may have different levels of fluency in different modalities or even within the same modality. Each communication modality, however, is an alteration from the standardized administration on which the normative sample information was gathered. Examiners should consider the degree to which each access provision (i.e., alteration from standard procedures) fundamentally alters the intellectual construct that the Index/subtest/item purports to measure. The greater the alteration or modification of the underlying test construct, the greater the need for caution when interpreting results using the normative data provided. For example, the sign-language hand-shape similarities between certain numbers and letters add an additional level of confusion and complexity to the Letter-Number Sequence subtest.

Even when signs are not used, a hard-of-hearing individual's unique profile of hearing abilities and inabilities (both aided and unaided), as displayed on his or her audiogram, should be examined as an essential component of the test selection process. Students are often classified in regard to the overall average degree of loss in terms of their ability to perceive pure tone averages across a range of frequencies, and this process results in classifications that can be misleading. Since spoken-language phonemes vary by the frequencies in which they are transmitted and perceived, students with different profiles may perceive different sounds. Students with greater difficulty perceiving high-frequency sounds may experience greater difficulty with items containing such sounds as "f," "s," and "th," whereas students with greater difficulty perceiving low-frequency sounds may experience greater difficulties with items containing such sounds as "j," "z," and "v." The acoustic environment in which these students are assessed is another variable to consider, especially when ALDs are used.

It is important to remember that a student's ability to speak clearly should not be used as an estimate of his or her intellectual functioning. The administration guidelines published in the WISC-IV manual seek to provide assistance in this decision process. In order to use those guidelines an examiner must know both how and how well an examinee communicates across modalities prior to administering any or all parts of the WISC-IV. Prior to administering the WISC-IV, examiners should also decide which components of the test (e.g., PRI subtests) can be made administratively accessible to an examinee without altering the underlying construct those components are intended to measure. Examiners should also decide whether WISC-IV test results should be supplemented with tests that permit task access without modifying the test construct, if such tests are available.

Communication Demands of the WISC-IV

Careful consideration of the characteristics of the instrument, the individual, and the examiner is necessary for effective communication and administration. Administration of the WISC-IV to individuals who do not hear clearly, if at all, or do not communicate via spoken English means that the administration of the test will not be conducted following standardization procedures. While there are specialists in the deaf and hard-of-hearing populations as well as examiners who have the skills to communicate fluently, the vast majority of examiners do not. Many examiners will need to utilize the services of a professional sign-language interpreter or cued-speech transliterator. Access through the use of an interpreter/transliterator can satisfy legal and ethical requirements, but such use can be problematic. Examiners must remain aware that use of an interpreter injects an additional layer of complexity and adds an additional variable into the administration. The clinical rapport between the examiner and examinee can be affected when an interpreter is used. It can also be affected by the manner in which the interpreter relates to both the examiner and the examinee. Examiners should also be aware that the demands of communication in a different language directly or via an interpreter can increase the overall test administration time. Furthermore, as with many other languages, there is not always a one-to-one correspondence between English and ASL signs. It is also important to remember that the signs used in sign language are not used uniformly throughout the country. Many children use signs for basic communication needs that are based on gestures used at home or at school. Both examiner training on the effective use of interpreters *and* interpreter training on the proper interpretation of test directions are highly recommended because they will likely result in an interpreting process that retains the cognitive constructs that underlie the WISC-IV.

Examiner Qualifications

The final set of variables to consider when assessing a deaf or hard-of-hearing student concerns the qualifications of the examiner. While a sensitive examiner with adequate resources may be able to meet the communication demands necessary for appropriate administration of the WISC-IV, clinically significant information may be missed, distorted, or lost when the examiner does not understand the examinee's communication needs fully. Therefore, it is recommended that whenever possible examiners consult with fellow professionals and national professional organizations that offer specialized training and support in serving members of these populations. When using the WISC-IV or any other cognitive assessment battery, qualified examiners should possess training and/or background experience in the genetic, developmental, psychological, and sociological aspects of deafness. They should also have formal training and knowledge in assessing cultural, behavioral, motor, visual, and linguistic factors related to deafness. Skills in communicating with deaf and hard-of-hearing students in their primary languages or preferred communication modes, or the use of an interpreter or transliterator according to the student's communication mode so that an effective psychologist-examinee rapport can be developed, are essential but not sufficient. Rapid Reference 6.15 lists several points that examiners should remember when assessing deaf or hard-of-hearing individuals.

≡ Rapid Reference 6.15

Points to Remember When Assessing Deaf or Hard-of-Hearing Children

- All modifications to the standard WISC-IV administration, especially variations in communication, need to be documented in the interpretive report.
- Depending on the referral question(s), individual characteristics, and communication modality of the assessment administration, subtests from the WISC-IV may need to be supplemented or replaced with other measures.
- ASL, simultaneous communication, signed exact English, cued speech, and other visual communication modalities differ in how they alter WISC-IV test items and their function.
- Examiners should remember that ASL is not universal. Even within the United States there are geographic, ethnic, educational, and generational variations in signs used.
- When interpreting WISC-IV results, an examiner must consider the degree to which an interpreter or transliterator affected the assessment process and should document any findings related to this effect in the interpretive report.
- Interpreters vary in terms of their skill levels as well as their abilities to meet the needs of the examiner and examinee in the assessment situation. Hence, examiners should clarify roles and needs prior to an assessment session.

Conclusions

While the WISC-IV manual is the first edition to provide administrative guidelines for test selection and use for children who are deaf and hard-of-hearing, these guidelines should be considered a first critical step toward establishing the usefulness of the WISC-IV with these children. Until validity data are available, these guidelines and the recommendations discussed here should be considered preliminary.

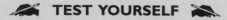 **TEST YOURSELF**

1. **Coding, though historically a "Performance" subtest, is a language-like task that requires a written code and the use of symbols, and it may pose difficulty for children with language disorders.** True or False?

2. **A child with ADHD would likely perform the best on which of the following subtests?**
   (a) Arithmetic
   (b) Cancellation
   (c) Word Reasoning
   (d) Coding

3. **Children with Asperger's Syndrome and Autism demonstrated their poorest performance on which of the following WISC-IV Indexes?**
   (a) VCI
   (b) PSI
   (c) WMI
   (d) POI

4. **Historically, specific patterns on Wechsler subtests have not been effective for differentially diagnosing Mental Retardation.** True or False?

5. **Which of the following variables needs to be considered when assessing children who are deaf or hard-of-hearing?**
   (a) Mode(s) of communication
   (b) Comorbid conditions
   (c) Stability of hearing loss
   (d) All of the above

6. **American Sign Language is universal.** True or False?

Answers: 1. True; 2. c; 3. b; 4. True; 5. d; 6. False

Seven

CLINICAL APPLICATIONS
Assessment of Gifted, Learning Disabled, and
Culturally and Linguistically Diverse Populations

IDENTIFICATION OF GIFTED STUDENTS WITH THE WISC-IV

Martin A. Volker and LeAdelle Phelps

In a broad sense, *gifted* is a term applied to productive people who show rare, demonstrable, high-level abilities that are valued within a given cultural context (Sternberg, 1993, 1995). Thus, the nature of giftedness varies across cultures to the extent that different abilities or domains of excellence are valued by different cultures. Within the United States, federal law defines *gifted* and *talented* children as those who demonstrate high performance capability in general intellectual ability, creative or productive thinking, visual or performing arts, leadership, or specific academic areas (Educational Amendment of 1978; Jacob K. Javits Gifted and Talented Students Education Act of 1988; Marland, 1972). These children are assumed to require services not typically provided in schools in order to fully develop their abilities.

Though all five domains listed under the federal definition are important and valued areas of functioning within our culture, intelligence tests are most relevant to the identification and assessment of intellectual giftedness. Therefore, the term "gifted" will be used in the rest of this section to refer to intellectually gifted people. Although intelligence tests in general have been criticized on grounds of cultural bias (Tyerman, 1986), low test ceilings (Harrington, 1982; Kaufman, 1993), overemphasis on speed of performance (Kaufman, 1992, 1994; Sternberg, 1982), difficulties evaluating children with more "nontypical" profiles (Sparrow & Gurland, 1998, p. 63), and frequent lack of strong fluid ability measures (Carroll, 1997; McGrew & Flanagan, 1996), each of these issues can be reasonably well addressed by a competent examiner using reliable and valid instruments. Though intelligence tests are not perfect instruments, they are currently the best general predictors of academic achievement (Kaufman & Harrison, 1986; Sparrow & Gurland), they are the most technically sound psychometric instruments

The sections that make up Chapter 7 were written by invited contributors. Dawn Flanagan and Alan Kaufman edited the text and developed Rapid References 7.1–7.3.

available, and they can potentially identify gifted children who might otherwise go undetected due to behavior problems, learning disabilities, or other issues that might negatively bias those who work with them (Kaufman & Harrison).

The identification of gifted children is often associated with the use of specific cutoff scores. For example, a FSIQ greater than or equal to 2 SDs above the normative mean (The Psychological Corporation, 2003; Winner, 1997, 2000) or a FSIQ greater than 125 (Kaufman & Lichtenberger, 2000) may be among the selection criteria used in some areas for gifted programs. However, what is most important is that the examiner not rigidly adhere to a single cutoff score or criterion. The examiner should be attentive to other sources of information and show special sensitivity to the examinee's cultural background; possible physical, sensory, or learning disabilities; known errors in measurement associated with the test (Kaufman & Harrison, 1986); and known population prevalence of uneven development in different ability areas or expressions of intelligence (e.g., verbal vs. nonverbal; Sparrow & Gurland, 1998; Wechsler, 1991).

National surveys of school psychologists have typically shown that the Wechsler scales are the most frequently used individually administered intelligence tests for the identification of gifted students (e.g., Klausmeier, Mishra, & Maker, 1987). Given that the WISC-IV is likely to continue this trend, it is very important that it be thoroughly evaluated for this purpose. To this end, the remainder of this section will evaluate the WISC-IV in terms of testing time and speed-of-performance issues, subtest ceilings, cultural bias, use with nontypical gifted children, assessment of fluid reasoning, and an evaluation of the gifted validation study reported in the *WISC-IV Technical and Interpretive Manual* (The Psychological Corporation, 2003).

Testing Time

School psychologists have many responsibilities and need to test efficiently. Long tests can be costly. Ideally, tests need to comprehensive, yet able to be completed in a reasonable period of time. In the WISC-IV, all 10 subtests needed to calculate the FSIQ and the four Index scores are included in the standard battery. The technical and interpretive manual indicated that although the time required for the administration of the standard battery is similar for the WISC-III and WISC-IV, the WISC-III required the administration of additional supplemental subtests to derive scores for the two smaller factors. Thus, the WISC-IV administration is more efficient, allowing the derivation of all scores in less time. Given that assessments of the intellectually gifted tend to take longer than those of typical children (e.g., 90% of gifted children completed the tests in 104 minutes, vs. 90% of the normative sample completing the test in 94 minutes; *WISC-IV Technical and Interpretive*

Manual, The Psychological Corporation, 2003, p. 12) and that best practices dictates thorough consideration of scores and other information beyond the FSIQ, this greater efficiency is a decided advantage of the WISC-IV over its predecessor.

Speed of Performance

The WISC-III has been criticized by those who assess intellectually gifted children because of its perceived overemphasis on speed of performance (Kaufman, 1992, 1994; Sparrow & Gurland, 1998). Among the subtests contributing to the WISC-III FSIQ, scores for Coding, Block Design, Picture Arrangement, Object Assembly, and Arithmetic all included time bonuses. These scores could be adversely impacted by more methodical, reflective, motor-impaired, or otherwise slower response styles, especially for older children for whom the time bonuses were essential for Above Average scores. The fact that the preponderance of these time-laden tasks contributed to the PIQ may have contributed to significant Verbal versus Performance IQ differences in many gifted profiles. The authors of the WISC-IV attempted to address this issue by removing the Object Assembly and Picture Arrangement subtests, making Arithmetic a supplemental subtest without time bonuses, and reducing the time bonus scoring of Block Design. With the exception of Symbol Search, the subtests that were brought into the WISC-IV standard battery to replace those that were removed do not include a significant time component.

Despite these subtest adjustments, slower performance may still affect a gifted child's score; hence, the examiner should attend to the potential involvement of slower response speed on Coding, Symbol Search, and Block Design. For example, the PSI was the lowest average composite score for the group of gifted children tested in the WISC-III validity study (Wechsler, 1991) and a general area of relative weakness for this population (i.e., FSIQ = 128.7 vs. PSI = 110.2). The validity study with gifted children reported in the *WISC-IV Technical and Interpretive Manual* shows essentially the same pattern (i.e., FSIQ = 123.5 vs. PSI = 110.6; The Psychological Corporation, 2003). Furthermore, a relative weakness in Processing Speed on the WISC-IV has more direct bearing on the interpretation of the FSIQ, because Coding and Symbol Search are used in the calculation of both composites.

Though the time bonuses for Block Design on the WISC-IV were reduced relative to the WISC-III, they can still have a significant effect on a child's scores. As a child gets older, time bonuses become essential for Above Average performance on Block Design. Table 7.1 illustrates that without time bonuses, children above 8 years of age cannot achieve a Block Design score at least 2 SDs above the mean. Children above age 11 cannot achieve a Block Design score even outside the Average range without time bonuses. Thus, examiners should always check

Table 7.1   Highest WISC-IV Block Design Standard Score Possible without Time Bonuses

				Age in Years				
	6	7	8	9	10	11	12	13/14	15/16
Block Design maximum standard score	18	17	16	15	14	13	12	11	10

Source: Material used in this table was adapted from Appendix A of the *WISC-IV Administration and Scoring Manual* (Wechsler, 2003).

for relatively weaker performance on the Processing Speed and Block Design subtests in assessing the impact of speed of performance on the scores of potentially gifted children.

A number of things can be done to examine and offset the possible negative effects of speed of performance. First, if the examiner anticipates *a priori* that an examinee will have difficulties with speed-oriented subtests, the examiner could specifically select the most appropriate test that minimizes or eliminates such issues for the examinee. Second, the examiner should focus interpretation at the level of the WISC-IV factor index scores. Be aware that gifted students in the validity study reported in the technical and interpretive manual showed the following mean factor index profile: VCI = 124.7, PRI = 120.4, WMI = 112.5, and PSI = 110.6 (The Psychological Corporation, 2003, p. 77). Though exact discrepancy frequencies were not available, it would not be unusual to find that the PSI and WMI scores were significantly lower than the VCI and PRI scores with these students. As already noted, a lower Block Design score coupled with a relatively lower PSI score could suggest speed-of-performance issues. Fortunately, the WISC-IV has been designed with several process scores that attempt to systematically alter the conditions of testing or scoring in order to give the examiner more interpretive information. A Block Design No Time Bonus process score is available to help the examiner assess whether speed of performance made a difference on this subtest. Third, the WISC-IV makes several supplemental subtests available that could conceivably be used to replace problematic core subtests. For example, if Block Design is expected to be problematic for a child with motor difficulties, it could be replaced with Picture Completion. The Processing Speed subtests cannot be replaced with nonspeeded subtests because they are designed to measure quick and correct performance. However, focusing on interpretations at the factor-index level allows the examiner to account for and remove their influence, if necessary, in the identification decision. Fourth, testing the limits on time-laden tasks following a complete, standardized administration of the WISC-IV can yield a rough estimate of an examinee's accuracy and problem-solving skills in the absence of time pressure. Finally, if test results lead an examiner to conclude that speed of performance was problematic for the examinee, the WISC-IV results can be supplemented with other measures (see Flanagan & Ortiz, 2001, and Kaufman, 1994, for examples).

Subtest Ceilings

Subtest ceilings are problematic when there are too few difficult items at the top of the subtest and too many examinees are able to respond correctly to all of the items. When this *ceiling effect* occurs, it means that the subtest cannot adequately discriminate among those who score at the top of the subtest. Kaufman (1992) described the subtests of the WISC-III as having excellent ceilings for distinguishing among gifted children between the ages of 6 and 14, with all core subtests allowing standard scores up to 3 SDs above the mean. Though all of the core subtests had ceilings that went at least 2 SDs above the mean even at age 16, it was considered less than optimal that several core subtests could not yield scores 3 SDs out at the top age for the test. In general, Kaufman described the WISC-III subtest ceilings as ranging from excellent to adequate.

In the WISC-IV, subtest ceilings were refined. More-difficult items were added to several subtests in order to expand the range of possible raw scores and push the subtest ceilings further. Now all subtests in the WISC-IV standard battery can yield standard scores up to 3 SDs above the mean at all ages covered by the test. Among the five supplemental subtests, the Word Reasoning subtest begins to show a lower ceiling starting at age 14, but all four other supplemental subtests can yield scores 3 SDs out up through age 16:11. Thus, the WISC-IV has excellent subtest ceilings that allow it to more accurately discriminate among higher functioning examinees.

Cultural Bias

It is generally incumbent upon the producer of an intelligence test to demonstrate that it does not significantly favor one group over another for noncognitive reasons, and it is incumbent upon the user of the test to be informed about its appropriate use with various populations (see American Educational Research Association [AERA], 1999). At the item level, the expectation is that a test should be designed in such a way as to minimize the likelihood that items might be easier or more difficult for individuals from different cultural or subcultural backgrounds. It appears that the authors of the WISC-IV took all reasonable steps to minimize the influence of cultural bias on the test within the general English-speaking population of the United States. The standardization was careful and thorough, matching the 2000 Census numbers across five major demographic variables. A combination of formal expert review and empirical bias analyses were performed to identify and delete or modify problematic items. Experts came from multicultural research and intelligence testing, while empirical analyses included traditional Mantzel-Haenszel and item response theory bias-analysis techniques. Items were reportedly reviewed on three occasions between the test development and standardization phases (The Psychological Corporation, 2003). Additionally, the Information and Picture Arrangement subtests, which have been criticized for their more culture-laden content, were relegated to supplemental status or deleted from the battery, respectively.

Despite all of the care taken in the standardization and bias analyses, there is no completely culture-free test (Sattler, 2001). Thus, it is up to the examiner to understand when and how it is appropriate to use the WISC-IV. You should be informed and compassionate, and use common sense. When you are faced with an examinee for whom the standardization sample is not an appropriate comparison group or for whom certain subtest tasks are not meaningful because of differences related to culture, language, ethnicity, or disability, it behooves the examiner to select an appropriate alternative test, use only appropriate sections of the test, supplement testing with other pieces of information (e.g., other test scores, grades, records, background information from parents and teachers, and behavioral observations), and to make reasonable accommodations or modifications to make sure that the examinee understands the tasks and is given every reasonable opportunity to respond.

Nontypical Gifted Test Profiles

As Winner (2000) stated, gifted children often show uneven test profiles. Consistent with this statement, Sparrow and Gurland (1998) reported that significant and even substantial WISC-III Verbal IQ versus Performance IQ discrepancies were not that unusual within the gifted population. Given the factor index profile reported earlier for the WISC-IV validity study with gifted children, significant differences among the factor scores do not appear to be unusual on the WISC-IV. Based on the validity study, it appears that the two smaller factors (i.e., PSI and WMI) are the most likely to stand out with relatively lower scores than the two larger VCI and PRI factors.

The precise reasons for this will need to be clarified by further research, but certainly the two larger factors are more psychometrically robust, have stronger construct validity, and are more g loaded than the two smaller factors (see Appendix C). From the CHC perspective (McGrew, 1997), three of the four factor indexes could be ranked according to their theoretical relationship to g. The VCI, reflecting Crystallized Ability *(Gc)*, would be first; the PRI reflecting, Visual Processing *(Gv)* and Fluid Reasoning *(Gf)*, second; and the PSI, reflecting Processing Speed *(Gs)*, third. The exact position and status of the WMI are unclear, as Working Memory appears to be a broader construct than CHC theory's Stratum II Short-Term Memory *(Gsm)* factor (see McGrew & Flanagan, 1998, pp. 21–23). However, the WMI notwithstanding, the relative positions of these broad factors from CHC theory in relation to *g* at the third stratum appear to generally correspond to the relative rankings of the mean WISC-IV factor index scores for gifted children.

It is also noteworthy that Keith (1997) suggested that the memory and speed-of-processing tasks available on conventional intelligence tests like the WISC-III were only distantly similar to the more *g*-laden laboratory tasks designed to measure the same constructs. He concluded that memory and processing-speed tasks on the WISC-III were less related to *g* than tasks included on the test that assessed Crystallized Intelligence *(Gc)* and Quantitative Reasoning *(Gq)*. The best measure of *Gq* on the WISC-III and WISC-IV is the Arithmetic subtest. The removal of this subtest from among the core WMI subtests on the WISC-IV may have reduced the *g* loading of the WMI and made it less important for identifying gifted children. In any event, whether because of theoretical factors, statistical regression, or both, the PSI tends to be the lowest relative score for gifted examinees and the highest relative score for mentally retarded examinees (The Psychological Corporation, 2003).

The fact that discrepancies among the WISC-IV Indexes do not appear to be unusual in the gifted population, lends further credence to the notion that all scores should be considered when evaluating a potentially gifted child. The WISC-IV is well suited to giving useful information beyond the FSIQ, and it is clear that the separate Indexes should not be ignored. In the absence of meaningful discrepancies between Indexes, a FSIQ may reflect an accurate and useful overall estimate of an examinee's ability. However, this should never be assumed to be the case without taking all available scores and other relevant outside information into account.

Fluid Reasoning

Three new subtests to the WISC-IV (i.e., Matrix Reasoning, Picture Concepts, and Word Reasoning) are purported measures of Fluid Reasoning *(Gf)*. *Fluid Reasoning* (or *fluid intelligence*) refers to mental operations or problem-solving approaches a person may use when faced with relatively novel tasks. Both inductive and deductive reasoning are considered to be narrower aspects of this domain (McGrew & Flanagan, 1998). From a CHC perspective, Fluid Reasoning *(Gf)* bears the strongest relationship to *g* of all the CHC factors at the broad Stratum-

II level (Carroll, 1993; McGrew & Flanagan, 1998). Thus, one would expect these subtests to be highly relevant to gifted identification.

The inclusion of *Gf* subtests on the WISC-IV is clearly an attempt to address the criticism that the Wechsler scales have traditionally not measured fluid intelligence well (Carroll, 1997; McGrew & Flanagan, 1996). If one ranks the means for the set of 15 WISC-IV subtests from the gifted group described in the *WISC-IV Technical and Interpretive Manual* (The Psychological Corporation, 2003), the three Fluid Reasoning tasks are among the top 10 subtest means. However, none of them are among the top five subtest means. Assessment of Fluid Reasoning *(Gf)* using WISC-IV subtests was discussed in Chapter 4, and norms for a *Gf* cluster are provided in Appendix H.

Validity Study

There were a number of concerns regarding the WISC-IV validity study reported in the *WISC-IV Technical and Interpretive Manual* (The Psychological Corporation, 2003). Although discussed in Chapter 6, these concerns deserve further elaboration here. The study included 63 students previously identified as intellectually gifted by a score ≥ 2 SDs above the mean on a standardized measure of cognitive ability. The specific cognitive measures used to initially identify these children are not reported. The study reported significant differences favoring gifted students over matched controls on all core and supplemental subtests, except the nonsignificant difference for the Cancellation subtest. Gifted students also scored significantly higher on the FSIQ and all Indexes compared to matched controls. However, the WISC-IV FSIQ ($M = 123.5$) and Indexes (reported earlier) for the gifted sample were lower than expected. It is not unusual for the Flynn effect (1987) and statistical regression to the mean to lead to lower scores for an extreme scoring group upon retesting with a new cognitive measure. The mean FSIQ in the WISC-III gifted validity study was 128.7 (Wechsler, 1991, p. 210). The fact that the mean dropped below the original 130 cutoff score for the gifted sample upon retesting with the new measure seems readily explainable in terms of the Flynn effect and statistical regression. However, the WISC-IV mean FSIQ for the gifted sample is too low to be due solely to these factors.

There are several possible alternative explanations. First, it is possible that the original measure or measures used to identify the children as gifted were excessively varied or less than adequately related to the WISC-IV. It is not clear what individually administered or group-administered test or tests were used to initially identify these children. If the children were initially identified by a group-administered test, this might easily explain the difference. Second, the difference may be due to the changes in the WISC-IV core subtest battery relative to the WISC-III. Digit Span, Picture Concepts, Letter-Number Sequencing, Matrix Reasoning, and Symbol Search are all new to the core battery. When all 15 subtest scores are ranked from highest to lowest for the gifted sample, four of the five supplemental subtests show up in the top 10. These include Arithmetic, Information, and Picture Completion, which were originally in the core WISC-III battery but are relegated to the supplemental section of the WISC-IV. It is also telling that the two core PSI subtests (i.e., Coding and Symbol Search) and two core WMI subtests (i.e., Digit Span and Letter-Number Sequencing) were among the five lowest subtest scores in the gifted sample. A third possibility lies with the normalization and smoothing procedures used in the calibration of the FSIQ and Indexes. These procedures, which are only vaguely described in the *WISC-IV Technical and Interpretive Manual* (The Psychological Corporation, 2003), appear to have pulled in the tails of the IQ distribution to some extent. To illustrate, a direct linear transformation of the WISC-IV sum of subtest scores into the deviation quotient distribution would suggest an IQ distribution ranging from approximately 35 to 165. However, the manual reports values ranging from 40 to 160. The largest deviation from expectation based on a direct linear transformation occurs beyond the 3rd SD from the mean. Now, the range of 4 SDs to either side of the mean is excellent in and of itself. However, it is narrower than expected. Thus, it is possible that the normalization and smoothing procedures may have led to more extreme scores' being pulled in closer to the center of the distribution. Whatever the reason, the need for further studies to examine the relationship between the WISC-IV and other cognitive measures with gifted children is clear. The study made it evident that gifted children score significantly higher on the WISC-IV when compared to matched controls. Yet we are left uncertain about how well their WISC-IV scores would compare to their scores on other cognitive measures.

In conclusion, the WISC-IV has reduced speed-of-performance demands, excellent subtest ceilings for the core subtests across the entire age range covered by the test, solid standardization and reasonable minimization of cultural bias, a variety of scores beyond the FSIQ to assist in the evaluation of uneven abilities, and improved coverage of fluid ability. The gifted validity study reported in the *WISC-IV Technical and Interpretive Manual* (The Psychological Corporation, 2003) showed that the WISC-IV discriminates well between gifted and nongifted matched controls. However, further research on the WISC-IV with gifted children is required to clarify how well gifted children perform on this test relative to other cognitive tests.

USE OF THE WISC-IV AND WIAT-II WITHIN THE CONTEXT OF A MODERN OPERATIONAL DEFINITION OF LEARNING DISABILITY

Jennifer T. Mascolo

The WISC-IV and the Wechsler Individual Achievement Test–Second Edition (WIAT-II) together measure a range of cognitive and academic abilities that are important to assess when evaluating children suspected of having a learning disability (LD). Although these and other major cognitive and academic batteries provide many of the tests necessary for conducting the type of comprehensive evaluation that is required to identify and diagnose LD, the manner in which these tools are used varies widely. Having reliable and valid tests, such as those that comprise the WISC-IV/WIAT-II, is only part of the LD evaluation equation. In the field of LD, it has long been recognized that such tools should be used within the context of an operational definition of LD (see Flanagan et al., 2002; Kavale & Forness, 2000, for a review).

To use the WISC-IV/WIAT-II within the context of an operational definition of LD, you need to be able to make decisions related to the sufficiency of a WISC-IV/WIAT-II evaluation, identify normative and personal strengths and weaknesses, evaluate potential mitigating factors on test performance, and evaluate underachievement. The information presented here serves as one model for addressing LD referrals using the WISC-IV and WIAT-II.

Assessing Individuals Referred for Learning Difficulties with the WISC-IV and WIAT-II

Table 7.2 describes the operational definition of LD developed by Flanagan and colleagues (2002). The WISC-IV/WIAT-II may be used within the context of this operational definition for LD referrals. The essential elements in defining LD, as illustrated in this table, include (1) interindividual academic ability analysis (Level I-A); (2) evaluation of mitigating and exclusionary factors (Levels I-B and II-B); (3) interindividual cognitive ability analysis (Level II-A); and (4) integrated ability analysis (Level III). These elements together form an operational definition of LD. The WISC-IV/WIAT-II can be used effectively to gather information and test hypotheses at each level of this operational definition. It is only when the criteria at each of these levels of the operational definition are met that you can be reasonably confident that a diagnosis of LD is appropriate.

It is assumed that the levels of evaluation depicted in Table 7.2 are undertaken after prereferral intervention activities have been conducted with little or no suc-

Table 7.2 Operational Definition of Learning Disability

Essential Element	Focus of Assessment	Examples	Criteria	Learning Disability Determination
Level I-A: Interindividual academic ability analysis	Performance in academic skills and acquired knowledge	Performance on standardized tests, evaluation of work samples, clinical observations of academic skill performance, task analysis, etc.	Performance in one or more academic ability domains falls *outside and below normal limits.*	Necessary
Level I-B: Evaluation of exclusionary factors	Evaluation of potential primary causes of observed manifest academic ability deficits	Mental retardation, cultural or linguistic difference, sensory impairment, insufficient instruction or opportunity to learn, organic or physical health factors, emotional or psychological disturbance, etc.	Performance cannot be *primarily* attributed to other factors.	
Level II-A: Interindividual cognitive ability analysis	Performance in abilities/processes and learning efficiency	Performance on standardized tests, evaluation of work samples, clinical observations of cognitive ability performance, task analysis, etc.	Performance in one or more cognitive ability or processing domains *related to academic deficits falls outside and below normal limits.*	
Level II-B: Reevaluation of exclusionary factors	Evaluation of potential primary causes of observed manifest cognitive ability deficits	Mental retardation, cultural or linguistic difference, sensory impairment, insufficient instruction or opportunity to learn, organic or physical health factors, emotional or psychological disturbance, etc.	Performance cannot be *primarily* attributed to other factors.	
Level III: Integrated ability analysis	Evaluation of underachievement	Identification of deficits in related academic and cognitive abilities along with performance on other abilities within normal limits; OR global ability Within Normal Limits or higher and significantly discrepant from academic ability.	Below Average aptitude-achievement consistency AND other broad abilities are Within Normal Limits or higher; OR ability-achievement discrepancy AND global ability are Within Normal Limits or higher.	Sufficient

Source: From Flanagan, Keiser, Bernier, and Ortiz, *Diagnosis of Learning Disability in Adulthood.* Published by Allyn & Bacon, Boston, MA. Copyright © 2002 by Pearson Education. Adapted by permission of the publisher.

cess and, therefore, a focused evaluation of specific abilities and processes through standardized testing was deemed necessary. Moreover, prior to your beginning LD assessment with the WISC-IV/WIAT-II, other significant data sources could have (and probably should have) already been uncovered within the context of these intervention activities. These data may include results from informal testing, direct observation of behaviors, work samples, reports from people familiar with the child's difficulties (e.g., teachers, parents), and perhaps information provided by the child. In principle, Level I-A assessment should begin only after the scope and nature of a child's learning difficulties have been documented. It is beyond the scope of this book to provide a detailed discussion of assessment and interpretation-related activities for each level of the operational definition. Therefore, only a brief summary of each level follows (see Flanagan et al., 2002, for a comprehensive description of this LD model).

Level I-A, Interindividual Academic Ability Analysis with the WIAT-II: Performance in Academic Skills and Acquired Knowledge

Level I-A focuses on the basic concept of LD: that learning is somehow disrupted from its normal course on the basis of some type of internal disorder or dysfunction. Although the specific mechanism that inhibits learning is not directly observable, one can proceed on the assumption that it manifests itself in observable phenomena, particularly academic achievement. Thus, the first component of the operational definition of LD involves documenting that some type of *learning* deficit exists. Accordingly, the process at Level I-A involves comprehensive measurement of the major areas of academic achievement (e.g., reading, writing, and math abilities) or any subset of abilities that form the focus and purpose of the evaluation.

The academic abilities that are generally assessed at this level in the operational definition include the seven areas of achievement specified in the federal definition of LD as outlined in the Individuals with Disabilities Education Act (IDEA; PL 105-17). These seven areas are math calculation, math reasoning, basic reading, reading comprehension, written expression, listening comprehension, and oral expression. Most of the abilities measured at Level I-A represent an individual's stores of acquired knowledge. These specific knowledge bases (e.g., Quantitative Knowledge, Reading, Writing) develop largely as a function of formal instruction, schooling, and educationally related experiences. Rapid Reference 7.1 lists the WIAT-II subtests that correspond to the seven achievement areas specified in the federal definition of LD. This Rapid Reference includes a list of subtests from the Woodcock-Johnson Tests of Achievement–Third Edition (WJ III ACH) and the Kaufman Test of Educational Achievement–Second Edition,

≡ Rapid Reference 7.1

Representation of Academic Abilities by Learning Disability Area on the WIAT-II and Other Comprehensive Achievement Batteries

Learning Disability Area Listed in IDEA Definition	WIAT-II	KTEA-II	WJ III ACH
Basic reading skills	Word Reading (RD) Pseudoword Decoding (RD, PC:A)	Letter and Word Recognition (RD) Nonsense Word Decoding (RD, PC:A) Phonological Awareness (PC:A) Timed Nonsense Word Decoding (RD, RS, PC:A) Timed Word Recognition (RD, RS) Fluency (Semantic and Phonological) (RS) Rapid Automatized Naming (Glr-NA)	L-W Identification (RD) Word Attack (RD, PC:A) Sound Awareness (PC:A, PC:S) Reading Fluency (RS)
Reading comprehension	Reading Comprehension (RC)	Reading Comprehension (RC) Reading Vocabulary (V, VL)	Passage Comprehension (RC, CZ)
Math calculation	Numerical Operations (A3)	Math Computation (A3) Calculation (A3)	Math Fluency (N, A3)

Math reasoning	Math Reasoning (Gf-RQ)	Math Concepts and Applications (Gf-RQ, A3) Quantitative Concepts (KM, Gf-RQ)	Applied Problems (A3, KM, Gf-RQ)
Written expression	Spelling (SG) Written Expression (WA)	Spelling (SG) Written Expression (WA)	Spelling (SG) Writing Samples (WA) Editing (Gc-MY, EU) Punctuation and Capitalization (EU) Spelling of Sounds (SG, PC:A, PC:S) Writing Fluency (R9)
Oral expression	Oral Expression (CM)	Oral Expression (CM)	Story Recall (LS; Glr-MM) Picture Vocabulary (Language Development, VL)
Listening comprehension	Listening Comprehension (LS)	Listening Comprehension (LS)	Understanding Directions (LS, Gsm-WM) Oral Comprehension (LS)

Note: WIAT-II = Wechsler Individual Achievement Test–Second Edition; KTEA-II = Kaufman Test of Educational Achievement–Second Edition, Comprehensive Form; WJ III ACH = Woococck-Johnson Tests of Achievement–Third Edition. See Appendix A for C–HC broad and narrow ability definitions. Narrow ability classifications are based on expert consensus (see Caltabiano & Flanagan, 2004) and information presented in the test manuals of each achievement battery. Story Recall–Delayed (Glr-MM) and Handwriting Legibility Scale are two supplemental measures on the WJ III ACH not included in this table. A3 = Math Achievement; EU = English Usage Knowledge; KM = Math Knowledge; LS = Listening Ability; MM = Meaningful Memory; N = Number Fluency; NA= Naming Facility; PC:A = Phonetic Coding: Analysis; PC:S = Phonetic Coding: Synthesis; RC = Reading Comprehension; RD = Reading Decoding; RQ = Quantitative Reasoning; RS = Reading Speed; SG = Spelling Ability; V = Verbal (Printed) Language Comprehension; VL = Lexical Knowledge; WA = Writing Ability; CM = Communication Ability; CZ = Cloze Ability; MY = Grammatical Sensitivity; R9 = Rate-of-test-taking.

Comprehensive Form (KTEA-II; Kaufman & Kaufman, 2004b) that may be used to supplement the WIAT-II, if necessary, via the Cross-Battery method (see Flanagan et al., 2002 for a detailed review of Cross-Battery procedures).

Once you select and administer achievement tests (see Rapid Reference 7.1), evaluate performance to determine whether an academic *Normative Weakness* is present. This is accomplished through an *interindividual academic ability analysis*. This type of analysis involves making normative-based comparisons of the child's WIAT-II (or any other achievement test) performance against a representative sample of same-age or -grade peers from the general population. If Normative Weaknesses in the child's academic achievement profile are not identified, then the issue of LD is likely moot because such weaknesses are a necessary component of the definition. Therefore, the presence of a Normative Weakness established through standardized testing as well as by other means, such as clinical observations of academic performance, work samples, and so forth, is a necessary but insufficient condition for LD determination. By definition, dysfunction in learning as manifest in significant academic difficulties forms the foundation of all prevailing LD definitions. Therefore, when a Normative Weakness in academic performance or learning is found (irrespective of the particular method by which it is identified), a necessary but not sufficient condition for LD is established and you can advance to Level I-B.

Level I-B, Evaluation of Exclusionary Factors

The criterion at Level I-B involves evaluating whether any documented Normative Weakness found through Level I-A analysis is or is not *primarily* the result of factors that are largely external to the child or are noncognitive in nature. Because there can be many reasons for deficient academic performance, you should be careful not to ascribe causal links to LD prematurely and should develop reasonable hypotheses related to other potential causes. For example, cultural and linguistic differences are two common factors that can affect both test performance and academic skill acquisition adversely and result in achievement data that appear to suggest LD (this topic is discussed in the next section of this chapter). In addition, lack of motivation, emotional disturbance, performance anxiety, psychiatric disorders, sensory impairments, and medical conditions (e.g., hearing or vision problems) also need to be ruled out as potential explanatory correlates to any Normative Weaknesses identified on WIAT-II (or other) subtests at Level I-A. The crux of the criterion at this level rests on the extent to which any external or noncognitive factor or factors are determined to be the primary reason for the Normative Weakness in academic performance that was uncovered at Level I-A. If performance cannot be attributed primarily to other factors, then the second criterion necessary for establishing LD according to the operational definition is met, and assessment may continue to the next level.

It is important to recognize that, although external factors may be present and may affect evaluation of performance, LD can also be present. Certainly, children who may have vision problems, chronic illnesses, limited English proficiency, and so forth, may well possess some type of LD. Therefore, when these or other factors at Level I-B are present or even when they are determined to be contributing to poor performance, LD should not be ruled out automatically. Rather, only when such factors are determined to be *primarily* responsible for Normative Weaknesses in learning and academic performance, not merely *contributing* to them, should LD, as an explanation for dysfunction in performance, be discounted. Examination of exclusionary variables is necessary to ensure fair and equitable interpretation of the data collected for LD determination and is not intended to rule in LD but rather to specifically rule out other possible explanations for deficient academic ability. You should remember that the final determination of LD is made only after all criteria from each and every level are met, irrespective of how dramatic any particular datum or pattern of data may appear initially.

One of the major reasons for placing evaluation of exclusionary factors at this point in the assessment process is to provide a mechanism that is efficient in both time and effort and that may prevent the unnecessary administration of tests or imposition of further invasive and unneeded evaluative procedures. Use of standardized tests, in particular IQ tests, cannot be considered a benign process. The implications and ramifications that can result from their use demands that you carefully and selectively apply them only when absolutely necessary. We recognize, of course, that it may not be possible to completely and convincingly rule out all of the numerous potential exclusionary factors at this stage in the assessment process. For example, the data gathered at Levels I-A and I-B may be insufficient to draw conclusions about such conditions as Mental Retardation, which often requires more thorough and direct cognitive assessment. Therefore, proper assessment must seek to uncover and evaluate as many possibilities as is practical or necessary. When exclusionary factors have been carefully evaluated and eliminated as possible *primary* explanations for poor Level I-A performance— at least those that can be reliably assessed at this level—assessment may advance to the next level.

Level II-A, Interindividual Cognitive Ability Analysis with the WISC-IV: Performance in Cognitive Abilities and Processes

The criterion at this level is similar to the one specified in Level I-A except that it is evaluated with data from an assessment of cognitive abilities and processes (e.g., from the WISC-IV). Analysis of data generated from the administration of standardized tests represents the most common method available by which cognitive functioning in children can be evaluated. However, this does not preclude the use of other types of information and data relevant to cognitive performance. In keeping with good assessment practices, you should actively seek out and gather data from other sources as a means of providing corroborating evidence for whatever conclusions you reach. In general, the assessment process at Level II-A, as with the measurement of abilities at Level I-A, proceeds with the expectation that a child's cognitive performance will be *Within Normal Limits* unless otherwise indicated by careful analysis of all available data. This is true even when actual, verifiable academic Normative Weaknesses are identified at Level I-A. Rapid Reference 7.2 identifies the CHC abilities measured by the WISC-IV as well as by other major intelligence batteries.

A particularly salient aspect of any operational definition of LD is the concept of a neurologically-based dysfunction in a cognitive ability or process that presumably underlies the difficulties in academic performance or skill development observed at Level I-A. Because nearly all LD definitions either specify directly or imply that the relationship between the cognitive dysfunction and the manifest learning problems are not random but rather causal in nature, data analysis at this level should seek to ensure that identified Normative Weaknesses on cognitive tests bear an empirical or logical relationship to those Normative Weaknesses previously identified on achievement tests. It is this very notion that makes it necessary to draw upon cognitive theory and research to inform LD definitions and increase the reliability and validity of the LD determination process. Theory and its related research base not only specify the relevant constructs in LD determination (e.g., constructs that ought to be measured at Levels I-A and II-A), but also predict the manner in which they are related. Therefore, application of current theory and research serves to guide data analysis at all levels, including this one, and provides a substantive empirical foundation from which interpretations and conclusions may be drawn. Table 7.3 provides a summary of the relations between CHC cognitive abilities and reading, math, and written language achievement. This table may assist in organizing assessments at Levels I-A and II-A as well as aid in determining whether Level II-A criteria have been met.

Meeting the criterion at Level II-A requires the identification of interindividual cognitive ability or processing deficits that are empirically or logically related to the corresponding Normative Weaknesses previously identified in academic performance at Level I-A. When evaluation of cognitive performance is comprehensive and sufficient in terms of measuring the areas of suspected dysfunction and no Normative Weaknesses in cognitive functioning are found, then poor

≡ Rapid Reference 7.2

CHC Abilities Measured by Major Intelligence Tests

Broad Ability	WISC-IV	KABC-II	WJ III COG
Gf	Picture Concepts (I) Matrix Reasoning (I, RG) Word Reasoning (I) Arithmetic (RG)	Pattern Reasoning (I, Gv-Vz) Story Completion (I, RG, Gc-K0, Gv-Vz)	Concept Formation (I) Analysis Synthesis (RG)
Gc	Similarities (LD, VL) Picture Concepts (K0) Vocabulary (VL) Comprehension (K0) Picture Completion (K0) Information (K0) Word Reasoning (VL)	Riddles (VL, LD, Gf-RG) Expressive Vocabulary (VL) Verbal Knowledge (VL, K0)	Verbal Comprehension (VL, LD) General Information (K0)
Ga	—	—	Incomplete Words (PC:A) Sound Blending (PC:S) Auditory Attention (US/U3)

(continued)

Broad Ability	WISC-IV	KABC-II	WJ III COG
Gv	Block Design (SR) Picture Completion (CF)	Conceptual Thinking (Vz, Gf-I) Block Counting (Vz, Gq-A3) Face Recognition (MV) Triangles (SR, Vz) Rover (SS, Gf-RG, Gq-A3) Gestalt Closure (CS)	Spatial Relations (Vz, SR) Picture Recognition (MV)
Gsm	Digit Span (MS, WM) Letter-Number Sequencing (WM)	Word Order (MS, WM) Number Recall (MS) Hand Movements (Ms, Gv-MV)	Memory Words (MS) Numbers Reversed (WM) Auditory Working Memory (WM)
Glr	—	Atlantis (MA, LI) Rebus (MA) Atlantis Delayed (MA, LI) Rebus Delayed (MA, LI)	Visual Auditory Learning (MA, MM) Visual-Auditory Learning Delayed (MA) Retrieval Fluency (FI, FA) Rapid Picture Naming (NA)
Gs	Coding (R9) Symbol Search (P, R9) Cancellation (P, R9)	—	Visual Matching (P, R9) Decision Speed (N)
Gq	Arithmetic (A3)	—	—

Source: Narrow ability classifications are based on expert consensus (see Caltabiano & Flanagan, 2004) and information presented in the test manuals of each cognitive battery.

Note: WISC-IV = Wechsler Intelligence Scale for Children–Fourth Edition; KABC-II = Kaufman Assessment Battery for Children–Second Edition; WJ III COG = Woodcock-Johnson Tests of Cognitive Abilities–Third Edition. A3 = Math Achievement; I = Inductive Reasoning; K0 = General (Verbal) Information; MA = Associative Memory; MM = Meaningful Memory; MS = Memory Span; N = Number Facility; NA = Naming Facility; P = Perceptual Speed; PCA = Phonetic Coding: Analysis; PCS = Phonetic Coding: Synthesis; RG = General Sequential Reasoning; RQ = Quantitative Reasoning; VL = Lexical Knowledge; SR = Spatial Relations; CF = Flexibility of Closure; MV = Visual Memory; WM = Working Memory; R9 = Rate-of-test-taking; Vz = Visualization; SS = Spatial Scanning; CS = Closure Speed; L = Learning Abilities; US/U3 = Speech/General Sound Discrimination; FI = Ideational Fluency; FA = Associational Fluency. See Appendix A for CHC broad and narrow ability definitions.

Table 7.3 Relations between CHC Cognitive Abilities and Academic Achievement

CHC Ability	Reading Achievement	Math Achievement	Writing Achievement
Gf	Inductive (I) and General Sequential (RG) Reasoning abilities play a moderate role in reading comprehension.	**Inductive (I) and General Sequential (RG) Reasoning abilities are consistently very important at all ages.**	Inductive (I) and General Sequential (RG) Reasoning abilities are related to basic writing skills primarily during the elementary school years (e.g., ages 6 to 13) and consistently related to written expression at all ages.
Gc	**Language Development, Lexical Knowledge (VL), and Listening Ability (LS) are important at all ages. These abilities become increasingly more important with age.**	**Language Development, Lexical Knowledge (VL), and Listening Abilities (LS) are important at all ages. These abilities become increasingly more important with age.**	**Language Development, Lexical Knowledge (VL), and General Information (K0) are important primarily after age 7. These abilities become increasingly more important with age.**
Gsm	**Memory Span (MS) is important especially when evaluated within the context of working memory.**	**Memory Span (MS) is important especially when evaluated within the context of working memory.**	Memory Span (MS) is important to writing, especially for spelling skills, whereas Working Memory (WM) has shown relations with advanced writing skills (e.g., written expression).
Gv		May be important primarily for higher-level or advanced mathematics (e.g., geometry, calculus).	
Ga	**Phonetic Coding (PC) or "phonological awareness/processing" is very important during the elementary school years.**		**Phonetic Coding (PC) or "phonological awareness/processing" is very important during the elementary school years for both basic writing skills and written expression (primarily before age 11).**

(continued)

Table 7.3 (Continued)

CHC Ability	Reading Achievement	Math Achievement	Writing Achievement
Glr	**Naming Facility (NA)** or **"rapid automatized naming" is very important during the elementary school years.** Associative Memory (MA) may be somewhat important at select ages (e.g., age 6).		Naming Facility (NA) or "rapid automatized naming" has demonstrated relations with written expression, primarily the fluency aspect of writing.
Gs	**Perceptual Speed (P) abilities are important during all school years, particularly the elementary school years.**	**Perceptual Speed (P) abilities are important during all school years, particularly the elementary school years.**	**Perceptual Speed (P) abilities are important during all school years for basic writing and related to all ages for written expression.**

Source: Information in this table was reproduced from McGrew and Flanagan (1998), Flanagan and colleagues (2000), and Flanagan and colleagues (2002) with permission from Allyn & Bacon. All rights reserved.

Note: The absence of comments for a particular CHC ability and achievement area (e.g., *Ga* and mathematics) indicates that the research reviewed either did not report any significant relations between the respective CHC ability and the achievement area, or if significant findings were reported, they were weak and were for only a limited number of studies. Comments in bold represent the CHC abilities that showed the strongest and most consistent relations with the respective achievement domain.

academic performance alone, as identified at Level I-A, is not sufficient to establish the presence of LD. Likewise, when a Normative Weakness in cognitive functioning is identified at Level II-A but the area of dysfunction is not logically or empirically related to the Normative Weakness at Level I-A, then the presence of LD is indeterminate.

Level II-B, Reevaluation of Exclusionary Factors

Because new data (i.e., WISC-IV data) were gathered at the previous level, reevaluation of mitigating or exclusionary factors, as conducted at Level I-B, should be undertaken again at this point. Although establishing the presence of a Normative Weakness in cognitive functioning that is related to an identified Normative Weakness in academic performance (as done in Level II-A) is fundamental to the operational definition of LD, it should be reasonably determined that such a Normative Weakness is not the primary result of external or exclusionary factors. Reevaluation of mitigating and exclusionary hypotheses at this level illustrates the recursive nature of this component of the LD determination process. Reliable and valid measurement of LD depends partly on being able to exclude the many factors that could play a part in affecting WISC-IV performance adversely. When it can be reasonably determined that the Normative Weaknesses in cognitive functioning identified at Level II-A cannot be ascribed primarily to external or noncognitive factors, then the necessary criterion at this level is met and advancement to the next level of assessment is appropriate.

Level III, Integrated Ability Analysis with the WISC-IV and WIAT-II: Evaluation of Underachievement

Integrated ability analysis revolves specifically around theory- and research-guided examination of a child's WISC-IV/WIAT-II performance across both cognitive and academic ability domains in order to establish the condition of underachievement. When the process of evaluating LD has reached this level, three necessary criteria for LD determination have already been met: (1) One or more Normative Weaknesses in academic performance have been identified; (2) one or more Normative Weaknesses in cognitive abilities or processes that are related to the area(s) of academic weakness have been identified; and (3) exclusionary factors have been ruled out as the primary causes of the identified Normative Weaknesses in academic and cognitive performance. What has not been determined, however, is whether the pattern of results supports the notion of underachievement in a manner that suggests LD. The nature of underachievement, within the context of the operational definition presented here, suggests that not only does a child possess specific, circumscribed, and related academic and cognitive Normative Weaknesses, but that these weaknesses exist within an otherwise *normal ability* profile. Determining whether this criterion is met usually takes one of two forms—consistency analysis or discrepancy analysis.

Aptitude-Achievement Consistency Analysis   If the cognitive and achievement data generated in assessment were evaluated within the context of current theory and research (e.g., CHC theory), then evaluation of data at this level can take the form of aptitude-achievement *consistency* analysis. *Analysis of consistency* refers to examination of the degree to which a Normative Weakness in academic ability (achievement) is *consistent* or positively correlated with a *related* cognitive ability, which by definition is an *aptitude* (see Flanagan et al., 2002). Inclusion of measures of specific aptitudes is central to this form of analysis because it allows one to investigate whether two or more abilities that are known to correlate highly with one another actually do; hence the term "aptitude-achievement consistency analysis." Note also that, in general, this type of analysis is not concerned with consistency between scores that tend to fall Within Normal Limits or higher, but rather, with performance that is outside *and* below normal limits—the ability range that is associated with dysfunction or disability. Therefore, consistency analysis within the context of LD determination generally focuses on the evaluation of consistency among related cognitive and achievement scores within the Below Average or lower range of functioning. The information in Table 7.3 depicts important cognitive ability and achievement relationships.

It is important to understand that discovery of consistencies among cognitive and academic abilities in the Below Average or lower range could result from mental retardation or generally low cognitive ability. Therefore, identification of LD cannot rest on consistency analysis alone. A child must also demonstrate evidence of intact functioning (e.g., Within Normal Limits or higher) on WISC-IV and WIAT-II measures, for example, that are largely unrelated to the presenting problem. For example, in the case of a child with reading decoding difficulties, it would be necessary to determine that performance in areas largely unrelated to this skill (e.g., *Gf,* math ability) are not identified as Normative Weaknesses. If these abilities are Within Normal Limits or higher relative to same-age or -grade peers from the general population, you can be reasonably confident that the observed Below Average consistency between aptitude and achievement is not due to a more pervasive form of dysfunction (e.g., mental retardation). Such a pattern therefore reinforces the notion of underachievement—that the child could in all likelihood perform within normal limits in whatever achievement skill he or she was found to be deficient (as he or she demonstrated the ability to do in other areas of achievement) if not for a specific cognitive deficit. The finding of Normative Weaknesses in such a circumscribed set of related (i.e., domain-specific) cognitive and academic ability domains within an otherwise normal ability profile is, for all intents and purposes, convincing evidence of LD. If, however, Normative Weaknesses are evident in a child's other abilities (in addition to the abilities that comprise the Below Average aptitude-achievement consistency), then it is more likely that overall WIAT-II and WISC-IV performance is due primarily to broader causes, such as low general intelligence or cognitive ability. In sum, underachievement is established through the aptitude-achievement consistency method only on the basis of two necessary conditions: (1) a consistency between specific cognitive abilities (aptitude) as measured by the WISC-IV (and/or other cognitive tests) and one or more WIAT-II (and/or other) achievement tests that are both related to one another and generally confined to the Below Average or lower range of ability; and (2) performance in some cognitive or achievement areas that is Within Normal Limits or higher.

This pattern of normal or average performance in abilities apart from already identified consistent Normative Weaknesses between aptitude and achievement may also be investigated and established via examination of other data, such as measures of adaptive behavior, work samples, classroom observations, teacher reports, curriculum-based measures, interviews, or criterion-referenced methods. In some cases, generally average or normal ability might also be established by examination of comprehensive global ability scores (i.e., WISC-IV FSIQ) or by an abbreviated measure of general intellectual functioning (e.g., WISC-IV General Ability Index [GAI]). But use of such scores to evaluate the expected level of WIAT-II achievement can be misleading because they are generally not designed to predict development or acquisition of specific academic skills (e.g., reading decoding). Additionally, such general ability scores may be attenuated by the inclusion of abilities in which the individual is deficient, resulting in scores that do not provide an accurate picture of overall ability. This problem is further explained in the following discussion of another type of procedure often used to establish underachievement, called "ability-achievement discrepancy analysis."

Ability-Achievement Discrepancy Analysis   Evaluation of underachievement is probably most often accomplished via *ability-achievement discrepancy analysis,* particularly when standardized tests are used. Cognitive assessment (such as that conducted at Level II-A) very often must generate some type of global ability score (as opposed to specific aptitude scores), to comply with current legal or diagnostic requirements for the identification of LD (see Flanagan et al., 2002, for a comprehensive discussion). Given the flaws in the logic of this approach and the extent to which it has been discredited in the literature, practitioners would seem to be better served by avoiding it altogether. Despite the logical, empirical, and theoretical advantages of aptitude-achievement consistency analysis over ability-achievement discrepancy analysis, the latter method remains in widespread use. (For a complete treatment of the fallibilities of ability-achievement discrepancy analysis, see Flanagan et al.).

In the operational definition of LD presented here, we accommodate the use of ability-achievement discrepancy analysis in the LD determination process, in light of practical constraints (i.e., while school districts phase out this analysis vis à vis the reauthorization of IDEA), but it is not required. More importantly, the finding of a significant ability-achievement discrepancy is neither a necessary nor a sufficient condition for LD determination. In contrast, ability-achievement consistency analysis can be used in combination with other data to determine LD and represents a far more defensible method for LD determination in light of the research base that supports it. Therefore, it should be considered the first-line method of analysis at Level III in the operational definition. In short, the criterion at Level III is met when it is demonstrated reliably that underachievement exists for the child as established either by a Below Average or lower aptitude-achievement consistency in a pattern of Average Range or higher performance in other abilities, or by an ability-achievement discrepancy coupled with global ability Within Normal Limits or higher.

Summary of the Operational Definition of Learning Disability

The preceding paragraphs provided a brief summary of the major components of a modern operational definition of LD that is designed specifically to assist clinicians in the evaluation of LD. The operational definition presented here provides a common foundation for the practice of LD determination and will likely be most effective when it is informed by cognitive theory and research that supports (1) the identification and measurement of constructs associated with LD, (2) the relationship between selected cognitive and academic abilities, and (3) a defensible method of interpreting results. The operational definition is based primarily on the work of Flanagan and colleagues (2002) and was adapted here for use with the WISC-IV and WIAT-II. Of the many important components of the definition, the central focus revolved around specification of criteria at the various levels of assessment that should be met to establish the presence of LD. These criteria included identification of logically or empirically related interindividual academic and cognitive ability Normative Weaknesses, evaluation of exclusionary factors, identification of a pattern of underachievement, and identification of intact functioning.

In keeping with the conclusions of Flanagan and colleagues, when the criteria specified at each level of the operational definition are met (as depicted in Table 7.2), it may be concluded that the data gathered are sufficient to support a diagnosis of LD. Because the conditions outlined in Table 7.2 are based on current LD research, the operational definition presented here represents progress toward a more complete and defensible approach to the process of evaluating LD. We believe that an operational definition of this type has the potential to increase agreement among professionals with respect to who does and does not have a specific LD. Toward that end, we have undertaken a distillation of the criteria inherent in our operational definition of LD that may help simplify and clarify the goals of assessment for practitioners. Rapid Reference 7.3 lists the five questions that guide the specific LD assessment activities within the scope of the operational definition. The questions are phrased in a straightforward manner and together provide an indication of both the type of data that may need to be collected

≡ Rapid Reference 7.3

Summary of Guiding Questions Implied by the Operational Definition of Learning Disability

Question 1 Does the child demonstrate one or more interindividual deficits in one or more academic abilities (e.g., in reading, writing, mathematics, etc.)?

Question 2 Can the academic skill deficits be attributed *primarily* to mitigating or exclusionary factors such as sensory impairment, emotional disturbance, inadequate schooling or instruction, limited familiarity with the language used in the test items, low motivation or energy, etc.?

Question 3 Does the child demonstrate interindividual deficits in one or more cognitive abilities that are empirically or logically related to the development or acquisition of the academic ability found to be deficient?

Question 4 Can the cognitive ability deficits be attributed *primarily* to mitigating or exclusionary factors such as sensory impairment, emotional disturbance, inadequate schooling or instruction, limited familiarity with the language used in the test items, low motivation or energy, etc.?

Question 5 Is there evidence of underachievement that can be established either through a Below Average or lower aptitude-achievement consistency *and* other abilities Within Normal Limits or higher *or* an ability-achievement discrepancy *and* global ability Within Normal Limits or higher?

Source: These questions are based on the operational definition presented in Flanagan and colleagues (2002).

as well as the manner in which the data should be interpreted as being sufficient to meet the respective criteria at each level.

A Comprehensive Framework for Learning Disability Determination

Broadly speaking, *LD assessment* can be defined as an exercise in decision making. This was evident in the previous discussion of the operational definition of LD. However, the decision-making process extends beyond the confines of the specifications of the operational definition to the broader process of assessment as a whole. Whether focusing directly on criteria related to the operational definition of LD or not, the general process of psychological assessment involves a broader set of questions or conditions that should be attended to in order to establish a firm basis for defending any final interpretations and conclusions. For example, issues related to the degree that the collected data respond appropriately to the specific referral questions, the sufficiency of the evaluation of any abilities that may have been measured, and the nature and type of intervention and remediation that may be required, represent components of any comprehensive assessment, particularly those centered on LD determination.

Attention to the general aspects of LD assessment is important for several reasons. First, and perhaps most importantly, careful attention to the operational criteria for establishing LD does not automatically validate the entire assessment process. For example, identifying a specific LD in reading comprehension serves little purpose if the referral concern centered on difficulties in mathematical computation. Failure to collect data that can be used to answer the questions that precipitated the referral, no matter how meticulously the data were gathered, represents an inefficient use of time and effort. Second, practitioners often take for granted that the abilities they sought to measure were in fact the abilities that *were* measured. Unless you carefully evaluate the sufficiency of your evaluative efforts (i.e., the degree to which you actually measured the relevant and precise abilities in question), interpretations and conclusions made from the collected data may be much less valid than you had originally believed. Although it is logical to assume that a test of reading comprehension does in fact measure reading comprehension, you should not take for granted that any test will in fact measure what it is purported to measure with equal reliability and validity for every individual and across every age group. Even tests that are presumed to measure the same ability may vary simply as a function of slight differences in task characteristics (e.g., feedback given or not given, verbal responding vs. pointing). Accordingly, you should be familiar with the qualitative and quantitative characteristics of any tests used (e.g., task characteristics, reliability at different ages, specificity, validity, floors and ceilings) to further substantiate your impressions (see the appendices of this book). Third, identification of LD or other problems does not represent an end in and of itself. Rather, it represents the beginning of a new set of assessment activities that seek to link the results of the evaluation to appropriate types of intervention and remediation. Moreover, what might constitute an appropriate remedial strategy or accommodation for a particular type of disability in one child does not imply that the same is true for another child with the same disability. The manner in which LD is manifest in children can vary considerably, even when two children share essentially the same difficulties or diagnosis (e.g., LD in mathematical computation or reading comprehension).

In sum, defensible evaluation of LD cannot rest on simply meeting the criteria set forth in the operational definition described here—or in any other definition, for that matter. Careful attention to the issues and questions that make up the activities of the assessment process as a whole, within which the operational definition is embedded, is also required so that proper and defensible decisions can be made. This broader process of LD assessment is illustrated graphically as a decision-based flowchart and is presented in Figure 7.1. Much like the proposed operational definition described previously, the comprehensive assessment framework shown in Figure 7.1 is adapted primarily from the work of Flanagan and colleagues (2002). The flowchart is easily navigated via the specification of particular assessment activities and evaluation procedures that proceed on the basis of answers to "yes-or-no" questions. A more comprehensive discussion of the major aspects and decision points involved in the process may be found in Flanagan and colleagues. Decisions in the case of Ryan in Chapter 8 of this book were made, in part, following the operational definition presented here.

Conclusion

This section presented an operational definition of LD that can be used with the WISC-IV and WIAT-II and that was based primarily on the work of Flanagan and colleagues (2002). In broad terms, the operational definition described in this section consists of various levels that specify the necessary criteria required for LD determination. Meeting these particular criteria and evaluating the components of the broader process of assessment (Figure 7.1) are necessary for making a diagnosis of LD, and constitute a best-practices approach to the assessment of learning difficulties in children. In sum, the resulting operational definition and comprehensive framework provide practitioners and researchers with an inherently practical method for LD assessment that is believed to be more reliable and defensible than that represented by most traditional methods and practices.

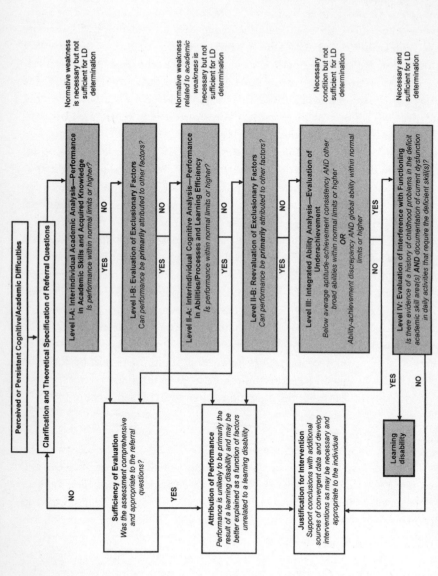

Figure 7.1 Flowchart of Evaluation Procedures Necessary for LD Determination

From D. P. Flanagan, S. O. Ortiz, V. C. Alfonso, J. T. Mascolo, *The Achievement Test Desk Reference: Comprehensive Assessment and Learning Disability.* Published by Allyn & Bacon, Boston, MA. Copyright © 2002 by Pearson Education. Reproduced by permission of the Publisher.

BILINGUAL-MULTICULTURAL ASSESSMENT WITH THE WISC-IV

Samuel O. Ortiz

With the possible exception of the Army Alpha and Beta tests (Brigham, 1922; Gould, 1981) and the translated Binet scales (Terman, 1916), perhaps no other tests have been administered more frequently to individuals from diverse cultural and linguistic backgrounds as the venerable Wechsler scales. Certainly within the last 50 years it is hard to imagine any battery having been applied more often to the task of evaluating the intelligence or cognitive capabilities of diverse children than the Wechsler family of instruments. It is interesting to note, however, that the reasons for their popularity in this particular application were not built upon issues of established fairness or cross-cultural validity per se, but rather on the lack of technically adequate tests in languages other than English, the paucity of competent and qualified bilingual-bicultural professionals, and the absence of any systematic framework or guiding principles for addressing bilingual-multicultural issues in assessment (Ortiz, 2001). Even where a test in a language other than English might be available (e.g., Escala de Inteligencía Wechsler para Niños–Revisada [EIWN-R]), the vast majority of intelligence testing on non–English speaking children has continued to be conducted in English (i.e., with the WISC) and is a common practice that persists to the present day (Ochoa, Powell, & Robles-Piña, 1996).

How and in what manner the WISC-IV may be used to assess and evaluate more fairly and equitably the intelligence and cognitive capabilities of children from diverse cultural and linguistic backgrounds are the very issues that constitute the focus and purpose of this section. Readers are cautioned from the outset, however, that the procedures described herein are not, in and of themselves, a complete answer to the obstacles extant in assessing diverse children and do not, by themselves, constitute the only—or even a sufficient—solution for establishing definitively the intelligence of such children. It is believed, however, that the procedures described here represent a significant advancement in the assessment of culturally and linguistically diverse children, particularly as compared to the methods historically and presently employed with the first publication and subsequent revisions of the WISC.

Traditional Practices and Procedures

Understanding any approach to the assessment of intelligence in diverse populations with the WISC-IV requires knowledge regarding why certain practices or procedures are or are not equitable or appropriate. There have been many prescriptions regarding how to administer a WISC to children from diverse cultural or linguistic backgrounds, from adding acculturation points to the FSIQ (Mercer,

1979) to administration of translated WISCs that are normed on individuals from other countries or other special populations (e.g., the WISC-R-PR, which was normed on Puerto Rican children living in the United States). Some legal prescriptions have even gone so far as to restrict or entirely eliminate the use of any intelligence test with certain populations (e.g., Larry P. vs. Riles, 1979).

None of these methods have been widely adopted, perhaps because each has significant problems. The System of Multicultural Pluralistic Assessment (SOMPA; Mercer, 1979) was roundly criticized for various reasons and never recovered from the maelstrom that decried any alteration of the sacred IQ. The use of native-language tests seemed rather promising, especially because the WISC-III had been adapted and standardized in 16 different countries. Still, significant problems remained.

According to information available online from The Psychological Corporation, these tests are suitable primarily for children whose families have recently immigrated to the United States. No caution is given, however, with regard to consideration of the immigrant's educational history, socioeconomic status, type of current instructional program, and emerging *bilingual* development—all of which are crucial factors that should be considered when attempting to evaluate such children. Because children in school in the United States are expected to learn and are specifically taught English, they become circumstantial bilinguals and as such constitute a group that is far different than the monolingual children on whom these foreign-language adaptations were normed (Figueroa & Hernandez, 2000; Flanagan & Ortiz, 2001; Ortiz, 2001, 2002; Valdes & Figueroa, 1994). Moreover, use of such adapted tests obviously requires an examiner who possesses both the fluency required for administration as well as the competency in nondiscriminatory assessment that provides the real basis for equitable interpretation. Thus, although a Spanish version of the WISC-IV is currently under development, its publication will do little to assist the vast majority of practitioners who do not speak Spanish, those who need to evaluate children in languages other than Spanish, and those who do not possess specific training and education in nondiscriminatory assessment. In order to reach the great majority of professionals currently faced with evaluating the intelligence and cognitive abilities of diverse children in the schools, other methods will need to be employed.

Perhaps the most common practice for assessing the intelligence of children from culturally and linguistically diverse backgrounds has been the clinical prescription to simply administer only the subtests that make up the PIQ (Figueroa, 1990). Previous versions of the WISC utilized the original dichotomous organization of subtests segregated into the Verbal and Performance categories. It seemed reasonable and simple enough to suggest that children who had limited

English proficiency should be administered the subtests within the Performance category, for several reasons: (1) The Verbal subtests obviously relied heavily on language development and ability, (2) the Performance subtests relied far less on language development and ability, and (3) the reduction in language demands on the Performance tests should result in an IQ (i.e., the PIQ) that was a fairer estimate of the child's intelligence.

This method has been exceedingly popular and continues to be taught in the present day, but it is problematic for many reasons. First, in the event that a child's dysfunction was language based or related to verbal abilities, use of the Performance tests alone would not provide any information in this regard. Second, although the Performance subtests rely less on language demands than the Verbal tests, they are not devoid of language demands nearly to the extent that they may appear. Block Design, for example, requires no verbal expression to provide a response, yet it requires considerable linguistic comprehension to understand the instructions, which are quite verbally laden. And third, the reduction of language demands provided by the use of Performance tests may appear to yield a fairer estimate of intelligence but only because they are measuring a narrow range of abilities—primarily visual processing and processing speed (Flanagan et al., 2000; Flanagan & Ortiz, 2001). If the child's abilities in these areas are intact, the estimate of intelligence suggested by the PIQ is misleading because it suggests average global intelligence while ignoring a substantial number of other abilities that make up intelligence. Likewise, if the child's abilities in these areas are deficient, the PIQ is again misleading because it will be interpreted as low general ability (similar to low FSIQ) when it may in fact reflect weaknesses in these two areas (i.e., Visual Processing and Processing Speed), but not in others that remained untested.

Clearly, the use of the PIQ as an estimate of the intelligence of children from diverse backgrounds is problematic, but it continues to exist, primarily via clinical lore. But the practice may soon cease as it has effectively been rendered moot by the WISC-IV, which no longer adheres to the old VIQ-PIQ structure of its predecessors. Practitioners concerned with the evaluation of children from culturally and linguistically diverse backgrounds will need to look beyond this outdated and superficial practice and instead learn a more modern and systematic approach if they seek to continue utilizing the WISC. The remainder of this section provides such an approach.

The Fundamental Objective in Assessment

It should be acknowledged that there is no way in which the WISC-IV, or any other test for that matter, can be applied in a completely valid and nondiscriminatory manner when evaluating the intelligence of children from diverse backgrounds. Totally unbiased assessment is an illusion, and attempting to remove all the discriminatory components in any evaluation is both an impossible task and an inappropriate professional goal. A more reasonable objective for practitioners engaged in such pursuits is to evaluate the degree to which the results from such assessment have been affected by cultural or linguistic factors. By determining the relative extent to which experiential differences in culture or language may have affected test results, practitioners are in a better position to defend the validity of any conclusions and inferences drawn from the obtained data. For example, in cases where it can be established that cultural or linguistic factors are not likely to have had a primary or systematic influence on the results, the viability of alternative explanations and hypotheses is increased and may be pursued with a greater degree of confidence. Conversely, in cases where cultural or linguistic factors are believed to have had a primary or systematic influence on the test results, the validity of the obtained data remains questionable and further interpretation cannot be defended adequately. Thus, the first step in conducting fairer and more equitable assessments, particularly when using the WISC-IV or similar tests, rests primarily on being able to answer the question, "To what extent are the obtained results a reflection of cultural or linguistic differences or actual measured ability?" Until this determination is made, the data will be of little, if any, value.

The CHC Culture-Language Matrix and Classifications

The manner in which this fundamental question of bilingual-multicultural assessment can be answered has been formalized in a systematic, research-based approach found in the cultural and linguistic extensions of the CHC Cross-Battery approach (Flanagan et al., 2000; Flanagan & Ortiz, 2001; Ortiz, 2001). In general, the approach rests on two interrelated components: the CHC Culture-Language Classifications and the CHC Culture-Language Matrix. Although the foundation of the approach and the classifications offered by Flanagan and Ortiz rest primarily on the CHC theory-based mental ability constructs measured by various subtests from a wide range of intelligence batteries, additional classifications based on test characteristics were provided and form the basis for examining the relative influence of language and culture on test performance through the use of a matrix (Flanagan & Ortiz, 2001).

It has long been established that tests such as the WISC-IV rarely exhibit psychometric forms of bias, particularly the reliability indexes (Figueroa, 1990; Jensen, 1980; Sandoval, Frisby, Geisinger, Scheuneman, & Grenier, 1998; Valdes & Figueroa, 1994). However, this does not mean that bias does not exist or is not operating, as there are other definitions of bias that may well be established. To what extent tests are or are not biased, particularly with respect to issues of validity, remains debatable among researchers (e.g., Figueroa & Hernandez, 2000; Sandoval, 1979; Sandoval et al., 1998). But what is not in dispute is the fact that tests, whether culturally or linguistically *biased* or not, are most assuredly culturally and linguistically *loaded* (Jensen; Scarr, 1978; Sanchez, 1934; Sattler, 1992). Taking this body of research into account, classifications of current tests of intelligence and cognitive abilities were established on the basis of two characteristics: (1) the degree to which a particular test or subtest contains or requires familiarity, specific knowledge, or an understanding of U.S. mainstream culture; and (2) the degree to which a particular test or subtest requires expressive or receptive language skills, either because the ability being measured is language based, the correct response requires verbal competency, or appropriate administration rests upon adequate verbal comprehension by the examinee. Through the application of a simple, three-level (Low, Moderate, and High) system, tests were thus classified according to the degree of cultural loading and degree of linguistic demand, including those from the Wechsler scales. Additional research is currently in progress to establish these classifications for the WISC-IV; however, because some tests were retained from the WISC-III, and because other new tests are similar to existing ones that have already been classified, enough information exists with which to provide preliminary classifications. Accordingly, Figure 7.2 presents the most probable Culture-Language classifications for the WISC-IV.

Degree of Cultural Loading	Degree of Linguistic Demand		
	Low	Moderate	High
Low	Matrix Reasoning Cancellation	Block Design Symbol Search Digit Span Coding	Letter-Number Sequencing
Moderate		Arithmetic Picture Concepts	
High	Picture Completion		Information Similarities Vocabulary Comprehension Word Reasoning

Figure 7.2 Cultural Loading and Linguistic Demand Classifications of the WISC-IV Subtests

Note: The culture-language classifications for the WISC-IV are only preliminary and are still in the process of evaluation.

By themselves, the WISC-IV classifications in Figure 7.2 already provide practitioners with one option for reducing some of the potentially discriminatory aspects of assessment. Decades of research on issues related to bias has shown that tests that are lower in cultural content (more abstract or process dominant) and lower in linguistic demands (less verbally laden, with more manipulatives, pictures, etc.) tend to yield results that are more equitable for diverse individuals, although they still are not completely fair (Jensen, 1980; Sandoval et al., 1998; Valdes & Figueroa, 1994). Thus, users of the WISC-IV may well decide to administer only those tests with the lowest cultural loading and linguistic demands (e.g., Matrix Reasoning and Cancellation). This would be similar to the practice of using only the subtests that made up the old PIQ. Unfortunately, while there is some merit to this approach, it suffers from the same flaws as before, including a limited range of abilities being measured, an inability to derive any of the four Indexes (i.e., VCI, PRI, PSI, WMI), and lack of information regarding abilities that may be of importance (e.g., verbal abilities and their relationship to suspected reading difficulties). Thus, such practice is not recommended.

The greatest benefit from use of the WISC-IV classifications listed in Figure 7.2 comes from application of the Culture-Language Matrix (Flanagan & Ortiz, 2001). The matrix represents a tool with which practitioners can evaluate the systematic influence of cultural and linguistic differences on test performance—hence addressing the fundamental question regarding the validity of the obtained results. Flanagan and Ortiz recommend converting the usual Wechsler scaled scores to the common deviation IQ metric (helpful in cases where subtests from other batteries may be included) and calculating an arithmetic average for all tests within each of the nine cells of the matrix. An example illustrating how this is accomplished is presented in Figure 7.3, using WISC-IV data.

It is important to note that the derivation of the cell averages or means is done only for the purpose of examining patterns in the data. The average score in each cell does not represent any particular construct and *must not* be interpreted as such. The score is simply an indication of average performance on a collection of tests (sometimes even just one test) that share similar characteristics in terms of cultural loading and linguistic demand. As noted previously, scores for diverse individuals on subtests that are less affected by cultural content or language differences tend to be higher than scores on subtests that are more influenced by these variables. The arrangement of WISC-IV subtests in the matrix, where the cells in the upper left corner are those with the lowest cultural loading and linguistic demand and the cells in the lower right corner are those with the highest, allows for direct examination of whether, for example, the obtained results follow a declining pattern. If the primary influence on the test results is due to cultural or lin-

Degree of Cultural Loading	Degree of Linguistic Demand		
	Low	Moderate	High
Low	Matrix Reasoning (SS = 11) 105 Cancellation (SS = 9) 95 $X = 100$	Block Design (SS = 8) 90 Symbol Search (SS = 11) 105 Digit Span (SS = 7) 85 Coding (SS = 10) 100 $X = 95$	Letter-Number Sequencing (SS = 8) 90 $X = 90$
Moderate		Arithmetic (SS = 7) 85 Picture Concepts (SS = 7) 85 $X = 85$	
High	Picture Completion (SS = 8) 90 $X = 90$		Information (SS = 6) 80 Similarities (SS = 4) 70 Vocabulary (SS = 5) 75 Comprehension (SS=6) 80 Word Reasoning (SS = 4) 70 $X = 75$

Figure 7.3 Culture-Language Matrix Incorporating WISC-IV Data

Note: X = mean; SS = Scaled Score; IQ Metric is the converted scaled score (having a mean of 100 and a standard deviation of 15).

guistic factors, then a systematic decline in performance across the matrix from the top-left cells to the bottom-right cells should be evident. Conversely, if the primary influence on the test results is anything other than cultural or linguistic in nature (e.g., fatigue, improper administration, etc.) then there is no reason to expect a systematic pattern of degradation in performance across the cells from top left to bottom right. That is, when cultural and linguistic differences are not factors operating systematically upon the data, then any other pattern, or no pattern at all, may emerge. In either case it can be reliably ascertained that test performance was not influenced primarily by the cultural loading or linguistic demand of the WISC-IV tests given, and alternative explanations regarding the obtained results (e.g., measured deficit in processing speed, uncooperative test behavior, inattention and lack of effort, etc.) may be reasonably entertained as valid.

The WISC-IV data presented in Figure 7.3 illustrate the expected pattern of decline that would be typical of an individual with a culturally and linguistically diverse background. It should be noted, however, that "typical" does not imply that the pattern is always identical to that which is portrayed in the table. Although the same relative pattern of decline from top left to bottom right remains the hallmark of the systematic influence of cultural and linguistic variables on test performance, differences in levels of acculturation and English-language proficiency can alter the resulting averages. That is, the more "different" an individual is with respect to these two variables, the lower the scores will be overall as compared to an individual whose acculturation or English-language skills are better. Yet, the pattern of decline will be evident in both cases. Unfortunately, it is impossible within the scope of this section to fully detail the manner in which even differences in acculturation and language proficiency affect the observed pattern of decline; the reader is referred to Flanagan and Ortiz (2001) for a more in-depth treatment of such issues.

The data contained in Figure 7.3 show a consistent and systematic decline in performance across the matrix with the best performance seen on the tests with the lowest cultural loading and linguistic demand (Matrix Reasoning and Cancellation; $X = 100$) and the worst performance evident on the tests with the highest cultural loading and linguistic demand (Information, Similarities, Vocabulary, Comprehension, and Word Reasoning; $X = 75$). Because such a pattern of performance would be unlikely to have occurred as a function of other extraneous factors or influences, the most reasonable conclusion is that the results are likely a reflection of cultural and linguistic differences. As such, the temptation to interpret scores in the usual manner, such as through examination of WISC-IV FSIQ or Indexes, should be resisted as there is no defensible basis for drawing inferences from these scores. On the other hand, had there not been any systematic pattern of decline in the WISC-IV scores, interpretation may proceed in the normal manner because cultural and linguistic variables were evaluated systematically and ruled out as the *primary* influence on test performance.

Conclusion

The determination as to whether results obtained from the WISC-IV and the Culture-Language Matrix indicate the presence of culture or language differences or perhaps something else requires some degree of clinical skill and application of professional judgment. In this way, such determinations are not unlike other clinical decisions that rest on one's level of experience, training, and education. Nonetheless, users of the WISC-IV who have a need to evaluate the intelligence or cognitive abilities of children from culturally and linguistically diverse backgrounds have at their disposal a systematic method supported by scientific knowledge that is defensible within the context of nondiscriminatory assessment and consistent with the best standards of practice. Moreover, the fact that practitioners need not be fluent in another language puts the ability to make crucial determinations regarding the effect of cultural and linguistic variables on test performance within the reach of all professionals, not just those with highly specialized skills. Bilingual-multicultural assessment can be overwhelming and confusing for many practitioners. Through the use of the Culture-Language Classifications and Matrix, one of the most critical aspects in such assessment—evaluating the relative influence of cultural and linguistic differences on test performance—is now something that can be readily accomplished using the WISC-IV.

✍ TEST YOURSELF ✍

1. Gifted children show little variability across the four WISC-IV Indexes and, as such, these Indexes have little meaning for this population. True or False?

2. Establishing Normative Weaknesses in a child's academic functioning is a necessary condition in the operational definition of LD. True or False?

3. Which of the following CHC abilities demonstrate(s) a significant relationship with reading achievement?

   (a) Auditory Processing *(Ga)*

   (b) Short-Term Memory *(Gsm)*

   (c) Processing Speed *(Gs)*

   (d) All of the above

(continued)

4. **The nature of underachievement, within the context of the operational definition of LD, suggests that not only does a child possess specific, circumscribed, and related academic and cognitive Normative Weaknesses, but that these weaknesses exist within an otherwise *normal ability* profile.** True or False?

5. **Administering only those subtests with the lowest cultural loadings and linguistic demands to culturally and linguistically diverse populations is not recommended because**

   (a) it results in a narrow range of abilities being measured.

   (b) it precludes the calculation of the four Indexes.

   (c) it results in a lack of information regarding other abilities that may be important in understanding the referral concern.

   (d) All of the above.

6. **Which of the following subtests can be described as having a low cultural loading, but a high linguistic demand?**

   (a) Digit Span

   (b) Letter-Number Sequencing

   (c) Arithmetic

   (d) Block Design

Answers: 1. False; 2. True; 3. d; 4. True; 5. d; 6. b

Eight

ILLUSTRATIVE CASE REPORTS

This chapter presents case studies of two children who were referred for psychoeducational evaluations. The WISC-IV profile of Ryan was included in Chapter 4 to exemplify how to utilize the interpretive approach advocated in this book. The other case report describes the profile of a 14-year-old girl with HIV who was referred for evaluation of suspected learning disability.

The goal of this chapter is to bring all facets of this book together to show how

---

CAUTION

Common Errors to Avoid in Report Writing

- Including inappropriate or excessive detail
- Using unnecessary jargon or technical terms
- Using vague language
- Making abstract statements
- Not supporting hypotheses with sufficient data
- Making generalizations from isolated information, such as a single outlier scaled score
- Inserting value judgments
- Discussing the test itself rather than the child's abilities
- Using poor grammar
- Presenting behavior or test scores without interpreting them
- Failing to adequately address reasons for referral
- Failing to provide confidence intervals or otherwise denote that all obtained test scores have a band of error
- Giving test results prematurely (e.g., in the "Appearance and Behavioral Characteristics" section)

Source: From A. S. Kaufman & E. O. Lichtenberger, *Essentials of WISC-III and WPPSI-R Assessment.* Copyright © 2000 John Wiley & Sons, Inc. This material is used by permission of John Wiley & Sons, Inc.

the WISC-IV may be used as a core battery in assessment. The case reports demonstrate the cross-validation of hypotheses with behavioral observations, background information, and supplemental tests. Each report includes the following information about the child: reason for referral, background information, physical appearance of the child, and behavioral observations during the assessment, evaluation procedures, test results and interpretation, diagnostic impressions, and recommendations.

PSYCHOLOGICAL REPORT

Name: Ryan S.	DOB: 1/16/94
Age: 10	Grade: 5th
Date of Testing: 2/26/04	Date of Report: 3/01/04

Referral and Background Information

Ryan was referred for a psychoeducational evaluation by his elementary school's building intervention team (BIT) due to academic difficulties, primarily in the area of reading. More specifically, his teacher noted that he is unable to recognize certain words that he is otherwise expected to know, and he exhibits difficulty decoding unfamiliar words. Additionally, Ryan's reading comprehension is not commensurate with that of his classmates. For instance, he often misses the main points to class reading assignments, and fails to identify details accurately. Despite this difficulty, Ryan's teacher described Ryan's comprehension as "inconsistent" and stated that he seems to perform better when reading about familiar topics. In addition to reading difficulties, Ryan also demonstrates difficulties in the area of writing. That is, Ryan's teacher reported that although he has good ideas and can communicate them verbally, his written products generally contain spelling errors and are relatively bland and lack variety (e.g., he uses the same words repeat-

> ### DON'T FORGET
>
> **Pertinent Information to Include in Identifying Information Section**
>
> - Name
> - Date of birth
> - Age
> - Grade in school (if applicable)
> - Date(s) of testing
> - Date of report
>
> Source: From A. S. Kaufman & E. O. Lichtenberger, Essentials of WISC-III and WPPSI-R Assessment. Copyright © 2000 John Wiley & Sons, Inc. This material is used by permission of John Wiley & Sons, Inc.

edly and includes minimal descriptive words in his writing). Finally, Ryan has recently begun experiencing difficulties in math, a subject in which he has historically performed average or better.

Information from Ryan's parents, Mr. and Mrs. S., revealed that Ryan, who was born via caesarean section, met developmental milestones within normal limits. Other than an asthma episode at age 5, Ryan's health history is unremarkable and he is currently reported to be in good health. Ryan's parents describe him as a "delightful, energetic, and well-behaved" child. Ryan attends school regularly and reportedly has a "good attitude" toward school. Parental concerns are consistent with teacher reports and center largely on Ryan's inability to decode words and comprehend written text consistently.

> **DON'T FORGET**
> ....
>
> ### Pertinent Information to Include in Reason for Referral Section
>
> A. Who referred the child
>   1. List name and position of referral source.
>   2. List questions and concerns of referral source.
> B. Specific symptoms and concerns
>   1. Summarize current behaviors and relevant past behaviors.
>   2. List any separate concerns that the child has.
>
> Source: From A. S. Kaufman & E. O. Lichtenberger, Essentials of WISC-III and WPPSI-R Assessment. Copyright © 2000 John Wiley & Sons, Inc. This material is used by permission of John Wiley & Sons, Inc.

In terms of educational history, Ryan attended a preschool program that focused on teaching precursor skills thought to be necessary for kindergarten success (e.g., letter identification, development of basic concepts, and color and shape recognition). Ryan reportedly liked preschool and especially enjoyed the social opportunities afforded by this setting.

In kindergarten, Ryan's performance was described as "average," with specific areas of concern. Although he seemed to do well with number concepts and color and shape identification, he had difficulty in other areas, such as letter recognition and rhyming. These difficulties continued throughout Ryan's early elementary school years and, based on the results of a district-wide reading assessment in third grade, Ryan was provided with remedial reading services twice a week. These services focused primarily on developing Ryan's sight-word vocabulary and teaching him how to use context cues to obtain meaning from a passage.

In fourth grade, Ryan's reading difficulties became more pronounced. It was around this time that Mr. and Mrs. S. noted that Ryan was inconsistent in his completion of reading assignments, and generally only completed readings that focused on topics he enjoyed or was familiar with. Mr. and Mrs. S. also noticed that Ryan required more assistance to complete his homework. For example, they often had to read directions to him and assist him with decoding words in his content-area texts (e.g., science and social studies).

Presently, Ryan continues to receive remedial reading services, but Mr. and Mrs. S., along with Ryan's teacher, are concerned that Ryan's difficulties are not being sufficiently addressed. Their primary concern is that Ryan is not making gains that are commensurate with the type of intervention being offered. Additionally, Ryan's parents and teacher are concerned that if Ryan continues to experience frustration on academic tasks, his interest and positive attitude toward school will diminish.

Despite Ryan's parents' and teacher's concerns, information from a recent interview with Ryan revealed that he likes school but is having difficulty with reading and completing his class work on time.

Ryan's favorite subjects are math and science. Ryan is particularly fond of math because he is "good at it." However, consistent with his teacher's report, he noted that math has recently become more difficult for him. Ryan's least favorite sub-

---

DON'T FORGET

Pertinent Information to Include in Background Information Section

Present in paragraph form the information you have obtained from all sources, including referral source, child, family members, social worker, teachers, medical records, etc. State pertinent information only, not needless details.

The following information may be included:

- Current family situation (parents, siblings, etc.—*no* gossip)
- Other symptoms
- Medical history (including emotional disorders)
- Developmental history
- Educational history
- Previous treatment (educational or psychological)
- New or recent developments (including stressors)
- Review of collateral documents (past evaluations)

Source: From A. S. Kaufman & E. O. Lichtenberger, *Essentials of WISC-III and WPPSI-R Assessment.* Copyright © 2000 John Wiley & Sons, Inc. This material is used by permission of John Wiley & Sons, Inc.

jects are reading, spelling, and writing. Ryan stated that he does not like the books that he has to read in school, and thus he does not enjoy reading. Nevertheless, Ryan reported that when he is at home he enjoys reading "joke books" with his father and looking at comic books with his friends. Furthermore, Ryan reported that spelling and writing are difficult for him, but he also stated that he is able to do better with these tasks if his mother and father help him and if he can use the "spell check" feature on his parents' computer. Despite Ryan's difficulties, he does not describe school as stressful. When Ryan feels stress, however, he attempts to cope with it positively by seeking out his parents' support.

In terms of Ryan's social and emotional functioning as it relates to school, he feels that he is an integrated member of the school, and feels that others are nice to him. Ryan reports getting along with his peers, and having several close friends that he socializes with on a daily basis. Furthermore, he has no reservations about interacting with others and participating in classroom activities. For instance, he is comfortable asking and answering questions, and talking to his classmates.

Appearance and Behavioral Observations

Ryan was neatly groomed and presented as a well-mannered child. Rapport was easily established and was maintained throughout the evaluation process. Furthermore, Ryan communicated his ideas and feelings in a thoughtful and meaningful way. He was particularly conversant about video games and movies, and was quite good at summarizing the plots for some of his favorite, most-often-watched movies.

Ryan appeared engaged and motivated during most of the tasks administered. He liked to ask questions and discuss various topics that came up during the evaluation, and often brought up other topics that interested him. For instance, he tended to offer detailed explanations for how he knew certain things and often told stories about personal experiences that related to certain questions. Ryan was very persistent when working through the math-related tasks, and he often commented on how he enjoyed figuring out some of the more difficult items, while pointing out that he was glad that he did not have to read any of the word problems. Unlike Ryan's approach to math tasks, during the vocabulary-based tasks he appeared less enthusiastic. For instance, many of his answers on vocabulary items were brief. Finally, Ryan used a very slow and labor-intensive approach to processing speed tasks. Overall, the results of this assessment are considered a valid indication of Ryan's current level of cognitive and academic ability.

DON'T FORGET

Pertinent Information to Consider Including in Appearance and Behavioral Observations Section

- Talk about significant patterns or themes you see going on during testing.
- Sequence information in order of importance, rather than in order of occurrence. (Don't just make a chronological list.)
- Describe the behavioral referents to your hypotheses (and provide specific examples).
- Describe what makes this child unique. (Paint a picture for the reader.)
- Suggested areas to review (in addition to significant behavior):

Appearance
- Size: height and weight
- Facial characteristics
- Grooming and cleanliness
- Posture
- Clothing style
- Maturity: Does the person look his or her age?

Behavior
- Speech articulation, language patterns
- Activity level (foot wiggling, excessive talking, nail biting, tension, etc.)
- Attention span/distractibility
- Cooperativeness or resistance
- Interest in doing well
- How does the child go about solving problems?
- Does the child use a trial-and-error approach?
- Does the child work quickly or reflectively?
- Does the child check his or her answers?
- How does the child react to failure or challenge?
- Does the child continue to work until time is up?
- Does the child ask for direction or help?
- Did failure reduce interest in the task or lead to avoidance of other tasks?
- When frustrated, is the child aggressive or dependent?
- What is the child's attitude toward self?
- Does the child regard self with confidence, have a superior attitude, feel inadequate, or appear defeated?
- How did the child strive to get approval and respond to your praise of effort?

Evaluation Procedures

Wechsler Intelligence Scale for Children–Fourth Edition (WISC-IV)
Woodcock-Johnson Tests of Cognitive Abilities, Third Edition (WJ III), select subtests
Wechsler Individual Achievement Test–Second Edition (WIAT-II)
School observation—Reading class
Interview with teachers
Interview with parents
Interview with child

Reading Class Observation

Ryan was observed in his reading class in the morning. There were approximately 13 students in the classroom, and the desks were arranged in several rows facing the chalkboard. Ryan sits in the front row, close to where the teacher usually stands while presenting a lesson. On this day, the teacher was leading a discussion pertaining to a reading homework assignment concerning erosion. Upon starting the discussion, the teacher asked volunteers to read various passages from the text to the class. Ryan sat quietly while a majority of his classmates enthusiastically volunteered by raising their hands. Despite his silence, Ryan appeared to listen carefully to what his classmates were reading. A discussion followed about erosion and weathering, in which the teacher asked how the process of erosion takes place. At this point, Ryan was asked to read a passage pertaining to this topic. Ryan read slowly and in a labor-intensive manner. Furthermore, he made many mistakes that distorted the meaning of what he was reading. More specifically, he frequently omitted words and inserted words that were not in the text. Additionally, he altered word endings and switched words around. For instance, he changed "something" to "someone," and read "when the rain hits the rock" as "when the rock hits the rain." Ryan also demonstrated limited sight-word vocabulary in his reading repertoire, but demonstrated a rudimentary level of decoding skill to decipher simpler words. When Ryan encountered a more difficult word that he was unable to decode, he tended to skip it. At times Ryan lost his place and mistakenly read an entire sentence over again, and other times he skipped entire sentences. As a result, Ryan demonstrated very limited comprehension of what he read.

TEST RESULTS AND INTERPRETATION

Cognitive Performance

WISC-IV

The WISC-IV groups an individual's ability into four global areas: Verbal Comprehension Index (VCI), which measures verbal ability; Perceptual Reasoning Index (PRI), which involves the manipulation of concrete materials or pro-

DON'T FORGET

Pertinent Information to Include in Test Results and Interpretation Section

- Use paragraph form.
- Put numbers in this section, including IQs and Indexes with confidence intervals and percentile ranks. Do not include raw scores.
- Tie in behaviors with results to serve as logical explanations or reminders wherever appropriate.
- With more than one test, attempt to explain similarities in performances and differences (discrepancies) if you have sufficient information to do so.
- Support hypotheses with multiple sources of data, including observed behaviors.
- Do not contradict yourself.
- Be sure that you are describing the Indexes, not just naming them. Remember, the reader has no idea what "Perceptual Reasoning" means.
- Describe the underlying abilities that the Indexes are measuring.
- Talk about the child's abilities, not about the test.
- Be straightforward in your writing. Do not be too literary, and avoid writing in metaphors.

Source: From A. S. Kaufman & E. O. Lichtenberger, Essentials of WISC-III and WPPSI-R Assessment. Copyright © 2000 John Wiley & Sons, Inc. This material is used by permission of John Wiley & Sons, Inc.

cessing of visual stimuli to solve problems nonverbally; Working Memory Index (WMI), which measures short-term memory; and Processing Speed Index (PSI), which measures cognitive processing efficiency.

On the WISC-IV, Ryan earned a Full Scale IQ (FSIQ) of 83, which ranks his overall ability at the 13th percentile and classifies his global IQ as falling within the Average Range. There is a 95% chance that his true FSIQ is between 79 and 88. However, this estimate of his general intellectual ability on the WISC-IV cannot be interpreted meaningfully and should be deemphasized because he displayed considerable variability among the four Indexes that constitute this full scale score. Ryan's Indexes ranged from 70 on the PSI (2nd percentile) to 98 on the VCI (45th percentile), suggesting that Ryan's intelligence is best understood by his performance on the separate WISC-IV Indexes, namely, Verbal Comprehension, Perceptual Reasoning, Working Memory, and Processing Speed. The table on page 264 [Table 8. 1] lists Ryan's cognitive performance on the WISC-IV.

Because Ryan's WISC-IV FSIQ could not be interpreted and his Verbal Comprehension (98) and Perceptual Reasoning (90) Indexes were similar, these Indexes were combined to yield a General Ability Index (GAI). The GAI differs from the FSIQ in that it is not influenced directly by Ryan's performance on working memory and processing speed tasks.

Ryan earned a GAI of 93, classifying his general level of intellectual ability as in the Average Range/Within Normal Limits. The chances are good (95%) that Ryan's true GAI is somewhere within the range of 87 to 99. His GAI is ranked at the 33rd percentile, indicating that he scored higher than 33% of other children of the same age in the standardization sample.

Before discussing Ryan's Indexes on the four scales, one must first determine whether each Index is interpretable—that is, does it measure a reasonably unitary trait for Ryan, or do his scaled scores on the subtests that constitute the Index include substantial variability? Three of Ryan's WISC-IV Indexes are considered "interpretable." The largest discrepancy among his subtest scaled scores within an Index was 6 points (the difference between his scaled scores of 13 on Comprehension and 7 on Vocabulary for the VCI). To be considered *not* interpretable, discrepancies between the highest and lowest subtest scaled scores within an Index must be greater than or equal to 5 points. Discrepancies within the other three Indexes were 4 points (PRI), 0 points (WMI), and 1 point (PSI). Consequently, Ryan's PRI, WMI, and PSI are all considered to provide good estimates of his skill on the abilities measured by each scale.

The PSI, a measure of Processing Speed *(Gs)*, represents Ryan's ability to perform simple, clerical-type tasks quickly. Ryan's *Gs* ability was assessed with two tasks—one required Ryan to quickly copy symbols that were paired with

Table 8.1 Summary of Cognitive Performance: WISC-IV

Index/Subtest	Score	95% CI	Percentile Rank	Descriptive Category
Verbal Comprehension	98	[91–105]	45th	Average Range/Within Normal Limits
Similarities	9		38th	
Vocabulary	7		16th	
Comprehension	13		84th	
(Information)	12		75th	
(Word Reasoning)	6		9th	
Perceptual Reasoning	90	[83–98]	25th	Average Range/Within Normal Limits
Block Design	6		9th	
Picture Concepts	10		50th	
Matrix Reasoning	9		38th	
(Picture Completion)	8		25th	
Working Memory	83	[77–92]	13th	Below Average/Normative Weakness
Digit Span	7		16th	
Letter-Number Sequencing	7		16th	
(Arithmetic)	11		65th	
Processing Speed	70	[65–83]	2nd	Below Average/Normative Weakness
Coding	5		5th	
Symbol Search	4		2nd	
(Cancellation)	5		5th	
Full Scale IQ	83	[79–88]	13th	Below Average/Normative Weakness
General Ability Index	93	[87–99]	33rd	Average Range/Within Normal Limits

Note: Tests appearing in parentheses are supplemental measures. CI = Confidence Interval.

numbers according to a key (Coding), and the other required him to identify the presence or absence of a target symbol in a row of symbols (Symbol Search). The difference between Ryan's performances on these two tasks (Coding scaled score of 5 minus Symbol Search scaled score of 4 equals 1) was not significant (i.e., ≥ 5), indicating that his PSI is a good estimate of his processing speed. Ryan obtained a PSI of 70 (65–83), which is ranked at the 2nd percentile and is classified as Below Average/Normative Weakness. Ryan's processing speed is a significant weakness as compared to other individuals his age in the normative population. In addition, his ability in this area is significantly lower than his abilities in other areas. Overall, Ryan's processing speed is a notable weakness and suggests that he has a disorder in this basic psychological process, a finding that should play an essential role for developing educational interventions.

The WMI, a measure of Short-Term Memory *(Gsm)*, represents Ryan's ability to apprehend and hold, or transform, information in immediate awareness and then use it within a few seconds. Ryan's *Gsm* ability was assessed by two tasks— Digit Span, which required him to repeat a sequence of numbers in the same order as presented by the examiner (Digit Span Forward) and also in the reverse order (Digit Span Backward), and Letter-Number Sequencing, which required him to listen to a sequence of numbers and letters and recall the numbers in ascending order and the letters in alphabetical order. Ryan obtained a WMI *(Gsm)* of 83 (77–92), which is ranked at the 13th percentile and is classified as Below Average/ Normative Weakness. Ryan's working memory is considered a significant weakness compared to other children his age in the normative population. Like processing speed, Ryan's working memory is a notable weakness and suggests that he has a disorder in this basic psychological process, a finding that should play an essential role for developing educational interventions.

The PRI, a measure of Visual Processing and Fluid Reasoning *(Gv/Gf)*, represents Ryan's ability to analyze and synthesize visual stimuli as well as to reason with it. Ryan's *Gv/Gf* ability was assessed by tasks that required him to recreate a series of modeled or pictured designs using blocks (Block Design), identify the missing portion of an incomplete visual matrix from one of five response options (Matrix Reasoning), and select one picture from each of two or three rows of pictures to form a group with a common characteristic (Picture Concepts). Ryan obtained a PRI *(Gv/Gf)* of 90 (83–98), which is ranked at the 25th percentile and is classified as Average Range/Within Normal Limits.

The VCI, a measure of Crystallized Intelligence *(Gc)*, represents Ryan's ability to reason with previously learned information. One's *Gc* ability develops largely as a function of both formal and informal educational opportunities and experiences and is highly dependent on exposure to mainstream U.S. culture. Ryan's *Gc* was assessed by tasks that required him to define words (Vocabulary, scaled score = 7), draw conceptual similarities between words (Similarities, scaled score = 9), and answer questions involving knowledge of general principles and social situations (Comprehension, scaled score = 13). The variability among Ryan's performances on these tasks was significant (i.e., scaled score range was equal to or greater than 5 points), indicating that his overall *Gc* ability cannot be summarized in a single score (i.e., the VCI). Ryan's Crystallized Intelligence is discussed further below.

Planned Clinical Comparisons

In addition to the 10 core-battery subtests of the WISC-IV, Ryan was administered five supplemental subtests. The administration of these supplemental subtests allowed for further examination of Ryan's cognitive abilities. Specifically, these supplemental subtests were combined into several clinical clusters. These clusters are listed in the table below [Table 8.2]. Similar to the WISC-IV Index analyses, Planned Clinical Comparisons can be made using the clinical clusters only when the subtests constituting each cluster in the comparison are unitary (i.e., the difference between the highest and lowest subtest scaled scores in the cluster is less than 5). In Ryan's case, all clinical clusters were determined to be unitary, with the

Table 8.2 Summary of Clinical Cluster Performance

Clinical Cluster	Standard Score
Fluid Reasoning (*Gf*) Cluster Matrix Reasoning + Picture Concepts + Arithmetic	100
Visual Processing (*Gv*) Cluster Block Design + Picture Completion	83
Nonverbal Fluid Reasoning (*Gf*-nonverbal) Cluster Matrix Reasoning + Picture Concepts	97
Verbal Fluid Reasoning (*Gf*-verbal) Cluster Similarities + Word Reasoning	86
Lexical Knowledge (*Gc*-VL) Cluster Word Reasoning + Vocabulary	81
General Information (*Gc*-K0) Cluster Comprehension + Information	114
Long-Term Memory (*Gc*-LTM) Cluster Vocabulary + Information	Not Interpretable
Short-Term Memory (*Gsm*-MW) Cluster Letter-Number Sequencing + Digit Span	83

exception of the Gc-LTM Cluster. Therefore, four of the six possible Planned Clinical Comparisons were conducted, the results of which appear next.

Gc-VL versus Gc-K0

The difference between Ryan's General Information (Gc-K0) Cluster of 114 (83rd percentile; Average Range/Within Normal Limits) and his Lexical Knowledge (Gc-VL) Cluster of 81 (11th percentile; Below Average/Normative Weakness) is unusually large (differences as large as Ryan's discrepancy of 33 points occur less than 10% of the time in the normative population). Higher standard scores on Gc-K0 than Gc-VL can occur for many reasons. For example, some children might have an adequate fund of information but lack a strong vocabulary knowledge base and therefore have difficulty reasoning with words. Not only is Ryan's lexical knowledge ability less well developed than his general information ability, it is also in the Below Average range of functioning relative to his age mates and, therefore, is a Normative Weakness.

Gf versus Gv

The difference between Ryan's Gf Cluster of 100 (50th percentile; Average Range/Within Normal Limits) and his Gv Cluster of 83 (13th percentile; Below Average/Normative Weakness) was not unusually large, indicating that it is not uncommon to find a difference of this magnitude in the normative population. Nevertheless, it is important to recognize that Ryan's ability to analyze and synthesize visual information fell within the Below Average range of functioning compared to his age mates and, therefore, represents a Normative Weakness. Overall, the difference between Ryan's Gf ability and his abilities in other cognitive domains and his Gf-verbal and Gf-nonverbal abilities were not uncommon in the normative population.

WJ III Cognitive—Select Subtests

In addition to the WISC-IV, Ryan was administered select tests from the WJ III (see Table 8.3). These tests measured abilities that were not measured by the WISC-IV, namely, Auditory Processing (Ga) and Long-Term Retrieval (Glr).

Auditory Processing (Ga) involves the ability to discriminate, analyze, and synthesize auditory stimuli. Ryan's auditory processing was assessed through phonetic tasks that required him to listen to a series of separated syllables or phonemes (e.g., "m-oth-er") and blend the sounds into a complete word (e.g., "mother"; Sound Blending) and identify a complete word (e.g., "record") that was initially presented with one or more missing phonemes (e.g., "re_ord"; Incomplete Words). These tasks primarily measured Ryan's skill in synthesizing and analyzing speech sounds. Ryan obtained a Phonemic Awareness Cluster of 76 (70–82), which is ranked at

Table 8.3 Summary of Cognitive Performance: WJ III

Cluster/Subtest	Score	68% CI	Percentile Rank	Descriptive Category
Phonemic Awareness (_Ga_)	**76**	**[70–82]**	**5th**	**Below Average/Normative Weakness**
Sound Blending	83	[77–89]	13th	
Incomplete Words	80	[72–87]	9th	
Long-Term Retrieval (_Glr_)	**88**	**[82–94]**	**21st**	**Average Range/Normal Limits**
Visual-Auditory Learning	93	[88–99]	32nd	
Retrieval Fluency	85	[78–91]	15th	

the 5th percentile and is classified as Below Average/Normative Weakness. Ryan's observed difficulty with phonetic coding has had a negative impact on his development of basic reading skills (e.g., decoding words). This weakness will likely become even more salient as Ryan's reading material progresses and he is presented with an increased number of unfamiliar (and multisyllabic) words.

Long-Term Retrieval (_Glr_) involves the ability to store information efficiently and retrieve it later through association. Ryan's _Glr_ ability was assessed through tasks that required him to learn and recall a series of rebuses (i.e., pictographic representations of words; Visual-Auditory Learning) and name as many examples as possible from a series of three categories (i.e., things to eat or drink, first names of people, and animals) within a 1-minute time period (Retrieval Fluency). More specifically, these tasks assessed Ryan's ability to learn, store, and retrieve a series of associations as well as his ability to fluently retrieve information from stored knowledge.

Although Ryan's overall _Glr_ performance suggests that his efficiency in transferring and storing information to be recalled later is adequate (SS = 88 [82–94]; 21st percentile; Average Range/Within Normal Limits), his Ideational Fluency performance as measured by the WJ III Retrieval Fluency test was at the lower end of the Average Range and was ranked at the 15th percentile, suggesting that he indeed had difficulty with this task. Ryan's observed difficulty with Ideational Fluency may be partly related to his weakness in processing speed given that the Retrieval Fluency test is timed. Children who have difficulty retrieving information quickly often have difficulty acquiring basic reading skills.

Achievement Assessment

In addition to an assessment of cognitive functioning, Ryan was administered tests from the WIAT-II (see Table 8.4). The WIAT-II comprises subtests that al-

Table 8.4 Summary of Academic Performance: WIAT-II

Composite/Subtest	Score	95% CI	Percentile Rank
Reading Composite	**82**	**[79–85]**	**12th**
Word Reading	83		13th
Reading Comprehension	87		19th
Pseudoword Decoding	82		12th
Math Composite	**95**	**[88–102]**	**38th**
Numerical Operations	98		45th
Math Reasoning	95		38th
Written Language Composite	**90**	**[82–98]**	**25th**
Spelling	87		19th
Written Expression	96		40th
Oral Language Composite	**92**	**[81–103]**	**29th**
Oral Expression	98		45th
Listening Comprehension	92		29th
Total Achievement	**87**	**[83–91]**	**19th**

Note: Tests appearing in parentheses are supplemental measures. CI = Confidence Interval.

low for the derivation of four domain-specific composite scores, namely, Reading, Writing, Mathematics, and Oral Language. In addition to these domain-specific composites, the WIAT-II provides a Total Achievement score, which is based on an aggregate of an individual's subtest scores that make up each domain-specific composite. Ryan obtained a Total Achievement Composite of 87 (83–91), which is ranked at the 19th percentile and is classified as Average Range/Within Normal Limits. Ryan's performances in math, writing, and oral language are within normal limits as compared to same-aged peers from the normative population. Conversely, Ryan's reading performance represents a significant normative weakness. A more complete description of Ryan's performance within each academic domain appears in the following sections.

Reading
Ryan's performance in the area of reading reflects his skill in identifying words presented in isolation (Word Reading, scaled score = 83), applying structural and phonic analysis to decode a series of nonsense words (Pseudoword Decoding, scaled score = 82), and reading and understanding connected text (Reading Comprehension, scaled score = 87). Ryan obtained a Reading Composite of 82 (79–85), which is ranked at the 12th percentile and is classified as Below Average/

Normative Weakness. Ryan's overall reading achievement is consistent with referral concerns. His basic reading skills as well as his ability to apply his knowledge to comprehend written discourse appear to be equally underdeveloped. His primary area of difficulty appears to be related to an inability to accurately decode words, which, in turn, negatively impacts his ability to obtain meaning from written text. For instance, an error analysis suggested that although Ryan could generally identify initial letter sounds, he did not consistently attend to medial or final sounds when attempting to read the word (e.g., he read "goal" as "go"). Moreover, when Ryan attended to initial and final sounds, he often confused medial sounds and either added sounds not in the initial word or omitted sounds (e.g., he read "during" as "doing"). Finally, although Ryan attempted to apply phonetic strategies to decode words, he often broke down each word into separate parts without fully blending the word after decoding those parts. For instance, when presented with the word "carefully," Ryan broke it down into two separate words, "careful" and "fully." While Ryan's reading decoding difficulties may be related to his weaknesses in working memory, processing speed, and fluency, his reading comprehension is likely most strongly impacted by his weakness in lexical knowledge, as evidenced by his performance on the *Gc*-VL Cluster (standard score = 81).

Mathematics
In the area of mathematics, Ryan was required to perform basic mathematical computations (e.g., addition, subtraction) to solve problems (Numerical Operations, standard score = 98), as well as solve more involved word problems *that were read to him* by the examiner (Math Reasoning, standard score = 95). Ryan's overall performance in math (Math Composite standard score = 95 [88–102]; 38th percentile) is consistent with his academic record review, which revealed generally average math performance. Although Ryan's teacher indicated that he has recently begun to struggle with specific math tasks, it is likely that this is a result of the nature of his present math instruction (e.g., the current curriculum is focused almost exclusively on word problems) and may also be related in part to his weaknesses in the areas of processing speed and working memory—abilities that have both demonstrated a consistent relationship to math achievement.

Written Language
Ryan's performance in the area of writing reflects his ability to accurately spell a series of isolated words that are presented orally by the examiner (Spelling, standard score = 87); and to write words fluently, combine words, and generate connected text using contextual cues (e.g., pictures) or verbal prompts (Written Expression, standard score = 96). Ryan obtained a Written Language Composite of

90 (82–98), which is ranked at the 25th percentile and is classified as Average Range/Within Normal Limits. Although Ryan performed Within Normal Limits on the spelling subtest, he demonstrated several noteworthy errors. That is, although Ryan's misspellings generally approximated the orally presented word, in that he wrote phonetic representations of the word, there were instances, similar to his reading performance, wherein Ryan either added sounds not presented in the original word or omitted sounds. Other errors resulted in approximations of only the initial sound of the word. Although the former errors likely will not detract from the content of Ryan's written work and will interfere only minimally with its readability, the latter types of errors, wherein Ryan spells only the initial letter-sound correctly, could exert more of an impact on the readability of Ryan's written work. A review of Ryan's classroom writing samples supports this finding. More specifically, although some of Ryan's work was easily read despite multiple spelling errors, when Ryan could not spell a word phonetically, he tended to write words using only their initial sounds (e.g., he wrote "destroy" as "distrude"), which seriously detracted from the readability of his work and disrupted the continuity of his writing.

Oral Language

Ryan's performance in the area of Oral Language reflects his ability to name words, generate stories, or provide directions when given visual or verbal cues (Oral Expression, standard score = 98), as well as generate words based on visual or verbal descriptions and select pictures that match a specific word or sentence (Listening Comprehension, standard score = 92). Ryan's expressive and receptive language skills are Average, as reflected by his obtained Oral Language Composite of 92 (81–103; 29th percentile). Although Ryan performed Within Normal Limits on both tasks that make up this domain, he demonstrated difficulty on specific aspects of each task. For instance, on the expressive language task, Ryan had difficulty when he was asked to quickly name words that were associated with specific semantic categories (similar to his difficulties on the WJ III Retrieval Fluency test). On the receptive language task, Ryan's difficulty centered on an inability to state single words that reflected a definition presented by the examiner. Ryan's difficulty on this specific task appears to be directly related to his weakness in lexical knowledge.

Diagnostic Impressions

Data obtained from the administration of the WISC-IV, WIAT-II, and select tests from the WJ III, coupled with information from select comparisons among

Ryan's cognitive abilities, suggest that he demonstrates Below Average to Average Range functioning across the various cognitive and academic domains that were evaluated. Ryan's intact areas of functioning include his associative memory, general language development and reasoning abilities, and oral language ability. His overall global intellectual ability was classified as Average Range/Within Normal Limits. Ryan demonstrated specific cognitive weaknesses in processing speed, working memory, fluency, lexical knowledge, phonetic coding, and visual processing—all of which contribute to his reported academic difficulties, particularly in the areas of reading and writing. For instance, although Ryan appears to have a sufficient amount of information available to him (Gc-K0) to read and understand age-appropriate reading passages and compose written text, his inability to efficiently process (Gs) and retain information in immediate awareness long enough to encode or transform it (Gsm-WM), coupled with his weaknesses in Lexical Knowledge (Gc-VL), and specific aspects of Visual Processing (Gv) and Auditory Processing (Ga-PC) negatively impact his ability to decode specific words, consistently comprehend written text, and communicate his thoughts effectively in written form.

Although Ryan has good knowledge of factual information, he lacks facility with words and, therefore, has difficulty reasoning with words. This difficulty constrains his ability to communicate his thoughts effectively in writing, despite having adequate knowledge of a topic. Ryan's weak vocabulary also impacts his ability to comprehend what he reads. This finding is consistent with his teacher's description of his comprehension skills as "inconsistent."

Ryan's weakness in the areas of processing speed and retrieval fluency inter-

---

DON'T FORGET

Pertinent Information to Include in Summary and Diagnostic Impressions Section

- State summary information early in the body of the report.
- Include summary of referral, key background, or behavioral observation points.
- Summarize the most important interpretations of global scores and strengths and weaknesses.
- Defend your diagnosis, if one is made.

Source: From A. S. Kaufman & E. O. Lichtenberger, *Essentials of WISC-III and WPPSI-R Assessment.* Copyright © 2000 John Wiley & Sons, Inc. This material is used by permission of John Wiley & Sons, Inc.

fere with his ability to process information efficiently and is likely partly responsible for his self-reported difficulty with completing tasks on time. These weaknesses also impact his ability to read fluently, which leads to a deterioration in reading comprehension. Weaknesses in processing speed and fluency may also impact Ryan's written expression. For example, he may have difficulty generating ideas quickly, copying notes from the board, and taking notes during an oral presentation. As a result, Ryan may have difficulty keeping up with his classmates.

Ryan's performance on various measures of achievement is consistent with referral concerns, and is both consistent with and logically related to the outcomes found in the evaluation of his cognitive abilities. Ryan demonstrated weak word-attack and word-recognition skills. His spelling and reading comprehension skills, although not considered Normative Weaknesses, represent areas of difficulty for him. It is important to note that the tests administered to Ryan included many context cues. For instance, on the writing test, Ryan was sometimes provided with a picture that he needed to write about and/or was *provided with* sentences that he had to connect using specific words (e.g., conjunctions). Additionally, this writing test required Ryan to generate relatively short paragraphs rather than lengthy ones.

Similarly, the reading comprehension test that was administered to Ryan allowed him to refer back to the text when answering questions, which reduced the demands on Ryan's short-term memory. The demands of Ryan's current curriculum clearly exceed those that were required to complete the academic tests administered during this evaluation.

In summary, Ryan's pattern of related cognitive and academic weaknesses within an otherwise normal ability profile is consistent with a specific reading disability. His performance suggests that he has a disorder in two basic psychological processes, namely processing speed and short-term memory, that interfere with his ability to read individual words in isolation. Ryan's weaknesses in vocabulary, retrieval fluency, and phonetic coding also contribute to his reading difficulties. It is likely that the same cognitive processes and abilities that contributed to Ryan's reading difficulty, as well as poor reading ability in and of itself, have contributed to the difficulties that Ryan demonstrates in other academic domains (e.g., spelling, written language). Hence, it is recommended that the current assessment results be presented before the Committee on Special Education to determine whether there is agreement that a disabling condition, as defined by the Individuals with Disabilities Education Act (IDEA), exists, and to discuss the appropriate supports and services that should be provided to Ryan in an effort to circumvent the impact that his Normative Weaknesses have on his ability to learn and achieve at a level commensurate with his same-age peers.

Recommendations

The primary purpose of psychoeducational assessment is not so much diagnostic as it is to generate data that may be used to develop effective interventions to resolve the issues that led to the referral in the first place. Because of the close relationship that exists between theory and assessment, the resulting data provide a significant foundation from which learning difficulties can be clearly understood and appropriate instructional interventions developed. Regardless of the types of interventions that are developed, ongoing evaluation of their effectiveness should remain a part of whatever plan is developed to ameliorate the observed academic difficulties and concerns. The integration of corroborative information from standardized tests, teacher and parent reports, and prereferral data provided the basis for the following recommendations for Ryan:

1. To address Ryan's identified difficulty in the area of word knowledge, it may be beneficial to provide specific supports that can be used during the completion of academic tasks. Such supports may include, but are not limited to, the following: (a) provide Ryan with a word bank for written expression tasks; (b) provide a glossary of terms that Ryan can refer to when completing reading assignments; (c) ensure that test questions do not include vocabulary terms that are unknown; (d) review or teach vocabulary words when Ryan is asked to read from content-area texts; (e) write key words and terms on the board when lecturing on new content areas; (f) ensure that instructions contain words that Ryan knows; (g) simplify instructions by extending upon unknown words with words that are familiar to Ryan, or define terms when initially presenting them (e.g., "the *composition* of igneous rock, that is, *what it is made up of,* is . . . ."); and (h) teach Ryan to use a thesaurus when completing writing tasks.

2. Ryan's short-term memory weaknesses are most appropriately addressed through specific instructional modifications and self-implemented strategies. For instance, Ryan's teachers should avoid the use of elaborate or multistep instructions whenever possible. Additionally, Ryan's teachers should sequence material from simple to more complex. His teachers can also provide frequent opportunities for practice and review of newly learned material, including systematic review within a few hours of learning. In terms of self-implemented strategies, Ryan should be encouraged to request repetition of instruc-

tions or statements when necessary, and should be taught to use mnemonic aids and verbal mediation strategies (e.g., saying the information to be remembered while looking at it) that he can apply when trying to retain new information.

3. To address Ryan's visual processing difficulties, it may be beneficial to (a) avoid excessive reliance on visual models, diagrams, and demonstrations; (b) accompany visual demonstrations with oral explanations; and (c) break down spatial tasks into component parts (e.g., providing a set of verbal instructions to match each part). Additionally, because Ryan may have trouble forming a visual representation of a concept in his mind (e.g., a mental image), manipulatives or hands-on, concrete learning experiences may be beneficial when learning about an abstract concept that is visual in nature (e.g., the rotation of the planets in the solar system). Concrete or hands-on experiences should also be supplemented with verbal information.

4. Ryan's teacher can attempt to circumvent any adverse impact caused by his processing speed weakness in several ways, including (a) providing him with additional time to complete tasks; (b) shortening the length of in-class assignments; (c) allowing him to complete unfinished seatwork at home; (d) assisting Ryan in generating ideas and listing them prior to completing writing assignments; (e) utilizing a guided-notes (i.e., fill-in-the-blank) system that Ryan can use during classroom lectures or lessons.

5. Ryan's auditory processing weaknesses negatively impact his reading performance and can potentially interfere with his ability to accurately process orally presented information (e.g., instructions, class discussions). To address these difficulties, it may be beneficial to (a) encourage Ryan to physically orient himself toward the teacher during the provision of oral instructions ("seeing" what is being stated supports the processing of auditory information); (b) ensure that words are clearly enunciated during the presentation of oral information (e.g., dictation of spelling words); (c) check for understanding of orally presented directions by asking Ryan to paraphrase what he heard; and (d) provide Ryan with direct instruction regarding the use of word-attack skills and context cues to decode words.

Jennifer T. Mascolo, PsyD
Examiner

PSYCHOLOGICAL REPORT

Name: Cheryl J.　　　　　　　　　　　　DOB: 4/15/89
Chronological age: 14 years, 11 months　Grade: 9
Date of Testing: 3/27/04　　　　　　　Date of Report: 4/2/04

Referral and Background Information

Cheryl was referred for evaluation by her parents, Mr. and Mrs. J., and by Dr. Ronald F., a hematologist. Dr. F. and Mr. and Mrs. J. would like to gain some insight into Cheryl's cognitive and achievement abilities and current level of functioning; they suspect that she might have a learning disability. Cheryl has been experiencing difficulty with her ninth-grade schoolwork and has a history of reading and spelling problems. Her school grades have been deteriorating, and she has been having more difficulty as the demands in school have become greater. In the recent past, Cheryl has been noncompliant in taking her medication for HIV; both her medical condition and her noncompliance have been great concerns to her parents, physicians, and therapist.

　　Cheryl, adopted at the age of 2 months, was diagnosed with an "unknown blood disorder" at age 6 months, and as being HIV-positive at age 18 months. Virtually nothing is known about her biological parents. A referral was made from Cheryl's therapist, Dr. Judy S., for psychological testing. Dr. S., Dr. F., and Cheryl's parents suspect that Cheryl may have a learning disability that is making school extraordinarily difficult for her and may be related to her noncompliance with her medications.

　　Cheryl lives at home with her brother and sister and both of her adoptive parents in San Bernardino, CA. She is the youngest of the three children, all of whom were adopted as infants. Her brother, Milton, is 19, and her sister, Candace, is 17; Cheryl is almost 15. Both parents, Milton, and Cheryl are Caucasian; Candace is African American.

　　Cheryl's birth history is unknown and her early developmental history is unremarkable. She reached all developmental milestones within a normal time frame. Since the diagnosis of HIV-positive at age 18 months, Cheryl has required close blood monitoring, with frequent visits to the doctor's office for blood tests. Based on occasional abnormalities revealed by the blood tests, she has had blood transfusions her whole life, sometimes several times a year. She has also had many medical "emergencies" throughout her life because every infection or cold is legitimate cause for concern. During the past two years, her failure to take prescribed medications has led to three visits to the emergency room at a nearby hospital. No other major illnesses or injuries were reported, but Cheryl's mother stated that Cheryl's health has been at the forefront of their parenting efforts since the diagnosis of her disease.

It is her parents' belief that Cheryl has just recently begun to take more responsibility for her own health care. Cheryl is also currently being seen by a health team that assists in taking care of her physical and emotional needs in relation to her HIV and health maintenance.

Cheryl attended preschool from age 2 to age 4½. Mrs. J. reported that Cheryl was very tearful when she first began school and that she cried often even though her older sister, Candace, was at school with her. When Cheryl went to kindergarten she reportedly enjoyed school more and did not cry when school began. Mrs. J. also reported that Cheryl was younger and less mature than the other children in the classroom "because of her late birthday." When Cheryl went into the first grade she experienced "stomach aches" and did not like school. Her parents then placed her in a kindergarten–first grade combination classroom at a private school for the second semester. The following autumn, Cheryl began the first grade again, at a new public school, and apparently did better and felt more comfortable.

Mrs. J. reported that Cheryl had difficulty with phonics at an early age and that she was eventually tested by a school psychologist when she was in second grade. Mrs. J. stated that the school psychologist said that Cheryl had a "high IQ" but that she was immature for her age.

Throughout Cheryl's education, she has had moderate difficulties with her schoolwork, but her health care, rather than her school difficulties, has typically been the focus of her problems. Recently, however, her schoolwork has become more demanding and difficult and has become a pressing concern to her; it has also assumed more importance to her parents. In the summer before the ninth grade, Cheryl expressed some doubt in her own ability to achieve academically. She was beginning to recognize that she was having problems completing assignments, especially writing and spelling. Cheryl agreed to this testing and expressed a desire to improve her schoolwork and obtain a better understanding of her academic and intellectual strengths and weaknesses.

Cheryl, Mrs. J., and several of Cheryl's teachers reported that she is a very social adolescent. Mrs. J. stated that there had been a change in her peer group to a "less academically oriented" group, with whom she spends a great deal of time. Her counselor and two teachers describe one of her strengths as her extremely personable nature and ability to get along well with others. Cheryl's math teacher stated that she "talks too much in class and is out of her seat a lot." In comparison, Cheryl's history teacher reported that Cheryl was "withdrawn" and "not socializing." The amount of time that Cheryl spends socializing in class may be related to the peers that are in each of her classes with whom she can socialize. Both Mrs. J. and Cheryl reported that outside of school, Cheryl's time is mostly spent on the phone with friends or going out with her friends. Cheryl also added that most of her friends are older than she. When asked why her friends were older she said that they just were and did not offer any further explanation.

At the beginning of the second (and final) testing session, the examiner asked Cheryl how she was doing in school and asked her if she had any questions. Cheryl reported that she was having great difficulty in school and that she spent 4–5 hours per night doing homework. Whereas she undoubtedly does not spend this amount of time on homework each night, it does suggest that Cheryl feels academically overwhelmed. She said that she just cannot keep up and that it takes her a lot longer to do her schoolwork than it does the other students. She reported that she did not feel that her social life interfered with her schoolwork; however, most adolescents would provide a similar response.

Appearance and Behavioral Observations

Cheryl is an attractive adolescent girl with brown eyes and straight, dark-blond hair cut bluntly above her shoulders. She was well groomed and dressed casually and she wore many earrings in her ears. Cheryl appeared her stated age of almost 15 and her overall presentation of herself was consistent with that of an independent adolescent. She made very little eye contact, her posture was poor, and she did not converse easily with the examiner. Cheryl seemed to feel relatively uncomfortable during most of the testing and even though she complied with all that was requested of her, it was apparent that she retained her sense of privacy and minimal social involvement with the examiner. At one point during the testing, Cheryl's pager went off and she asked if she could use the phone. When she was asked to wait, she did, and returned to the task without any difficulty. It should be noted that Cheryl's behavior is not unusual for an adolescent.

Cheryl arrived for her appointments on time and was cooperative and pleasant. She spoke softly and she often had her hands in front of her mouth while she was speaking. Although Cheryl seemed to be uninterested, especially during the first testing session, she appeared to be trying her best. Cheryl was a little anxious, as evidenced by her excessive psychomotor activity. She tapped her foot on the ground repeatedly, moved around in her seat, and engaged in a number of self-stimulating behaviors. For example, she continually engaged in the following behaviors: running her hands through her hair, playing with her necklace, playing with strings on her clothing, touching her face, touching her neck, and pulling or biting on her lips. These behaviors did not seem to distract her from what she was doing but rather seemed to soothe her emotionally and reduce her anxiety.

While solving problems and answering test questions, Cheryl continued to speak softly. The tone of her speech lacked confidence, as her answers were often stated in more of a questioning tone. Cheryl also bit her nails when she seemed unsure of herself. Despite her apparent lack of confidence, she was able to say when she did know an answer and would ask questions if she did not know something or did not understand what was being asked of her. In general, she responded well to feedback and encouragement from the examiner.

Evaluation Procedures

Wechsler Intelligence Scale for Children–Fourth Edition (WISC-IV)
Kaufman Assessment Battery for Children–Second Edition (KABC-II)
Kaufman Test of Educational Achievement–Second Edition, Comprehensive Form (KTEA-II, Form A)
Clinical interview with Mrs. J.
School observation
Interviews with teachers
Interview with school counselor
Interview with Dr. Judy S.
Home visit and observation

Test Results and Interpretation

During the first testing session, Cheryl was administered the core battery of the Wechsler Intelligence Scale for Children–Fourth Edition (WISC-IV), and about half of the Kaufman Test of Educational Achievement–Second Edition, Comprehensive Form (KTEA-II, Form A). At the second session, five days later, she was administered the remainder of the KTEA-II and the core battery of the Kaufman Assessment Battery for Children–Second Edition (KABC-II). The WISC-IV and KABC-II are each individually administered tests of a child's intellectual and processing ability, and each provides scales to identify the child's cognitive strengths and weaknesses. The KTEA-II measures school achievement in reading, math, oral language, and written language.

Cognitive Assessment

WISC-IV
The WISC-IV groups an individual's ability into four global areas: Verbal Comprehension Index (VCI), which measures verbal ability; Perceptual Reasoning Index (PRI), which involves the manipulation of concrete materials or pro-

cessing of visual stimuli to solve nonverbal problems; Working Memory Index (WMI), which measures short-term memory; and Processing Speed Index (PSI), which measures cognitive processing efficiency.

On the WISC-IV, Cheryl earned a Full Scale IQ (FSIQ) of 114, which ranks her overall ability at the 82nd percentile and classifies her global IQ as falling within the Average Range. There is a 95% chance that her true FSIQ is between 109 and 119. However, this estimate of her general intellectual ability on the WISC-IV cannot be interpreted meaningfully and should be deemphasized because she displayed considerable variability in the four Indexes that constitute this full scale score. Her Indexes ranged from 88 on the WMI (21st percentile) to 119 on the VCI (90th percentile), suggesting that Cheryl's intelligence is best understood by her performance on the separate WISC-IV Indexes, namely, Verbal Comprehension, Perceptual Reasoning, Working Memory, and Processing Speed.

Before discussing Cheryl's Indexes on the four scales, one must first determine whether each Index is interpretable—that is, does it measure a reasonably unitary trait for Cheryl, or do her scaled scores on the subtests that make up the Index include substantial variability? In fact, all four of Cheryl's WISC-IV Indexes are considered "interpretable." The largest discrepancy among her subtest scaled scores was 4 points on the VCI (the difference between her scaled scores of 15 on Similarities and 11 on Vocabulary). Discrepancies on the other three Indexes were 3 points (PRI), 2 points (PSI), and 0 points (WMI). None of these values met or exceeded the critical value needed for each of these scales. Consequently, Cheryl's PRI, VCI, WMI, and PSI are all considered to provide good estimates of the abilities measured by each scale.

The PRI, a measure of Visual Processing and Fluid Reasoning *(Gv/Gf)*, represents Cheryl's ability to reason using visual stimuli. Cheryl's *Gv/Gf* ability was assessed by tasks that required her to recreate a series of modeled or pictured designs using blocks (Block Design), identify the missing portion of an incomplete visual matrix from one of five response options (Matrix Reasoning), and select one picture from each of two or three rows of pictures to form a group with a common characteristic (Picture Concepts). Cheryl obtained a PRI *(Gv/Gf)* of 117 (108–123), which ranks her at the 87th percentile and classifies her PRI as Above Average/Normative Strength. Cheryl's perceptual reasoning ability is considered a significant strength compared to other individuals her age in the normal population. In addition, her ability in this area is significantly higher than her abilities in other areas. Therefore, Cheryl's perceptual reasoning ability is a notable integrity, a finding that may play an essential role in developing educational interventions.

The VCI, a measure of Crystallized Intelligence *(Gc)*, represents Cheryl's ability to reason with previously learned information. An individual's *Gc* ability develops largely as a function of formal and informal educational opportunities and experiences and is highly dependent on exposure to mainstream U.S. culture. Cheryl's *Gc* ability was assessed by tasks that required her to define words (Vocabulary), draw conceptual similarities between words (Similarities), and answer questions involving knowledge of general principles and social situations (Comprehension). Cheryl obtained a VCI *(Gc)* of 119 (111–125), which ranks her at the 90th percentile and classifies her VCI as Above Average/Normative Strength. Cheryl's crystallized intelligence is considered a significant strength compared to other individuals her age in the normal population. In addition, her ability in this area is significantly higher than her abilities in other areas. Therefore, Cheryl's crystallized intelligence is a notable integrity, a finding that may play an essential role in developing educational interventions.

The WMI, a measure of Short-Term Memory *(Gsm)*, represents Cheryl's ability to apprehend and hold, or transform, information in immediate awareness and then use it within a few seconds. Cheryl's *Gsm* ability was assessed by two tasks—Digit Span required Cheryl to repeat a sequence of numbers in the same order as presented by the examiner (Digit Span Forward) and also in the reverse order (Digit Span Backward), and Letter-Number Sequencing required her to listen to a sequence of numbers and letters and recall the numbers in ascending order and the letters in alphabetical order. Cheryl obtained a WMI *(Gsm)* of 88 (81–97), which ranks her at the 21st percentile and classifies her WMI as Average Range/Within Normal Limits. Cheryl's short-term memory is considered a significant weakness compared to her abilities in other areas. In fact, the difference between her short-term memory and her abilities in other areas is so large that it is not commonly found in the normal population of children her age. Therefore, Cheryl's short-term memory is a notable personal weakness, a finding that may play an essential role in developing educational interventions.

The PSI, a measure of Processing Speed *(Gs)*, represents Cheryl's ability to fluently and automatically perform cognitive tasks, especially when under pressure to maintain focused attention and concentration. Cheryl's *Gs* ability was assessed by two tasks—one required Cheryl to quickly copy symbols that were paired with numbers according to a key (Coding), and the other required her to identify the presence or absence of a target symbol in a row of symbols (Symbol Search). Cheryl obtained a PSI *(Gs)* of 112 (102–120), which ranks her at the 79th percentile and classifies her PSI as Average Range/Within Normal Limits.

As noted, Cheryl's WISC-IV FSIQ could not be interpreted because she demonstrated considerable variability in her performance across the four Indexes that make up this score, namely the Verbal Comprehension, Perceptual Reasoning, Working Memory, and Processing Speed Indexes. However, it is often useful to provide a global estimate of an individual's current level of functioning. Because Cheryl's performance on the Verbal Comprehension and Perceptual Reasoning Indexes was similar, these Indexes can be combined to yield a General Ability Index (GAI). The GAI differs from the FSIQ in that it is not influenced directly by Cheryl's performance on working memory and processing speed tasks.

Cheryl earned a GAI of 120, classifying her general level of intellectual ability as Above Average/Normative Strength. The chances are good (95%) that Cheryl's true GAI is somewhere within the range of 114 to 126. Her GAI is ranked at the 91st percentile, indicating that she scored higher than 91 percent of other children of the same age in the standardization sample. Table 8.5 summarizes Cheryl's performance on all tests administered.

KABC-II

The KABC-II, like the WISC-IV, provides a comprehensive measure of cognitive abilities. Ordinarily, examiners opt to administer a single measure of comprehensive cognitive ability to a child, and supplement that measure with selected tasks to enrich the breadth of the cognitive assessment. For Cheryl, a second comprehensive test was administered for several reasons: (1) as noted, Cheryl seemed to be uninterested in the testing, especially during the first session, so validation of the results was warranted; (2) the WISC-IV PRI combines *Gf* and *Gv* abilities—the KABC-II provides *separate* scales to measure *Gf* and *Gv*, which might offer additional insights; (3) the KABC-II measures Learning Ability *(Glr)*, an important skill to assess for individuals with learning problems in school; and (4) the KABC-II is a new test—the best way for examiners to understand the clinical aspects of new instruments is to administer them alongside traditional tests such as Wechsler's.

The KABC-II is based on a double theoretical foundation: Luria's neuropsychological model and the Cattell-Horn-Carroll (CHC) psychometric theory. It offers five scales, each given a label that reflects both theoretical models: Sequential/*Gsm*, Simultaneous/*Gv*, Learning/*Glr*, Planning/*Gf*, and Knowledge/*Gc*. Examiners who opt to administer the Luria model of the KABC-II give only four of these scales (Knowledge/*Gc* is excluded when the Luria model is used because measures of language ability and acquired knowledge may not provide fair assessment of the cognitive abilities of some children—e.g., those from non-mainstream backgrounds or those with receptive/expressive language disorders). Cheryl was administered the CHC model of the KABC-II, which comprises

Table 8.5 Psychometric Summary for Cheryl J.

Wechsler Intelligence Scale for Children–Fourth Edition (WISC-IV)

Index/Subtest	Standard Score (mean = 100; SD = 15)	95% CI	Percentile Rank
Verbal Comprehension	119	[111–125]	90th
Similarities = 15			
Vocabulary = 11			
Comprehension = 14			
Perceptual Reasoning	117	[108–123]	87th
Block Design = 11			
Picture Concepts = 13			
Matrix Reasoning = 14			
Working Memory	88	[81–97]	21st
Digit Span = 8			
Letter-Number Sequencing = 8			
Processing Speed	112	[102–120]	79th
Coding = 13			
Symbol Search = 11			
Full Scale IQ	114	[109–119]	82nd
General Ability Index	120	[114–126]	91st

(continued)

all five areas of cognitive ability (with each area measured by two subtests). She earned a KABC-II Fluid-Crystallized Index (FCI) of 120, ranking her at the 91st percentile and classifying her overall cognitive ability as Above Average/Normative Strength.

Cheryl's FCI of 120 is the same as her GAI that was computed on the WISC-IV. However, like Cheryl's WISC-IV FSIQ, her FCI is not very meaningful in view of the considerable variability among Cheryl's Indexes on the KABC-II. Her range of Indexes on the KABC-II was greater than the 2-SD range on the WISC-IV, extending from 94 on Sequential/*Gsm* (34th percentile) to 135 on Planning/*Gf* (99th percentile). Quite clearly, the best understanding of Cheryl's strengths and weaknesses will come from an integration of her Indexes on both the WISC-IV and KABC-II.

On the KABC-II, four of Cheryl's five Indexes are considered "interpretable." That is to say, she performed with reasonable consistency on the subtests that constitute four of the KABC-II scales, but her scores were too variable on the fifth

Table 8.5 (Continued)

Kaufman Assessment Battery for Children–Second Edition (KABC-II) Cattell-Horn-Carroll (CHC) Model

Scale/Subtest	Standard Score (mean = 100; SD = 15)	95% CI	Percentile Rank
Sequential/*Gsm*	94	[85–103]	34th
Number Recall = 10			
Word Order = 8			
Simultaneous/*Gv*	106	[96–116]	66th
Rover = 13			
Block Counting = 9			
Learning/*Glr*	126	[117–133]	96th
Atlantis = 16			
Rebus = 13			
Planning/*Gf*	135	[120–144]	99th
Story Completion = 17			
Pattern Reasoning = 14			
Knowledge/*Gc*	115	[106–122]	84th
Verbal Knowledge = 11			
Riddles = 15			
Fluid-Crystallized Index	120	[115–125]	91st

scale—Knowledge/*Gc*. The largest discrepancy in her scores was 4 points (the difference between her highest and lowest subtest scaled scores on a scale), and that discrepancy occurred twice—on the Simultaneous/*Gv* scale (where she earned 13 on Rover and 9 on Block Counting) and on the Knowledge/*Gc* scale (where she earned 11 on Verbal Knowledge and 15 on Riddles). The difference of 4 points on Simultaneous/*Gv* is smaller than the critical value of 6 points to determine "uninterpretability" for ages 13–18 years. However, for Knowledge/*Gc*, the critical value for ages 13–18 years is 4 points, exactly equal to Cheryl's subtest score variability on that scale. Consequently, all of Cheryl's scale Indexes—except Knowledge/*Gc*—are able to be interpreted. (The critical values for each scale denote subtest scaled-score differences that are so large that they occurred less than 10% of the time in the normative sample; such differences render a scale Index uninterpretable.)[1]

---

[1] Note that the critical values for determining scale interpretability differ for the WISC-IV and KABC-II.

Table 8.5 (Continued)

Kaufman Test of Educational Achievement–Second Edition (KTEA-II), Comprehensive Form (Form A)

Composite/Subtest	Standard Score	Percentile Rank
Reading Composite	**105**	**63rd**
Letter and Word Recognition	89	23rd
Reading Comprehension	120	91st
(Nonsense Word Decoding)	(85)	(16th)
(Decoding Composite)	**(87)**	**(19th)**
Mathematics Composite	**112**	**79th**
Mathematics Concepts and Applications	112	79th
Mathematics Computation	111	77th
Oral Language Composite	**121**	**92nd**
Listening Comprehension	117	87th
Oral Expression	124	95th
Written Language Composite	**88**	**21st**
Written Expression	91	27th
Spelling	88	21st
Total Battery Composite	**108**	**70th**

Note: Subtests and Composites in parentheses are supplemental.

On the KABC-II, Cheryl's Planning/*Gf* Index of 135 (120–144) ranks her performance at the 99th percentile relative to adolescents her age and classifies her ability as Upper Extreme/Normative Strength. To perform at this high level, Cheryl had to solve nonverbal problems rapidly where these problems require Fluid Reasoning *(Gf)*, executive functioning (generating and evaluating hypotheses), verbal mediation, and planning ability. One of these tasks required her to complete series of abstract patterns (Pattern Reasoning), and the other required her to complete a story told with pictures (Story Completion). Cheryl's strong *Gf* reflects both a Normative Strength (relative to others her age) and a Personal Strength (relative to her own level of ability); furthermore, the difference between her Index of 135 and her own average Index is "uncommonly large" (i.e., differences that large occurred less than 10% of the time in the normative population). Therefore, Cheryl's *Gf* ability is a Key Asset for her, a finding that should play an essential role in developing educational interventions.

Cheryl's Learning/*Glr* Index of 126 (117–133) ranks her performance at the 96th percentile relative to adolescents her age and classifies her ability as Above

Average/Normative Strength. Cheryl demonstrated the ability to use her Long-Term Storage and Retrieval *(Glr)* to learn new material that is taught by the examiner in a standardized, structured manner (two paired-associate learning tasks—Atlantis required her to learn the nonsense names of fish, plants, and shells; Rebus Learning required her to "read" words that are paired with symbols). Her ability to learn new material *(Glr)* is both a Normative Strength and a Personal Strength for Cheryl, a finding that should play an essential role in developing educational interventions—especially since the ability to learn new material translates directly to the classroom.

Cheryl's Simultaneous/*Gv* Index of 106 (96–116) ranks her performance at the 66th percentile relative to adolescents her age and classifies her ability as Average Range/Within Normal Limits. Cheryl demonstrated the ability use her simultaneous and Visual Processing *(Gv)* on two tasks, one requiring her to use executive functioning and visualization to solve problems (getting "Rover" to a bone on a checkerboard-like grid using the shortest path), and the other (Block Counting) requiring her to count an array of blocks where some blocks are hidden or partially hidden. Though her *Gv* ability is in the Average Range relative to other adolescents her age, it represents a Personal Weakness for Cheryl, a finding that may play an essential role in developing educational interventions.

Cheryl's Sequential/*Gsm* Index of 94 (85–103) ranks her performance at the 34th percentile relative to adolescents her age and classifies her ability as within the Average Range/Within Normal Limits. Cheryl demonstrated her Short-Term Memory *(Gsm)* and sequential processing on Word Order, which required her to point in sequence to pictures named by the examiner, sometimes with an intervening interference task (color naming), and Number Recall (forward digit span). Although her *Gsm* ability is in the Average Range relative to other adolescents her age, it represents an "uncommon" Personal Weakness for Cheryl—i.e., her Index of 94 is below her Indexes on other KABC-II scales by an unusually large number of points (a magnitude that occurred less than 10% of the time in the normal population). This finding should play an essential role in developing educational interventions.

Integrating Test Scores from the WISC-IV and KABC-II

Cheryl's scores on the two comprehensive tests of cognitive abilities are basically quite consistent with one another. She displayed wide variability on both instruments, but her strengths and weaknesses on both tests combine to paint a fairly clear picture of Cheryl's cognitive strengths and weaknesses. Despite her apparent lack of interest in the assessment process during the first session (when the WISC-IV was given), her similar level of performance on the KABC-II, during the second session when interest level was more optimal, suggests that her WISC-IV profile provides a valid estimate of her functioning.

The WISC-IV PRI measures a blend of Gf and Gv, making the nature of Cheryl's Normative and Personal Strengths unclear. When viewed in the context of Cheryl's KABC-II profile, it is evident that Cheryl's PRI of 117 (87th percentile) is the approximate midpoint of her exceptional Gf ability (Planning/Gf Index = 135, 99th percentile) and her average Gv ability (Simultaneous/Gv = 106, 66th percentile). In fact, on the KABC-II, Cheryl had a *Personal Weakness* in her Gv ability. Examination of Cheryl's PRI subtest scaled scores indicates consistency with stronger Gf than Gv—she performed at the 91st and 84th percentiles on the two subtests that are primarily measures of Gf (Matrix Reasoning and Picture Concepts, respectively) compared to the 65th percentile on Block Design (primarily Gv). In fact, Cheryl's exceptional fluid reasoning ability was evident throughout the subtest profiles of both the WISC-IV and KABC-II, most notably on the Gc scales. On the VCI, Cheryl performed better on Comprehension and Similarities (91st and 95th percentiles, respectively), both of which require Gf for successful performance, than on Vocabulary (65th percentile). Similarly, on the Knowledge/Gc scale, Cheryl scored higher on Riddles (95th percentile) than on Verbal Knowledge (65th percentile). Riddles requires Gf to integrate verbal clues to solve each "riddle"; Verbal Knowledge measures word knowledge and factual information, neither of which requires Gf. The Knowledge/Gc Index was not interpretable for Cheryl, undoubtedly because its component tasks differ in the amount of Gf each demands. Cheryl's strong Gf, evidenced on both comprehensive tests, has implications for Cheryl's educational intervention.

The WISC-IV and KABC-II also help document Cheryl's relative weakness in short-term memory, as she earned a WMI of 88 and a similar Sequential/Gsm Index of 94. Both of these Indexes are Within Normal Limits, but both are clear-cut weaknesses for Cheryl relative to her other cognitive abilities. This finding of a Gsm personal weakness on two different instruments has implications both diagnostically and for planning Cheryl's educational interventions.

In addition to the integration of test results on the WISC-IV and KABC-II to better understand her strengths and weaknesses on abilities measured by both tests, each test contributes information on a unique CHC ability. On the WISC-IV, Cheryl earned a PSI of 112, indicating that her processing speed was Average Range/Within Normal Limits. On the KABC-II, she displayed a Personal Strength and Normative Strength on the Learning/Glr Scale (Index = 126), indicating that her learning ability and long-term storage and retrieval are areas of strength for her, important information for planning educational interventions.

Based on scores on both batteries, the following standard scores are the best estimates of her performance on six CHC abilities (*Gf*, *Glr*, and *Gv* are from KABC-II; *Gc* and *Gs* are from WISC-IV; *Gsm* is the average of her two pertinent Indexes).

CHC Broad Ability	Standard Score	Percentile Rank
Fluid Reasoning/*Gf*	135	99th
Long-Term Storage and Retrieval/*Glr*	126	96th
Crystallized Ability/*Gc*	115	84th
Processing Speed/*Gs*	112	79th
Visual Processing/*Gv*	106	66th
Short-Term Memory/*Gsm*	91	27th

Achievement Assessment

KTEA-II Comprehensive Form A
Cheryl's standard scores on the KTEA-II Form A (based on grade norms) were extremely varied. Her overall Test Battery Composite of 108 (70th percentile) was nothing more than a midpoint of her separate composite standard scores, which ranged from 88 to 121: Oral Language (121, 92nd percentile), Mathematics (112, 79th percentile), Reading (105, 63rd percentile), and Written Language (88, 21st percentile). Her Reading Composite of 105 suggests an average level of reading ability, but that standard score is misleading. Cheryl performed in the Above Average category on Reading Comprehension (120), but had great difficulty with basic reading fundamentals (89 on Letter and Word Recognition). Her phonetic abilities, in particular, are a significant weakness for her; she earned a standard score of 85 (16th percentile) on the supplementary Nonsense Word Decoding subtest, a task that required her to decode nonsense words by making use of principles of phonics. Her standard score of 87 (19th percentile) on the supplementary KTEA-II Decoding Composite (Letter and Word Recognition + Nonsense Word Decoding) provides an overview of this area of weakness.

Cheryl performed strikingly better in her Oral Language (121) than Written Language (88). She is notably better in expressing her ideas orally (124 on Oral Expression) than via writing (91 on Written Expression). However, she is about equally able to comprehend information whether it is presented orally (117 in Listening Comprehension) or in printed form (120 in Reading Comprehension). Her performance on both of these "Comprehension" subtests was facilitated by the strong fluid reasoning that she displayed on the cognitive batteries.

Cheryl's performance in mathematics reveals intact functioning in the basic skills of computation and quantitative concepts (111) and also in the ability to apply mathematical principles to solve word problems (112).

The KTEA-II provides a systematic error analysis to help examiners identify specific academic areas of strength and weakness. Cheryl's responses on several subtests were further examined by this error-analysis procedure.

The K-TEA-II error analysis for Spelling classifies spelling errors into 15 categories, and compares the number of errors that Cheryl made to the number made by other adolescents in Grade 9 who attempted the same number of items. Relative to her peers, Cheryl was classified as Weak in 7 of the 15 categories. The most noteworthy area of weakness, in which she made seven to eight errors (when the average person in her grade made two to four errors), were Suffixes and Word Endings, Long Vowels, Silent Letters, and Single and Double Consonants. For example, she spelled "construction" as "constructine," a problem with word endings; she spelled "while" as "whyle," a problem with long vowels; and she spelled "regretted" as "regretid," a problem with both long vowels and suffixes and word endings.

Further error analysis in the areas of Letter/Word Recognition and Nonsense Word Decoding revealed similar skill-weakness error patterns when Cheryl read words and nonsense words aloud. Again, the Weak skill areas included Suffixes and Word Endings, Long Vowels, and Silent Letters. For example, she pronounced the word "truth" with a short "u" sound; and "gigantic" with a short "i" sound in the first syllable, both examples of long vowel errors; she read "revolutionary" as "revolutinry," a problem with suffixes and word endings. In Nonsense Word Decoding, she pronounced "trame" with a short "a" sound as well as pronouncing the silent "e" as a long e sound, a problem with both long vowels and silent letters; "plewness" was read as "plewrest," a problem with suffixes and word endings.

The KTEA-II error analysis for Written Expression classifies writing errors into five categories: task, structure, word form, capitalization, and punctuation. When compared to her same-age peers, Cheryl made significantly more capitalization and punctuation errors (6 and 16, respectively) than her same-grade peers, who averaged only 0–2 errors in capitalization and 6–11 errors in punctuation.

Diagnostic Impressions

In view of Cheryl's extreme fluctuation in her performance on both cognitive batteries, it was difficult to find a "best estimate" of her current level of functioning. For the purposes of evaluating discrepancies between Cheryl's ability and achievement, her GAI of 120 on the WISC-IV, derived from her VCI and PRI, will be used. That score is significantly and substantially higher than her standard scores on the KTEA-II Decoding Composite (88), Written Language Composite (88), and both subtests that compose the Written Language Composite—Written Expression (91) and Spelling (88). These discrepancies are approximately 2 SDs, strongly supportive of a learning disorder. Based on these discrepancies, on a possible processing disorder in sequential processing or short-term memory, on the results of the error analysis, and on clear-cut areas of integrity in fluid reasoning, planning abilities, learning ability, and long-term storage and retrieval, Cheryl appears to demonstrate a learning disorder. This disorder appears to manifest in reading decoding, writing mechanics, written expression, and spelling, and is perhaps related to the sequential and memory Personal Weaknesses that she evidenced on the cognitive tests. This learning disorder undoubtedly explains many of the reading, writing, and spelling difficulties she has experienced in school, but it cannot explain all of her academic problems. For example, her mathematics ability is at the high end of the Average Range (which is consistent with her intellectual ability), and is evenly developed in different areas such as computational ability and math reasoning. The "D" that she is receiving after five weeks of class is probably related to the "bad citizenship" that was noted by her math teacher.

Cheryl's phonics problem and general difficulty with other basic reading skills are of less concern than her difficulties in written-language mechanics and spelling. She has compensated well for her reading-skill deficiencies, as attested by her Above Average performance on KTEA-II Reading Comprehension. The ability to understand what we read is quite dependent on reasoning ability. Cheryl has spontaneously been able to apply her exceptional reasoning and problem-solving abilities to gain understanding of material that she reads.

Although Cheryl's school and learning difficulties have been the focus of this assessment, it is important to address her emotional and social functioning and how it relates to her academic abilities and achievement. This assessment suggests that Cheryl is both anxious and oppositional. Her approach to many of the tasks and her interactions with the examiner, as well as some of her teachers reports, suggest that she is angry and that she does not relate to adults as well as she should. Cheryl's attitude and emotions significantly affect her school performance. Her relatively weak short-term memory likely makes school considerably more difficult for her than other students; however, she has compensated for her personal weaknesses well. Furthermore, Cheryl's poor citizenship grades and teacher reports about her socializing in class suggest that some of Cheryl's school problems stem from behavioral difficulties and her negative and angry attitude.

It is important to note that many of Cheryl's difficulties may also be related to her HIV status. That is, individuals infected with HIV, especially those who are perinatally exposed, often have cognitive, affective, and behavioral symptomatology directly resulting from the disease. Cognitive impairments generally include language deficits (especially expressive language), short-term memory impairments, visual-spatial processing difficulties, and phonological awareness deficits. These impairments in perinatally exposed children are due to the inability of the child's brain to make appropriate neuronal connections due to the introduction of the virus at a time when the brain is not fully developed. Although many children reach developmental milestones within normal limits, as Cheryl has, subtle cognitive difficulties can become evident over time due to the progressive nature of the disease. Although antiretroviral medications can delay, and sometimes reverse, the manifestation of these subclinical deficits, these deficits can still exert a negative impact on the child's functioning. Additionally, certain antiretroviral medications and protease inhibitors, which are commonly used to treat HIV-infected children and adolescents, can have negative effects over time. An unfortunate feature of these medications is that many are ototoxic. That is, they can impact a child's hearing and cause subtle hearing loss. This feature may partly explain Cheryl's reported history of difficulty with phonics as well as her observed weakness on phonologically based measures. Another common reason for phonological difficulties in HIV-infected children is the fact that these children often experience frequent colds and ear infections, which can compromise their hearing during sensitive periods of development. In essence, their frequent, and often lengthy, infections cause them to lose important linguistic information (e.g., subtle phonemic distinctions) and effectively delay appropriate development of phonological abilities.

In addition to the previously mentioned cognitive difficulties, affectively, HIV-infected individuals often manifest an increased level of anxiety and depression and, behaviorally, these individuals often have difficulties maintaining attention and are sometimes described as highly distractible.

Although Cheryl's cognitive *(Gsm)* and behavioral difficulties clearly have a negative impact on her academic functioning, the primary causes of her academic difficulties—that is, cognitive, behavioral, medical—cannot be determined. As such, Cheryl cannot be diagnosed as learning disabled under the Individuals with Disabilities Education Act (IDEA). That is, the exclusionary criteria that must be considered in learning-disability referrals requires the examiner to demonstrate that certain factors, such as a medical condition, are not the *primary* cause of the child's academic difficulties. Given that Cheryl's reported and observed difficulties are common consequences of HIV infection, it is difficult to rule out her health status as a primary cause of her current academic difficulties.

Because IDEA generally does not apply to individuals with communicable diseases, such as HIV, Cheryl may not meet criteria for classification of "Other Health Impaired" under IDEA because her physical condition appears to directly impact her ability to learn. Therefore, her health status cannot be ruled out as a *primary* cause for her learning difficulties. Nonetheless, individuals like Cheryl are protected under Section 504 of the Americans with Disabilities Act if there is evidence that the individual is "experiencing academic difficulty (below grade level performance), and it is suspected that the medical condition is or will adversely affect classroom functioning." Clearly, Cheryl meets this criterion. Thus, it is recommended that Cheryl receive a 504 accommodation plan to address her current academic difficulties through the provision of special education supports and services, as described in the next section.

Recommendations

The following recommendations have been made to assist both Cheryl and her parents with Cheryl's cognitive, academic, emotional, and behavioral difficulties. This assessment suggests that Cheryl's difficulties are the result of a complex set of variables and dynamics and, therefore, should be addressed from a multimodal approach.

1. Cheryl should receive remedial tutoring to help with her learning difficulties. The school system will probably not be capable of providing Cheryl with the amount of help that she needs. Cheryl needs to be tutored in spelling, grammar, written expression, and the mechanics of reading decoding and writing. The following local Learning Specialists will be able to provide the help that Cheryl needs: (a) Andrea P. and (b) Annabelle M. The following book also provides some useful suggestions for intervention that take into account Cheryl's strengths in planning and reasoning ability and her weaknesses in short-term memory and sequential processing: Naglieri, J. A., & Pickering, E. B. (2003), *Helping children learn: Intervention handouts for use in school and at home,* Baltimore: Paul H. Brookes.

2. If the decision is made to send Cheryl to another school, it should be a school that has a low student-teacher ratio and provides a very structured environment. The school should also have teachers who are certified in teaching special education. We suggest that it is important for Mr. and Mrs. J. to verify credentials documenting both the school and the teaching staff.

3. Cheryl needs to be encouraged to take responsibility for her health care and her schoolwork. If she feels that she is being forced to do something because someone else wants her to do it, she is less likely to

follow through. If Cheryl chooses not to follow through with taking care of her health and schoolwork she needs to experience the consequences herself. It will be very important for Cheryl to feel that she has the emotional support and structure that she will need from her parents because she will be dealing with new demands and responsibilities. The additional stress in the household will be best handled by Mr. and Mrs. J.'s setting firm limits for Cheryl with predetermined consequences, both positive and negative.

4. Cheryl's emotional and behavioral difficulties need to be addressed by a trained therapist such as Dr. S., who reported that Cheryl views therapy with her as a "punishment" for not adhering to her health care regimen. Dr. S.'s area of expertise in combining psychotherapy and HIV health care management is invaluable. Therefore, it is recommended that Cheryl continue seeing Dr. S. on a regular basis, but perhaps only once a month while Cheryl still views this as punishment. In addition, it is recommended that Cheryl work with an art therapist. Cheryl is a creative and artistic individual who would benefit from expressing herself though her artistic talent. Art therapy is often seen as a less threatening, less verbal, and more hands-on and creative form of therapy. Mr. Alex O., a local art therapist, may be helpful.

5. Cheryl's oppositional behavior can be both frustrating and overwhelming. Cheryl will need firm and consistent limits to be set by both parents in order to help her take responsibility and make the best use of learning remediation and therapy. Therefore, it is recommended that Mr. and Mrs. J. continue in family therapy with Dr. S. as well as attend a parenting support group.

Nadeen L. Kaufman, EdD
Examiner

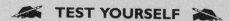 **TEST YOURSELF**

1. List five topics to include in the "Background Information" section of the report.

2. Every single behavior that was noticed during the assessment session should be described in detail in the "Appearance and Behavioral Characteristics" section of the report. True or False?

3. Besides a description of the child's physical appearance and behavioral observations, what else should be mentioned in the "Appearance and Behavioral Characteristics" section of the report?

    (a) Test scores

    (b) Referral question

    (c) A statement about the validity of the results

    (d) Brief recommendations

4. The least meaningful type of score metric, and therefore the one that should not be used in case reports, is the

    (a) raw score.

    (b) percentile rank.

    (c) standard score.

    (d) scaled score.

5. If you forget to mention some of the test results in the "Test Results and Interpretation" section, there is no need to worry because you can simply write about them in the "Summary" section of the report. True or False?

6. Which of the following is highly recommended in writing your report?

    (a) Using a lot of metaphors

    (b) Listing as many observed behaviors as possible

    (c) Using technical terms

    (d) Omitting confidence intervals, as they are too confusing

    (e) None of the above

Answers: 1. See *Don't Forget 8.3;* 2. False; 3. c; 4. a; 5. False; 6. e

Source: From A. S. Kaufman & E. O. Lichtenberger, *Essentials of WISC-III and WPPSI-R Assessment.* Copyright © 2000 John Wiley & Sons, Inc. This material is used by permission of John Wiley & Sons, Inc.

Appendix A

Definitions of CHC Abilities

CHC THEORY AND THE STRUCTURE OF COGNITIVE AND ACADEMIC ABILITIES

In this section the definitions of the broad and some of the narrow abilities included in the CHC model are presented. These definitions are consistent with those presented in Flanagan and Ortiz (2001), Flanagan and colleagues (2000), and McGrew and Flanagan (1998). They were derived from an integration of the writings of Carroll (1993), Gustafsson and Undheim (1996), Horn (1991), McGrew (1997), McGrew, Woodcock, and Werder (1991), and Woodcock (1994). Given the number of narrow abilities within the model (more than 70), it is not practical to include definitions of all these abilities in this text. Practitioners are referred to Flanagan and Ortiz and Flanagan and colleagues for detailed descriptions of all narrow abilities.

Fluid Intelligence (Gf)

Fluid Intelligence *(Gf)* refers to mental operations that an individual uses when faced with a relatively novel task that cannot be performed automatically. These mental operations may include forming and recognizing concepts, perceiving relationships among patterns, drawing inferences, comprehending implications, problem solving, extrapolating, and reorganizing or transforming information. Inductive and deductive reasoning are generally considered to be the hallmark narrow ability indicators of *Gf*. The WISC-IV provides three distinct reasoning tests: Picture Concepts and Word Reasoning (which involve the use of inductive reasoning) and Matrix Reasoning (which involves the use of general sequential reasoning, i.e., deductive reasoning). Select *Gf* narrow abilities are defined in Table A.1.

Crystallized Intelligence (Gc)

Crystallized Intelligence (Gc) refers to the breadth and depth of a person's acquired knowledge of a culture and the effective application of this knowledge. This store

Table A.1 Description of Select *Gf* Narrow Ability Definitions

Narrow Ability (Code)	Definition
General Sequential Reasoning (RG)	Ability to start with stated rules, premises, or conditions, and to engage in one or more steps to reach a solution to a novel problem.
Induction (I)	Ability to discover the underlying characteristic (e.g., rule, concept, process, trend, class membership) that governs a problem or a set of materials.
Quantitative Reasoning (RQ)	Ability to inductively and deductively reason with concepts involving mathematical relations and properties.

Source: Narrow ability definitions were adapted from McGrew (1997) with permission from Guilford. All rights reserved. Two-letter factor codes (e.g., RG) are from Carroll (1993).

of primarily verbal or language-based knowledge represents those abilities that have been developed largely through the "investment" of other abilities during educational and general life experiences (Horn & Noll, 1997).

Gc includes both declarative (static) and procedural (dynamic) knowledge. *Declarative knowledge* is held in long-term memory *(Glr)* and is activated when related information is in working memory *(Gsm)*. Declarative knowledge includes factual information, comprehension, concepts, rules, and relationships, especially when the information is verbal in nature. *Procedural knowledge* refers to the process of reasoning with previously learned procedures in order to transform knowledge. For example, a child's knowledge of his or her street address would reflect declarative knowledge, while a child's ability to find his or her way home from school would require procedural knowledge. Declarative knowledge refers to knowledge "that something is the case, whereas procedural knowledge is knowledge of how to do something" (Gagne, 1985, p. 48). The WISC-IV measures many different aspects of *Gc*. For example, the WISC-IV Verbal Comprehension Index (VCI), which is composed of Vocabulary, Similarities, and Comprehension, provides an assessment of several *Gc* narrow abilities, including Lexical Knowledge (VL), Language Development (LD), and General Information (K0). The WISC-IV Information (K0), Word Reasoning (VL), Picture Concepts (K0), and Picture Completion (K0) subtests also involve the use of specific *Gc* narrow abilities. The breadth of *Gc* is apparent from the number of narrow abilities (i.e., 11) that it subsumes. Select *Gc* narrow abilities are defined in Table A.2.

A rather unique aspect of *Gc* not seen in the other broad abilities is that it appears to be both a store of acquired knowledge (e.g., lexical knowledge, etc.) as well

Table A.2 Description of Select Gc Narrow Ability Definitions

Narrow Ability (Code)	Definition
Language Development (LD)	General development, or the understanding of words, sentences, and paragraphs (*not* requiring reading), in spoken native language skills.
Lexical Knowledge (VL)	Extent of vocabulary that can be understood in terms of correct word meanings.
Listening Ability (LS)	Ability to listen to and comprehend oral communications.
General (verbal) Information (K0)	Range of general knowledge.
Information about Culture (K2)	Range of cultural knowledge (e.g., music, art).

Source: Narrow ability definitions were adapted from McGrew (1997) with permission from Guilford. All rights reserved. Two-letter factor codes (e.g., LD) are from Carroll (1993).

as a collection of processing abilities (oral production and fluency, etc.). Although *Gc* is probably most often conceptualized much like *Gq* and *Grw* as an ability that is highly dependent upon learning experiences (especially formal, classroom-type experiences), it also seems to encompass a few abilities that are more process oriented. General Information, as one example of a narrow ability, is clearly a repository of learned information. Yet, Listening Ability, as another example of a narrow ability under *Gc* not only appears to represent learned material but reflects an ability as well—the ability to comprehend information presented orally. Although comprehension is of course dependent on knowledge of the words being presented, the natures of these abilities are clearly not identical. Assessment of *Gc* abilities therefore may require that closer attention be paid to the narrow abilities that subsume it. Despite the interrelatedness of all narrow abilities under *Gc,* there may well be times when focus on the abilities that are more process oriented as opposed to those that are more knowledge oriented is important.

Quantitative Knowledge (Gq)

Quantitative Knowledge represents an individual's store of acquired quantitative declarative and procedural knowledge. The *Gq* store of acquired knowledge represents the ability to use quantitative information and manipulate numeric symbols. *Gq* abilities are typically measured by achievement tests. For example, most com-

Table A.3 Description of Select *Gq* Narrow Ability Definitions

Narrow Ability (Code)	Definition
Mathematical Knowledge (KM)	Range of general knowledge about mathematics.
Mathematical Achievement (A3)	Measured mathematics achievement.

Source: Narrow ability definitions were adapted from McGrew (1997) with permission from Guilford. All rights reserved. Two-letter factor codes (e.g., KM) are from Carroll (1993).

prehensive tests of achievement included measures of math calculation, applied problems, and general math knowledge. Although intelligence batteries (e.g., the Wechsler Scales and SB-IV) have measured aspects of *Gq,* they typically do not measure them comprehensively. The WISC-IV contains one *Gq* subtest, namely, Arithmetic, which measures primarily Math Achievement (A3).

It is important to understand the difference between *Gq* and the Quantitative Reasoning (RQ) ability that is subsumed by *Gf.* On the whole, *Gq* represents an individual's store of acquired mathematical knowledge, including the ability to perform mathematical calculations correctly. Quantitative Reasoning represents only the ability to reason inductively and deductively when solving quantitative problems. Recall that RQ is a narrow ability that is typically found to fall under *Gf.* However, because RQ, as discussed previously, is dependent on possession of basic mathematical concepts and knowledge, it seems to be as much a narrow ability under *Gq* as it is under *Gf.* Quantitative Reasoning is most evident when a task requires mathematical skills and general mathematical knowledge (e.g., knowing what the square root symbol means). Quantitative Reasoning would be required in order to solve for a missing number in a number-series task (e.g., 3, 6, 9, ___). Although most achievement batteries measure specific math skills and general math knowledge, some also require individuals to solve quantitative problems through inductive or deductive reasoning. Therefore, it may be best to conceptualize RQ as being a narrow ability that falls under both *Gf* and *Gq* broad abilities. Select *Gq* narrow abilities are defined in Table A.3.

Short-Term Memory (*Gsm*)

Short-Term Memory (Gsm) is the ability to apprehend and hold information in immediate awareness and then use it within a few seconds. It is a limited-capacity system, as most individuals can retain only seven "chunks" of information (plus or minus two chunks) in this system at one time. The ability to remember a telephone number long enough to dial it, or the ability to retain a sequence of spoken directions long enough to complete the tasks specified in the directions, are examples of *Gsm*. Given the limited amount of information that can be held in short-term memory, information is typically retained for only a few seconds before it is lost. As most individuals have experienced, it is difficult to remember an unfamiliar telephone number for more than a few seconds unless one consciously uses a cognitive learning strategy (e.g., continually repeating or rehearsing the numbers) or other mnemonic device. When a new task requires an individual to use his or her *Gsm* abilities to store new information, the previous information held in short-term memory is either lost or must be stored in the acquired stores of knowledge (i.e., *Gc, Gq, Grw*) through the use of *Glr*.

In the CHC model, *Gsm* subsumes the narrow ability of working memory, which has received considerable attention recently in the cognitive psychology literature. *Working Memory* is considered to be the "mechanism responsible for the temporary storage and processing of information" (Richardson, 1996, p. 23). It has been referred to as the "mind's scratchpad" (Jensen, 1998, p. 220), and most models of working memory postulate a number of subsystems or temporary "buffers." The phonological or articulatory loop processes auditory-linguistic information, while the visuospatial sketch- or scratchpad (Baddeley, 1986, 1992; Logie, 1996) is the temporary buffer for visually processed information. Most working memory models also posit a central executive or processor mechanism that coordinates and manages the activities and subsystems in working memory.

Carroll (1993) is skeptical of the working memory construct, as reflected in his conclusion that "although some evidence supports such a speculation, one must be cautious in accepting it because as yet there has not been sufficient work on measuring working memory, and the validity and generality of the concept have not yet been well established in the individual differences research" (p. 647). Notwithstanding those doubts, the working memory construct has been related empirically to a variety of different outcomes, including many specific reading and math skills. Therefore, despite the questions that have been raised regarding its validity as a measurable construct, Flanagan and colleagues (2000) included working memory in the CHC taxonomy in light of the current literature that argues strongly for its predictive utility. Nevertheless, given that Carroll has raised questions about the validity of the construct of working memory, it is important to remember that this construct was included in current CHC theory primarily for practical application and ease of communication. Additional research is necessary before definitive decisions can be reached about the inclusion or exclusion of working memory in CHC theory. Even so, the WISC-IV Letter-Number Sequencing subtest is purported to measure working memory and the WISC-IV Digit Span subtest is pur-

Table A.4 Description of Select *Gsm* Narrow Ability Definitions

Narrow Ability (Code)	Definition
Memory Span (MS)	Ability to attend to and immediately recall temporally ordered elements in the correct order after a single presentation.
Working Memory (WM)	Ability to temporarily store and perform a set of cognitive operations on information that requires divided attention and the management of the limited capacity of short-term memory.

Source: Narrow ability definitions were adapted from McGrew (1997) with permission from Guilford. All rights reserved. Two-letter factor codes (e.g., MS) are from Carroll (1993).

ported to measure memory span, in addition to working memory (viz., Digits Backward). Select *Gsm* narrow abilities are defined in Table A.4.

Visual Processing (Gv)

Visual Processing (Gv) is the ability to generate, perceive, analyze, synthesize, store, retrieve, manipulate, transform, and think with visual patterns and stimuli (Lohman, 1992). These abilities are measured frequently by tasks that require the perception and manipulation of visual shapes and forms, usually of a figural or geometric nature (e.g., a standard Block Design task). An individual who can mentally reverse and rotate objects effectively, interpret how objects change as they move through space, perceive and manipulate spatial configurations, and maintain spatial orientation would be regarded as having a strength in *Gv* abilities. The WISC-IV provides two *Gv* measures, including Block Design, which assesses the *Gv* narrow ability of Spatial Relations (SR); and the Picture Completion subtest, which assesses primarily Flexibility of Closure (CF). Select *Gv* narrow abilities are defined in Table A.5.

Auditory Processing (Ga)

In the broadest sense, *auditory abilities* "are cognitive abilities that depend on sound as input and on the functioning of our hearing apparatus" (Stankov, 1994, p. 157) and reflect "the degree to which the individual can cognitively control the perception of auditory stimulus inputs" (Gustafsson & Undheim, 1996, p. 192). *Auditory Processing (Ga)* is the ability to perceive, analyze, and synthesize patterns

Table A.5 Description of Select *Gv* Narrow Ability Definitions

Narrow Ability (Code)	Definition
Spatial Relations (SR)	Ability to rapidly perceive and manipulate relatively simple visual patterns or to maintain orientation with respect to objects in space.
Visual Memory (MV)	Ability to form and store a mental representation or image of a visual stimulus and then recognize or recall it later.
Closure Speed (CS)	Ability to quickly combine disconnected, vague, or partially obscured visual stimuli or patterns into a meaningful whole, *without knowing in advance* what the pattern is.
Visualization (Vz)	Ability to mentally manipulate objects or visual patterns and to "see" how they would appear under altered conditions.
Flexibility of Closure (CF)	Ability to find, apprehend, and identify a visual figure or pattern embedded in a complex visual array, *when knowing in advance* what the pattern is.
Spatial Scanning (SS)	Ability to accurately and quickly survey a spatial field or pattern and identify a path through the visual field or pattern.
Serial Perceptual Integration (PI)	Ability to apprehend and identify a pictorial or visual pattern when parts of the pattern are presented rapidly in serial or successive order.

Source: Narrow ability definitions were adapted from McGrew (1997) with permission from Guilford. All rights reserved. Two-letter factor codes (e.g., SR) are from Carroll (1993).

among auditory stimuli, and discriminate subtle nuances in patterns of sound (e.g., complex musical structure) and speech when presented under distorted conditions. While *Ga* abilities do not require the comprehension of language *(Gc)* per se, they may be very important in the development of language skills. Auditory Processing subsumes most of those abilities referred to as "phonological awareness/processing" and, therefore, tests that measure these abilities (viz., phonetic coding) are found typically on achievement batteries. In fact, the number of tests specifically designed to measure phonological processing has increased significantly in recent years, presumably as a result of the consistent finding that phonological awareness/processing appears to be the core deficit in individuals with reading difficulties (e.g., Morris et al., 1998; Vellutino, Scanlon, & Lyon, 2000). However, the *Ga* domain is very broad (i.e., it contains many narrow abilities subsumed by *Ga*), and, thus, extends far beyond phonetic coding ability.

In CHC theory, Carroll's Phonetic Coding (PC) narrow ability was split into separate analysis (PC:A) and synthesis (PC:S) abilities. Support for two different PC abilities comes from a growing number of sources. First, in a sample of kindergarten students, Yopp (1988) reported evidence in favor of two phonemic awareness factors: simple phonemic awareness (required one operation to be performed on sounds) and compound phonemic awareness (required holding sounds in memory while performing another operation on them). Second, in what appears to be one of the most comprehensive *Ga* factor analytic studies, Stankov and Horn (1980) presented evidence for seven different auditory abilities, two of which had tests of sound blending (synthesis) and incomplete words (analysis) as factor markers. Third, the WJ-R Sound Blending and Incomplete Words tests (which are almost identical in format to the tests used by Stankov & Horn) correlated only moderately (.37 or 13.7% shared or common variance) across the kindergarten to adult WJ-R norm sample, a correlation that suggests that these tests are measuring different aspects of PC. Fourth, using confirmatory factor analytic methods, Wagner, Torgesen, Laughton, Simmons, and Rashotte (1993) presented a model of phonological processing that included separate auditory analysis and synthesis factors.

Although the features of these different auditory factors across respective studies are not entirely consistent, there are many similarities. For example, Yopp's (1988) simple phonemic factor appears to be analogous to Wagner and colleagues' (1993) synthesis factor and the factor Stankov and Horn (1980) identified with the aid of sound-blending tasks. Also, Yopp's compound phonemic factor bears similarities to Wagner and colleagues' analysis factor and the Stankov and Horn factor, identified, in part, by an incomplete words task. Presently, it appears that Wagner and colleagues' analysis/synthesis distinction is likely the most useful. According to Wagner and colleagues, *analysis* and *synthesis* can be defined as "the ability to segment larger units of speech into smaller units" and "the ability to blend smaller units of speech to form larger units" (p. 87), respectively. The analysis/synthesis distinction continues to be empirically supported, as demonstrated by the separate Phonetic Coding: Analysis and Phonetic Coding: Synthesis tests included in the new WJ III (Woodcock et al., 2001). Select *Ga* narrow abilities are defined in Table A.6.

Long-Term Storage and Retrieval (*Glr*)

Long-Term Storage and Retrieval (Glr) is the ability to store information in and fluently retrieve new or previously acquired information (e.g., concepts, ideas, items, names) from long-term memory. *Glr* abilities have been prominent in creativity research, where they have been referred to as idea production, ideational fluency,

Table A.6 Description of Select *Ga* Narrow Ability Definitions

Narrow Ability (Code)	Definition
Phonetic Coding: Analysis (PC:A)	Ability to segment larger units of speech sounds into smaller units of speech sounds.
Phonetic Coding: Synthesis (PC:S)	Ability to blend smaller units of speech together into larger units of speech.
Speech Sound Discrimination (US)	Ability to detect differences in speech sounds under conditions of little distraction or distortion.
Resistance to Auditory Stimulus Distortion (UR)	Ability to understand speech and language that has been distorted or masked in one or more ways.
Memory for Sound Patterns (UM)	Ability to retain, on a short-term basis, auditory events such as tones, tonal patterns, and voices.
General Sound Discrimination (U3)	Ability to discriminate tones, tone patterns, or other musical elements with regard to pitch, intensity, duration, and rhythm.

Source: Narrow ability definitions were adapted from McGrew (1997) with permission from Guilford. All rights reserved. Two-letter factor codes (e.g., PC:A) are from Carroll (1993).

or associational fluency. It is important not to confuse *Glr* with *Gc, Gq,* and *Grw,* an individual's stores of acquired knowledge: *Gc, Gq,* and *Grw* represent *what* is stored in long-term memory, while *Glr* is the *efficiency* by which this information is initially stored in and later retrieved from long-term memory.

It is important to note that different processes are involved in *Glr* and *Gsm.* Although the expression "long-term" frequently carries with it the connotation of days, weeks, months, and years in the clinical literature, long-term storage processes can begin within a few minutes or hours of performing a task. Therefore, the time lapse between the initial task performance and the recall of information related to that task is not necessarily of critical importance in defining *Glr.* More important is the occurrence of an intervening task that engages short-term memory before the attempted recall of the stored information (e.g., *Gc;* Woodcock, 1993). Although *Glr* is measured directly by several major intelligence batteries, the WISC-IV does not assess *Glr.* In the present CHC model, 13 narrow memory and fluency abilities are included under *Glr.* Select *Glr* narrow abilities are defined in Table A.7.

Processing Speed (Gs)

Processing Speed (Gs), or mental quickness, is often mentioned when one is talking about intelligent behavior (Nettelbeck, 1992). *Processing speed* is the ability to flu-

Table A.7 Description of Select *Glr* Narrow Ability Definitions

Narrow Ability (Code)	Definition
Associative Memory (MA)	Ability to recall one part of a previously learned but unrelated pair of items when the other part is presented (i.e., paired-associative learning).
Meaningful Memory (MM)	Ability to recall a set of items where there is a meaningful relation between items or the items comprise a meaningful story or connected discourse.
Free Recall Memory (M6)	Ability to recall as many unrelated items as possible, in any order, after a large collection of items is presented.
Ideational Fluency (FI)	Ability to rapidly produce a series of ideas, words, or phrases related to a specific condition or object. Quantity, not quality, is emphasized.
Associational Fluency (FA)	Ability to rapidly produce words or phrases associated in meaning (semantically associated) with a given word or concept.
Expressional Fluency (FE)	Ability to rapidly think of and organize words or phrases into meaningful, complex ideas under highly general or more specific cueing conditions.
Naming Facility (NA)	Ability to rapidly produce names for concepts when presented with a pictorial or verbal cue.
Word Fluency (FW)	Ability to rapidly produce words that have specific phonemic, structural, or orthographic characteristics (independent of word meanings).
Figural Fluency (FF)	Ability to rapidly draw or sketch several examples or elaborations when given a starting visual or descriptive stimulus.

Source: Narrow ability definitions were adapted from McGrew (1997) with permission from Guilford. All rights reserved. Two-letter factor codes (e.g., MA) are from Carroll (1993).

ently and automatically perform cognitive tasks, especially when under pressure to maintain focused attention and concentration. "Attentive speediness" encapsulates the essence of *Gs, which* is measured typically by fixed-interval, timed tasks that require little in the way of complex thinking or mental processing. The WISC-IV provides three *Gs* tasks, namely, Coding, Symbol Search, and Cancellation.

Recent interest in information-processing models of cognitive functioning has resulted in a renewed focus on *Gs* (Kail, 1991; Lohman, 1989). A central construct in information-processing models is the idea of limited processing re-

Table A.8 Description of Select Gs Narrow Ability Definitions

Narrow Ability (Code)	Definition
Perceptual Speed (P)	Ability to rapidly search for and compare known visual symbols or patterns presented side by side or separated in a visual field.
Rate-of-Test-Taking (R9)	Ability to rapidly perform tests that are relatively easy or that require very simple decisions.
Number Facility (N)	Ability to rapidly and accurately manipulate and deal with numbers, from elementary skills of counting and recognizing numbers to advanced skills of adding, subtracting, multiplying, and dividing numbers.

Source: Narrow ability definitions were adapted from McGrew (1997) with permission from Guilford. All rights reserved. Two-letter factor codes (e.g., R9) are from Carroll (1993).

sources (e.g., the limited capacities of short-term or working memory). That is, "many cognitive activities require a person's deliberate efforts and . . . people are limited in the amount of effort they can allocate. In the face of limited processing resources, the speed of processing is critical because it determines in part how rapidly limited resources can be reallocated to other cognitive tasks" (Kail, p. 152). Woodcock (1993) likens *Gs* to a valve in a water pipe. The rate in which water flows in the pipe (i.e., *Gs*) increases when the valve is opened wide and decreases when the valve is partially closed. Three different narrow speed of processing abilities are subsumed by *Gs* in the present CHC model. Select *Gs* narrow abilities are defined in Table A.8.

Appendix B

CHC Abilities Measured by Major Intelligence Tests

Broad	WPPSI-III	WISC-IV	WAIS-III	SB:5	KABC-II	WJ III COG	WJ III COG DS
Gf	Matrix Reasoning (I, RG) Picture Concepts (I, Gc-K0)	Picture Concepts (I, Gc-K0) Matrix Reasoning (I, RG) Arithmetic (RQ, Gq-A3)[1]	Matrix Reasoning (I, RG)	Nonverbal Fluid Reasoning (I, Gv-Vz) Nonverbal Quantitative Reasoning (RQ, Gq-A3) Verbal Fluid Reasoning (RG) Verbal Quantitative Reasoning (RQ, Gq-A3)	Pattern Reasoning (I, Gv-Vz) Story Completion (I, RG, Gc-K0, Gv-Vz)	Concept Formation (I) Analysis Synthesis (RG)	Number Series (RQ) Number Matrices (RQ)
Gc	Information (K0) Vocabulary (VL) Word Reasoning (VL, Gf-I) Comprehension (K0, LD) Similarities (LD, VL, Gf-I) Receptive Vocabulary (VL, K0) Picture Naming (VL, K0)	Similarities (LD, VL, Gf-I) Vocabulary (VL) Comprehension (K0, LD) Information (K0) Word Reasoning (VL, Gf-I)	Vocabulary (VL) Similarities (LD, VL, Gf-I) Information (K0) Comprehension (K0, LD)	Nonverbal Knowledge (K0) Verbal Knowledge (VL, Gf-I)	Riddles (VL, LD, Gf-RG) Expressive Vocabulary (VL) Verbal Knowledge (VL, K0)	Verbal Comprehension (VL, LD) General Information (K0)	Bilingual Verbal Comprehension (VL, LD)
Ga	—	—	—	—	—	Incomplete Words (PC:A) Sound Blending (PC:S) Auditory Attention (US/U3)	Sound Patterns–Voice (US) Sound Patterns–Music (US)

Gv	Block Design (SR, Vz) Picture Completion (CF, Gv-K0) Object Assembly (CS, SR)	Block Design (SR, Vz) Picture Completion (CF, Gv-K0)	Picture Completion (CF, Gv-K0) Block Design (SR, Vz) Picture Arrangement (Vz, Gv-K0) Object Assembly (CS, SR)	Nonverbal Visual-Spatial Processing (Vz, SR) Verbal Visual-Spatial Processing (Vz, Gv-LS, LD)	Block Counting (Vz, Gq-A3) Conceptual Thinking (Vz, Gf-I) Face Recognition (MV) Triangles (SR, Vz) Rover (SS, Gf-RG, Gq-A3) Gestalt Closure (CS)	Spatial Relations (Vz, SR) Picture Recognition (MV)	Visual Closure (CF) Block Rotation (SR, Vz)
Gsm	—	Digit Span (MS, WM) Letter-Number Sequencing (WM)	Digit Span (MS, WM) Letter-Number Sequencing (WM)	Nonverbal Working Memory (WM, Gq-Vz) Visual Working Memory (WM, MS)	Word Order (MS, WM) Number Recall (MS) Hand Movements (MS, Gv-MV)	Memory for Words (MS) Numbers Reversed (WM) Auditory Working Memory (WM)	Memory for Sentences (MS)
Glr	—	—	—	—	Atlantis (MA, L1) Rebus (MA) Atlantis Delayed (MA, L1) Rebus Delayed (MA, L1)	Visual Auditory Learning (MA) Visual Auditory Learning Delayed (MA) Retrieval Fluency (FI) Rapid Picture Naming (NA)	Memory for Names (MA) Memory For Names Delayed (MA)
Gs	Symbol Search (P, R9) Coding (R9)	Symbol Search (P, R9) Coding (R9) Cancellation (P, R9)	Symbol Search (P, R9) Digit Symbol/Coding (R9)	—	—	Visual Matching (P, R9) Decision Speed (R4)	Cross Out (R9)
Gq	—	—	Arithmetic (A3, Gf-RQ)	—	—	—	—

Source: Narrow ability classifications are based on expert consensus (see Caltabiano & Flanagan, 2004) and information presented in the test manuals of each cognitive battery.

Note: WPPSI-III = Wechsler Preschool and Primary Scale of Intelligence; WISC-IV = Wechsler Intelligence Scale for Children–Fourth Edition; WAIS-III = Wechsler Adult Intelligence Scale; SB5 = Stanford-Binet Intelligence Scale, Fifth Edition; KABC-II = Kaufman Assessment Battery for Children–Second Edition; WJ III COG = Woodcock-Johnson Tests of Cognitive Abilities–Third Edition; WJ III COG DS = Woodcock-Johnson Tests of Cognitive Abilities–Third Edition, Diagnostic Supplement; A3 = Math Achievement; CF = Flexibility of Closure; CS = Closure Speed; FA = Associational Fluency; FI = Ideational Fluency; I = Inductive Reasoning; K0 = General (Verbal) Information; L1 = Learning Abilities; LD = Language Development; LS = Listening Ability; MA = Associative Memory; MS = Memory Span; MV = Visual Memory; NA = Naming Facility; P = Perceptual Speed; PC:A = Phonetic Coding: Analysis; PC:S = Phonetic Coding: Synthesis; R9 = Rate-of-Test-Taking; RG = General Sequential Reasoning; RQ = Quantitative Reasoning; SR = Spatial Relations; SS = Spatial Scanning; U3 = Resistance to Auditory Stimulus Distortion; US = Speech Sound Discrimination; VL = Lexical Knowledge; VZ = Visualization; WM = Working Memory. See Appendix A for CHC broad and narrow ability definitions.

[1] The primary classification of Arithmetic as Gf is based on the factor analyses of Keith and colleagues (2004).

Appendix C

WISC-IV Subtest g-Loadings, by Age Group and Overall Sample

Table C.1 WISC-IV Subtest g-Loadings, by Age Group

Subtest, by Index	6–7	8–9	10–11	12–13	14–16	All
Verbal Comprehension Index (VCI)						
Similarities	.76	.79	.78	.78	.81	.79
Vocabulary	.77	.83	.83	.83	.84	.82
Comprehension	.70	.63	.72	.70	.74	.70
(Information)	.78	.80	.78	.80	.81	.79
(Word Reasoning)	.67	.73	.71	.73	.68	.70
Perceptual Reasoning Index (PRI)						
Block Design	.60	.66	.70	.70	.68	.67
Picture Concepts	.60	.54	.55	.56	.58	.57
Matrix Reasoning	.65	.69	.76	.67	.66	.68
(Picture Completion)	.57	.69	.66	.63	.61	.63
Working Memory Index (WMI)						
Digit Span	.52	.56	.54	.45	.51	.51
Letter-Number Sequencing	.56	.61	.61	.62	.63	.60
(Arithmetic)	.76	.71	.76	.76	.74	.74
Processing Speed Index (PSI)						
Coding	.38	.54	.52	.43	.51	.48
Symbol Search	.61	.63	.59	.55	.53	.58
(Cancellation)	.24	.28	.25	.25	.24	.25

Source: Wechsler Intelligence Scale for Children–Fourth Edition. Copyright © 2003 by Harcourt Assessment, Inc. Reproduced by permission of the publisher. All rights reserved. "Wechsler Intelligence Scale for Children" and "WISC" are trademarks of Harcourt Assessment, Inc., registered in the United States of America and/or other jurisdictions.

Note: These g-loadings are the unrotated loadings on the first factor using the principal factor analysis method. Supplemental subtests appear in parentheses.

Table C.2 WISC-IV Subtest g-Loadings, Based on Overall WISC-IV Standardization Sample

Subtest	Principal Factor Analysis Model (1)	CFA Nested Factors Model (2)
Vocabulary	.82	.75
(Information)	.79	.75
Similarities	.79	.73
(Arithmetic)	.74	.77
(Word Reasoning)	.70	.65
Comprehension	.70	.65
Matrix Reasoning	.68	.69
Block Design	.67	.67
(Picture Completion)	.63	.62
Letter-Number Sequencing	.60	.62
Symbol Search	.58	.57
Picture Concepts	.57	.58
Digit Span	.51	.53
Coding	.48	.45
(Cancellation)	.25	.21

Source: Wechsler Intelligence Scale for Children–Fourth Edition. Copyright © 2003 by Harcourt Assessment, Inc. Reproduced by permission of the publisher. All rights reserved. "Wechsler Intelligence Scale for Children" and "WISC" are trademarks of Harcourt Assessment, Inc., registered in the United States of America and/or other jurisdictions.

Note: These g-loadings are the unrotated loadings on the first factor using the principal factor analysis method. Supplemental subtests appear in parentheses. WISC-IV subtests are listed in order of their individual g-loadings (from highest to lowest). Column (1) contains g-loadings based on the overall WISC-IV standardization sample. Column (2) contains results of a confirmatory factor analysis conducted by Timothy Z. Keith (2004). The loadings in this column were derived from analyses using a nested factors model, which simply assumes that each subtest measures both g and a broad ability (factor). CFA = confirmatory factor analysis.

Appendix D

Psychometric, Theoretical, and Qualitative Characteristics of the WISC-IV

Table D.1 Evaluation of WISC-IV Test Characteristics

Subtest	Reliability		g-Loading	CHC Classification	Cultural Loading/ Linguistic Demand	Most Probable Factors Influencing Test Performance
	Internal Consistency	Test-Retest				
Block Design	Medium (6–16)	Low (6–9) Medium (10–16)	Medium	Gv-SR,VZ	Low/Moderate	Reflectivity/impulsivity Field dependence/independence Flexibility/inflexibility Planning Ability to perform under time pressure
Similarities	Medium (6–16)	Medium (6–11, 14–16) High (12–13)	High	Gc-VL, LD Gf-I	High/High	Language stimulation Environmental stimulation Cultural opportunities/experiences Educational opportunities/ experiences
Digit Span	Medium (6–15) High (16)	Low (8–9) Medium (6–7, 10–16)	Medium	Gsm-MS, WM	Low/Moderate	Attention span/distractibility Concentration Distractibility Verbal rehearsal Visual elaboration Organization

Subtest						Influences
Picture Concepts	Low (15–16) Medium (6–14)	Low (6–9, 12–16) Medium (10–11)	Medium	*Gf*-I, *Gc*-K0	Moderate/Moderate	Environmental stimulation Language stimulation Alertness to the environment Educational opportunities/experiences
Coding	Low (6–7) Medium (8–16)	Low (6–7) Medium (8–16)	Low	*Gs*-R9	Low/Moderate	Concentration Distractibility Visual acuity Reflectivity/impulsivity Verbal elaboration Visual elaboration Planning Ability to perform under time pressure
Vocabulary	Medium (6–9, 11) High (10, 12–16)	Medium (6–7) High (8–16)	High	*Gc*-VL	High/High	Language stimulation Environmental stimulation Intellectual curiosity Educational opportunities/experiences Alertness to the environment Cultural opportunities/experiences
Letter-Number Sequencing	Medium (10, 13, 15–16) High (6–9, 11–12,14)	Medium (6–16)	Medium	*Gsm*-WM	Low/High	Attention span/distractibility Concentration Distractibility Verbal rehearsal Visual elaboration
Matrix Reasoning	Medium (6–7, 10–11, 13–16) High (8–9, 12)	Low (14–16) Medium (6–9, 12–13) High (10–11)	Medium	*Gf*-I, RG	Low/Low	Reflectivity/impulsivity Field dependence/independence Flexibility/inflexibility Planning
Comprehension	Low (7–8) Medium (6, 9–16)	Low (10–13) Medium (6–9, 14–16)	Medium	*Gc*-K0, LD	High/High	Language stimulation Environmental stimulation Alertness to the environment Educational opportunities/experiences Cultural opportunities/experiences

(continued)

Table D.1 (Continued)

Subtest	Reliability		g-Loading	CHC Classification	Cultural Loading/ Linguistic Demand	Most Probable Factors Influencing Test Performance
	Internal Consistency	Test-Retest				
Symbol Search	Low (6–7, 12–16) Medium (8–11)	Low (6–7, 12–16) Medium (8–11)	Medium	Gs-P, R9	Low/Moderate	Attention span Concentration Distractibility Visual acuity Reflectivity/impulsivity Verbal elaboration Visual elaboration Planning Ability to perform under time pressure
Picture Completion	Medium (6–16)	Low (6–7) Medium (8–16)	Medium	Gv-CF, Gc-K0	High/Low	Vision difficulties Alertness to the environment Visual acuity Field dependence/independence
Cancellation	Low (8–9, 12–16) Medium (6–7, 10–11)	Low (8–9, 12–16) Medium (6–7, 10–11)	Low	Gs-P, R9	Low/Low	Attention span Concentration Distractibility Visual Acuity Reflectivity/impulsivity Verbal elaboration Visual elaboration Planning Ability to perform under time pressure

Subtest					
Information	Low (7) Medium (6, 8–14) High (15–16)	Medium (6–9, 12–13) High (10–11)	High	Gc-K0	High/High	Environmental stimulation Educational opportunities/experiences Intellectual curiosity Cultural opportunities/experiences Alertness to the environment
Arithmetic	Medium (6, 8, 11–14) High (7, 9–10, 15–16)	Low (6–9) Medium (10–16)	High	Gf-RQ Gq-A3	Moderate/Moderate	Math difficulties Educational opportunities/experiences Hearing difficulties Attention span/distractibility Concentration Visual elaboration
Word Reasoning	Low (6, 10–12, 16) Medium (7–9, 13–15)	Low (6–7, 12–13) Medium (8–11, 14–16)	Medium	Gc-VL, Gf-I	High/ High	Language stimulation Environmental stimulation Educational opportunities/experiences

Source: All ratings included in this table are based on criteria presented in *The Intelligence Test Reference: Gf-Gc Cross-Battery Assessment* (McGrew & Flanagan, 1998). CHC classifications are based on expert consensus (i.e., Caltabiano & Flanagan, 2004) and information contained in the WISC-IV manuals. G-loadings are courtesy of Timothy Z. Keith (personal communication, October 14, 2003).

Note: Subtests in bold are new; subtests in italic are supplemental; subtests in bold and italic are new supplemental tests. All WISC-IV subtests have adequate floors and ceilings.

Table D.2 Definitions of Psychometric, Theoretical, and Qualitative Test Characteristics, Evaluative Criteria, and Interpretive Relevance

Category/Characteristic	Evaluative Criteria	Definition	Interpretive Relevance
Psychometric			
Reliability		The precision of a test score (i.e., its freedom from errors of measurement).	Important for making accurate educational and/or diagnostic decisions.
	High	Coefficients of .90 or above.	Test scores are sufficiently reliable and can be used to make diagnostic decisions.
	Medium	Coefficients from .80 to .89 inclusive.	Test scores are moderately reliable and can be used to make *screening* decisions or can be combined with other tests to form a composite with high reliability.
	Low	Coefficients below .80.	Test scores are not sufficiently reliable and cannot be used to make important screening and/or diagnostic decisions. Must be combined with other tests to form a composite with medium or high reliability.
g-loading		Each test's loading on the first unrotated factor or component in principal factor or component analysis with all other tests from a specific intelligence battery.	Important indicator of the degree to which a test of an individual battery measures general intelligence. Aids in determining the extent to which a test score can be expected to vary from other scores within a profile.
	High	A loading of .70 or higher.	Tests with high *g*-loadings are not expected to vary greatly from the mean of the profile and are considered good indicators of general intelligence.
	Medium	A loading of .51 to .69.	Tests with medium *g*-loadings may vary from the mean of the profile, as tests with this classification are considered fair indicators of general intelligence.
	Low	A loading of .50 or lower.	Tests with low *g*-loadings can be expected to vary from the mean of the profile, as tests with this classification are considered poor indicators of general intelligence.

Test floor		The test contains a sufficient number of easy items to reliably distinguish between individuals functioning in the Average, Below Average, and Lower Extreme ranges of ability.	
	Adequate	A raw score of 1 is associated with a standard score that is more than 2 SDs below the normative mean of the test.	A test with an adequate floor can distinguish reliably between individuals functioning in the Average, Below Average, and Lower Extreme ranges of ability. Moreover, tests with adequate floors can discriminate reliably between various degrees of Mental Retardation (i.e., mild, moderate).
	Inadequate	A raw score of 1 is associated with a standard score that is *not* more than 2 SDs below the normative mean of the test.	A test with an inadequate floor, or an insufficient number of easy items, may not distinguish reliably between individuals functioning in the Average, Below Average, and Lower Extreme ranges of ability. Moreover, tests with inadequate floors cannot discriminate reliably between various degrees of Mental Retardation (i.e., mild, moderate).
Test ceiling		The test contains a sufficient number of difficult items to reliably distinguish between individuals functioning in the Average, Above Average, and Upper Extreme ranges of ability.	
	Adequate	The maximum raw score for the test is associated with a standard score that is more than 2 SDs above the normative mean of the test.	A test with an adequate ceiling can distinguish reliably between individuals functioning in the Average, Above Average, and Upper Extreme ranges of intellectual ability. Moreover, tests with adequate ceilings can discriminate reliably between various levels of giftedness.
	Inadequate	The maximum raw score is associated with a standard score that is *not* more than 2 SDs above the normative mean of the test.	A test with an inadequate ceiling, or an insufficient number of difficult items, will not distinguish reliably between individuals who function in the Average, Above Average, and Upper Extreme ranges of intellectual ability. A test with an inadequate ceiling cannot discriminate reliably between various levels of giftedness.

(continued)

Table D.2 (Continued)

Category/Characteristic	Evaluative Criteria	Definition	Interpretive Relevance
Item Gradients[1]		A test with good item gradient characteristics has items that are approximately equally spaced in difficulty along the entire test scale, and the spacing between items is small enough to allow for reliable discrimination between individuals on the latent trait measured by the test. An item gradient *violation* occurs when a 1-unit increase in raw score points results in a change of more than one-third of a standard deviation in standard score values. Item gradient violations are identified for each test by calculating the standard score change for every possible raw score change in the test.	
	Good	≤ 5% violations	Items are approximately equally spaced in difficulty along the entire test scale and spacing between items is small enough to allow for reliable discrimination between individuals on the latent trait measured by the test.
	Fair	> 5% to ≤ 15% violations	Items are not equally spaced in difficulty at certain points along the entire test scale, resulting in fair discrimination between individuals on the latent trait measured by the test.
	Poor	> 15% violations	Items are inconsistently spaced in difficulty at various points along the entire test scale, resulting in generally unreliable discrimination between individuals on the latent trait measured by the test.

Theoretical

CHC broad (Stratum II) ability classification		A description of the broad abilities that underlie intelligence tests based on an examination of appropriately designed CHC confirmatory cross-battery factor analysis research studies.	Useful for guiding interpretation and discussing performance at the broad level of ability (viz., in terms of the basic, long-standing ability underlying a specific cluster of tests).
CHC narrow (Stratum I) ability classification[2]		A description of the narrow abilities that underlie intelligence tests based on expert content-validity consensus.	Important in interpreting performance in terms of the specific ability or abilities measured by the test.
Degree of cultural loading		The degree to which U.S. cultural knowledge or experience is required to perform the task. It is assumed that an examinee's level of acculturation to mainstream U.S. culture will affect his or her performance to a greater extent on tests that are dependent upon accumulated knowledge and acquired experiences (that result from exposure to U.S. culture) than on tests that measure basic learning processes.	Important in determining the extent to which knowledge of cultural information and/or conventions can impact test performance.
	High	Test performance is highly influenced by exposure to mainstream U.S. culture.	Scores obtained from examinees with minimal exposure to U.S. culture should not be interpreted as a valid estimate of ability, as they are likely to be spuriously low.
	Medium	Test performance is moderately influenced by exposure to mainstream U.S. culture.	Scores obtained from examinees with minimal exposure to U.S. culture should be interpreted with caution, as they may be spuriously low.
	Low	Test performance is minimally influenced by exposure to mainstream U.S. culture.	Scores obtained from examinees with minimal exposure to U.S. culture may be considered minimally affected.
Degree of linguistic demand		The extent to which a test requires expressive/receptive language skills to be properly administered, as well as the degree of language proficiency required by the examinee in order to understand the test instructions and provide an appropriate response.	Important in determining the extent to which the language demands necessary to perform a test may compromise optimal performance.

(continued)

Table D.2 (Continued)

Category/Characteristic	Evaluative Criteria	Definition	Interpretive Relevance
	High	Test administration requires a high level of expressive/receptive language. Optimal test performance requires a high level of language proficiency on the part of the examinee.	Test scores obtained from examinees with limited English proficiency may not be valid indicators of ability.
	Medium	Test administration requires a moderate level of expressive/receptive language. Optimal test performance requires a moderate level of language proficiency on the part of the examinee.	Test scores obtained from examinees with limited English proficiency should be interpreted with caution, as scores may be spuriously low.
	Low	Test administration has minimal expressive/receptive language requirements. Test performance is less dependent on the examinee's level of language proficiency.	Test scores obtained from examinees with limited English proficiency are minimally influenced by language demands. Therefore, scores may be interpreted as estimates of their respective underlying cognitive abilities when supported by other sources of data.
Background/ Environmental Influences			
Hearing difficulties		A past history of significant problems in the perception of auditory stimuli that may affect the extent to which an examinee can accurately discriminate auditory stimuli.	Important when interpreting scores obtained on tests that require the examinee to process or discriminate auditory stimuli effectively prior to providing a response.
Vision difficulties		A past history of significant problems in the perception of visual stimuli that may affect the extent to which an examinee can accurately discriminate visual stimuli.	Important when interpreting scores obtained on tests that require the examinee to perceive and/or discriminate visual information effectively prior to providing a response (e.g., WISC-IV Matrix Reasoning).
Reading difficulties		A past history of significant problems with reading.	Important when interpreting scores obtained on tests in which the examinee's ability to read information can impact directly on his or her ability to respond and/or the quality of response.

Math difficulties	A past history of significant problems with mathematics.	Important when interpreting scores obtained on tests requiring the examinee to perform and/or comprehend mathematical operations or rules (e.g., Wechsler Arithmetic tests).
Language stimulation	The extent to which an examinee's verbal communication skills have been influenced by frequent interaction with the environment.	Important when interpreting scores obtained on tests involving a moderate to high degree of verbal stimuli (e.g., Wechsler Vocabulary tests).
Cultural opportunities and experiences	The extent to which an examinee has been exposed to a wide array of opportunities and experiences that impart knowledge of mainstream U.S. culture.	Important when interpreting scores obtained on tests that contain items that (directly or indirectly) assume knowledge of specific and/or general cultural conventions or facts on the part of the examinee (e.g., Wechsler Comprehension tests).
Educational opportunities and experiences	The extent to which an examinee has been exposed to a wide array of formal and informal educational experiences.	Important when interpreting scores obtained on tests measuring general (verbal) information acquired through both direct and indirect instruction (e.g., Wechsler Information tests).
Alertness to the environment	The extent to which an examinee is attentive to his or her surroundings.	Important when interpreting scores obtained on tests measuring knowledge that is acquired informally by individuals who are alert to their surroundings (e.g., Wechsler Comprehension tests).
Intellectual curiosity	The extent to which an examinee displays a tendency to seek out and explore knowledge and new learning.	Important when interpreting scores obtained on tests involving information that is often acquired through informal instruction and learning experiences (e.g., WISC-IV Matrix Reasoning).
Individual/Situational Influences		
Attention span/ distractibility	An examinee's ability to focus on two or more competing stimuli simultaneously (divided attention) or a specific stimulus under distracting conditions (selective attention).	Important when interpreting scores obtained on tests on which attentiveness can either facilitate or inhibit an examinee's performance to a significant degree, or on which competing and/or distracting stimuli can significantly affect performance (e.g., WISC-IV Digit Span, Coding, Symbol Search, Letter-Number Sequencing).

(continued)

Table D.2 (Continued)

Category/Characteristic	Evaluative Criteria Definition	Interpretive Relevance
Concentration	An examinee's ability to focus on stimuli for a sustained period of time (sustained attention).	Important when interpreting scores obtained on tests in which optimal performance requires a sustained, concentrated effort on the part of the examinee (e.g., WISC-IV Coding, WAIS-III Digit-Symbol Coding).
Ability to perform under time pressure	The extent to which an examinee is capable of maintaining an optimal level of performance during a specified period of time (vigilance).	Important when interpreting scores obtained on speeded tests from the Wechsler Performance Scales (e.g., WISC-IV Symbol Search).
Visual-motor coordination	An examinee's ability to coordinate the movement of his or her eyes, hands, and fingers when holding and/or manipulating objects.	Important when interpreting scores obtained from certain Wechsler Performance Scale (and Perceptual Reasoning) tests (e.g., WISC-IV Block Design).
Color blindness	A congenital visual defect that results in an examinee's inability to identify and distinguish certain colors from other colors.	Important when interpreting scores obtained from tests that require the accurate perception of chromatic stimuli (e.g., WISC-IV Matrix Reasoning).
Reflectivity vs. impulsivity	An examinee's consistent tendency to respond either deliberately (reflectively) or quickly (impulsively) when confronted with problem-solving situations.	Important when interpreting scores obtained from tests on which performance can be facilitated or inhibited by the examinee's carefulness in responding (e.g., timed tests involving problem solving, such as WISC-IV Block Design).
Field dependence vs. independence	The examinee's tendency to be significantly affected (dependent) or not affected (independent) by irrelevant factors or stimuli in a perceptual field.	Important when interpreting scores obtained on tests that are moderately to highly susceptible to performance errors when irrelevant stimuli become the focus of the examinee's attention (e.g., WISC-IV Picture Completion).

Term	Definition	Interpretation note
Verbal rehearsal	The strategy of verbally repeating (covertly or overtly) information in short-term memory to facilitate the immediate use of the information.	Important when interpreting scores obtained on tests in which the examinee's use of verbal rehearsal strategies can facilitate performance (e.g., WISC-IV Digit Span; Letter-Number Sequencing).
Verbal elaboration	The strategy of verbally relating new information to already existing information to facilitate the transfer of the information to the stores of acquired knowledge (i.e., Gc, Gf, Grw).	Important when interpreting scores obtained on tests on which novel stimuli can be encoded verbally to facilitate performance (e.g., WISC-IV Coding; associative memory tasks).
Visual elaboration	The strategy of visually relating new information to already existing information to facilitate the transfer of the information to the stores of acquired knowledge (i.e., Gc, Gf, Grw).	Important when interpreting scores obtained on tests on which visual representations of test stimuli can be used to facilitate performance (e.g., WISC-IV Letter-Number Sequencing; associative memory tasks).
Organization	The strategy of grouping together several different "chunks" or clusters of information to aid in the encoding and retrieval of information.	Important when interpreting scores obtained on tests that require the examinee to encode, and later retrieve, moderate amounts of information (e.g., WISC-IV Letter-Number Sequencing).
Planning	The process of developing efficient methods or solutions (i.e., plans or "forward thinking") to a problem prior to starting the solution.	Important when interpreting scores obtained on tests on which optimal performance may be facilitated through careful contemplation of the task prior to responding.
Monitoring/regulating	The process of assessing how well a selected strategy or plan is working, and then deciding whether to continue, modify, or discontinue the strategy or plan.	Important when interpreting scores obtained from tests on which the examinee has an opportunity to modify or retain his or her current mode of responding to facilitate performance.

[1] This test characteristic is often referred to as *item density*.

[2] CHC narrow (Stratum I) ability definitions can be found in Carroll (1993), McGrew (1997), McGrew and Flanagan (1998), and Appendix A of this text.

Appendix E

WISC-IV Interpretive Worksheet

STEP 1. Report the Child's WISC-IV Standard Scores (Full Scale IQ and Indexes) and Subtest Scaled Scores

For IQ and Indexes, report standard score, confidence interval, percentile rank, and descriptive category. For subtests, report scaled scores and percentile ranks only. (See Rapid Reference 4.1, "Location of Information in *WISC-IV Administration and Scoring Manual* and *WISC-IV Technical and Interpretive Manual* Needed for Score Conversions"; see Rapid Reference 4.4 for descriptive categories.)

Index Subtest	Score	95% CI	Percentile Rank	Descriptive Category
Verbal Comprehension				
Similarities				
Vocabulary				
Comprehension				
(Information)				
(Word Reasoning)				
Perceptual Reasoning				
Block Design				
Picture Concepts				
Matrix Reasoning				
(Picture Completion)				
Working Memory				
Digit Span				
Letter-Number Sequencing				
(Arithmetic)				
Processing Speed				
Coding				
Symbol Search				
(Cancellation)				
Full Scale IQ				

Note: Tests appearing in parentheses are supplemental measures. CI = Confidence Interval.

STEP 2. Determine the Best Way to Summarize Overall Intellectual Ability

Step 2a. To determine whether the FSIQ is interpretable, subtract the lowest Index from the highest Index.

Index names:
Index standard scores: _____ − _____ = _____
               (Highest)   (Lowest)   (Difference)

Is the size of the difference less than 1.5 SDs (i.e., < 23 points)?   Yes   No

- If YES, then the FSIQ may be interpreted as a reliable and valid estimate of a child's overall intellectual ability.
- If NO, then proceed to Step 2b.

See Rapid Reference 4.5 for an example of how to describe the FSIQ in a psychological report.

Step 2b. To determine whether the General Ability Index (GAI) may be used to summarize overall intellectual ability, calculate the difference between the VCI and PRI.

Index standard scores: _____ − _____ = _____
               (VCI)   (PRI)   (Difference)

Is the size of the difference less than 1.5 SDs (i.e., < 23 points)?   Yes   No

- If YES, then the GAI can be calculated and interpreted as a reliable and valid estimate of the child's overall intellectual ability.
- If NO, then proceed to Step 3.

To calculate the GAI, sum the VCI and PRI standard scores and locate the GAI that corresponds to this sum in Appendix F.

Index standard scores: _____ + _____ = _____ = _____
               (VCI)   (PRI)   (Sum of Standard Scores)   (GAI)

See Rapid Reference 4.6 for an example of how to describe the GAI in a psychological report. Proceed to Step 3.

STEP 3. Determine Whether Each of the Four Indexes is Unitary and Thus Interpretable

Step 3a. Calculate the difference between the highest and lowest VCI subtest scaled scores.

VCI subtest scaled scores: _____ − _____ = _____
               (Highest)   (Lowest)   (Difference)

Is the difference between the highest and lowest VCI subtest scaled scores < 5?   Yes   No

- If YES, interpret the VCI as representing a unitary Index.
- If NO, do not interpret the VCI as representing a unitary Index.

Proceed to Step 3b.

Step 3b. **Calculate the difference between the highest and lowest PRI subtest scaled scores.**

PRI subtest scaled scores: _____   –   _____   =   _____
                      (Highest)   (Lowest)   (Difference)

Is the difference between the highest and lowest PRI subtest scaled scores < 5?   Yes   No

- If YES, interpret the PRI as representing a unitary Index.
- If NO, do not interpret the PRI as representing a unitary Index.

Proceed to Step 3c.

Step 3c. **Calculate the difference between the WMI subtest scaled scores.**

WMI subtest scaled scores: _____   –   _____   =   _____
                      (Highest)   (Lowest)   (Difference)

Is the difference between the highest and lowest WMI subtest scaled scores < 5?   Yes   No

- If YES, interpret the WMI as representing a unitary Index.
- If NO, do not interpret the WMI as representing a unitary Index.

Proceed to Step 3d.

Step 3d. **Calculate the difference between the PSI subtest scaled scores.**

PSI subtest scaled scores: _____   –   _____   =   _____
                      (Highest)   (Lowest)   (Difference)

Is the difference between the highest and lowest PSI subtest scaled scores < 5?   Yes   No

- If YES, interpret the PSI as representing a unitary Index.
- If NO, do not interpret the PSI as representing a unitary Index.

Proceed to Step 4. If all four Indexes are not interpretable, refer to pages 133, 135, 136, and Step 7 for additional interpretive options.

STEP 4. Determine Normative Strengths and Normative Weaknesses in the Index Profile

Enter the name of each interpretable Index in the table below. Record the standard score for each interpretable Index. Place a checkmark in the box corresponding to the appropriate normative category for each Index.

Interpretable Index	Standard Score	Normative Weakness < 85	Within Normal Limits 85–115	Normative Strength > 115

STEP 5. Determine Personal Strengths and Personal Weaknesses in the Index Profile

Step 5a. Compute the mean of the child's Indexes and round to the nearest 10th of a point. Note that all Indexes (interpretable and noninterpretable) are included in the computation of the mean.

$$\frac{}{\text{(VCI)}} + \frac{}{\text{(PRI)}} + \frac{}{\text{(WMI)}} + \frac{}{\text{(PSI)}} = \frac{}{\text{(Sum)}} \div 4 = \frac{}{\text{(Index Mean)}}$$

Step 5b. Fill in the table below as follows:

- Record the name of each interpretable Index in Column (1).
- Record each interpretable Index standard score in Column (2).
- Record the rounded mean of all Indexes (from Step 5a) in Column (3).
- Record the difference score (i.e., standard score minus mean) in Column (4).
- Record the critical value needed for the difference score to be considered significant in Column (5) (these values are included in the "Personal Strength/Weakness Table for Ages 6 through 16").
- If the difference score equals or exceeds the critical value, record a "PS" for a positive (+) difference score or a "PW" for a negative (–) difference score.

Interpretable Index (1)	Standard Score (2)	Rounded Mean of All Indexes (3)	Difference Score (4)	Critical Value Needed for Significance (5)	Personal Strength or Personal Weakness (PS or PW) (6)
			+/–		
			+/–		
			+/–		
			+/–		

Personal Strength/ Weakness Table for Ages 6 through 16

	6	7	8	9	10	11	12	13	14	15	16
VCI	7.9	7.7	7.3	7.1	7.1	6.9	6.1	6.6	6.2	6.2	6.2
PRI	7.9	7.7	7.1	10.9	10.9	6.9	6.8	6.9	7.2	7.2	7.5
WMI	7.6	8.2	7.6	7.7	7.7	7.2	6.8	7.5	6.9	7.2	6.9
PSI	9.8	10.3	8.4	8.5	8.2	7.8	8.0	8.1	8.0	7.7	8.0

Note: The critical values listed in this table are at the $p < .05$ level of significance. For critical values at the $p < .01$ level of significance, see Table 4.3.

Are there any Personal Strengths or Weaknesses evident in the child's Index profile?   Yes   No

- If YES, go to Step 5c.
- If NO, proceed directly to Step 6.

Step 5c. **Determine whether the Personal Strength/Weakness is uncommon (base rate < 10%) in the general population.**

Index	Difference Score (from Step 5b)	PS or PW (from Step 5b)	Critical Value	Uncommon (U) or Not Uncommon (NU)
VCI			≥14	
PRI			≥13.5	
WMI			≥15	
PSI			>17	

Note: Difference scores are entered into this table only for *unitary* Indexes that were identified as Personal Strengths (PS) or Personal Weaknesses (PW) in Step 5b. Difference scores that are equal to or exceed the critical value listed in the fourth column of this table should be denoted Uncommon (U). Difference scores that are less than the critical value should be denoted Not Uncommon (NU).

Are there any uncommon personal strengths or weaknesses evident in the child's Index profile?   Yes   No

- If YES, go to Step 5d.
- If NO, proceed directly to Step 6.

Step 5d. **Determine whether any of the Interpretable Indexes are Key Assets or High-Priority Concerns.**

Review your findings from Steps 4, 5b, and 5c. In the following table, for each relevant Index place a checkmark in the column that accurately describes the findings for that Index. An Index that is both a Normative Strength and an Uncommon Personal Strength should be identified as a "Key Asset." An Index that is both a Normative Weakness and an Uncommon Personal Weakness should be identified as a "High-Priority Concern."

Index	NS (Step 4)	NW (Step 4)	PS (Step 5b)	PW (Step 5b)	Uncommon (Step 5c)	Key Asset	High-Priority Concern
VCI							
PRI							
WMI							
PSI							

Note: NS = Normative Strength; NW = Normative Weakness; PS = Personal Strength; PW = Personal Weakness.

Proceed to Step 6.

STEP 6. Interpret Fluctuations in the Child's Index Profile

Use Rapid Reference 4.10 for definitions of the various terms used to classify Indexes (e.g., High-Priority Concern, Key Asset, etc.). Include a paragraph in your report that defines these terms for the reader.

See Rapid Reference 4.11 for descriptions of the 12 possible combinations that Steps 3–5 can yield.

Interpret each index in a separate paragraph. Begin with strengths (including Key Assets), followed by weaknesses (including High-Priority Concerns), and then describe those Indexes that are neither strengths nor weaknesses, as well as those that are uninterpretable.

Note: You may find the summary sheet in Appendix G useful for recording all WISC-IV findings, including your clinical impressions and suggestions for clinical comparisons between the new WISC-IV Clinical Clusters. If you administered any or all WISC-IV supplemental subtests for the purpose of making Planned Clinical Comparisons or if, in your clinical judgement, you believe Post Hoc Clinical comparisons based on the administration of supplemental subtests would yield useful information, then proceed to Step 7.

STEP 7. (Optional) Conduct Select Clinical Comparisons

There are six possible clinical comparisons. Select which of the six (if any) make sense to compare based on either the referral question(s) or assessment results (see Rapid Reference 4.12).

Step 7a. **Determine whether each clinical cluster is unitary. Using the table below (at left), record the scaled score (SS) for each relevant subtest. On the lines to the right of the table, subtract the lowest from the highest scaled scores to compute the differences. If a difference equals or exceeds 5 points (i.e., 1.5 SDs), the related clinical cluster is not unitary and cannot be used to conduct clinical comparisons. If a difference is less than 5 points, then the clinical cluster is unitary. Clinical comparisons may be made *only* when both clusters that make up the comparison are unitary.**

Subtest	SS
MR	
PCn	
AR	
BD	
PCm	
SI	
WR	
VO	
CO	
IN	
LNS	
DS	

Fluid Reasoning (*Gf*) Cluster
Matrix Reasoning + Picture Concepts + Arithmetic

$\overline{\text{(Highest)}}$ − $\overline{\text{(Lowest)}}$ = $\overline{\text{(Difference)}}$

Visual Processing (*Gv*) Cluster
Block Design + Picture Completion

$\overline{\text{(Highest)}}$ − $\overline{\text{(Lowest)}}$ = $\overline{\text{(Difference)}}$

Nonverbal Fluid Reasoning (*Gf*-nonverbal) Cluster
Matrix Reasoning + Picture Concepts

$\overline{\text{(Highest)}}$ − $\overline{\text{(Lowest)}}$ = $\overline{\text{(Difference)}}$

Verbal Fluid Reasoning (*Gf*-verbal) Cluster
Similarities + Word Reasoning

$\overline{\text{(Highest)}}$ − $\overline{\text{(Lowest)}}$ = $\overline{\text{(Difference)}}$

Lexical Knowledge (*Gc*-VL) Cluster
Word Reasoning + Vocabulary

$\overline{\text{(Highest)}}$ − $\overline{\text{(Lowest)}}$ = $\overline{\text{(Difference)}}$

General Information (*Gc*-K0) Cluster
Comprehension + Information

$\overline{\text{(Highest)}}$ − $\overline{\text{(Lowest)}}$ = $\overline{\text{(Difference)}}$

Long-Term Memory (*Gc*-LTM) Cluster
Vocabulary + Information

$\overline{\text{(Highest)}}$ − $\overline{\text{(Lowest)}}$ = $\overline{\text{(Difference)}}$

Short-Term Memory (*Gsm*-WM) Cluster
Letter-Number Sequencing + Digit Span

$\overline{\text{(Highest)}}$ − $\overline{\text{(Lowest)}}$ = $\overline{\text{(Difference)}}$

Step 7b. For unitary clusters only, sum the scaled scores for the subtests that compose the cluster. Convert the sums of scaled scores to clinical clusters (i.e., standard scores having a mean of 100 and SD of 15) using Appendix H.

Subtest	SS
MR	
PCn	
AR	
BD	
PCm	
SI	
WR	
VO	
CO	
IN	
LNS	
DS	

$$\underline{\text{(MR)}} + \underline{\text{(PCn)}} + \underline{\text{(AR)}} = \underline{\hphantom{xxxx}}_{\text{(Sum of Scaled Scores)}} = \underline{\hphantom{xx}}\ \textit{Gf}\ \text{Cluster}$$

$$\underline{\text{(BD)}} + \underline{\text{(PCm)}} = \underline{\hphantom{xxxx}}_{\text{(Sum of Scaled Scores)}} = \underline{\hphantom{xx}}\ \textit{Gv}\ \text{Cluster}$$

$$\underline{\text{(MR)}} + \underline{\text{(PCn)}} = \underline{\hphantom{xxxx}}_{\text{(Sum of Scaled Scores)}} = \underline{\hphantom{xx}}\ \textit{Gf}\text{-nonverbal Cluster}$$

$$\underline{\text{(SI)}} + \underline{\text{(WR)}} = \underline{\hphantom{xxxx}}_{\text{(Sum of Scaled Scores)}} = \underline{\hphantom{xx}}\ \textit{Gf}\text{-verbal Cluster}$$

$$\underline{\text{(WR)}} + \underline{\text{(VO)}} = \underline{\hphantom{xxxx}}_{\text{(Sum of Scaled Scores)}} = \underline{\hphantom{xx}}\ \textit{Gc}\text{-VL Cluster}$$

$$\underline{\text{(CO)}} + \underline{\text{(IN)}} = \underline{\hphantom{xxxx}}_{\text{(Sum of Scaled Scores)}} = \underline{\hphantom{xx}}\ \textit{Gc}\text{-K0 Cluster}$$

$$\underline{\text{(VO)}} + \underline{\text{(IN)}} = \underline{\hphantom{xxxx}}_{\text{(Sum of Scaled Scores)}} = \underline{\hphantom{xx}}\ \textit{Gc}\text{-LTM Cluster}$$

$$\underline{\text{(LNS)}} + \underline{\text{(DS)}} = \underline{\hphantom{xxxx}}_{\text{(Sum of Scaled Scores)}} = \underline{\hphantom{xx}}\ \textit{Gsm}\text{-WM Cluster}$$

Step 7c. Conduct Planned Clinical Comparisons.

Calculate the difference between the clusters in the comparison. If the size of the difference is equal to or greater than the value reported in the table below, then the difference is uncommon; If the size of the difference is less than the table value, then the difference is not uncommon.

Clinical Comparison	Difference Score (use values from Step 7b to calculate difference scores)	Critical Value	Uncommon (U) or Not Uncommon (NU)
Gf versus *Gv*		≥ 21	
Gf-nonverbal versus *Gv*		≥ 24	
Gf-nonverbal versus *Gf*-verbal		≥ 24	
Gc-VL versus *Gc*-K0		≥ 17	
Gc-LTM versus *Gsm*-WM		≥ 24	
Gc-LTM versus *Gf*-verbal		≥ 17	

Note: Difference scores that are equal to or exceed the critical values listed in the third column of this table should be denoted Uncommon (U). Difference scores that are less than these critical values should be denoted Not Uncommon (NU).

Step 7d. Describe results of Planned Clinical Comparisons.

Regardless of the outcome of Step 7c, review Rapid Reference 4.13 to identify an example of an interpretive statement that most appropriately describes the results of the child's clinical cluster comparison. If the child demonstrated a Normative Weakness in any clinical cluster, refer to Rapid Reference 4.14 for hypotheses about the meaning of such findings. Rapid Reference 4.14 also provides suggestions for educational interventions and instructional strategies that may be useful for children who demonstrate uncommon patterns of performance on the WISC-IV clinical clusters.

Appendix F

General Ability Index (GAI) Conversion Table Based on Sum of Verbal Comprehension Index (VCI) and Perceptual Reasoning Index (PRI) Standard Scores

Table F.1

Sum of VCI + PRI	GAI	Percentile Rank	95% CI	Sum of VCI + PRI	GAI	Percentile Rank	95% CI
90	40	.01	34–46	125	58	.25	52–64
91	40	.01	34–46	126	59	.30	53–65
92	40	.01	34–46	127	59	.30	53–65
93	41	.01	35–47	128	60	.36	54–66
94	41	.01	35–47	129	61	.49	55–67
95	42	.01	36–48	130	61	.49	55–67
96	42	.01	36–48	131	62	1	56–68
97	43	.01	37–49	132	62	1	56–68
98	43	.01	37–49	133	63	1	57–69
99	44	.01	38–50	134	63	1	57–69
100	45	.01	39–51	135	64	1	58–70
101	45	.01	39–51	136	64	1	58–70
102	46	.01	40–52	137	65	1	59–71
103	46	.01	40–52	138	66	1	60–72
104	47	.02	41–53	139	66	1	60–72
105	47	.02	41–53	140	67	1	61–73
106	48	.03	42–54	141	67	1	61–73
107	48	.03	42–54	142	68	2	62–74
108	49	.04	43–55	143	68	2	62–74
109	49	.04	43–55	144	69	2	63–75
110	50	.05	44–56	145	69	2	63–75
111	51	.06	45–57	146	70	2	64–76
112	51	.06	45–57	147	71	3	65–77
113	52	.07	46–58	148	71	3	65–77
114	52	.07	46–58	149	72	3	66–78
115	53	.09	47–59	150	72	3	66–78
116	53	.09	47–59	151	73	3	67–79
117	54	.11	48–60	152	73	3	67–79
118	54	.11	48–60	153	74	4	68–80
119	55	.16	49–61	154	74	4	68–80
120	56	.16	50–62	155	75	5	69–81
121	56	.16	50–62	156	76	5	70–82
122	57	.20	51–63	157	76	5	70–82
123	57	.20	51–63	158	77	6	71–83
124	58	.25	52–64	159	77	6	71–83

(continued)

Table F.1 (Continued)

Sum of VCI + PRI	GAI	Percentile Rank	95% CI	Sum of VCI + PRI	GAI	Percentile Rank	95% CI
160	78	7	72–84	205	103	57	97–109
161	78	7	72–84	206	103	57	97–109
162	79	8	73–85	207	104	62	98–110
163	79	8	73–85	208	104	62	98–110
164	80	9	74–86	209	105	65	99–111
165	81	11	75–87	210	106	65	100–112
166	81	11	75–87	211	106	65	100–112
167	82	12	76–88	212	107	67	101–113
168	82	12	76–88	213	107	67	101–113
169	83	13	77–89	214	108	70	102–114
170	83	13	77–89	215	108	70	102–114
171	84	14	78–90	216	109	73	103–115
172	84	14	78–90	217	109	73	103–115
173	85	16	79–81	218	110	75	104–116
174	86	17	80–92	219	111	77	105–117
175	86	17	80–92	220	111	77	105–117
176	87	19	81–93	221	112	79	106–118
177	87	19	81–93	222	112	79	106–118
178	88	21	82–94	223	113	81	107–119
179	88	21	82–94	224	113	81	107–119
180	89	23	83–95	225	114	83	108–120
181	89	23	83–95	226	114	83	108–120
182	90	25	84–96	227	115	84	109–121
183	91	27	85–97	228	116	86	110–122
184	91	27	85–97	229	116	86	110–122
185	92	29	86–98	230	117	87	111–123
186	92	29	86–98	231	117	87	111–123
187	93	33	87–99	232	118	88	112–124
188	93	33	87–99	233	118	88	112–124
189	94	35	88–100	234	119	89	113–125
190	94	35	88–100	235	119	89	113–125
191	95	38	89–101	236	120	91	114–126
192	96	40	90–102	237	121	92	115–127
193	96	40	90–102	238	121	92	115–127
194	97	43	91–103	239	122	92	116–128
195	97	43	91–103	240	122	92	116–128
196	98	45	92–104	241	123	94	117–129
197	98	45	92–104	242	123	94	117–129
198	99	48	93–105	243	124	95	118–130
199	99	48	93–105	244	124	95	118–130
200	100	50	94–106	245	125	95	119–131
201	101	52	95–107	246	126	96	120–132
202	101	52	95–107	247	126	96	120–132
203	102	55	96–108	248	127	97	121–133
204	102	55	96–108	249	127	97	121–133

Table F.1   (Continued)

Sum of VCI + PRI	GAI	Percentile Rank	95% CI	Sum of VCI + PRI	GAI	Percentile Rank	95% CI
250	128	97	122–134	280	144	99.84	138–150
251	128	97	122–134	281	145	99.87	139–151
252	129	97	123–135	282	146	99.89	140–152
253	129	97	123–135	283	146	99.89	140–152
254	130	98	124–136	284	147	99.93	141–153
255	131	98	125–137	285	147	99.93	141–153
256	131	98	125–137	286	148	99.93	142–154
257	132	98	126–138	287	148	99.93	142–154
258	132	98	126–138	288	149	99.94	143–155
259	133	99	127–139	289	149	99.94	143–155
260	133	99	127–139	290	150	99.95	144–156
261	134	99	128–140	291	151	99.96	145–157
262	134	99	128–140	292	151	99.96	145–157
263	135	99	129–141	293	152	99.97	146–158
264	136	99	130–142	294	152	99.97	146–158
265	136	99	130–142	295	153	99.98	147–159
266	137	99	131–143	296	153	99.98	147–159
267	137	99	131–143	297	154	99.99	148–160
268	138	99	132–144	298	154	99.99	148–160
269	138	99	132–144	299	155	99.99	149–161
270	139	99.57	133–145	300	156	99.99	150–162
271	139	99.57	133–145	301	156	99.99	150–162
272	140	99.64	134–146	302	157	99.99	151–163
273	141	99.70	135–147	303	157	99.99	151–163
274	141	99.70	135–147	304	158	99.99	152–164
275	142	99.75	136–148	305	158	99.99	152–164
276	142	99.75	136–148	306	159	99.99	153–165
277	143	99.80	137–149	307	159	99.99	153–165
278	143	99.80	137–149	308	160	99.99	154–166
279	144	99.84	138–150	309	160	99.99	154–166
				310	160	99.99	154–166

Source: Wechsler Intelligence Scale for Children–Fourth Edition. Copyright © 2003 by Harcourt Assessment, Inc. Reproduced by permission of the publisher. All rights reserved. *Wechsler Intelligence Scale for Children* and *WISC* are trademarks of Harcourt Assessment, Inc., registered in the United States of America and/or other jurisdictions.

Note: CI = Confidence Interval.

This table was developed based on data provided in the *WISC-IV Technical and Interpretive Manual* (The Psychological Corporation, 2003, Table 5.1), and on a statistical technique for linear equating provided by Tellegen and Briggs (1967, Formula 4). This equation permits computation of a composite standard score based on the intercorrelations

(continued)

Table F.1 (Continued)

among the components that make up the composite. The GAI is a composite based on the sum of the VCI and PRI. Therefore, based on the intercorrelation between VCI and PRI (.62 for the total sample aged 6–16), the technique of linear equating produced the following formula: GAI standard score = .555 x − 11, where x = sum of VCI and PRI. This table was developed from that formula, using mean = 100 and SD = 15. A single formula was appropriate for the entire WISC-IV age range because the correlations between VCI and PRI were close to the value for the total sample (.62 ± .05) for each separate age group between 6 and 16 years (The Psychological Corporation, 2003, Appendix A).

Appendix G

Summary of Analyses of WISC-IV Indexes

Name:

Date of testing:

Age:

WISC-IV Index	Standard Score	INTERPRETIVE STEP				
		(STEP 3) Is Index Standard Score Interpretable?	(STEP 4) Normative Strength (NS) or Normative Weakness (NW)?	(STEP 5b) Personal Strength (PS) or Personal Weakness (PW)?	(STEP 5c) Is PS or PW Uncommon?	(STEP 5d) Key Asset (KA) or High-Priority Concern (HPC)?
VCI						
PRI						
WMI						
PSI						

Clinical Impressions and Suggested (Post Hoc) Clinical Comparisons:

Appendix H

Norms Tables for Clinical Clusters

Table H.1 Fluid Reasoning (*Gf*) Cluster Equivalent of Sums of Scaled Scores for Matrix Reasoning, Picture Concepts, and Arithmetic

Sum of Scaled Scores	*Gf* Cluster	95% Confidence Interval	Percentile Rank
3	50	42–58	.05
4	52	44–60	.07
5	54	46–62	.11
6	55	47–63	.16
7	57	49–65	.20
8	59	51–67	.30
9	61	53–69	.49
10	62	54–70	1
11	64	56–72	1
12	66	58–74	1
13	67	59–75	1
14	69	61–77	2
15	71	63–79	3
16	73	65–81	3
17	75	67–83	5
18	77	69–85	6
19	78	70–86	7
20	80	72–88	9
21	82	74–90	12
22	84	76–92	14
23	86	78–94	17
24	88	80–96	21
25	90	82–98	25
26	92	84–100	29
27	94	86–102	35
28	96	88–104	40
29	98	90–106	45
30	100	92–108	50

Table H.1 (Continued)

Sum of Scaled Scores	Gf Cluster	95% Confidence Interval	Percentile Rank
31	102	94–110	55
32	104	96–112	62
33	106	98–114	65
34	109	101–117	73
35	111	103–119	77
36	113	105–121	81
37	115	107–123	84
38	117	109–125	87
39	119	111–127	89
40	121	113–129	92
41	123	115–131	93
42	125	117–133	95
43	127	119–135	97
44	129	121–137	97
45	131	123–139	98
46	132	124–140	98
47	134	126–142	99
48	136	128–144	99
49	137	129–145	99
50	139	131–147	99.57
51	141	133–149	99.70
52	142	134–150	99.75
53	144	136–152	99.84
54	146	138–154	99.89
55	147	139–155	99.93
56	149	141–157	99.94
57	150	142–158	99.95

Table H.2 Visual Processing (Gv) Cluster Equivalent of Sums of Scaled Scores for Block Design and Picture Completion

Sum of Scaled Scores	Gv Cluster	95% Confidence Interval	Percentile Rank
2	50	41–59	.05
3	53	44–62	.09
4	56	47–65	.16
5	59	50–68	.30
6	62	53–71	1
7	65	56–74	1
8	67	58–76	1
9	70	61–79	2
10	72	63–81	3
11	75	66–84	5
12	78	69–87	7
13	80	71–89	9
14	83	74–92	13
15	86	77–95	17
16	88	79–97	21
17	91	82–100	27
18	94	85–103	35
19	97	88–106	43
20	100	91–109	50
21	103	94–112	57
22	106	97–115	65
23	108	99–117	71
24	111	102–120	77
25	114	105–123	83
26	117	108–126	87
27	120	111–129	91
28	123	114–132	93
29	126	117–135	96
30	130	121–139	98
31	133	124–142	99
32	135	126–144	99
33	138	129–147	99
34	140	131–149	99.64
35	143	134–152	99.80
36	145	136–154	99.87
37	148	139–157	99.93
38	150	141–159	99.95

Table H.3 Nonverbal Fluid Reasoning (*Gf*-nonverbal) Cluster Equivalent of Sums of Scaled Scores for Matrix Reasoning and Picture Concepts

Sum of Scaled Scores	*Gf*-nonverbal Cluster	95% Confidence Interval	Percentile Rank
2	50	41–59	.05
3	53	44–62	.09
4	55	46–64	.16
5	58	49–67	.25
6	61	52–70	.49
7	64	55–73	1
8	67	58–76	1
9	69	60–78	2
10	71	62–80	3
11	74	65–83	4
12	77	68–86	6
13	79	70–88	8
14	82	73–91	12
15	85	76–94	16
16	88	79–97	21
17	91	82–100	27
18	94	85–103	35
19	97	88–106	43
20	100	91–109	50
21	103	94–112	57
22	106	97–115	65
23	109	100–118	73
24	112	103–121	79
25	115	106–124	84
26	118	109–127	88
27	121	112–130	92
28	124	115–133	95
29	127	118–136	97
30	130	121–139	98
31	133	124–142	99
32	135	126–144	99
33	138	129–147	99
34	140	131–149	99.64
35	143	134–152	99.80
36	145	136–154	99.87
37	148	139–157	99.93
38	150	141–159	99.95

Table H.4 Verbal Fluid Reasoning (*Gf*-verbal) Cluster Equivalent of Sums of Scaled Scores for Similarities and Word Reasoning

Sum of Scaled Scores	*Gf*-verbal Cluster	95% Confidence Interval	Percentile Rank
2	50	40–60	.05
3	52	42–62	.07
4	55	45–65	.16
5	58	48–68	.25
6	61	51–71	.49
7	63	53–73	1
8	66	56–76	1
9	69	59–79	2
10	72	62–82	3
11	75	65–85	5
12	78	68–88	7
13	81	71–91	11
14	84	74–94	14
15	86	76–96	17
16	89	79–99	21
17	92	82–102	29
18	94	84–104	35
19	97	87–107	43
20	100	90–110	50
21	102	92–112	55
22	105	95–115	65
23	108	98–118	71
24	111	101–121	77
25	113	103–123	81
26	116	106–126	86
27	120	110–130	91
28	123	112–133	93
29	126	116–136	96
30	129	119–139	97
31	132	122–142	98
32	135	125–145	99
33	137	127–147	99
34	140	130–150	99.64
35	142	132–152	99.75
36	145	135–155	99.87
37	147	137–157	99.93
38	150	140–160	99.95

Table H.5 Lexical Knowledge (Gc-VL) Cluster Equivalent of Sums of Scaled Scores for Word Reasoning and Vocabulary

Sum of Scaled Scores	Gc-VL Cluster	95% Confidence Interval	Percentile Rank
2	50	41–59	.05
3	53	44–62	.09
4	56	47–65	.16
5	59	50–68	.30
6	62	53–71	1
7	65	56–74	1
8	68	59–77	2
9	71	62–80	3
10	74	65–83	4
11	76	67–85	5
12	79	70–88	8
13	81	72–90	11
14	84	75–93	14
15	86	77–95	17
16	89	80–98	21
17	91	82–100	27
18	94	85–103	35
19	96	87–105	40
20	99	90–108	48
21	102	93–111	55
22	105	96–114	65
23	108	99–117	71
24	110	101–119	75
25	113	104–122	81
26	116	107–125	86
27	120	111–129	91
28	123	114–132	93
29	126	117–135	96
30	129	120–138	97
31	132	123–141	98
32	135	126–144	99
33	137	128–146	99
34	140	131–149	99.64
35	142	133–151	99.75
36	145	136–154	99.87
37	147	138–156	99.93
38	150	141–159	99.95

Table H.6 General Information (Gc-K0) Cluster Equivalent of Sums of Scaled Scores for Comprehension and Information

Sum of Scaled Scores	Gc-K0 Cluster	95% Confidence Interval	Percentile Rank
2	50	40–60	.05
3	53	43–63	.09
4	56	46–66	.16
5	59	49–69	.30
6	62	52–72	1
7	65	55–75	1
8	68	58–78	2
9	71	61–81	3
10	73	63–83	3
11	76	66–86	5
12	78	68–88	7
13	81	71–91	11
14	83	73–93	13
15	85	75–95	16
16	88	78–98	21
17	91	81–101	27
18	94	84–104	35
19	97	87–107	43
20	99	89–109	48
21	102	92–112	55
22	105	95–115	65
23	108	98–118	71
24	111	101–121	77
25	114	104–124	83
26	117	107–127	87
27	120	110–130	91
28	123	113–133	93
29	126	116–136	96
30	129	119–139	97
31	131	121–141	98
32	133	123–143	99
33	136	126–146	99
34	139	129–149	99.57
35	142	132–152	99.75
36	145	135–155	99.87
37	148	138–158	99.93
38	150	140–160	99.95

Table H.7 Long-Term Memory (Gc-LTM) Cluster Equivalent of Sums of Scaled Scores for Vocabulary and Information

Sum of Scaled Scores	Gc-LTM Cluster	95% Confidence Interval	Percentile Rank
2	50	42–58	.04
3	54	46–62	.11
4	57	49–65	.20
5	60	52–68	.36
6	63	55–71	1
7	66	58–74	1
8	69	61–77	2
9	72	64–80	3
10	74	66–82	3
11	77	69–85	6
12	79	71–87	8
13	81	73–89	11
14	84	76–92	14
15	87	79–95	19
16	89	81–97	21
17	91	83–99	27
18	94	86–102	35
19	97	89–105	43
20	99	91–107	48
21	102	94–110	55
22	105	97–113	65
23	108	100–116	71
24	111	103–119	77
25	113	105–121	81
26	116	108–124	86
27	119	111–127	89
28	122	114–130	92
29	125	117–133	95
30	127	119–135	97
31	130	122–138	98
32	133	125–141	99
33	136	128–144	99
34	138	130–146	99
35	141	133–149	99.70
36	144	136–152	99.84
37	147	139–155	99.93
38	150	142–158	99.95

Table H.8 Short-Term Memory (*Gsm*-WM) Cluster Equivalent of Sums of Scaled Scores for Letter-Number Sequencing and Digit Span

Sum of Scaled Scores	*Gsm*-WM Cluster	95% Confidence Interval	Percentile Rank
2	50	42–58	.05
3	52	44–60	.07
4	54	46–62	.11
5	56	48–64	.16
6	59	51–67	.30
7	62	54–70	1
8	65	57–73	1
9	68	60–76	2
10	71	63–79	3
11	74	66–82	4
12	77	69–85	6
13	80	72–88	9
14	83	75–91	13
15	86	78–94	17
16	88	80–96	21
17	91	83–99	27
18	94	86–102	35
19	97	89–105	43
20	99	91–107	48
21	102	94–110	55
22	104	96–112	62
23	107	99–115	67
24	110	102–118	75
25	113	105–121	81
26	116	108–124	86
27	120	112–128	91
28	123	115–131	94
29	126	118–134	96
30	129	121–137	97
31	132	124–140	98
32	135	127–143	99
33	138	130–146	99
34	141	133–149	99.70
35	144	136–152	99.84
36	146	138–154	99.89
37	148	140–156	99.93
38	150	142–158	99.95

Note: The *Gsm*-WM Cluster is identical to the WISC-IV Working Memory Index (WMI).

References

Ackerman, P. T., & Dykman, R. A. (1995). Reading-disabled students with and without co-morbid arithmetic disability. *Developmental Neuropsychology, 11,* 351–371.

Alfonso, V. C., Flanagan, D. P., & Radwan, S. (in press). The impact of Cattell-Horn-Carroll (CHC) theory on test development and the interpretation of cognitive and academic abilities. In D. P. Flanagan & P. L. Harrison (Eds.), *Contemporary intellectual assessment: Theories, tests, and issues* (2nd ed.). New York: Guilford.

Alfonso, V. C., Oakland, T., LaRocca, R., & Spanakos, A. (2000). The course on individual cognitive assessment. *School Psychology Review, 29,* 52–64.

American Educational Research Association. (1999). *Standards for educational and psychological testing.* Washington, DC: Author.

American Psychiatric Association. (1994). *Diagnostic and statistical manual of mental disorders* (4th ed.). Washington, DC: Author.

American Psychiatric Association. (2000). *Diagnostic and statistical manual of mental disorders* (4th ed., Text Rev.). Washington, DC: Author.

Anastasi, A. (1988). *Psychological testing* (6th ed.). New York: Macmillan.

Anastasi, A., & Urbina, S. (1997). *Psychological testing* (7th ed.). Upper Saddle River, NJ: Prentice Hall.

Attwood, T. (1998). *Asperger's Syndrome: A guide for parents and professionals.* Philadelphia: Jessica Kingsley.

Baddeley, A. (1986). *Working memory.* Oxford: Oxford University Press.

Baddeley, A. (1992). Is working memory working? The fifteenth Bartlett Lecture. *Quarterly Journal of Experimental Psychology, 44A,* 1–31.

Bannatyne, A. (1974). Diagnosis: A note on recategorization of the WISC scaled scores. *Journal of Learning Disabilities, 7,* 272–274.

Barnhill, G., Hagiwara, T., Myles, B. S., & Simpson, R. L. (2000). Asperger Syndrome: A study of 37 children and adolescents. *Focus on Autism and Other Developmental Disabilities, 15*(3), 146–153.

Binet, A., & Simon, T. (1905). Méthodes nouvelles pour le diagnostique du niveau intellectuel des anormaux [New methods for the diagnosis of the intellectual level of abnormals]. *L'Année Psychologique, 11,* 191–244.

Binet, A. (1916). New methods for the diagnosis of the intellectual level of subnormals. In E. S. Kite (Trans.), *The development of intelligence in children.* Vineland, NJ: Publications of the Training School at Vineland. (Originally published 1905 in *L'Année Psychologique, 11,* 191–244)

Binet, A., & Simon, T. (1908). Le développment de l'intelligence chez les enfants [The development of intelligence in children]. *L'Année Psychologique, 14,* 1–90.

Bolen, L. M. (1998). WISC-III score changes for EMR students. *Psychology in the Schools, 35*(4), 327–332.

Bower, A., & Hayes, A. (1995). Relations of scores on the Stanford-Binet Fourth Edition and Form L-M: Concurrent validation study with children who have Mental Retardation. *American Journal on Mental Retardation, 99*(5), 555–563.

Bracken, B. A., & McCallum, R. S. (1998) *The Universal Nonverbal Intelligence Test.* Chicago: Riverside Publishing Company.

Braden, J. P. (1994). *Deafness, deprivation, and IQ.* New York: Plenum Press.

Braden, J. P. (1995). Review of Wechsler Intelligence Scale for Children—Third Edition. In J. V. Mitchell (Ed.), *The tenth mental measurement yearbook* (vol. 1, pp. 1098–1103). Lincoln, NE: Buros Institute of Mental Measurement.

Braden, J. P., & Niebling, B. C. (in press). Evaluating the validity evidence for intelligence tests using the joint test standards. In D. P. Flanagan & P. L. Harrison (Eds.), *Contemporary intellectual assessment: Theories, tests, and issues* (2nd ed.). New York: Guilford.

Brauer, B. A., Braden, J. P., Pollard, R. Q., & Hardy-Braz, S. T. (1998). Deaf and hard of hearing people. In J. Sandoval, C. L. Frisby, K. F. Geisinger, J. D. Scheuneman, & J. R. Grenier (Eds.), *Test interpretation and diversity: Achieving equity in assessment* (pp. 297–315). Washington, DC: American Psychological Association.

Brigham, C. C. (1922). *A study of American intelligence.* Princeton, NJ: Princeton University.

Caltabiano, L., & Flanagan, D. P. (2004). Content validity of new and recently revised intelligence tests: Implications for interpretation. Manuscript in preparation.

Canivez, G. L., & Watkins, M. W. (2001). Long-term stability of the Wechsler Intelligence Scale for Children–Third Edition among students with disabilities. *School Psychology Review, 30*(2), 438–453.

Carroll, J. B. (1993). *Human cognitive abilities: A survey of factor-analytic studies.* Cambridge, England: Cambridge University Press.

Carroll, J. B. (1997). Commentary on Keith and Witta's hierarchical and cross-age confirmatory factor analysis of the WISC-III. *School Psychology Quarterly, 12,* 108–109.

Carroll, J. B. (1998). Foreword. In K. S. McGrew & D. P. Flanagan, *The intelligence test desk reference (ITDR): Gf-Gc cross-battery assessment* (pp. xi–xii). Boston: Allyn & Bacon.

Cohen, J. (1952). A factor-analytically based rationale for the Wechsler-Bellevue. *Journal of Consulting Psychology, 16,* 272–277.

Cohen, J. (1959). The factorial structure of the WISC at ages 7-7, 10-6, and 13-6. *Journal of Consulting Psychology, 23,* 285–299.

Cohen, M. (1997). *Children's Memory Scale.* San Antonio, TX: The Psychological Corporation.

Daniel, M. H. (1997). Intelligence testing: Status and trends. *American Psychologist, 52*(10), 1038–1045.

Das, J. P., & Naglieri, J. A. (1997). *Cognitive Assessment System.* Itasca, IL: Riverside.

Diller, L., Ben-Yishay, Y., Gerstman, L. J., Goodkin, R., Gordon, W., & Weinberg, J. (1974). *Studies in cognitive and rehabilitation in hemiplegia,* Rehabilitation Monograph No. 50. New York: New York University Medical Center Institute of Rehabilitation Medicine.

Education for All Handicapped Children Act of 1975. Pub. L. No. 94-142. (1975).

Educational Amendment of 1978, Pub. L. No. 95-561 (1978).

Eisenmajer, R., Prior, M., Leekam, S., Wing, L., Gould, J. Welham, M., & Ong, B. (1996). Comparison of clinical symptoms in autism and Asperger's Disorder. *Journal of the American Academy of Child and Adolescent Psychiatry, 35,* 1523–1531.

Elliott (1990). *Differential Ability Scales.* San Antonio, TX: The Psychological Corporation.

Figueroa, R. A. (1990). Assessment of linguistic minority group children. In C. R. Reynolds and R. W. Kamphaus (Eds.), *Handbook of psychological and educational assessment of children: Vol. 1. Intelligence and achievement.* New York: Guilford.

Figueroa, R. A., & Hernandez, S. (2000). *Testing Hispanic students in the United States: Technical and policy issues.* Report to the President's Advisory Commission on Educational Excellence for Hispanic Americans. Washington DC: U.S. Department of Education, Office of Educational Research and Improvement (OERI).

Flanagan, D. P. (2000). Wechsler-based CHC cross-battery assessment and reading achievement: Strengthening the validity of interpretations drawn from Wechsler test scores. *School Psychology Quarterly, 15,* 295–329.

Flanagan, D. P., & Alfonso, V. C. (2000). Essentially, essential for WAIS-III users. *Contemporary Psychology, 45,* 528–539.

Flanagan, D. P., & Harrison, P. L. (Eds.). (in press). *Contemporary intellectual assessment: Theories, tests, and issues* (2nd ed.). New York: Guilford.

Flanagan, D. P., Harrison, P. L., & Genshaft, J. L. (Eds.). (1997). *Contemporary intellectual assessment: Theories, tests, and issues.* New York: Guilford.

Flanagan, D. P., Kaufman, A. S., & Mascolo, J. T. (2004). A review of the WISC-IV. *Journal of Psychoeducational Assessment.* Manuscript in preparation.

Flanagan, D. P., McGrew, K. S., & Ortiz, S. O. (2000). *The Wechsler intelligence scales and Gf-Gc theory: A contemporary approach to interpretation.* Boston: Allyn & Bacon.

Flanagan, D. P., & Ortiz, S. O. (2001). *Essentials of cross-battery assessment.* New York: Wiley.

Flanagan, D. P., & Ortiz, S. O. (2002a). Cross-battery assessment: A response to Watkins, Youngstrom, and Glutting (Part I). *Communique, 30*(7), 32–34.

Flanagan, D. P., & Ortiz, S. O. (2002b). Cross-battery assessment: A response to Watkins, Youngstrom, and Glutting (Part II). *Communique, 30*(8), 36–38.

Flanagan, D. P., Ortiz, S. O., Alfonso, V. C., & Mascolo, J. T. (2002). *The achievement test desk reference (ATDR): Comprehensive assessment and learning disabilities.* Boston, MA: Allyn & Bacon.

Floyd, R. G., Evans, J. J., & McGrew, K. S. (2003). Relations between measures of Cattell-Horn-Carroll (CHC) cognitive abilities and mathematics achievement across the school-age years. *Psychology in the Schools, 40*(2), 155–171.

Flynn, J. R. (1987). Massive IQ gains in 14 nations: What IQ tests really measure. *Psychological Bulletin, 101,* 171–191.

Gagne, E. D. (1985). *The cognitive psychology of school learning.* Boston, MA: Little & Brown.

Gallaudet Research Institute. (2003). *Regional and national summary report of data from the 2001–2002 annual Survey of Deaf and Hard of Hearing Children and Youth.* Washington, DC: GRI, Gallaudet University.

Gathercole, S. E., Hitch, G. J., Service, E., & Martin, A. J. (1997). Phonological short-term memory and new word learning in children. *Developmental Psychology, 33*(6), 966–979.

Ghaziuddin, M., Tsai, L. Y., & Ghaziuddin, N. (1992). Brief report: A comparison of the diagnostic criteria for Asperger Syndrome. *Journal of Autism and Developmental Disorders, 22,* 643–649.

Gilchrist, A., Green J., Cox, A., Burton, D., Rutter, M., & Le Couteur, A. (2001). Development and current functioning in adolescents with Asperger Syndrome: A comparative study. *Journal of Child Psychology and Psychiatry, 42*(2), 227–240.

Glutting, J. J., McDermott, P. A., & Konold, T. R. (1997). Ontology, structure, and diagnostic benefits of a normative subtest taxonomy from the WISC-III standardization sample. In D. P. Flanagan, J. L. Genshaft, & P. L. Harrison (Eds.), *Contemporary intellectual assessment: Theories, tests, and issues* (pp. 349–372). New York: Guilford.

Glutting, J. J., McDermott, P. A., Watkins, M. M., Kush, J. C., & Konold, T. R. (1997). The base rate problem and its consequences for interpreting children's ability profiles. *School Psychology Review, 26*(2), 176–188.

Gold, J. M., Carpenter, C., Randolph, C., Goldberg, T. E., & Weinberger, D. R. (1997). Auditory working memory and Wisconsin Card Sorting Test performance in schizophrenia. *Archives of General Psychiatry, 54,* 159–165.

Goldstein, G., Beers, S. R., Siegel, D. J., & Minshew, N. J. (2001). A comparison of WAIS-R profiles in adults with high-functioning autism or differing subtypes of learning disability. *Applied Neuropsychology, 8*(3), 148–154.

Goldstein, G., Minshew, N. J., Allen, D. N., & Seaton, B. E. (2002). High-functioning autism and schizophrenia: A comparison of an early and late onset neurodevelopmental disorder. *Archives of Clinical Neuropsychology, 17,* 461–475.

Gould, S. J. (1981). *The mismeasure of man.* New York: Norton.

Gustaffson, J. E., & Undheim, J. O. (1996). Individual differences in cognitive functions. In

D. C.Berliner & R. C. Cabfee (Eds.), *Handbook of educational psychology* (pp. 186–242). New York: MacMillan.

Hale, J. B., Fiorello, C. A., Kavanagh, J. A., Hoeppner, J. B., & Gaither, R. A. (2001). WISC-III predictors of academic achievement for children with learning disabilities: Are global and factor scores comparable? *School Psychology Quarterly, 16,* 31–55.

Hale, R. L. (1979). The utility of the WISC-R subtest scores in discriminating among adequate and underacheiving children. *Multivariate Behavioral Research, 14,* 245–253.

Hale, R. L., & Landino, S. A. (1981). Utility of the WISC-R subtest analysis in discriminating among groups of conduct problem, withdrawn, mixed, and non-problem boys. *Journal of Consulting and Clinical Psychology, 41,* 91–95.

Hale, R. L., & Saxe, J. E. (1983). Profile analysis of the Wechsler Intelligence Scale for Children—Revised. *Journal of Psychoeducational Assessment, 1,* 155–162.

Hardy-Braz, S. T. (1999). *School psychologists working with students who are deaf: Who are they and what are they doing that is different?* Poster presentation at the convention of the National Association of School Psychologists, Las Vegas, NV.

Hardy-Braz, S. T. (2003a). Enhancing school-based psychological services: Assessments and interventions with students who are deaf or hard-of-hearing. Workshop presented at the meeting of the National Association of School Psychologists, Toronto, Canada.

Hardy-Braz, S. T. (2003b). Testing children who are deaf or hard of hearing. In D. Wechsler (Ed.), *WISC-IV Administration and scoring manual* (pp. 12–18). San Antonio, TX: The Psychological Corporation.

Harrington, R. G. (1982). Caution: Standardized testing may be hazardous to the educational programs of intellectually gifted children. *Education, 103,* 112–117.

Harrison, P. L. (1990). Mental Retardation: Adaptive behavior assessment and giftedness. In A. S. Kaufman, *Assessing adolescent and adult intelligence* (pp. 533–585). Needham Heights, MA: Allyn & Bacon.

Hebben, N., & Milberg, W. (2002). *Essentials of neuropsychological assessment.* New York: Wiley.

Horn, J. L. (1991). Measurement of intellectual capabilities: A review of theory. In K. S. McGrew, J. K. Werder, & R. W. Woodcock, *Woodcock-Johnson Technical Manual* (pp. 197–232). Chicago: Riverside.

Horn, J. L., & Noll, J. (1997). Human cognitive capabilities: *Gf-Gc* theory. In D. P. Flanagan, J. L. Genshaft, & P. L. Harrison (Eds.), *Contemporary intellectual assessment: Theories, tests, and issues* (pp. 53–91). New York: Guilford.

Individuals with Disabilities Education Act, Pub. L. No. 105-17. (1991).

Jacob K. Javits Gifted and Talented Students Education Act of 1988, Pub. L. No. 100-297. (1988).

Jensen, A. R. (1980). *Bias in mental testing.* New York: Free Press.

Jensen, A. R. (1998). *The g factor: The science of mental ability.* CT: Praeger Publishers.

Kail, R. (1991). Developmental changes in speed of processing during childhood and adolescence. *Psychological Bulletin, 109,* 490–501.

Kamphaus, R. W. (1993). *Clinical assessment of children's intelligence.* Boston: Allyn & Bacon.

Kamphaus, R. W., Petoskey, M. D., & Morgan, A. W. (1997). A history of intelligence test interpretation. In D. P. Flanagan, J. L. Genshaft, & P. L. Harrison (Eds.), *Contemporary intellectual assessment: Theories, tests, and issues* (pp. 32–51). New York: Guilford.

Kamphaus, R. W., Winsor, A. P., Rowe, E. W., & Kim, S. (in press). A history of intelligence test interpretation. In D. P. Flanagan & P. L. Harrison (Eds.), *Contemporary intellectual assessment: Theories, tests, and issues* (2nd ed.). New York: Guilford.

Kaplan, E. (1988). A process approach to neuropsychological assessment. In T. J. Boll & B. K. Bryant (Eds.), *Clinical neuropsychology and brain function: Research, measurement, and practice* (pp. 129–167). Washington, DC: American Psychological Association.

Kaufman, A. S. (1975). Factor analysis of the WISC-R at 11 age levels between 6½ and 16½ years. *Journal of Consulting and Clinical Psychology, 43,* 135–147.

Kaufman, A. S. (1979). *Intelligent testing with the WISC-R.* New York: Wiley.

Kaufman, A. S. (1983). Intelligence: Old concepts—new perspectives. In G. W. Hynd (Ed.), *The school psychologist: An introduction* (pp. 95–117). Syracuse, NY: Syracuse University Press.

Kaufman, A. S. (1990). *Assessing adolescent and adult intelligence.* Boston: Allyn & Bacon.

Kaufman, A. S. (1992). Evaluation of the WISC-III and WPPSI-R for gifted children. *Roeper Review, 14*(3), 154–158.

Kaufman, A. S. (1993). King WISC the Third assumes the throne. *Journal of School Psychology, 31,* 345–354.

Kaufman, A. S. (1994). *Intelligent testing with the WISC-III.* New York: Wiley.

Kaufman, A. S. (2000a). Foreword. In D. P. Flanagan, K. S. McGrew, & S. O. Ortiz, *The Wechsler intelligence scales and Gf-Gc theory: A contemporary approach to interpretation* (pp. xiii–xv). Boston: Allyn & Bacon.

Kaufman, A. S. (2000b). Tests of intelligence. In R. J. Sternberg (Ed.), *Handbook of intelligence* (pp. 445–476). New York: Cambridge University Press.

Kaufman, A. S. (2003). Foreword. In J. Georgas, L. G. Weiss, F. J. R. van de Vijver, & D. H. Saklofske (Eds.), *Culture and children's intelligence: Cross-cultural analysis of the WISC-III* (pp. xix–xxiv). San Diego, CA: Academic Press.

Kaufman, A. S., & Harrison, P. L. (1986). Intelligence tests and gifted assessment: What are the positives? *Roeper Review, 8,* 154–159.

Kaufman, A. S., & Kaufman, N. L. (1993). *Manual for the Kaufman Adolescent and Adult Intelligence Test (KAIT).* Circle Pines, MN: American Guidance Service.

Kaufman, A. S., & Kaufman, N. L. (2004a). *Kaufman Assessment Battery for Children–Second Edition, Technical Manual.* Circle Pines, MN: American Guidance Service.

Kaufman, A. S., & Kaufman, N. L. (2004b). *Kaufman Test of Educational Achievement—Second Edition (KTEA-II).* Circle Pines, MN: American Guidance Service.

Kaufman, A. S., & Lichtenberger, E. O. (1999). *Essentials of WAIS-III assessment.* New York: Wiley.

Kaufman, A. S., & Lichtenberger, E. O. (2000). *Essentials of WISC-III and WPPSI-R assessment.* New York: Wiley.

Kaufman, A. S., & Lichtenberger, E. O. (2002). *Assessing adolescent and adult intelligence* (2nd ed.). Boston: Allyn & Bacon.

Kaufman, A. S., Lichtenberger, E. O., Fletcher-Janzen, E., & Kaufman, N. L. (in press). *Essentials of KABC-II assessment.* New York: Wiley.

Kavale, K. A., & Forness, S. R. (1984). A meta-analysis of the validity of Wechsler scale profiles and recategorizations: Patterns and parodies. *Learning Disabilities Quarterly, 7,* 136–156.

Kavale, K. A., & Forness, S. R. (2000). What definitions of learning disability say and don't say: A critical analysis. *Journal of Learning Disabilities, 33,* 239–256.

Keith, T. Z. (1988). Research methods in school psychology: An overview. *School Psychology Review, 17,* 502–520.

Keith, T. Z. (1997). What does the WISC-III measure? A reply to Carroll and Kranzler. *School Psychology Quarterly, 12,* 117–118.

Keith, T. Z., Fine, J. G., Taub, G. E., Reynolds, M. R., & Kranzler, J. H. (2004). *Hierarchical multi-sample, confirmatory factor analysis of the Wechsler Intelligence Scale for Children—Fourth Edition: What does it measure?* Manuscript submitted for publication.

Kelley M. F., & Surbeck, E. (1991). History of preschool assessment. In B. A. Bracken (Ed.), *The psychoeducational assessment of preschool children* (2nd ed., pp. 1–17). Boston: Allyn & Bacon.

Kelly, M., & Braden, J. P. (1990). Criterion-related validity of the WISC-R Performance Scale with the Stanford Achievement Test–Hearing Impaired Edition. *Journal of School Psychology, 28,* 147–151.

Klausmeier, K. L., Mishra, S. P., & Maker, C. J. (1987). Identification of gifted learners: A national survey of assessment practices and training needs of school psychologists. *Gifted Child Quarterly, 31,* 135–137.

Klin, A. (1994). Asperger Syndrome. *Child and Adolescent Psychiatric Clinics of North America, 3,* 131–148.

Klin, A., Sparrow, S. S., Marans, W. D., Carter, A., & Volkmar, F. R. (2000). Assessment issues in children and adolescents with Asperger Syndrome. In A. Klin, F. R. Volkmar, & S. S. Sparrow (Eds.), *Asperger Syndrome* (pp. 309–339). New York: Guilford.

Klin, A., Volkmar, F. R., Sparrow, S. S., Cicchetti, D. V., & Rourke, B. D. (1995). Validity and neuropsychological characterization of Asperger's Syndrome: Convergence with Nonverbal Learning Disabilities Syndrome. *Journal of Child Psychology and Psychiatry, 36,* 1127–1140.

Kohs, S. C. (1923). *Intelligence measurement.* New York: Macmillan.

Kramer, J. H. (1993). Interpretation of individual subtest scores on the WISC-III. *Psychological Assessment, 5,* 193–196.

Larry P. v. Wilson Riles. 343 F. Supp. 1306 (N. D. Cal. 1972) affr 502 F . 2d 963 (9th Cir. 1974); 495 F. Supp. 926 (N. D. Cal. 1979); appeal docketed, No. 80-4027 (9th Cir., Jan. 17, 1980).

Lincoln, A. J., Courchesne, E., Kilman, B. A., Elmasian, R., & Allen, M. (1988). A study of intellectual abilities in high-functioning people with autism. *Journal of Autism and Developmental Disorders, 18,* 505–524.

Little, S. G. (1992). The WISC-III: Everything old is new again. *School Psychology Quarterly, 7*(2), 148–154.

Logie, R. (1996). The seven ages of working memory. In J. Richardson, R. Engle, L. Hasher, R. Logie, E. Stoltzfus, & R. Zacks (Eds.), *Working memory and human cognition* (pp. 31–65). New York: Oxford.

Lohman, D. F. (1989). Human intelligence: An introduction to advances in theory and research. *Review of Educational Research, 59*(4), 333–373.

Lohman, D. F. (1994). Spatial ability. In R. J. Sternberg (Ed.), *Encyclopedia of human intelligence* (pp. 1000–1007). New York: Macmillan.

Luckasson, R., Borthwick-Duffy, S., Buntix, W. H. E., Coulter, D. L., Craig, E. M., Reeve, A., Schalock, R. L., Snell, M. E., Spitalnik, D. M., Spreat, S., & Tasse, M. J. (2002). *Mental Retardation: Definition, classification, and systems of supports* (10th ed.). Washington, DC: American Association on Mental Retardation.

Maller, S. (1996). WISC-III Verbal item invariance across samples of deaf and hearing children of similar measured ability. *Journal of Psychoeducational Assessment, 14,* 152–165.

Maller, S. (2003). Intellectual assessment of deaf people: A critical review of core concepts and issues. In M. Marschark & P. E. Spencer (Eds.), *Oxford handbook of deaf studies, language, and education* (pp. 451–463). New York: Oxford University Press.

Manjiviona, J., & Prior, M. (1995). Comparison of Asperger Syndrome and high-functioning autistic children on a test of motor impairment. *Journal of Autism and Developmental Disorders, 25,* 23–39.

Marland, S. P. (1972). *Education of the gifted and talented: Vol. 1. Report to the Congress of the United States by the U.S. Commissioner of Education.* Washington, DC: U.S. GPO.

Mather, N., & Jaffe, L. (2002). *Woodcock-Johnson III: Reports, recommendations, and strategies.* New York: Wiley.

Mayes, S. D., Calhoun, S. L., & Crites, D. L. (2001). Does *DSM-IV* Asperger's Disorder exist? *Journal of Abnormal Child Psychology, 29*(3), 263–271.

McDermott, P. A., Fantuzzo, J. W., & Glutting, J. J. (1990). Just say no to subtest analysis: A critique on Wechsler theory and practice. *Journal of Psychoeducational Assessment, 8,* 290–302.

McDermott, P. A., Fantuzzo, J. W., Glutting, J. J., Watkins, M. W., & Baggaley, R. A. (1992). Illusions of meaning in the ipsative assessment of children's ability. *Journal of Special Education, 25,* 504–526.

McGrew, K. S. (1994). *Clinical interpretation of the Woodcock-Johnson Tests of Cognitive Ability—Revised.* Boston: Allyn & Bacon.

McGrew, K. S. (1997). Analysis of the major intelligence batteries according to a proposed comprehensive *Gf-Gc* framework. In D. P. Flanagan, J. L. Genshaft, & P. L. Harrison (Eds.), *Contemporary intellectual assessment: Theories, tests, and issues* (pp. 151–180). New York: Guilford.

McGrew, K. S. (in press). The Cattell-Horn-Carroll (CHC) theory of cognitive abilities: Past, present and future. In D. P. Flanagan & P. L. Harrison (Eds.), *Contemporary intellectual assessment: Theories, tests, and issues* (2nd ed.). New York: Guilford.

McGrew, K. S., & Flanagan, D. P. (1996). The Wechsler Performance Scale debate: Fluid Intelligence *(Gf)* or Visual Processing *(Gv)*? *Communique, 24*(6), 14–16.

McGrew, K. S., & Flanagan, D. P. (1998). *The intelligence test desk reference (ITDR): Gf-Gc cross-battery assessment.* Needham Heights, MA: Allyn & Bacon.

McGrew, K. S., Flanagan, D. P., Keith, T. Z., & Vanderwood, M. (1997). Beyond *g:* The impact of *Gf-Gc* specific cognitive abilities research on the future use and interpretation of intelligence tests in the schools. *School Psychology Review, 26,* 177–189.

McGrew, K. S., Woodcock, R. W., & Werder, J. K. (1991). *Woodcock-Johnson Psycho-Educational Battery—Revised technical manual.* Chicago: Riverside.

McLaughlin-Cheng, E. (1998). Asperger Syndrome and autism: A literature review and meta-analysis. *Focus on Autism and Other Developmental Disabilities, 13*(4), 234–245.

Mercer, J. R. (1979). *The System of Multicultural Pluralistic Assessment: Technical manual.* New York: The Psychological Corporation.

Milberg, W. P., Hebben, N., & Kaplan, E. (1986). The Boston process approach to neuropsychological assessment. In K. Adams & I. Grant (Eds.), *Neuropsychological assessment of neuropsychiatric disorders* (pp. 65–86). New York: Oxford University Press.

Milberg, W. P., Hebben, N., & Kaplan, E. (1996). The Boston process approach to neuropsychological assessment. In K. Adams & I. Grant (Eds.), *Neuropsychological assessment of neuropsychiatric disorders* (2nd ed., pp. 58–80). New York: Oxford University Press.

Miller, J. N., & Ozonoff, S. (1997). Did Asperger's cases have Asperger Disorder? A research note. *Journal of Child Psychology and Psychiatry, 38,* 247–251.

Miller, J. N., & Ozonoff, S. (2000). The external validity of Asperger Disorder: Lack of evidence from the domain of neuropsychology. *Journal of Abnormal Psychology, 109*(2), 227–238.

Moran, J. L., & Mefford, R. B., Jr. (1959). Repetitive psychometric measures. *Psychological Reports, 5,* 269–275.

Morris, R. D., Stuebing, K. K., Fletcher, J. M., Shaywitz, S. E., Lyon, G. R., Shankweiler, D. P., Katz, L., Francis, D. J., & Shaywitz, B. A. (1998). Subtypes of reading disability: Variability around a phonological core. *Journal of Educational Psychology, 90*(3), 347–373.

Mueller, H. H., Dennis, S. S., & Short, R. H. (1986). A meta-exploration of WISC-R factor score profiles as a function of diagnosis and intellectual level. *Canadian Journal of School Psychology, 2,* 21–43.

Myhr, G. (1998). Autism and other pervasive developmental disorders: Exploring the dimensional view. *Canadian Journal of Psychiatry, 43,* 589–595.

Naglieri, J. A., & Pickering, E. B. (2003). *Helping children learn: Intervention handouts for use in school and at home.* Baltimore: Paul H. Brookes.

Nettlebeck, T. (1994). Speediness. In R. J. Sternberg (Ed.), *Encyclopedia of human intelligence* (pp. 1014–1019). New York: Macmillan.

Nyden, A., Billstedt, E., Hjelmquist, E., & Gillberg, C. (2001). Neurocognitive stability in Asperger Syndrome, ADHD, and Reading and Writing Disorder: A pilot study. *Developmental Medicine and Child Neurology, 43,* 165–171.

Ochoa, S. H., Powell, M. P., & Robles-Piña, R. (1996). School psychologists' assessment practices with bilingual and limited-English-proficient students. *Journal of Psychoeducational Assessment, 14,* 250–275.

Ortiz, S. O. (2001). Assessment of cognitive abilities in Hispanic children. *Seminars in Speech and Language, 22*(1), 17–37.

Ortiz, S. O. (2002). Best practices in nondiscriminatory assessment. In A. Thomas & J. Grimes (Eds.), *Best practices in school psychology IV.* Washington, DC: National Association of School Psychologists.

Ozonoff, S., Rogers, S. J., & Pennington, B. F. (1991). Asperger's Syndrome: Evidence of an empirical distinction from high-functioning autism. *Journal of Child Psychology and Psychiatry, 32,* 1107–1122.

Parker, F. (1981). Ideas that shaped American schools. *Phi Delta Kappan, 62,* 314–319.

Prifitera, A., & Saklofske, D. H. (Eds.). (1998). *WISC-III clinical use and interpretation: Scientist-practitioner perspectives.* San Diego, CA: Academic Press.

Prifitera, A., Saklofske, D. H., Weiss, L. G., & Rolfhus, E. (Eds.). (in press). *WISC-IV clinical use and interpretation: Scientist-practitioner perspectives.* San Diego, CA: Academic Press.

Psychological Corporation, The (2001). *Wechsler Individual Achievement Test–Second Edition.* San Antonio, TX: Author.

Psychological Corporation, The. (2002). *WPPSI-III technical and interpretive manual.* San Antonio, TX: Author.

Psychological Corporation, The. (2003). *WISC-IV technical and interpretive manual.* San Antonio, TX: Author.

Rapaport, D., Gill, M. M. & Schafer, R. (1945–46). *Diagnostic Psychological Testing* (2 vols.). Chicago: Yearbook Publishers.

Raven, J. C. (1938). *Progressive matrices: A perceptual test of intelligence.* San Antonio, TX: The Psychological Corporation.

Reynolds, C. R., & Kamphaus, R. W. (2003). *Reynolds Intellectual Assessment Scales (RIAS).* Tampa, FL: Psychological Assessment Resources.

Richardson, J. (1996). Evolving concepts of working memory. In J. Richardson, R. Engle, L. Hasher, R. Logie, E. Stoltzfus, & R. Zacks (Eds.), *Working memory and human cognition* (pp. 3–30). New York: Oxford.

Roid, G. H. (2003). *Stanford-Binet Intelligence Scales, Fifth Edition, Technical Manual.* Itasca, IL: Riverside.

Rumsey, J. M. (1992). Neuropsychological studies of high-level autism. In E. Schopler & G. B. Mesibov (Eds.), *High-functioning individuals with autism* (pp. 41–64). New York: Plenum Press.

Sanchez, G. I. (1934). Bilingualism and mental measures: A word of caution. *Journal of Applied Psychology, 18,* 765–772.

Sandoval, J. (1979). The WISC-R and internal evidence of test bias with minority groups. *Journal of Consulting and Clinical Psychology, 47,* 919–927.

Sandoval, J., Frisby, C. L., Geisinger, K. F., Scheuneman, J. D., & Grenier, J. R. (Eds.). (1998). *Test interpretation and diversity: Achieving equity in assessment.* Washington DC: American Psychological Association.

Sattler, J. (1992). *Assessment of children* (Rev. and updated 3rd ed.). San Diego, CA: Author.

Sattler, J. M. (2001). *Assessment of children: Cognitive applications* (4th ed.). La Mesa, CA: Author.

Sattler, J. M., & Dumont, R. (2004). *Assessment of children WISC-IV and WPPSI-III Supplement.* La Mesa, CA: Jerome M. Sattler.

Sattler, J. M., & Hardy-Braz, S. T. (2002). Hearing impairments. In J. M. Sattler (Ed.), *Assessment of children: Behavioral and clinical applications* (pp. 377–389). La Mesa, CA: Jerome M. Sattler.

Scarr, S. (1978). From evolution to Larry P., or what shall we do about IQ tests? *Intelligence, 2,* 325–342.

Schneider, W., & Shiffrin, R. M. (1977). Controlled and Automatic Human Information Processing: Detection, search, and attention. *Psychological Review, 84,* 1–66.

Schopler, E. (1996). Are autism and Asperger Syndrome (AS) different labels or different disabilities? *Journal of Autism and Developmental Disorders, 26,* 109–110.

Shapiro, E. (1996). *Academic skills problems: Direct assessment and intervention* (2nd. ed.). New York: Guilford Press.

Shaw, S. E., Swerdlik, M. E., & Laurent, J. (1993). Review of the WISC-III [WISC-III Monograph]. *Journal of Psychoeducational Assessment,* 151–160.

Siegel, D. J., Minshew, N. J., & Goldstein, G. (1996). Wechsler IQ profiles in diagnosis of high-functioning autism. *Journal of Autism and Developmental Disabilities, 26,* 398–406.

Slate, J. R. (1995). Discrepancies between IQ and index scores for a clinical sample of students: Useful diagnostic indicators? *Psychology in the Schools, 32,* 103–108.

Sparrow, S. S., & Gurland, S. T. (1998). Assessment of gifted children with the WISC-III. In A. Prifitera & D. Saklofske (Eds.), *WISC-III clinical use and interpretation: Scientist-practitioner perspectives* (pp. 59–72). San Diego, CA: Academic Press.

Spruill, J. (1998). Assessment of mental retardation with the WISC-III. In A. Prifitera & D. Saklofske (Eds.), *WISC-III clinical use and interpretation* (pp. 73–90). San Diego, CA: Academic Press.

Stankov, L., (1994). Auditory abilities. In R. J. Sternberg (Ed.), *Encyclopedia of human intelligence* (pp. 157–162). New York: Macmillan.

Stankov, L., & Horn, J. L. (1980). Human abilities revealed through auditory tests. *Journal of Educational Psychology, 72*(1), 21–44.

Sternberg, R. J. (1982). Lies we live by: Misapplication of tests in identifying the gifted. *Gifted Child Quarterly, 26,* 157–161.

Sternberg, R. J. (1993). Procedures for identifying intellectual potential in the gifted: A perspective on alternative "metaphors of mind." In K. A. Heller, F. J. Monks, & A. H. Passow (Eds.), *International handbook of research and development of giftedness and talent* (pp. 185–207). New York: Pergamon.

Sternberg, R. J. (1995). What do we mean by giftedness?: A pentagonal implicit theory. *Gifted Child Quarterly, 39,* 88–94.

Sternberg, S. (1966). High-Speed scanning in human memory. *Science, 153,* 652–654.

Stott, L., & Ball, R. (1965). Infant and preschool mental tests: Review and evaluation. *Monographs of the Society for Research in Child Development, 30,* 4–42.

Swanson, H. L., & Howell, M. (2001). Working memory, short-term memory, and speech rate as predictors of children's reading performance at different ages. *Journal of Educational Psychology, 9*(4), 720–734.

Szatmari, P., Archer, L., Fisman, S., Streiner, D. L., & Wilson, F. (1995). Asperger's Syndrome and autism: Differences in behavior, cognition, and adaptive functioning. *Journal of the American Academy of Child and Adolescent Psychiatry, 34,* 1662–1671.

Talland, G. A., & Schwab, R. S. (1964). Performance with multiple sets in Parkinson's Disease. *Neuropsychologia, 2,* 45–57.

Tellegen, A., & Briggs, P. F. (1967). Old wine in new skins: Grouping Wechsler subtests into new scales. *Journal of Consulting Psychology, 31,* 499–506.

Terman, L. M. (1916). *The measurement of intelligence: An explanation of and a complete guide for the use of the Stanford revision and extension of the Binet-Simon intelligence scale.* Boston: Houghton Mifflin.

Terman, L. M., & Merrill, M. A. (1937). *Measuring intelligence.* Boston: Houghton Mifflin.

Terman, L. M., & Merrill, M. A. (1960). *Stanford-Binet Intelligence Scale: Manual for the Third Revision Form L-M.* Boston: Houghton Mifflin.

Thompson, A. P. (1987). Methodological issues in the clinical evaluation of two- and four-subtest short forms of the WAIS-R. *Journal of Clinical Psychology, 43,* 142–144.

Thompson, A. P., Howard, D., & Anderson, J. (1986). Two- and four-subtest short forms of the WAIS-R: Validity in a psychiatric sample. *Canadian Journal of Behavioural Science, 26,* 492–504.

Tyerman, M. J. (1986). Gifted children and their identification: Learning ability not intelligence. *Gifted Education International, 4,* 81–84.

Valdes, G., & Figueroa, R. A. (1994). *Bilingualism and testing: A special case of bias.* Norwood, NJ: Ablex.

Vanderwood, M. L., McGrew, K. S., Flanagan, D. P., & Keith, T. Z. (2002). The contribution of general and specific cognitive abilities to reading achievement. *Learning and Individual Differences, 13,* 159–188.

Vellutino, F. R., Scanlon, D. M., & Lyon, G. R. (2000). Differentiating between difficult-to-remediate and readily remediated poor readers. *Journal of Learning Disabilities, 33,* 223–238.

Vig, S., Kaminer, R. K., & Jedrysek, E. (1987). A later look at borderline and mentally retarded preschoolers. *Journal of Developmental and Behavioral Pediatrics, 8,* 12–17.

Wagner, R. K., Torgesen, J. K., Laughton, P., Simmons, K., & Rashotte, C. A. (1993). Development of young readers' phonological processing abilities. *Journal of Educational Psychology, 85*(1), 83–103.

Watkins, M. W., & Kush, J. C. (1994). Wechsler subtest analysis: The right way, the wrong way, or no way? *School Psychology Review, 23,* 640–651.

Watkins, M. W., Youngstrom, E. A., & Glutting, J. J. (2002). Some cautions concerning cross-battery assessment. *Communique, 30*(5), 16–19.

Wechsler, D. (1939). *The measurement of adult intelligence.* Baltimore: Williams & Wilkins.

Wechsler, D. (1944). *The measurement of adult intelligence* (3rd ed.). Baltimore: Williams & Wilkins.

Wechsler, D. (1949). *Manual for the Wechsler Intelligence Scale for Children.* San Antonio, TX: The Psychological Corporation.

Wechsler, D. (1955). *Manual for the Wechsler Adult Intelligence Scale.* San Antonio, TX: The Psychological Corporation.

Wechsler, D. (1958). *The measurement and appraisal of adult intelligence* (4th ed.). Baltimore: Williams & Wilkins.

Wechsler, D. (1974). *Manual for the Wechsler Preschool and Primary Scale of Intelligence.* San Antonio, TX: The Psychological Corporation.

Wechsler, D. (1991). *Manual for the Wechsler Intelligence Scale for Children—Third Edition (WISC-III).* San Antonio, TX: The Psychological Corporation.

Wechsler, D. (2003) *Wechsler Intelligence Scale for Children-Fourth Edition (WISC-IV) administration and scoring manual.* San Antonio, TX: The Psychological Corporation.

Werner, H., & Kaplan, E. (1950). Development of word meaning through verbal context: An experimental study. *Journal of Psychology, 29,* 251–257.

Wing, L. (1998). The history of Asperger Syndrome. In E. Schopler, G. B. Mesibov, & L. J. Kunce (Eds.), *Asperger Syndrome or high-functioning autism?* (pp. 11–28). New York: Plenum.

Winner, E. (1997). Exceptionally high intelligence and schooling. *American Psychologist, 52*(10), 1070–1081.

Winner, E. (2000). The origins and ends of giftedness. *American Psychologist, 55*(1), 159–169.

Witt, J. C., & Gresham, F. M. (1985). Review of Wechsler Intelligence Scale for Children—Revised. In J. V. Mitchell (Ed.), *The ninth mental measurement yearbook* (vol. 2, pp. 1716–1719). Lincoln, NE: Buros Institute of Mental Measurement.

Wolf, M., & Bowers, P. (2000). The question of naming-speed deficits in developmental reading disability: An introduction to the Double-Deficit Hypothesis. *Journal of Learning Disabilities, 33,* 322–324. (Special issue on the Double-Deficit Hypothesis: Special Issue Editors: M. Wolf & P. Bowers)

Woodcock, R. W. (1993). An information processing view of *Gf-Gc* theory. *Journal of Psychoeducational Assessment* Monograph Series: WJ-R Monograph, 80–102.

Woodcock, R. W. (1994). Measures of fluid and crystallized intelligence. In R. J. Sternberg (Ed.), *The encyclopedia of human intelligence* (pp. 452–456). New York: Macmillan.

Woodcock, R. W., McGrew, K. S., & Mather, N. (2001). *Woodcock-Johnson III Tests of Achievement.* Itasca, IL: Riverside Publishing.

Yirmiya, N., & Sigman, M. (1991). High functioning individuals with autism: Diagnosis, empirical findings, and theoretical issues. *Clinical Psychology Review, 11,* 669–683.

Yopp, H. K. (1988). The validity and reliability of phonemic awareness tests. *Reading Research Quarterly, 23*(2), 159–177.

Zachary, R. A. (1990). Wechsler's intelligence scales: Theoretical and practical considerations. *Journal of Psychoeducational Assessment, 8,* 276–289.

Annotated Bibliography

Wechsler, D. (2003). *WISC-IV Administration and Scoring Manual.*

Includes the administration and scoring procedures for the WISC-IV as well as norms and conversion tables.

The Psychological Corporation. (2003). *WISC-IV Technical and Interpretive Manual.*

Includes information about the reliability and validity of the WISC-IV as well as other important psychometric characteristics of the test.

Flanagan, D. P., & Harrison, P. L. (Eds.). (in press). *Contemporary intellectual assessment: Theories, tests and issues* (2nd ed.). New York: Guilford.

A hard-cover edited book that includes chapters on all major intelligence tests, including the WISC-IV, as well as the prevailing theories of the structure of cognitive abilities and the nature of intelligence. In addition, a variety of new approaches to test interpretation are included alongside guidelines for using intelligence tests with different populations (e.g., preschool, learning disabled, gifted, culturally and linguistically diverse, etc.).

Flanagan, D. P., & Ortiz, S. O. (2001). *Essentials of cross-battery assessment.* New York: Wiley.

Provides a comprehensive set of guidelines and procedures for organizing assessments based on contemporary CHC theory and research, integrating test results from different batteries in a psychometrically defensible way, and interpreting test results within the context of research on the relations between cognitive and academic abilities and processes. Also includes guidelines for assessing culturally and linguistically diverse populations.

Flanagan, D. P., Ortiz, S. O., Alfonso, V. C., & Mascolo, J. T. (2002). *The achievement test desk reference (ATDR): Comprehensive assessment and learning disabilities.* Boston: Allyn & Bacon.

Reviews comprehensive, brief, and special purpose tests of achievement, including the WIAT-II, WJ III, specialized reading, math, and written language tests and tests of auditory and phonological processing. Demonstrates how to integrate findings from achievement tests with findings from intelligence tests following CHC theory and its research base. Offers an operational definition of Learning Disability and demonstrates how to incorporate this definition into everyday practice in the schools.

Lichtenberger, E. O., Mather, N., Kaufman, N. L., & Kaufman, A. S. (2004). *Essentials of assessment report writing.* New York: Wiley.

Covers the basics of writing psychological assessment reports. Uses the WISC-IV throughout for illustrative purposes.

Prifitera, A., Saklofske, D. H., Weiss, L. G., & Rolfhus, E. (Eds.). (in press). *WISC-IV use and interpretation: Scientist-practitioner perspectives.* San Diego, CA: Elsevier/Academic Press.

A hard-cover edited book that includes chapters on a variety of topics pertinent to the WISC-IV, such as clinical applications, psychometric properties, gifted assessment, LD assessment, and neuropsychological assessment.

Kaufman, A. S., Lichtenberger, E. O., Fletcher-Janzen, E., & Kaufman, N. L. (in press). *Essentials of KABC-II assessment.* New York: Wiley.

Covers thoroughly the interpretation of the KABC-II, including treatment of the integration of the KABC-II and WISC-IV. The case of Vanessa (age 11) integrates selected WISC-IV subtests and scales with the KABC-II. The interpretive system for the KABC-II (which is based on both Luria and CHC theories) parallels our WISC-IV interpretive system.

Kaufman, A. S., & Lichtenberger, E. O. (2002). *Assessing adolescent and adult intelligence* (2nd ed.). Boston, MA: Allyn & Bacon.

Provides a thorough theory-based, research-based, and clinically-based interpretation of tests of adult intelligence. This book features the WAIS-III, but also includes chapters on the KAIT, WJ III, and brief measures of adult intelligence.

Lichtenberger, E. O., & Kaufman, A. S. (2004). *Essentials of WPPSI-III assessment.* New York: Wiley.

Interprets the WPPSI-III in a systematic, thorough fashion, including integration of the WPPSI-III with the WISC-III and WISC-IV.

Index

Acknowledgments

We would like to acknowledge several people for their special and extraordinary contributions. We wish to express our deepest appreciation to Jennifer Mascolo, whose review of our work significantly enhanced the quality and utility of this book. Jennifer's unwavering dedication and commitment were truly remarkable. We are also particularly grateful to Nadeen Kaufman for providing a case report for inclusion in this book. Her vast knowledge and tremendous skill in assessment and interpretation made a significant contribution. We also appreciate the insightful comments and feedback of Vincent Alfonso and Jay Gassman, who dedicated their time and clinical expertise to ensure that this book would be maximally useful to practitioners. Our sincere gratitude is extended to Agnieska Dynda, Dan Oakley, and Jill Kelter for their many thoughtful insights and suggestions in their reviews of earlier drafts of this book. Our gratitude is also extended to Martin Volker for his assistance in formatting the WISC-IV interpretive worksheet and to Fotini Effie Kyvelos for her consultation on one of the case studies included in this book.

A special thanks is offered to Steven Hardy-Braz, Nancy Hebben, Elizabeth Lichtenberger, Jennifer Mascolo, Samuel Ortiz, LeAdelle Phelps, and Martin Volker, for graciously providing their expertise as it relates to the clinical applications of the WISC-IV. James Kaufman's research consultation is also most appreciated.

We would also like to thank Timothy Keith and Jack Naglieri for graciously providing the results of specific studies and analyses that are presented in the overview and interpretation chapters of this book. We are also grateful to Aurelio Prifitera, Jianjun Zhu, Larry Weiss, and other important members of The Psychological Corporation for conducting the several analyses we requested (included in Chapter 4 and Appendix H of this book).

Several of our students participated in the review of early drafts of this book, providing us with feedback regarding its utility and editorial comments regarding the accuracy and clarity of information presented in the administration, scoring, and interpretation chapters. Thank you Lisette Alvarez, Anya Levitin Barak, Ellenge Denton, Jessica Handy, Victoria Kristal, Estee Lieberman, Danielle Rannazzisi, Marina Treybick, Josephine Vitale, Angela Wilkos, Charles Yurkewicz, Ezra Zelkin, and Ayala Zoltan for your commitment to this book.

373

Finally, the contributions of Tracey Belmont, Susan Dodson, and the rest of the staff at Wiley are gratefully acknowledged. Their expertise and pleasant and cooperative working style made this book an enjoyable and productive endeavor.

Authors

Dawn P. Flanagan, PhD, St. John's University, Jamaica, NY
Alan S. Kaufman, PhD, Yale University School of Medicine, New Haven, CT

Contributors

Steven Hardy-Braz, PsyS, NCSP, President, North Carolina Association of School Psychologists
Nancy Hebben, PhD, ABPP-ABCN, Harvard Medical School, Boston, MA
Elizabeth O. Lichtenberger, PhD, The Salk Institute, La Jolla, CA
Jennifer T. Mascolo, PsyD, St. John's University, Jamaica, NY
Samuel O. Ortiz, PhD, St. John's University, Jamaica, NY
LeAdelle Phelps, PhD, State University of New York at Buffalo, Buffalo, NY
Martin A. Volker, PhD, State University of New York at Buffalo, Buffalo, NY